The New Country

The
New Country

A SOCIAL HISTORY
OF THE AMERICAN FRONTIER,
1776-1890

Richard A. Bartlett

OXFORD UNIVERSITY PRESS
London   Oxford   New York

Preface

I am quite sure that the date was May 24, 1938, when Jim and Merlin and I crawled through the rusted barbed-wire fence, sauntered across a rocky meadow, and entered an unpainted old barn. Its sides leaned windward at such an angle that one feared the next zephyr might blow it down. The bright sunlight cast its beams across air long undisturbed, and silver dust particles glittered in the stillness. The not unpleasant odor was of wood and hay and horse droppings, so long enclosed that all the smells had blended into one. But what commanded our attention as it stood there in the gleam of the Colorado sunshine was the old wagon—wheels, running gear, bed, bows, and tattered canvas: it was a genuine prairie schooner!

We examined it from tongue to grease bucket, mused, as high school boys will, about the people who had owned it, and from whence they had come, and where they had gone. And then we left, closing the rickety door that was almost too old to squeak, for we had a long way to go. (That morning we had set out westward from the Faculty Ranch, so called, on the North St. Vrain, and we had scrambled over many a mountain between there and Estes Park. I do remember that darkness overtook us and we had to wait on a ledge for the moon to rise to light our way back to the cabin.)

The next day was May 25, at that time a very important date in the Colorado year: the first day of fishing season. But I do not remember the trout, whether I caught any or not. Instead, I remember the old prairie schooner.

That was thirty-five years ago. In the three and a half decades since, I have pursued the study of America's great westward movement. I have also traveled widely over the United States, not only by jet from big city to big city, but by automobile from New England to California, from Florida to Colorado and Montana. I have taught college students in Texas, Florida, Nebraska, Tennessee, the Panama Canal Zone, and British Columbia. History research has led me from Tallahassee to Knoxville, Tucson, San Marino, Berkeley, Denver, Salt Lake, Helena, St. Paul, and Chicago. And always my thoughts have been on the westward movement—that great 114-year-long process, 1776-1890, that settled the heart of the North American continent.

Gradually I came to view this greatest element of America's Golden Age more realistically, I believe, and less romantically, than had my predecessors. I discovered that the most common phrase used by the pioneers to describe where they were going was not "to the frontier" or "to the tall timber" or "to the West": it was "to the new country." Now, writing more than eight decades after frontier's end, I feel that I can take a wider view of the process of settlement. I have come to look upon it not as a myriad of incidents, but as a great sweep westward, unbroken, inevitable, of epic proportions.

The result is this book. It is about humanity released from restrictions as never before, yet with the knowledge and technological skills of the nineteenth century. In the process of my research much of the old romance and mythology faded, but what emerged in its place was a poignant story of people elevating themselves to new affluence and dignity in a new country, in a new civilization of their own making. That story proved to be just as exciting as the old romance and mythology that was lost.

Such a broad study as this is based primarily upon an historian's career experiences. The challenge of teaching classes in the westward movement for nearly twenty years has helped me crystallize my thoughts. Many of my students have been remarkably perceptive and all of them have been a joy to teach. They have continually confronted me with problems of presentation and interpretation. I have also benefited from continuous association with my colleagues in the history department at Florida State University and from discussions with fellow members of the Western History Association. There have been lucrative chance meetings with historians of the West at such research centers as the Montana Historical Society, the Denver Public Library Western History Room, the Western History Research Center at the University of Wyoming, and the Huntington Library. Many have influenced my thoughts.

Sheldon Meyer of the Oxford University Press has shown patience, manifested continued interest, and given guidance when it was sorely needed; Stephanie Golden of that house worked with me beyond the call of duty; Mrs. Kathy Meffert helped with the typing. My wife, Marie C. Bartlett, and my four children have shown understanding toward a too-busy head of household. For any errors of fact or judgment, I of course take full responsibility.

Tallahassee, Florida   R.A.B.
June 1974

Contents

Maps

The New Country

I

This Land Is Ours:
The Sweep Across
the Continent

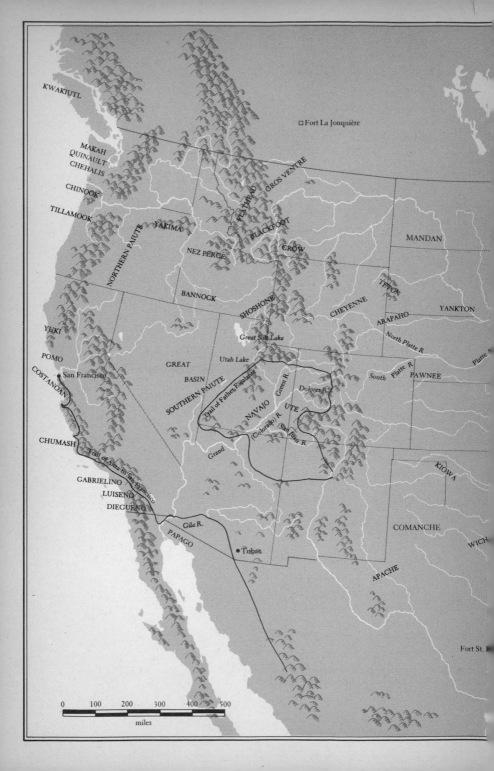

KWAKIUTL

MAKAH
QUINAULT
CHEHALIS

CHINOOK

TILLAMOOK

□ Fort La Jonquière

FLATHEAD
GROS VENTRE

MANDAN

YAKIMA
NEZ PERCE
BLACKFOOT

CROW

TETON

BANNOCK

SHOSHONE
CHEYENNE
ARAPAHO
YANKTON

North Platte R.

YUKI

GREAT
Great Salt Lake

Utah Lake
South Platte R.
PAWNEE

POMO
San Francisco

COSTANOAN

BASIN

SOUTHERN PAIUTE

Trail of Father Escalante

Green R.
Dolores R.

NAVAJO
UTE

(Colorado) R.
San Juan R.

CHUMASH

Trail of Anza to San Francisco

Grand

GABRIELINO
LUISEÑO
DIEGUEÑO

KIOWA

PAPAGO

Gila R.

Tubac

COMANCHE

WICH

APACHE

Fort St.

0   100   200   300   400   500

miles

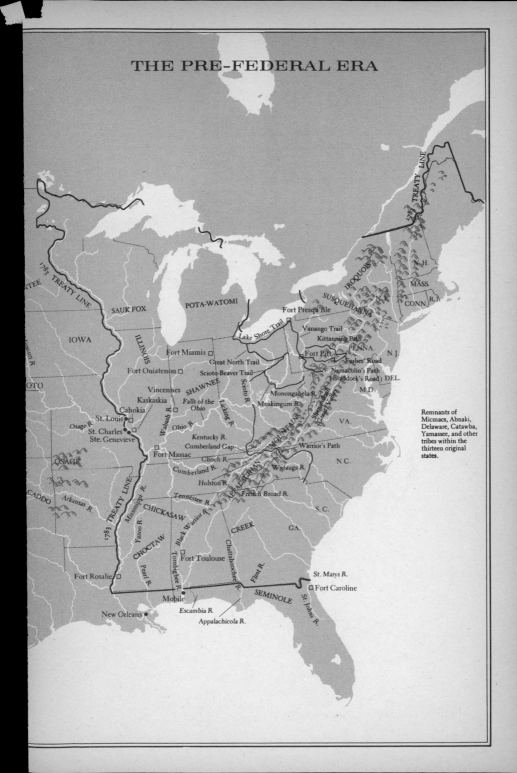

THE PRE-FEDERAL ERA

1783 TREATY LINE

N.H.

MASS.

CONN.   R.I.

IROQUOIS

SUSQUEHANNA

SAUK FOX

POTA-WATOMI

Fort Presqu'Isle

Vanango Trail

Kittanning Path

PENNA.   N.J.

Fort Miamis

IOWA

Great North Trail

Fort Pitt

Forbes' Road

Nemacolin's Path

(Braddock's Road) DEL.

Fort Ouiatenon

Scioto-Beaver Trail

Lake Shore Trail

ILLINOIS

M.D.

SHAWNEE

Vincennes

Monongahela R.

VA.

Kaskaskia

Falls of the Ohio

Muskingum R.

Cahokia

Osage R.

St. Louis

Ohio R.

St. Charles

Ste. Genevieve

Fort Massac

Kentucky R.

Cumberland Gap

Clinch R.

Warrior's Path

N.C.

OSAGE

Cumberland R.

Holston R.

Watauga R.

CADDO

Arkansas R.

Tennessee R.

French Broad R.

S.C.

CHICKASAW

Black Warrior R.

CREEK

GA.

CHOCTAW

Yazoo R.

Fort Rosalie

Pearl R.

Fort Toulouse

Chattahoochee R.

Flint R.

Mobile

Tombigbee R.

St. Marys R.

Fort Caroline

New Orleans

Escambia R.

SEMINOLE

St. Johns R.

Appalachicola R.

1783 TREATY LINE

Mississippi R.

APPALACHIAN MOUNTAINS

Great Valley

Shenandoah R.

Scioto R.

Licking R.

Wabash R.

Muskingum R.

Remnants of Micmacs, Abnaki, Delaware, Catawba, Yamassee, and other tribes within the thirteen original states.

Some Myths of the
American Frontier

Three myths have hindered the accurate portrayal of the sweep across the continent, and they should be destroyed. They are: (1) the myth of the unknown continent; (2) the myth of the trackless wilderness; (3) the myth of Indian invincibility.

First of all, the myth has somehow arisen that our eighteenth-century ancestors knew next to nothing about the North American land mass. They knew that somewhere far, far to the West, so the story goes, the land ended at the "South Sea" (as they called the Pacific), but no one had any inkling of what lay in between: lakes, mountains, rivers, forests, prairies, and deserts were but probabilities in the common colonial mind. Therein lies the justification for the mention of Lewis and Clark, Zebulon Pike, and Stephen H. Long in the pages of numerous history texts. If this ignorance of the continent really existed, then the American achievement in pushing towards the setting sun becomes all the greater, much more romantic, an even bolder venture than it actually was. Millions believe this myth of the unknown wilderness: that no one knew what lay out there, at least beyond the Mississippi.

This impression is, however, completely inaccurate. In fact, if all the accumulated knowledge of the English, Spanish, French, Dutch, and Russians concerning North America as of 1776 could be gathered, there would be few general geographical facts about the virgin land that were not known by Europeans.

For example, about 2,800 miles west of Philadelphia and just three months prior to July 4, 1776, a score of colonizers determined the sites for a presidio and chapel on the shores of San Francisco Bay. Their leader was Juan Bautista de Anza, a loyal servant to Carlos III, the Spanish king. Anza was probably the most successful colonizer in North American history.

The twenty men were the vanguard of 240 men, women, and chil-

Juan Bautista de Anza, 1728-88, portrait by Fray Orsi, 1774. (California Historical
Society, San Francisco)

dren whom he had escorted from Tubac, in present southern Arizona, to
Monterey, where they had arrived after 130 days on the trail. They had
lost a good many horses, mules, and cattle in crossing 1,400 miles of
terrible deserts and rugged mountains, but Anza brought them to Monterey with two more souls than he had started with. There had been
just one death, a mother in childbirth, but the infant survived, and
squalling lustily along with two other newborns, had been nursed by
other mothers along on the journey. And so Anza had carried out his
orders, despite hostile Indians, thirst, and freezing temperatures.

The twenty men returned to Monterey, and Anza returned to Tubac.
But he had shown the way, and by the end of June new colonizers had
arrived at San Francisco Bay, mass had been celebrated, and a mission
and a presidio were being built. San Francisco had its first white inhabitants.

But what American schoolchild knows of Anza's great achievement?
The presidio at the Golden Gate remained, and when Americans began

coming to California, there was a little town called Yerba Buena already in existence there. Later its name was changed to San Francisco.

In that same year of 1776 a Spanish sea captain named Heçeta reached the forty-ninth parallel and discovered the mouth of the Columbia River, while one Juan Perez had, two years before, explored the Nootka Sound on the west side of Vancouver Island in his ship, the *Santiago*.

Spanish geographers, government agents, and missionaries probably knew more about North America than anyone else in the eighteenth century. Their primary concern was the defense of the enormous piece of real estate to which their king laid claim. This was why they were at the Golden Gate, with a chain of missions running down California, eastward across Arizona, and into northern Mexico. It was part of their reason for being at the upper Rio Grande, where Santa Fe had been established in 1609. It lay behind Franciscan Father Francisco Silvestre Vélez de Escalante's explorations of the Great Basin in 1776. He and Father Francisco Atanasio Dominguez set out from Santa Fe on July 20, 1776, followed a trapper's trail past Mesa Verde, and ultimately turned west, hoping to blaze a new trail all the way to Monterey. They explored much of southwestern Colorado, discovered the Green River as well as sighted the San Juan, Dolores, Grand, and Colorado, and advanced into the Great Basin to Utah Lake and the lands south of Sevier Lake. By then it was October, and the party reluctantly gave up the quest for Monterey, and returned to Santa Fe.

It was fear of encroachment, most especially from the French, that led the Spanish to establish a line of missions and presidios across south Texas to the border of French Louisiana, and also to explore as far north as the Platte River. By the time Spain received Louisiana by the Peace of Paris (1763), she had pushed her trading activities at least as far up the Mississippi as Ste. Geneviève and St. Charles. In terms of lands claimed and settlement established, even though very sparsely, Spain as of 1776 was by far the greatest landowner in the part of North America that became the United States—although her borders, from San Francisco to St. Augustine, were always broken somewhere; between 1763 and 1783, for example, the Floridas were in British hands.

Spain was apprehensive and suspicious of others—of the French and British and Russians. Of these predatory powers, the most formidable to the Spanish for most of the eighteenth century were the French, who before 1763 not only held Canada and the Old Northwest (that vast section of land bounded by the Appalachians, the Ohio River, the Great Lakes, and the Mississippi), but had at one time or another penetrated other parts of North America as well.

The French knew all about northeast Florida, for example, because the Protestant Huguenots had been there and been brutally massacred in and about Fort Caroline in 1565 by the Spanish. In 1682, Jean Cavalier, Sieur de La Salle, reached the mouth of the Mississippi, several hundred miles west. In 1684 he established Fort St. Louis on Matagorda Bay, and, although it was abandoned in 1689, its very presence was sufficient to spur the Spanish to renew their defenses of east Texas. Early in the eighteenth century the French explored areas on both sides of the lower Mississippi, and by 1710 Mobile was the established capital of French colonization in that area. In 1713 a lieutenant of La Mothe Cadillac's, not to be outdone by his commander, who had founded Detroit, established a fur trading post at Natchitoches. It did not thrive, but it served as a further warning to the Spanish. In 1714 Fort Toulouse, near the junction of the Coosa and Talapoosa rivers (near present Montgomery, Alabama) was established for trade with the Upper Creeks; two years later Fort Rosalie was constructed at the present site of Natchez, Mississippi. In 1718 New Orleans was founded. For a time a thriving economy existed in New France south of Canada. North of these lower Mississippi settlements lay the Illinois country with Forts Cahokia, Kaskaskia, Vincennes, Ouiatanon, Miami, and Massac, and across the Mississippi, Ste. Geneviève and St. Charles; these were not even all of the French settlements there. Kaskaskia had a Jesuit school for white boys; Cahokia, a small school for Indians.

The vigor of French expansion is most noticeable in their explorations westward. Usually they advanced as traders. In 1717 a party of Frenchmen reached the Spanish town of San Juan Bautista. By 1719 other Frenchmen were up the Red River of the south; still others traded with the Osages along the river of the same name, and with the Pawnees on the Arkansas River. In 1721 Bernard de la Harpe reached Galveston Bay. By 1724 a Frenchman named Bourgmont made trade overtures to the Otos, the Iowas, and even the Padoucas of western Kansas. In 1734 a Frenchman had reached the Mandan villages via the Missouri; five years later the Mallet brothers crossed from the Platte southward across Nebraska, Kansas, and Colorado to Santa Fe. By the 1750's several routes to Santa Fe were known, and several French groups had arrived there, meeting variously with good trade or foul imprisonment, and had made treaties with some of the wild plains tribes, including the Comanches.

Meanwhile, in the 1730's, Gaultier de Varennes (better known as La Vérendrye) pushed westward across Canada; his successors pushed on, and finally Legardeur St. Pierre in 1752 founded Fort La Jonquière on the Saskatchewan at the foot of the Rockies. Nearly a decade before (1743) La Vérendrye's sons had reached some point, probably in Wyoming, from whence they could see one of the eastern ranges of the Rockies. "The French," commented historian Herbert Bolton, "had thus reached the Rockies by way of nearly every important stream between the Red River and the Saskatchewan."[1] No wonder the Spanish were apprehensive.

It is of course true that after 1763 the French were by treaty no longer in North America. Many of their fur-trading posts were abandoned and reverted to the wilderness. Yet Kaskaskia and Cahokia, Vincennes, St. Charles and Ste. Geneviève, Detroit, St. Joseph, and a few other isolated settlements remained, tiny pin-pricks of the French brand of Western civilization in the lonely land. Moreover, although the French were legally ousted, their *coureurs des bois* (literally, "runners of the woods" —unlicensed French fur traders and woods rovers), their half-bloods, and many of their traders remained and were a continuing source of information about the new country all the way to the Rockies. They knew the Indians, the beaver-populated streams, the passes, portages, fords, rapids, swamps, prairies, and lakes. It was hardly an unknown wilderness to them.

As for the Russians, they had pushed across Siberia during the seventeenth century. The Spanish had established the presidio at the Golden Gate as a result of news about Vitus Bering's explorations in the North Pacific. Bering, a Danish mariner in Russian employ, had in 1741 sailed south past Mt. St. Elias on the southern coast of Alaska, and by 1763 the Russians were conducting a vigorous trade down through the Aleutians, with posts at some of the larger islands. Their sailing ships had probed southward, down the Oregon coast.

And as for the British—in the same year, 1776, in which Anza established the presidio at San Francisco, the English were gravely concerned in the crisis involving their thirteen American colonies. And while British governmental affairs, including their colonial activities, left much to be desired in efficiency, integrity, and administrative wisdom, there were officials in His Majesty's service who knew a great deal about the new country west of the Proclamation Line of 1763 which had forbidden settlement west of the crest of the Appalachians. Englishmen were acutely aware of the area east of the Mississippi River which they had wrested from the French little more than a decade before. On their maps they had marked with some accuracy the Ohio, Wabash, Scioto, Muskingum, Great Kanawha, Tennessee, Kentucky, and Cumberland rivers, and even the mouth of the Missouri. The English also knew of the Pearl, Perdido, Escambia, Apalachicola, St. Johns, and St. Mary's, for since 1763 they had possessed the Floridas. There were authorities among the British who were quite aware of Spanish holdings at New Orleans, Natchitoches, San Antonio, Santa Fe, Taos, and of the chain of missions from Texas to Monterey. British traders had penetrated west of the Mississippi, especially along the lower reaches of the Arkansas and Osage.

The lobbying activities of land speculators, both British and colonials, and fur traders prevented the home government from ignoring the western country, at least to the Mississippi, for long. Not only were Scot fur-trading interests concerned with keeping the new country a wilderness, but in distinct opposition to them were those speculators who wanted great grants of land in order to open up the West to settlement. There were conflicting claims, some of them "sea to sea," made by the several colonies. Then there was the Indian menace, unsuccessfully dealt with by the Proclamation of 1763. Time and western activity had worked against the British, and their system of control of trade and settlement, based upon the Proclamation Line, collapsed. This was due, however, not to a lack of understanding of the geography so much as a failure to comprehend the forces that were building up pressure for westward advance.

These forces were all set in motion by the actual, permanent inhabitants of the new nation in North America. In 1763 they were still colonials, but by 1776 they were calling themselves Americans, or Continentals, and the thirteen colonies were now as many states. Thus they must be considered apart from the British. Before appraising their knowledge of the wilderness, we shall briefly note their condition as of 1776.

There were two and a half million white Americans and possibly three-fourths of a million black slaves in the thirteen states. Although the whites included Scotch-Irish, Germans, French Huguenots, and small representations of Dutch, Irish, and other European nationalities, the English language, English common law, and an English cultural context generally prevailed. Most of these people lived between seaside and fifty miles inland, although there were western extensions south of the Potomac, along the wide coastal plain and then into the upland piedmont, as much as 200 miles into the interior. Some of the easternmost mountain valleys, such as Virginia's Shenandoah, had also been settled. But for the most part the great Appalachian chain, even with its fertile valleys, remained a barrier to western settlement, restricting the population to an area between its eastern fringes and the sea. Beyond the mountains, or on their western fringes, the frontier settlements began. There was usually an actual geographical gap between the settled country and the new country, in some places extending 200 miles east to west, a wild span of mountains, valleys, and thick forests.

The country along the eastern seaboard had all the characteristics of a settled society. As many as five generations of unbroken occupation gave it a look of stability and maturity. There was no real threat from the Indians. There were towns and houses, and churches and grave-yards in which the tombstone inscriptions were difficult to read, so long ago had they been chiseled out, so old and weathered had the stones become. Because few Americans practiced scientific agriculture, there were areas of abandoned fields, barns, and outbuildings leaning with wind, unkept, unused, unpainted, and unoccupied. What of the owners of the farms? Had they simply died off leaving no progeny? Hardly, in that period of fruitful multiplication. Where had they gone? Quite probably they had gone West, to the new country. And where was the new country? What was known of it by Americans?

In a general way, we may say that Americans knew the main elements of its geography as far west as the "father of waters"—the Mississippi. That is to say, they knew the Appalachians, and they knew of the prairies of Kentucky, Indiana, and Illinois. By 1776 there were many "wilderness cosmopolites"—men who knew the western country from Michilimackinak to New Orleans, who were as at home in Philadelphia as at Fort Pitt, Vincennes, Detroit, or Pensacola. They knew the new country east of the Mississippi and west of the Appalachians, or large parts of it, like a book: Oliver Pollack, George Rogers Clark, Simon Kenton, Daniel Boone, Richard Henderson, John Sevier, and John Donelson are just a few of a substantial regiment of such men.

Surely, then, the continent was hardly unknown, at least as far west as the Mississippi. The average man would have known next to nothing of the lands beyond that great river, but educated persons such as Thomas Jefferson certainly possessed some knowledge of the rest of the continent—of Mexico and Texas and the far Pacific (the "South Sea") —and had some idea of high, formidable mountains and scorched deserts out there.

The Americans knew in a practical way much more than just the geographical elements of the country west to the Mississippi. They were aware that most of the land was thickly forested with deciduous trees —black walnut, oak, ash, elm, gum, maple, poplar, wild cherry, syca-more—that it was teeming with game, and was sparsely populated by Indians. And yet the flora and fauna of this vast region were, after all, no more than a richer, more primitive, and far more extensive version of the deciduous forests of western Europe and the British Isles, and the virgin stands remaining in the settled region east of the Appalachians.

This great forest, as some have called it, has been pictured as a virtu-ally impenetrable temperate zone jungle, so foreboding that men envel-oped in its midst felt as lonely as on the bounding sea, so dense and

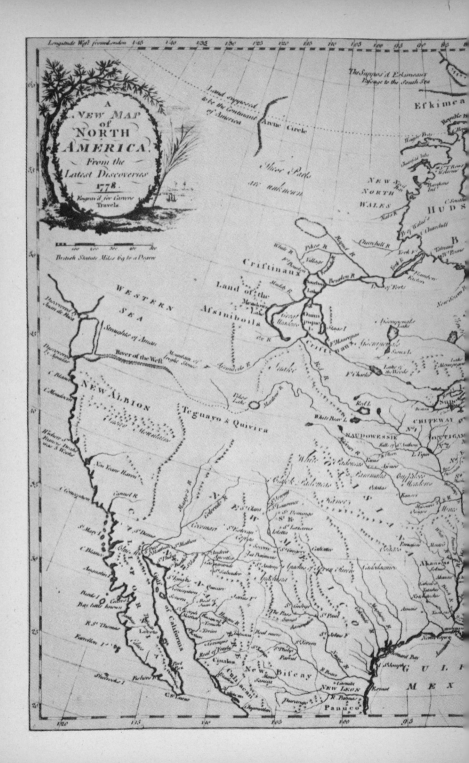

"A New map of North America From the Latest Discoveries in 1778," engraved for Jonathon Carver's *Travels Through the Interior Parts of North America.* (The National Archives)

wild did it appear. Theodore Roosevelt described it as "a region of sun-less, tangled forests . . . with underbrush . . . dense and rank, be-tween the boles of tall trees, making a cover so thick that it nowhere gave a chance for the human eye to see even as far as a bow could carry."[2]

If the great forest was such a menacing, impenetrable barrier, why did men plunge into it? Why would business-minded Virginians found the Ohio Company in 1747 and receive 200,000 acres under certain conditions, or form the Loyal Land Company in 1748, which received 800,000 acres from the Old Dominion? These are two out of dozens of speculative schemes involving the new country which sprouted down into Federalist times. Obviously the investors were ambitious to survey portions of the great forest and then sell the land to permanent settlers at great profit. Since from this vast, impenetrable forest men envisioned fields, meadows, gardens and orchards, homes, villages, roads, and bridges, it is clear that the terrible forest was hardly a deterrent to them.

For in truth, only parts of it grew so densely as to be nearly impene-trable. In many areas the great trees formed a sheltering canopy, high above the ground, that prevented brush from growing; the forest floor was like a green velveteen carpet of grass, brightened by wild flowers. Consisting mostly of deciduous trees, the entire region west of the mountains must in winter have been as gaunt and stark as a surrealist painting. Interspersed through these forested lands were glades and meadows, lakes and streams. A forest in which deer and bison could graze was something less than an impenetrable jungle. Indian encamp-ments were not lost in a jungle growth, but were established at glades, meadows, or other openings where sufficient sunshine came through for growing corn, beans, gourds, calabashes, and squashes. In a day's trek across primitive Ohio, Kentucky, or Tennessee, then, the pioneer might advance from glades to stream banks to salt licks to lakes, from a knoll into a valley, and, it is true, from time to time might be forced to plunge into a thick forest growth in which he did walk as in a perpetual gloam-ing.

The potential that the pioneer saw all around him far exceeded his fears. The trees he recognized; he knew that soil that would support them would support crops when they were felled. The abandoned In-dian villages, with their weed-covered patches where corn had been raised, bore promise of the fertility of the black soil. Dales and meadows where deer and bison grazed insured suitable meadow lands for sheep and cattle. The presence of wild boar proved that the domesticated pig could rut and grow fat on the mast of the forest. And the very forest itself, which must be destroyed, offered building materials and firewood.

The pioneer was not timid before his tasks. The forest invited him, dared him with his axe and his rifle. He willingly accepted the challenge; nor did he think of the forest as his enemy, as has sometimes been said. The woodsman learned its secrets: its herbs and berries, its fish, birds, and animals. He knew the heavy moss was on the north sides, the ragged branches on the northwest sides of the trees. He attacked the forest as unemotionally as a modern wrecker destroys an old house, or a bulldozer knocks over an old oak. He apparently felt no melancholy, no particular elation, no recognizable emotion save satisfaction at destroying it. If a shadow of regret flitted across the pioneer's mind when he thought of the land cover that *was* when he first arrived, and the farmsteads that were there now, he passed it off with a shrug. A shortage of timber? Inconceivable—but if it did happen, although he might have created it, he would never have to deal with it; let the next generation solve its own problems.

So much for the myth of the unknown continent.

Another false assumption is the myth of the trackless wilderness. Even the densest woods, with the more than 300 different varieties of trees, enormous vines, and thick undergrowth, were traversed by a maze of paths and trails. Most of these were animal-made, of course, and the biggest trails were made by the biggest animals, the buffalo. Usually such traces led to fords, salt licks, or meadows. Some of these trails were broad as a modern highway, others no wider than necessary for bison to make their way single file along the fringe of the forest. Sometimes, so constant were they in their travels, the trails were worn almost belly-deep into the ground.

The perambulations of generations of Indians had also hewn out primitive highways: the shortest and most direct routes from one village to another, portage paths from one stream or lake to another, traces from enemy to enemy, or paths from village to hunting grounds. Whatever the purpose, these trails took the high land, avoided swamps and cane brakes where possible, and, as if attracted by magnetism, forded at the easiest river crossings. They led the pedestrian to his destination with the greatest possible safety.

An Indian trail hoary with age, such as the Warrior's Path from Cherokee lands in North Carolina northward and westward, through Cumberland Gap, and northwestward to the Ohio, or the Iroquois war trail southward through western Pennsylvania, was of course easily followed. Typically it was twelve to eighteen inches in width, a single-file trail, and sometimes the moccasined feet of generations of red men had worn it a foot deep. Such a trail was called an Indian thoroughfare, and a runner could sometimes traverse a hundred miles of such a trail from sunrise to sunset. Lesser trails were not as well marked, and good woods lore was necessary to follow them.

Where possible, such trails followed the ridges, not exactly on the top, for such a trace would make the trespasser too easily seen by his enemies, but down a bit, on one side or the other. If the trail followed a watercourse, it cut across the elbows of the river, and thus shortened the distances. Crossings were often made at the mouth of a river, for here there was a sand or a mud bar extending far out into the main stream, thus narrowing the watery stretch that had to be crossed. Occasionally there were trail crossings along these Indian thoroughfares where an identifying post might be placed, a clearing made from the forest; and there, at certain times, Indian traders would barter with brethren from other tribes. Later, white traders "set up shop" at the same places, in a similar way, but with blue beads, calicos, firewater and falderal that appealed to the Indians.

The pioneers' knowledge and wide use of these trails through the new country attest to their importance in the march to the West. It is worth noting that there is hardly a railroad line that does not follow in approximation one of the great trails used by the Indians prior to the white man's occupation. Many automobile highways also follow them.

All of the trails received at least some use by the pioneers. The most northerly within the United States was the Iroquois Trail, the "water-level route" along the Mohawk River, stretching from the Hudson to Lake Erie. The Iroquois, through whose lands it ran, were, however, a deterrent to its use until the early nineteenth century. South of this route was the Kittanning Path, west from Philadelphia, up the Susquehanna, west on the Juniata (or West Branch of the Susquehanna), over the mountains by the Kittanning Gorge to the Allegheny River, and down that river to the Ohio. Forbes' Road, constructed from Carlyle to Pittsburgh during the French and Indian War, ran along an old trail known as the Raystown Path, south of the Kittanning.

Still farther south, linking the Potomac with the Ohio, was Nemacolin's Path, the main branch of which went as far as Pittsburgh. It was along this route that Braddock made his way until he was attacked by the French and Indians on July 9, 1755. Then there was the Warrior's Path which, because it had several branches as it made its way from North Carolina into Ohio, is hard to define with accuracy. The Virginia Warrior's Path went up the Shenandoah Valley to the Clinch River, then in a western direction through Cumberland Gap, northwest to the head of Rockcastle Creek, through present Crab Orchard and Danville, Kentucky, to the Falls of the Ohio at present Louisville.

Boone's Wilderness Road from Cumberland Gap northwest to the Kentucky River preempted some of this path; it was a major emigration route. On across the Ohio there was an Indian trail, a sort of continuation of the Warrior's Path, that wound westward, ultimately to St. Louis.

In the Old Northwest—Ohio and Indiana—there were a number of trails that carried Indians, then traders, then emigrants into the West. From Niagara to Detroit there was the Lake Shore Trail, from Fort Pitt to Detroit the Great Trail, then, deeper into the Ohio country, the Scioto-Beaver Trail, the Scioto-Monongahela Trail, the Venango Trail from Fort Pitt to Presqu'isle (Erie), and the Scioto Trail from Lake Erie down into Kentucky and Tennessee.

The tribes in the Far West, where trees became scarcer and rainfall skimpier, also followed long-established trails. Sometimes these could be more difficult to identify, for the prevalence of the buffalo, the dry climate, and the use by the Indians of ponies and travois, which could sometimes make their trails almost as wide as the horizon, all tended to blend the Indian trails with animal paths. Nevertheless, it is known that the Navajos and the Utes had well-marked traces through the rough, broken country north of the Grand Canyon. The Crossing of the Fathers, which Father Escalante used to ford the Colorado in 1776, was on a well-marked Indian trail. The various Pueblo Indians, we know, followed long trails to the sources of salt. There was a Great North Trail down the front range of the Rockies, dating back into the mists of earliest man in North America. There were trails through the Rockies, especially at the better passes. Both the Santa Fe and the Oregon trails followed logical routes used by Indians for generations before the coming of the white man.

The extent of Indian travels appears to have been remarkable. Plains Indians are known to have roamed up to 2,000 miles from their homelands, and the Blackfeet of Montana marauded into Colorado and the Great Salt Lake country. Iroquois warriors returned to their home country in central New York with Siouan captives they had apparently captured in a raid into South Dakota's Black Hills; the Iroquois also had attacked the Creeks as far south as north Florida. In fact it is probable that communication by Indian trails could be conducted through the length and breadth of the North American continent. This explains the use of sign language, which was understood throughout Indian America although there were hundreds of spoken dialects.

The water routes through the wilderness were also known. Rare was the frontiersman who was not aware of the river drainage of his own region. The settler in present West Virginia was acquainted with the Ohio and its tributaries to the south: the New, the Greenbriar, the Monongahela, the Great Kanawha, the Licking, and probably the Kentucky. Kentuckians certainly knew the Kentucky and the Cumberland, Tennesseeans knew their namesake plus its headwater streams, the Clinch, Holston, French Broad, and Watauga. So too were southern pioneers aware of the sluggish streams that flowed, or were tributary to streams that flowed, southward into the Gulf, like the Black Warrior, Tombigbee, Chattahoochee, Flint, Apalachicola, and Pearl, or into the Mississippi, like the Yazoo. Those northwest of the Ohio knew the Muskingum, Scioto, and the Wabash, and that the Allegheny and Monongahela joined at Fort Pitt to form the Ohio. If they had talked with traders, or with soldiers, or had read of Indian depredations (and most whites were literate in 1776), then they knew of the Great Lakes and the river and portage links connecting them. The vessels with which to navigate these western waters were readily available. The white men adopted the bark canoe in the north and the dugout canoe elsewhere—the flatboat and keelboat came later.

That these streams, especially those linked with the Ohio-Mississippi river system or those flowing into the Gulf out of Georgia and north Florida, were of use to the settler, was a fact not lost on those who hankered to stake their fortunes in the new country. The streams floated through the wilderness, inviting the settler with the lure of little effort and little work—of just floating down river, until the perfect place of settlement was found.

A third misconception is the myth of Indian invincibility.

The Indians are usually considered as having been a deterrent to frontier expansion. The folklore of American history has created a stock setting of the stalwart pioneer with a wife and children, from nursing babe to teenager, hacking out a home from the wilderness. The cabin is crude, perhaps a tiny log house eighteen feet by thirty, a chimney at one end, a single two-foot-square window, and a crude wooden door. The stealthy enemy creep up on these innocent, peaceful, God-fearing Christian people and commit horrible crimes. Then, their savage and bloody deeds accomplished, they disappear again into the darkness of the primeval forest.

Such dreadful happenings occurred often enough to place the stamp of validity on the folklore, and to make several thousand novels and western stories sound plausible. These are, however, border stories about the settlers on the cutting edge of the frontier, yarns of high adventure about a distinct minority of the settlers in the new country.

That edge was blunted within years and sometimes within months, as the human sickle swept west. If the pioneer was in danger of attack by the Indians, the reason may well have been because he had chosen to settle on Indian lands. He was thus committing an illegal act, but he and hundreds of his neighbors throughout the cutting edge of the frontier did it anyway. When an Indian agent rode through and informed him of the facts, the stock reply of the pioneer was that he did not know it, that the line of Indian ownership was not yet run, or it was disputed. Threats of forced removal or of Indian attack rarely deterred the squatter. He rationalized that God made the wilderness for the man who could use it best, and he as a white, civilized, Christian husbandman could certainly use it better than a few forest hunters. And so the Indians attacked, and those whites who somehow survived the barbarous assault lived to hate the Indian and swear to exterminate him. This attitude was behind the phrase, "The only good Indian is a dead Indian."

The red men are usually described as appearing like devils out of the forest, implying that where they lived was a mystery. Nothing could be further from the truth. If the lone settler did not know specifically, he knew approximately the region the Indians came from. He knew what Indians lived there, and he knew of the trails that led to their settlements.

Over at the "station," the nearest blockhouse, or the settlement at the crossroads or at the ford, the exact location of these Indian villages was even better known. This is partly because the Indians did not refuse to associate with the white man, as we are led to believe. On the contrary, the red men hung around the settlements, selling peltry, getting drunk, stealing horses, becoming nuisances; if they ceased to make an appearance, the frontiersman knew something was wrong.

Furthermore, the settlement would have merchants, among whom was an unscrupulous breed known as Indian traders. From the earliest times of settlement the Indian trader had made his presence known. He was an identifiable type in eighteenth- and nineteenth-century America, and was almost always described in the most derogatory terms. He brought to the Indians whiskey, disease, firearms, treachery and deceit; he destroyed their self-sufficiency. Because the Indians of the frontier West could gather furs which were in great demand, the Indian trader felt his way along the serpentine trails of the wilderness to haggle over and purchase the raw material for the coats and capes and hats of European dress. Following this line of reasoning to a logical conclusion, it can be argued that the Indian, and the commodity he could sell, actually hastened the settlement of the American West.

Most of the settlers in the new country never raised a rifle to aim at an Indian and probably never suffered an Indian scare. *Most* settlers in the new country possessed normal timidity, and waited until the Indians had been defeated in battle and then removed by treaty before advancing into what had become temporarily an area devoid of humanity. The great movements into the Old Northwest followed Anthony Wayne's victory at Fallen Timbers and the subsequent Treaty of Greenville in 1795, by which the Delaware, Miami, Shawnee, Wyandot, and other tribes were pushed west of the state of Ohio; later, the victory at the Battle of the Thames in 1813, in which Tecumseh was killed, paved the way for the Treaties of Portage des Sioux in 1815, whereby these same tribes, among others, gave up land extending to the banks of the Mississippi. The great migration into the Old Southwest followed Andrew Jackson's defeat of the Creeks at Horseshoe Bend in 1814 and the subsequent Treaty of Fort Jackson, by which these Indians lost about half their lands. Historically, the Indian was not so much of a deterrent to the sweep across the continent; but he posed a serious problem—how to get him off the white-coveted lands with as little bloodshed as possible, and with a semblance of Christian humaneness, to remove him without tarnishing too much the ideals of the Republic. It was a tough task, never well done, because the new country man refused to look upon the Indian as a human being who had a right to his home and land.

This idea of Indian invincibility, this assumption that the red man stood in the way of advancing civilization, is pretty much, then, a myth, which, like the myth of the unknown wilderness and the myth of the trackless wilderness, makes for great romance, but very poor history. But unlike the subjects of the first two myths, there is no question but that the Indian constituted a real problem.

The Problem of the
Native American

There are always discrepancies between ideals and realities. In the United States during the nineteenth century the most glaring of these was the existence of slavery in a free society. A close second to it was the treatment of the American Indian by a government whose citizens considered it the most humane on earth.

There is a tendency in our literature to make the Indian-in-general an enemy but the Indian-in-particular a noble savage. Cooper's Chingachgook, the ill-starred Indian lovers in Helen Hunt Jackson's *Ramona*, and even Tonto, the friend of the Lone Ranger in our own mass-media age, are all the noblest of people. Thomas Crawford's pediment on the north side of the national Capitol depicts "The Progress of American Civilization and the Decline of the Indian"; it has an idealized Indian mourning his dead.

In 1872 the painter George Catlin proposed that a permanent monument to the red man be constructed in the new Central Park in New York. He planned a sheet-iron replica of a Crow wigwam, seventy-five feet in height and of equal base diameter. Inside would be a real Crow tepee and a gallery containing 600 of Catlin's Indian paintings, plus artifacts he had collected. The proposal gained sufficient interest to warrant a front-page engraving of the proposed structure in *Frank Leslie's Illustrated Newspaper*.[1]

Eventually the noble savage became a symbol of liberty: he graced the Indian-head penny, 1859-1900, and the buffalo nickel, 1913-38; Sioux Chief One Papa glared out from the five-dollar silver certificate beginning in 1899; and in 1914 the Sioux warrior Hollow Horn Bear was pictured on the fourteen-cent postage stamp. In this way did the government commemorate a people who had been all but destroyed by the white man.

And yet at the same time the Indian-in-general was pictured as a barbarous deterrent to westward advance. Whether as Mingos, Hurons, Creeks, or Seminoles, or as warlike Sioux, fearless Comanches or cruel Apaches, always "the Indians" threatened danger and death, captivity and torture. Thousands of late-nineteenth-century dime novels, the pulp magazines of the 1920's and 30's, and today's paperback novels, motion pictures, and television scenarios have depicted the Indians in such sinister roles.

Clearly the Indian was, then, a complicated problem to be wrestled with while the American people swept across the continent. The presence of the red man created a psychological and moral dilemma which split the citizenry along political, geographical, and moral lines. Yet there remains throughout a callousness that is chilling. For the most part American society sighed at the red man's demise and then went on with the business of settling the new country the white man's way.

The number of Indians at any given time prior to the end of the frontier in 1890 is a matter of conjecture. A common estimate for the tribes north of the Ohio and east of the Mississippi, as of 1776, is 40,000 to 50,000. Some of these were Iroquois, rapidly weakening both in num-

George Catlin's design for the proposed Indian wigwam to be erected in Central Park, New York, from *Frank Leslie's Illustrated Weekly*.

Eastern woodlands Indians, Iroquois, painting by A. A. Jansson. (Courtesy American
Museum of Natural History)

bers and in purity of blood, and the various tribes of the Algonquian
tongue: Shawnee, Delaware, Chippewa, Wyandot, Potawatomi, Miami,
Ottawa, Winnebago, Monominee, Sauk, and Fox. Those south of the
Ohio and east of the Mississippi were primarily of the Five Civilized
Tribes: the Cherokee, Creek, Choctaw, Chickasaw, and Seminole.
There were probably 75,000 of them.

Just west of the Mississippi there were overflows of the eastern woods
Indians, but a little farther on the plains environment required a very different life style. Here the red men lived a nearly totally nomadic existence
within a given vast area that each tribe loosely considered its own. Before
the coming of the horse the plains Indian moved on his feet with nothing

greater as a beast of burden than dogs pulling travois or a stoical squaw carrying what little truk her nomadic spouse possessed. The horse emancipated these Indians and made them the white man's most troublesome contesters for the arid lands. The plains dwellers were not tempted by the white life style; they loved their equestrian, hunting existence. And the Sioux, Blackfeet, Bannock, Cheyenne, Kiowa, Comanche, Apache—to name the more warlike—for a brief period in the history of the frontier gave the white man a peck of trouble. Possibly there were 250,000 red men between the Mississippi and the Pacific coast in 1850, when Americans began to come in close and constant touch with them.

It is dangerous to generalize too much about the Indians, since this term covers such a wide variety of peoples. It has been said that the physical characteristics of the various Indian tribes, from the Puget Sound to southern Florida, from the Mojave Desert to the Aroostook Valley of Maine, actually varied more than the physical characteristics of the various races of white men. In terms of life style, the red men ranged from the Diggers of Nevada and Utah to the nomadic Sioux, Blackfeet, Crow, Cheyenne, Comanche, and Apache and the forest nomads of Algonquian stock surrounding the Great Lakes and southward to the Ohio, to the nearly sedentary Five Civilized Tribes of the southeast, Six Nations of the Iroquois in the northeast, and Pueblo Indians of the southwest.

Regardless of where they lived, the Indians were beautifully attuned to their environment. They were primarily hunters (save for the few sedentary tribes), and they were good at it. They were stone-age men who could be formidable adversaries in fighting for their land and way of life. Their warfare was barbaric, and, when occasion called for it, they could torture their victims mercilessly.

Nowhere was the Indians' adjustment to the environment more delicately balanced than on the Great Plains. The red men there blended into the ecology right along with the buffalo, wolf, and coyote. There were so many square miles for each Indian that his killing of an occasional bison, his use of a sheltered meadow or part of a river valley for his village and his horse herd, never upset nature's balance. The few patches of land the squaws put to beans, squash, and gourds were specks upon the grass sea, and the green meadows shorn of velvety fodder soon grew back again.

The Indian shelters were constructed from skins and dried wooden poles. With flaps at the pointed tops which helped draw the smoke from the tiny fire inside, little fuel was used, yet within two or three days after the tepee was pitched even the earthen floor was warmed to its elliptical circumference. When properly constructed by knowledgeable squaws and anchored down with stones, and with an inside fly which prevented condensation and also created a thin layer of air insulation, the dwelling was not only comfortable; it was capable of withstanding near-hurricane-force winds. When the game moved on or the village became dirty and the grass was closely cropped, it was but a matter of two or three hours to dismantle the tepees, pack them on travois, and move elsewhere. Then the cold wind blew, rain and snow dampened the bare spots, and spring brought new grass where the tepees had been. Where the small vegetable plots had been, a second growth of corn and beans, squash and gourds came amidst grasses and weeds. Before many seasons the area reverted to prairie.

Among some of the Shoshonian peoples of the mountains and the Great Basin, and among the Navajos and the Apaches, the wickiup, a brush shelter, was used instead of the tepee. Sometimes the wickiups were shaped like a tepee of limbs twenty or thirty feet high, with a circular "floor" twelve or fifteen feet in diameter, with pine and spruce boughs placed along the slanting sides to keep out the weather. When abandoned, they weathered and rotted in the rhythm of other natural things. The Navajo hogan may possibly be considered a sophisticated variety.

The Indian, then, did not destroy nature's rhythm; he was a part of it. But for this he needed space; and indeed, mobility was the key to his well-being. He followed the great herds of buffalo, making life adventurous by raiding the horse herds of his enemies or "counting coup"— i.e., touching an enemy. Only through mobility could he be assured of

Apache wickiup, Calva, Arizona. (Courtesy American Museum of Natural History)

Plains Indians. (Courtesy American Museum of Natural History)

good hunts; and so his free life on the unfenced plains depended entirely on the availability of the great open spaces. But the white man's culture demanded land ownership which gave the possessor absolute power over his real estate; he could fence it, burn it, mine it, plant it, graze it, and defend it with a gun from trespassers.

And so the conflict was inevitable. If the woods Indians of the Old Northwest had been willing to settle on a quarter section and learn the white man's agriculture, if the southeastern tribes had not resided on good cotton land, if the plains Indians had not been nomads whose existence depended on the hunting of the buffalo—in short, if they all had *not been Indians* occupying lands coveted by whites—then possibly a settlement could have been made.

And yet, the impression that the Indian was a friendless wretch suffering through "a century of dishonor" is not entirely just. Of the innumerable ambivalent policy situations in the history of the country, that of the Indian must certainly rate a prominent place. For in essence, the federal government assumed the position of moral agent, trying to defend the Indians from the acquisitiveness and blind hatred of the frontiersmen. Yet the federal position from which the rules and regulations for Indian matters were promulgated was itself uncertain, and therefore self-defeating. The government first tried assimilation, then by Andrew Jackson's time fostered segregation and removal, and by the Dawes Act of 1887 had returned to the concept of assimilation.

Indian policy, as it was gradually formulated, was uninspired. It had its origins with the British colonies; through the years the basic problems remained land intrusion by the whites and unscrupulous traders with their stock in trade, demon rum and rot-gut whiskey. The colonies passed ordinances regulating Indian matters, but in the back country colonial boundaries disappeared, and by 1755 the British had wisely assumed the control of Indian relations. They appointed a competent agent, Sir William Johnson, to look after the Iroquois and the tribes north of the Ohio, and John Stuart, another woods-wise Indian agent, to work with the Five Civilized Tribes south of the Ohio. These men, bolstered with ordinances, were able to do much to regulate trade, but the problem of intrusion by frontiersmen on the Indians' land remained.

This the British tried to solve in a temporary way with their Proclamation of 1763, which forbade settlement west of the Appalachian watershed. Since the colonial governments from earliest times, as well as the British government, recognized Indian title and ownership to Indian lands, this Proclamation (which had a precedent in a Pennsylvania act of 1758) merely crystallized a long-established assumption and delineated settled white man's country from Indian territory. Between 1765 and 1768 much of this Proclamation Line, which at first was only indicated on maps, was physically established; in 1768 the treaties of Fort Stanwix with the Iroquois and of Hard Labour with the Cherokee changed the line in accord with land speculation schemes.

Already the policy of guaranteeing the Indians their lands by solemn treaty, drawn up with their chiefs in a sober and honorable fashion (or signed by dishonorable government agents who knowingly cheated the Indians, on the one hand, and by disreputable drunks who could mark an "X," on the other) was in existence: but at the same time the white men knew full well that the frontier was inevitably going to advance westward, and that more treaties and more solemn promises would have to be made. This was, in fact, the crux of the whole problem.

Was this policy, then, sheer duplicity and chicanery? Some would insist it was. First, the white men knew that to recognize the Indian tribes as sovereign nations was absurd. Second, they knew that to conclude treaties with them which included boundary stipulations was totally unrealistic, since the Indians had a primitive sense of land ownership, and few tribes ever knew specifically the boundaries of their own lands since they were hunters, not agriculturalists. And finally, the guarantees written into the treaties promising the Indians the lands they retained for all time to come were barefaced lies, and the white men who most knew it were the very ones who participated in the negotiations.

But there is another way to look at the policy. First, there had evolved a theory concerning those lands. By the act of discovery, the Europeans reasoned, the white man gained a right to occupy the land. He thus claimed ownership and prevented a white national of some other European country from taking possession. Although the white man owned the land, the Indians retained the right of occupancy until such time as the white owners, by purchase or force, pushed the Indians out. This theory provided the legal basis for the system of Indian relations which grew through British colonial times and flowered in American Indian policy under the Constitution. The assumption of federal power is implicit in the very brevity of discussion concerning Indians at the Constitutional Convention, and by the simple, straightforward statement in Article I, Section 8, that Congress "shall have the power . . . to regulate commerce with foreign nations, and with the Indian tribes. . . ." Neither states, nor territories, nor individuals were allowed to make treaties, agreements, or land purchases with Indians, and no one could legally settle on lands stipulated as being in Indian country until the title had been formally cleared with the Indians. Attempts were also made—were continually being made—to control the traders and the whiskey traffic, to drive out squatters on Indian land, to punish crimes committed by whites against Indians. Thus, insofar as possible, the United States Government acted as a moral and civilizing agent, attempting to control the helter-skelter, rampaging rush of the frontiersmen toward the lands of the setting sun.

Attempts to augment the policy were numerous; there was the Indian Intercourse Act of 1793, a new one in 1796, and subsequent acts throughout most of the nineteenth century. They all failed. Leadership fell to the executive, as it should have, and with consistency presidents tried to administer these laws in good faith. Washington, in his Third Annual Address to Congress in the autumn of 1791, acknowledged the sense of Congress in desiring the defense and security of the western frontiers to be accomplished "on the most humane principles." He said that measures had been adopted to make even the most hostile tribes "sensible that a pacification was desired upon terms of moderation and justice."

Then the President listed the necessary measures to be included in the formulation of an Indian policy so that "all need of coercion in future may cease and that an intimate intercourse may succeed, calculated to advance the happiness of the Indians and to attach them firmly to the United States." It would seem necessary, he said, to give the Indians "the benefits of an impartial dispensation of justice"; to so define and regulate the alienation of their lands as "to obviate imposition and as far as may be practicable controversy"; to promote commerce with them under regulations to ensure them of fair treatment, to bring the blessings of civilization to them "as may from time to time suit their condition," and finally, to provide penalties and provision for levying them to those who infringed the treaties with the Indians "and endangered the peace of the Union." Then he added this justification for desiring such treatment for the Indians: "A system," he said, "corresponding with the mild principles of religion and philanthropy toward an unenlightened race of men, whose happiness materially depends on the conduct of the United States, would be as honorable to the national character as conformable to the dictates of sound policy."[2]

In his Seventh Annual Message of December 1795, Washington returned to the government's basic problem on the frontier—its inability to control the white frontiersmen. The law of 1793 had tried to deal with this problem. It stipulated that any "citizen or inhabitant of the United States," should he "go into any town, settlement, or territory, belonging to any nation or tribe of Indians, and shall there commit murder, robbery, larceny, trespass or other crime, against the person or property of any friendly Indian or Indians, . . . shall be subject to the same punishment, as if the offense had been committed within the state or district, to which he or she may belong. . . ." Moreover, any citizen settling on Indian lands, surveying such lands, or marking trees "for the purpose of settlement, he shall forfeit a sum not exceeding one thousand dollars . . . and suffer imprisonment not exceeding twelve months." Finally, "in order to promote civilization among the friendly Indian tribes," they were to be furnished with "domestic animals, and instruments of husbandry," and agents were to be stationed among the tribes.[3] The Act of 1796 empowered the President of the United States to "take such measures and to employ such military force, as he may judge necessary, to remove from land belonging . . . to any Indian tribe, any such citizen or other person, who has made or shall hereafter make, or attempt to make a settlement thereon. . . ."[4]

"We should not lose sight of an important truth which continually receives new confirmations," the President informed Congress, "namely, that the provisions heretofore made with a view to the protection of the Indians from the violences of the lawless part of our frontier inhabitants

are insufficient. . . . unless the murdering of Indians can be restrained
by bringing the murderers to condign punishment, all the exertions of
the Government to prevent destructive retaliations . . . will prove
fruitless. . . ."[5]

By "the lawless part" of the frontier elements, Washington was of
course referring to the actual murderers, thieves of the night, rapists,
and the like—the committers of crimes that have been crimes since man
came down out of the trees. But another lawless element was the squatters, always a poor and unmanageable class, who settled on Indian lands
in express violation of the law. A third element was that class of active
men with political power who have always exerted such a sinister and
powerful force on the well-meaning but tractable government of the
United States. In the new country, these men were the speculators,
often in the guise of bankers, lawyers, or just plain rich men. Their
chicanery, their barefaced violations of land laws, Indian treaties, and
restrictions on the Indian trade were the sources of much of the trouble
on the moving frontier.

The influence of this third frontier element extended to Congress,
which from the first was divided over Indian and frontier policy between hawks and doves. The hawks spoke of the gruesome realities of
Indian warfare, with substantiated cases of tomahawkings, scalpings, the
ripping of unborn infants from the bellies of frontier women, the horrors of death at the stake. Secretary of War Knox, in a report on the
Indian war in the Old Northwest (primarily the Ohio country) in the
1790's, estimated that 1,500 men, women, and children had been killed,
wounded, or taken into captivity between 1783 and 1790. To the hawks
such statistics demanded more military action.

But the doves had their say also. They insisted that the Indian war
had been "unjustly undertaken, . . . that depredations had been committed by the whites as well as by the Indians; and the whites were most
probably the aggressors, as they frequently made encroachments on the
Indian lands, whereas the Indians showed no inclination to obtain possession of our territory, or even to make temporary invasions of it until
urged to by a sense of their wrongs."[6]

Clearly the dilemma of the federal government was serious; it was
never solved, and indeed only ended with the near-destruction of the
Indian. The basic false premise behind the system of treaties was that
the nation would take centuries to occupy the land to the far shores of
the Pacific. Perhaps, if several hundred years rather than a single century had been involved, the system of treaties stipulating land sales by
the Indians to whites could have prevented bloodshed and hatred. Possibly there could have evolved a better solution, though it would still

have been inevitable that the Indians would eventually be deprived of their lands. But the movement into the new country was literally a tidal wave from east to west, and in its wake the best-laid plans of government were left behind as so much flotsam.

What else could the government do? It was able to insist upon a rational procedure for land acquisition. Every treaty was an expression of hope and a reiteration of good intentions. The United States commissioners stipulated the precise boundaries between the United States and lands of the tribe in question, the government "solemnly guaranteed" to the tribe "all their lands not hereby ceded," stated that anyone settling on the Indians' lands would "forfeit the protection of the United States," and in many cases granted to the Indians the right to have federal troops go in and drive such trespassers off their lands. Although the Indians were invariably deprived of something, usually land, they were always guaranteed protection of what lands they still retained or of the lands to which they were removed. The government appears to have realized that the chiefs did have the intelligence to understand the inevitable course of events and also that there did exist a sense of honor and obligation amongst the Indian leadership.

As President from 1801 to 1809, Thomas Jefferson also pushed provisions toward teaching the Indian how to live as an American farmer. It was a sort of Peace Corps plan, aimed at Indian assimilation, but it did not succeed. And even Jefferson, humanitarian that he was, reacted irritably, indicating that if the Indian would not learn, then he must be pushed west.

Besides the problems created by the white man's land hunger, the government had to cope with trade relations. The act of 1796 (which was revised in 1799 and 1802) established a system of government-operated Indian trading houses that limped along until private interests, led by John Jacob Astor, whose American Fur Company dominated the trade, and by one of his champions in the Senate, Thomas Hart Benton of Missouri, finally prevailed upon Congress to put an end to them in 1822. The government's system would have been a good one if it could have been soundly administered and the independent traders with their liquor restrained. But the federal government in the nineteenth century lacked the ability to administer properly these trading houses; it lacked law enforcement agencies on the frontier; and politically it could not cope with the power of such unscrupulous men as Astor. So the Indian was mercilessly exploited.

In 1834 there was passed a new, comprehensive Trade and Intercourse Act defining the constitutional right of Congress to administer to the tribes, specifying Indian country, and spelling out the regulations for conducting trade with the Indians. Much of this act remains as a basis of Indian policy today. Yet it simply continued policies that had failed before.

The frontiersman simply could not be controlled by the Great White Father. Thus, though the whiskey trade was a known cause of Indian discontent, the unscrupulous trader could not be contained. Neither could the squatter, the hunter, or the rich land speculator. There were instances when tribes were literally surrounded on their lands by frontier hamlets and the farms of the pioneers, and removing them was the only alternative to a total inundation of the enclave and possible massacre of the red men. If the reader questions how well-meaning men—well, more or less well-meaning—such as Lewis Cass in Michigan, William Clark in Missouri, or William Henry Harrison in Ohio and Indiana could conclude treaties depriving the hapless Indians of their ancestral lands, the answer lies here. Given the uncontrollable situation, the cession of these lands and the placing of the Indians somewhere else was the only way they could see to save the unfortunate people from obliteration. The Indians made things worse by going on the warpath, which was often done by uncontrollable young braves in violation of treaties. Besides this, the degradation caused by the white man's own liquor and diseases caused the Indians to appear in the worst possible light in the eyes of the whites.

Thus it is not surprising that the ink was hardly dry on the Louisiana Purchase agreement when President Jefferson conceived the idea of placing the Indians on some vast reservations west of the Mississippi. By the time of Monroe's administration (1817-25) the idea was gaining momentum. It was first applied, hesitatingly and using peaceful persuasion, to the southern tribes (Cherokee, Chickasaw, Choctaw, and Creek), because those tribes occupied lands that were coveted for growing cotton. The demand for these lands, upon which the highly profitable short-staple cotton could be so easily grown, was so great, the wealth of many of the planters so substantial, that the pressure to do something with those Indians could not be ignored. The fact that some of them were assimilating to the white man's world, living in cabins or frame houses, erecting fences around their fields, pursuing diversified agriculture and even owning slaves, did not deter the white settlers from insisting upon the removal of the "lesser" race to permit occupation by the more "advanced" one.

By the 1830's the concept of "Indian removal" (which by then meant removal west of the Mississippi and, in point of fact, primarily to present Oklahoma), had won over the government; it became a policy applicable to both the northern and southern tribes. President Jackson and his Secretary of War, Lewis Cass, supported removal as the only means of preserving the Indians from utter extinction. They argued that on their new lands the red men would be given time to adjust to the white man's ways; otherwise they would disappear. Jackson's political ploy of fusing humanitarian concern over Indian decline with the white man's desire for more of the Indian's lands would command the admiration of any twentieth-century politician. As Alexis de Toqueville said, "It is impossible to destroy men with more respect for the laws of humanity."[7]

Basing this solution of the "Indian problem" on the widely accepted concept that the lands west of the Mississippi constituted a wasteland, a Great American Desert in which the whites would or could not live, the federal government forcibly removed from their homelands the Five Civilized Tribes of the southeast, as well as the Sauk and Fox and many other northern tribes, some of which by then numbered less than a hundred survivors, and transferred them west. The years 1825-40 were the period of most extensive removal. Ultimately most of these eastern Indians went into Indian Territory, most of which is now the state of Oklahoma. (The Kiowa and Comanche, already in the western section of that region, took a dim view of the intrusion. Settling matters between the newcomers and natives took some delicate diplomacy on the part of federal officials.)

The removal of the tribes brought about the creation of a "permanent" Indian frontier, different from the boundaries created by previous treaties in that it stretched in a continuous line across much of the width of the United States. Its northern anchor was at Fort Snelling (south of Minneapolis). A chain of forts extended southward, including Leavenworth, Scott, Smith, and Towson. The dragoons, a force of mounted infantrymen, were expected to make protective marches and be a mobile force keeping unauthorized whites out of Indian Territory and the Indians west of white country. A valiant, though ultimately futile, attempt was made to enforce this "permanent" Indian frontier; but the situation changed as the frontier advanced to the Great Plains.

There is no date at which the destruction of the red men of the plains and mountains may be said to have begun. The enervating effect of liquor and the white man's diseases was well under way among the Indians of the Pacific Northwest when Lewis and Clark encountered them in the winter of 1805-6. The Spanish, with their mission system, had materially changed the way of life of many of the California Indians, as well as those of southern Arizona and especially of the upper Rio Grande Valley, prior to the Declaration of Independence. Most of the weak coastal tribes between El Camino Real (the trail from San

Antonio east to Nacogdoches) and the Gulf had ceased to exist by 1800.

Skirting the lakes and swamps, crossing the forests and forging west across the prairies of southern Canada had come the French *coureurs des bois* and occasional Scottish or English traders. When Lewis and Clark wintered with the Mandans in 1804-5, they encountered the signs of the white man's advance across Canada: there were blue-eyed, blond-haired Mandans and half-blood traders such as Toussaint Charbonneau, the husband of Sacajawea, the Shoshone woman who accompanied Lewis and Clark to the Pacific; and venereal disease was common.

These few men were vanguards of the destructive white intrusion which, in the next three decades, searched out not only the land but also all the Indians, traded with them, introduced them to liquor, made them dependent on the white man for blankets, gewgaws, and weaponry. Trappers such as Peter Skene Ogden and Alexander Ross from Fort Vancouver near the mouth of the Columbia approached them from the northwest, while the trappers' brigades out of St. Louis appeared from the southeast. So even before other tribes were pushed west onto the high plains, before the American settler (as apart from the trader) had yet shown himself, the destruction by alcohol, disease, and dependence upon the implements of civilization had already begun. In the years 1837-40 smallpox swept through the Arikarees, Mandans, Blackfeet, and other northern tribes, destroying whole villages and reducing the proud Mandans to a fragment of their past greatness, so that the survivors had to join other tribes.

Then came the Mexican War and the movements to Oregon and California. The Santa Fe Trail and the Platte River Trail to South Pass both cut across the Indians' open hunting grounds, and troubles began. In 1851 and 1853 the government concluded two "wagon road treaties," the Treaty of Fort Laramie and the Treaty of Fort Atkinson, which promised an annuity to the Indians, who on their part not only granted the white man trespass across Indian lands but even allowed him to erect military posts and bring Indian malefactors to justice. Moreover, in these treaties the white man specified the home territory of each tribe, which made it possible for the government to deprive one tribe of some or all of its specified lands without incurring the wrath of many tribes. This was an old American ruse, it was "dirty pool," but it worked very well.

Troubles were not long in coming. In 1854, as a result of the theft of a Mormon emigrant's cow and the foolishness of young lieutenant Grattan who had been sent to settle the matter, the Brulé Sioux killed the young officer and all but one of his detail of thirty men. The next year

General Harney, sent out to punish the Indians, defeated the Brulé Sioux at Ash Hollow in western Nebraska. The fact that none of those he fought had participated in the Grattan massacre or even knew about the Mormon's cow does not seem to have bothered the general. At the subsequent peace gathering the attempt was made to force this branch of the Sioux into a reservation in eastern Dakota with Fort Pierre as the headquarters. The Brulé Sioux resisted, and troubles continued sporadically. Meanwhile the Navajo in northwest New Mexico who were continuing the raids on ranches which had been a way of life under the Spanish and Mexicans, became the objects of the Americans' wrath; and in 1862 the Sioux in western Minnesota went on the warpath, killing more than 700 whites in the Minnesota River Valley before they were put to rout by General Sibley.

When the Civil War broke out many regulars were ordered East; the growing western settlements and the trails, still busy in spite of the war, were left virtually undefended. The Cheyenne, Arapaho, Kiowa, and Comanche were incensed over the continued presence of the whites, their widespread killing of the buffalo, and the continued deceit of their leaders. The Pike's Peak gold rush of 1859 and the gold discoveries at Coeur d'Alene and Alder Gulch in the northern Rockies only aggravated matters. The defeated and fiercely proud Sioux refugees from Minnesota spread over the plains and talked of war. From the Santa Fe Trail north to Mullan's Military Road in Montana, from just west of the Missouri River settlements to the Rockies, a vicious guerrilla warfare ensued. The Navajo were forced into a dry, desolate strip of land northeast of El Paso, the Bosque Redondo; they were only allowed to return to a fragment of their original homeland after a decade. The Cheyenne, Arapaho, Kiowa, and Comanche marauded far and wide across the central high plains from the North Platte south across the Smoky Hill River and down the Santa Fe Trail. Indians were shot by whites as so many mad dogs, and whites suffered burned wagons and coaches, mutilated corpses, and occasional humiliating captivity. The high plains became, in essence, a vast no-man's-land where no one was safe. To the whites the Indian stood as a threat to life and property, both of which, in the tradition of western society, were sacred and demanded protection by government at all costs. Yet no white man questioned his right to kill buffalo, settle, build fences, and shoot anyone who stole or violated "his" real estate even if he did not have clear title to it. To the Indian, the white man was occupying and destroying his one great possession: the land.

When emigrants trudging up the Platte River and Smoky Hill trails began to settle around stage stations, right in the midst of the buffalo

Cheyenne and Arapaho scouts for the U.S. Army. (Western History Collections, University of Oklahoma Library)

country, the Indian struck back with an understandable fury. When buffalo hunters armed with a special model Sharp's rifle entered his country and killed bison by the hundreds, skinned them, perhaps cut out their tongues, and left the carcasses on the prairie to rot and stench up the breeze, the Indian reacted with an understandable wrath. And as General Sherman pointed out, killing off the buffalo was the best way to bring the mobile, equestrian red man to bay: starve him into submission. This was a cheap policy for the army, since the bison were a natural resource to be exploited absolutely free, with no governmental supervision whatsoever. Moreover, the railroads made transportation of the smelly hides economically feasible, the Kansas Pacific and the Santa Fe being particularly fortuitous in running close to the favorite grazing grounds of the great southern herd. For several successive years in the early 1870's the hides shipped by the Santa Fe alone ran in excess of 100,000 a year; tourists commented on the piles of hides stacked for miles alongside the tracks.

Who killed the buffalo, and who purchased the hides? The truth is,

in a brief period of five (certainly no more than ten) years, many a future settler and substantial citizen participated in the mass slaughter. In
the 1870's, with very little investment—a Sharp's rifle, some ammunition, a skinning knife, a team of horses, and a wagon—a western farmer-
rancher or shopkeeper-to-be could kill fifty or sixty a day. Professionals
killed five to six thousand in a single season. At $2.50 a hide and 25
cents per tongue, a man could realize several hundred dollars in a few
weeks, a professional buffalo hunter eight or ten thousand dollars in a
season. This was when a dollar was worth three or four times its value
today. There existed no government strong enough, no incentive impressive enough, to halt the slaughter until the buffalo became so rare
that the hunters had for the most part entered other fields of endeavor.
Even then the rumor of a dozen survivors brought out the new country men by the hundreds.

And while the slaughter was at its worst, railroads were building,
cattle ranchers were settling while others were driving the longhorns up
the trails from Texas, and towns were beginning to appear out on the
windswept plains at rail junctions, or around military posts or stage stations. Wherever the red man went, he encountered the white man's rape
of the plains country. Here were the rotting carcasses of several dozen
buffalo, there the bleached bones of a hundred or so killed at a single
"stand"; here were the tracks of the railroad, there, down in a little valley, hidden among cottonwoods, was a ranch house, and not far off, the
corral and barn; up on the hill where buffalo once grazed, cattle content-
edly chewed their cuds; over there was the stage road, with a Concord
pulled by six half-broken horses raising a cloud of dust as it clattered by.

Most of the massacres of the whites by Indians were minor, although
occasionally a brash Captain Fetterman led his 81 men into a death
trap or a foolish Colonel Custer lost a total of 256. There were more
massacres of Indians: of the Cheyennes by Chivington at Sand Creek
and Custer on the Washita, or Major Baker's slaughter of the Piegans
on the Marias River in Montana, with the thermometer at thirty degrees below zero. More often the warfare consisted of skirmishes, such
as an emigrant wagon attacked, a stagecoach destroyed and its passengers scalped, or a troop of cavalry intercepting the line of march of
an Indian hunting party.

Bewildered by what his sense of honor told him was wrong, proud
of a way of life that he loved, the Indian witnessed the disruption of his
world. He fought back as best he knew how, savagely but futilely because his adversary enjoyed all the weapons of civilization. By December
of 1890, when the Sioux were massacred at Wounded Knee, the Indian
and his mainstay the buffalo were both in jeopardy of their very exist-

Heap Wolves, Comanche warrior, killed by the Osage in 1872. Photographed by Will Soule at Fort Sill, Oklahoma, *circa* 1870. (History Division, Natural History Museum of Los Angeles County)

ence. By then neither constituted a threat to the new way of life on the Great Plains.

Long after the end was in sight the hatred and the warfare continued. By 1865, however, a ground swell of humanitarianism had arisen. It was spurred by the revelations of the Sand Creek massacre of November 1864, which appeared in Congressional committee hearings, and undoubtedly aided by the end of the Civil War and the switch of humanitarians to a new cause. An Indian Peace Commission grappled with the problem of the vanishing American, men of the cloth served for a time as Indian agents, new reservations were set aside. In 1881 Helen Hunt Jackson presented the case of Indian maltreatment in her polemic *A Century of Dishonor*. The Dawes Act of 1887, a landmark in Indian policy, aimed once again toward assimilation. It urged Indians to become farmers, to act and live as white men, as Jefferson had advocated eighty years before. Under certain conditions land ownership was to be granted them: by 1934 nearly forty-one million acres had been allotted. It was hoped to turn them into sodbusting homesteaders, which would mean that hundreds of thousands of acres of reservation land would be left over. These acres would revert to the public domain, and then fall into the hands of eager white settlers. It was also hoped that tribal traditions would be destroyed. Yet, generally speaking, the Dawes Act was at best only a partial success: the Indian was not prepared to become a farmer, he was bewildered by the breakdown of his tribal society, and his morale was shattered by the loss of ninety million acres of tribal lands which, left over after allotment, reverted to the public domain.

The decade of the nineties, the first ten years after the frontier's official end, witnessed the nadir of Indian existence. Their population had decreased to an absolute low of 237,196 by 1900; yet they did recover and by 1960 numbered more than half a million. Segregated and morose, they were generally ignored by all but the Bureau of Indian Affairs. And, pushed down repeatedly until dejection and defeatism were a part of their children's upbringing, they were slow to rise up and protest. Only in the 1960's did members of the race begin to insist that they too deserved a share of American affluence. It is this new spirit that can lead the Indian to a legitimate place of respect in America, add to the nation's heterogeneity, and increase the diversity which has always spawned so much that is new, valuable, and different.

The Sweep Across the
Continent: First Phase

Inevitably, the frontier line was going to retreat westward. Viewed from eight decades after frontier's end in 1890, this one fact stands out stronger than any other, and one wonders how anyone could have been so naive as to believe the nation would stop its expansion short of the Pacific. In point of fact, few did. In the cock-o'-the-walk stance of a young nation that had experienced only success (Americans remembered Jackson's victory at New Orleans rather than the sack of Washington, D.C.), the politicians of the early nineteenth century anticipated control from the Atlantic to the shores of China, from the lands of the Aurora Borealis to Tierra del Fuego. Such flights of fancy demonstrated the American's faith in his system of government, his conviction that free Americans could conquer all. It was a belief bordering on certainty.

The government never really preceded the trapper and trader, the individualistic settler, religious congregation, or speculator. Freedom in America included the freedom to go. This meant movement into the public domain, the wilderness, as well as from state to state. The new country was a cynosure; it pulled men like a magnet. They could not resist it.

With its own explorers, its Indian commissioners and Indian agents, its pitifully small army, its surveyors, registers and receivers, governors, secretaries, and judges for the territories, the federal government trudged along behind. It arrived late, often just in time to avoid total chaos, calamity, or both. It avoided the one by providing for land survey, purchase, and territorial government, and the other by calming the Indians whose lands had been violated in total disregard of solemn treaties. In the refined salons of high diplomacy, its ministers drew up treaties or conventions or made deals for purchase, but long before the final ratifications or payments had been made, the lands in question had been violated by the rampaging Americans.

Let us begin with the Treaty of Paris of September 3, 1783, with Great Britain. By the terms of this incredibly favorable document the new nation was granted a northern boundary from Maine west to the "river Mississippi" via the lakes and waterways of the northern woodlands. Ignorance of the terrain brought on a good deal of litigation in years to come concerning the exact boundary, but the Convention of 1818 and the Webster-Ashburton Treaty of 1842, both with England, settled most of these matters, and on very favorable terms for the United States.

Then the boundary turned south, down the middle of the Mississippi river to the thirty-first parallel, east to the Chattahoochee, down that stream to its junction with the Flint (forming the Apalachicola), then straight east to the head of St. Mary's River, and down that stream to the Atlantic. This southern boundary was disputed with Spain, but the United States eventually won its claims.

Thus did the new nation acquire all the land between Canada and Florida. But how much had the British really lost? They were aware that for more than twenty years prior to the signing of the treaty the Americans had been pushing west of the Appalachians, particularly south of the Ohio. The pioneers had followed Daniel Boone's Wilderness Trail through the Cumberland Gap into Kentucky; or they had trekked to Pittsburgh and there purchased flatboats to float down the Ohio, then pole up the Kentucky, the Tennessee, and the Cumberland. If the English and their Indian allies could not drive out the few frontiersmen who held Kentucky during the war, then what chance had they to control these wildcats in time of peace?

Even in wartime the migration into Kentucky had continued. More than that, in the spring of 1780 John Donelson and his party of thirty frontier families had established themselves at the bend of the Cumberland, at a place they called Fort Nashborough (early Nashville). Also there were the frontiersman James Robertson and a similar contingent. This was far west of the early Tennessee settlements generally known as Watauga, located along the headwater rivers of the Tennessee system. Meanwhile, the settlement around the Forks of the Ohio had extended like tentacles up the Monongahela, Kanawha, Greenbriar, and other rivers in present West Virginia. All told, there were perhaps 100,000 souls west of the mountains. They were independent as wild horses but, with whatever patriotism they had, loyal to the country over the mountains to the east; they had come from there, and the link

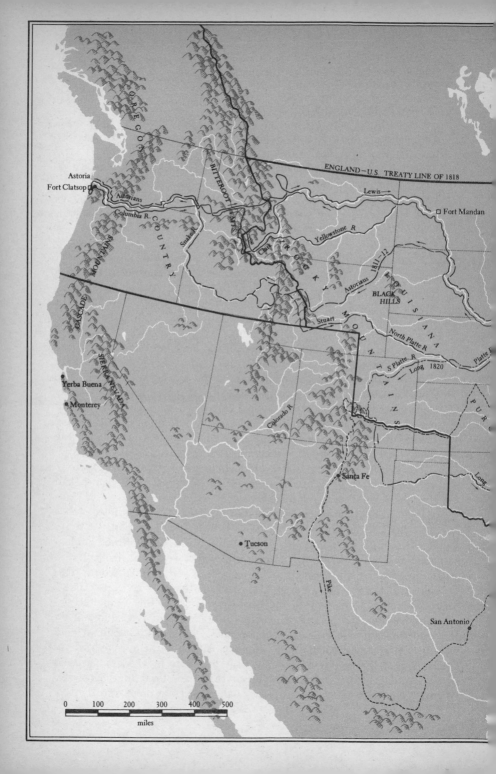

ENGLAND—U.S. TREATY LINE OF 1818

Astoria
Fort Clatsop
Astorians
Columbia R.
Snake R.
Lewis →
Fort Mandan
Yellowstone R.
Astorians
1811-12
BLACK HILLS
LOUISIANA
Stuart
North Platte R.
Platte R.
S. Platte R.
Long 1820
Long
Yerba Buena
Monterey
Colorado R.
Santa Fe
Tucson
Pike
San Antonio

OREGON COUNTRY
BITTERROOT
ROCKY MOUNTAINS
CASCADE MOUNTAINS
SIERRA NEVADA
MOUNTAINS
PUR

0   100   200   300   400   500
miles

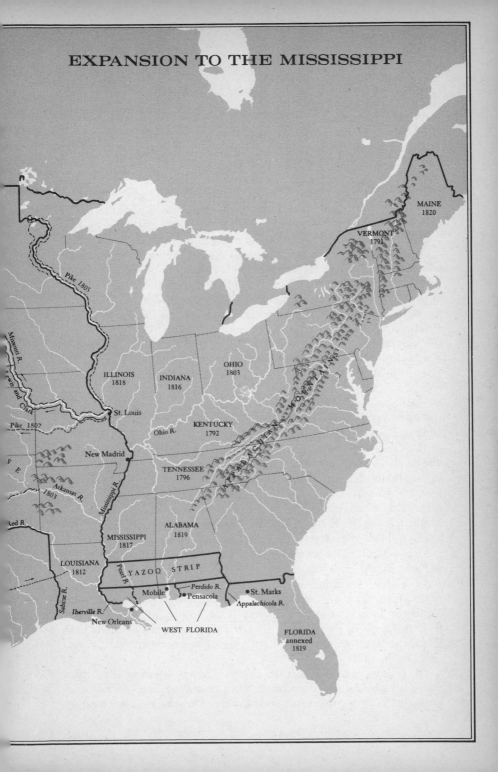

EXPANSION TO THE MISSISSIPPI

MAINE
1820

VERMONT
1791

OHIO
1803

ILLINOIS
1818

INDIANA
1816

KENTUCKY
1792

St. Louis

Ohio R.

Pike 1805

Missouri R.

Lewis and Clark

Pike 1807

New Madrid

Arkansas R.

1803

Red R.

TENNESSEE
1796

ALABAMA
1819

MISSISSIPPI
1817

LOUISIANA
1812

Pearl R.

YAZOO STRIP

Mobile

Perdido R.

Pensacola

St. Marks

Appalachicola R.

Sabine R.

Iberville R.

New Orleans

WEST FLORIDA

FLORIDA
annexed
1819

APPALACHIAN MOUNTAINS

Mississippi R.

of blood was bolstered by the links of common experience, common forms of government, common language, and a common heritage.

North of the Ohio, the Algonquian tribes, notably the Shawnee and the Miami, were for a time a deterrent to the white man's advance; so also were the six nations of the Iroquois and their close allies, the Mingos. As a result, north of the Ohio and west of the Alleghenies there was by 1783 little settlement. Furthermore, the British were in a position from which they could give aid to these Indians and incite them against the Americans. Seven forts on the American side of the border were held by the British during the war and were not surrendered—though they should have been by the terms of the 1783 treaty of Paris—until 1796. Some of this resistance was due to the lucrative fur trade, whose powerful lobby exerted pressure on the government in London to hold onto the lands north of the Ohio. It was even suggested that an Indian buffer state be created there. This idea died hard: the British diplomats meeting with the American commissioners in 1814 in Ghent, Belgium, to end the War of 1812 even suggested it. Finally there was the inertia of the English where they were already entrenched, plus a fear that to give signs of abandoning these posts—and thus their Indian allies—would result in an Indian massacre of the English in Canada.

Here also time was on the side of the Americans. True, the area was a wilderness, but before the Revolution began, even prior to 1763, speculative companies such as the Indiana Company, the Mississippi Company, and the Charlotina Company had sought large tracts north of the Ohio and east of the Mississippi. Now the war was over, and new land schemes appeared. Typical of these were the plans embodied in the Ohio and Scioto companies, which were granted a total of six and a half million acres in Ohio by the Confederation Congress. Though these plans ultimately failed, they indicate the interest in the region. Meanwhile the frontiersmen advanced, transforming the wilderness into a land of fields and cabins and settlements. Every blow of the pioneer's axe was a blow to the fur trade and to the Indians' domain. When the red men fought back, campaigns were launched against them. General Josiah Harmer failed in the campaign of 1790; Arthur St. Clair's troops were defeated in 1791; but General "Mad Anthony" Wayne's army defeated the Indians at Fallen Timbers (close to present Toledo, Ohio) in August 1794. In 1795 Wayne extracted the Treaty of Greenville from them; two-thirds of Ohio and a portion of southeastern Indiana was ceded to the whites.

The rapidity of change that the British observed south of the border, 1783-95, probably helped persuade them to a change of policy. They knew that their fur trade was on the wane, that the forts were expensive to maintain. In addition, the new United States under the Constitution appeared to be of a stable and lasting nature. So in 1794, when John Jay, a New Yorker, went to England to negotiate the treaty that bears his name (Jay's Treaty), he succeeded in gaining the British abandonment of the forts. Thus was most of Ohio and some of Indiana pacified and opened to settlement. By 1803 there was sufficient population for Ohio to achieve statehood, as the first of several states to be created in the Old Northwest.

The complex history of the Old Southwest—the area south of the Ohio, west of the Appalachians, and east of the Mississippi—involves the Americans, the Spanish, and the Five Civilized Tribes (Cherokee, Chickasaw, Choctaw, Creek, and Seminole). These peoples lived a sedentary existence. Their towns were surrounded by well-kept fields of corn, squash, beans, and gourds; they kept horses, hogs, and poultry; they feasted on the nuts of the forest, wild herbs, the fish of the streams, and the abundant game. They had no intention of giving up their lands. The half blood Creek leader Alexander McGillivray was a cohesive force in their resistance until his death in 1793; but difficulties continued for several decades thereafter. The defeat of the Creeks by Andrew Jackson's forces at the battle of Horseshoe Bend in central Alabama in March 1814 is a landmark in the Indians' decline; a few years later they were subject to removal westward.

As the Indians learned to their sorrow, nothing could stop the Americans. They were lounging on flatboats floating down the western waters, their vessels stacked with corn, flour, tobacco, hemp, wheat, salt pork, bear grease or oil, honey, tallow, furs, whiskey, and cotton—immense quantities of produce from the country above. They were crashing through the pine barrens of western Tennessee, northern Alabama, and Mississippi. Ambitious speculators such as William Blount, James Robertson, and John Sevier were staking out lands regardless of the illegality of their transactions. General James Wilkinson, an army officer whose western intrigues included dealings with both the British and the Spanish, was involved in many of the schemes.

Meanwhile, Georgia took measures to bring in revenue prior to its cession of western lands to the new nation. That state claimed all the lands from the American-claimed Florida line north to the Tennessee border and west all the way to the Mississippi. Its legislature, primarily the one meeting in 1795, persuaded by bribes and full of speculatively minded men, chose to sell most of these lands for paltry sums. Perhaps fifty million acres were thus disposed of by these so-called Yazoo land frauds (so named because much of the land was drained by the Yazoo River). The state created Bourbon County in the wilderness at the mouth of the Yazoo to aid the speculators. Before the eyes of the Spanish, the Indians, and the federal authorities, Georgia sold this land that was not its own—land that might have belonged to a foreign power, made treaties with Indians made irresponsible by liquor (to say nothing of the fact that Indian relations were now the sole responsibility of the federal authorities), then turned the resulting mess over to the national government and repudiated the Yazoo land sales. Out of this situation came the notable Supreme Court case of *Fletcher* v. *Peck* (1810), which upheld the legality of the sales as a contract to be fulfilled, and declared void a state law rescinding the original act providing for the sales. In 1814 the federal government paid Yazoo land claimants more than $4 million to settle the disputed land titles.

A further complicating factor in the history of the Old Southwest was Spain, which had substantial claim to Florida as far north as about 32° 28″, which is where the Yazoo flows into the Mississippi, and shadowy claims northward to the Tennessee and the Ohio. When England ceded Florida to Spain in 1783 in a separate peace settlement, the northern boundary was indefinite, but in the Treaty of Paris between England and the United States the boundary was specified at the thirty-first parallel. But Spain insisted that the land between 31° and 32° 28″, which came to be known as the Yazoo Strip, belonged to her. Along the Tombigbee River in Alabama the Spanish built Fort St. Stephens, about ninety miles north of Mobile, and Fort Confederation, above the line of 32° 28″. The Spanish also controlled the traffic of the Mississippi through their occupation of New Orleans and their strongholds at Baton Rouge, Natchez, Nogales (present Vicksburg), San Fernando (Chickasaw Bluffs, present Memphis), New Madrid, Ste. Geneviève, and St. Louis.

The Spanish authorities looked upon the new American states with suspicion; they knew that republicanism was a threat to monarchical institutions. Since the British had capitulated and given the Americans the land west to the Mississippi, it became a military problem for the Spanish to deter the American movement westward and thus protect the long exposed flank of Louisiana on the west side of the Mississippi.

They were, however, less realistic than the British. From 1783 until the mid-1790's the Spanish believed they could halt the American sweep westward. For a brief period they operated an unusually good program in Louisiana and West Florida, asserting a measure of control over the sparse population and consciously working with the disgruntled Indians. They brought McGillivray in on their side, allowed the successful British trading firm of Panton, Leslie and Company to trade with the Indians out of Pensacola and St. Marks, and endeavored to accomplish the most difficult task of all—to persuade the warring tribes to bury the hatchet and put up a strong united front against the Americans.

So successful did their initial efforts appear in 1784, barely a year after the Treaty of Paris, that the Spanish closed the Mississippi to American trade and suggested the negotiation of a treaty to settle the differences they had with the new nation. John Jay was the American negotiator. Ignorant of the explosive settlement activity going on west of the mountains and south of the Ohio, Jay blandly accepted the denial of American navigation of the Mississippi for twenty-five years. Possibly he felt that his insistence on the thirty-first parallel, rather than Spain's new claim to everything south of the Tennessee and west of the Hiwassee and Flint rivers, compensated for his submission to the other Spanish demands. There were also commercial clauses in the treaty that would help New England shipping. Jay soon discovered his error. His treaty, negotiated with the Spaniard Don Diego Gardoqui, engendered rage, sedition, and even treason amongst the men of the western waters. Their voices were heard back east, and only seven northern and middle states voted for the treaty. The southern states voted solidly against it, and it was never ratified.

The Spanish made the most of this reaction. They flirted with the Westerners, who were led by General James Wilkinson. In that same year of 1784, probably due at least in part to Wilkinson's efforts, the Spanish reopened the Mississippi to Americans under conditions involving 15 per cent taxation on exports, in 1793 the duty was reduced to 6 per cent. In 1788 the Spanish inaugurated a liberal immigration policy, believing they could assimilate and control the Americans. But it soon became clear that the frontiersmen were simply ambitious rogues who never seriously contemplated placing themselves under the yoke of Spanish authority. Morover, the Indians could not be managed—they were soon fighting among themselves—and the Americans were using this weakness to make greater and greater inroads into the wilderness. Between 1785 and 1795, the tide turned against the Spanish.

Moreover, by the Peace of Basle in July 1795, Spain ended her war with France but by so doing incurred the wrath of her ally, England. Possibly news of Jay's Treaty also made Spain nervous about the relations between the United States and England, along with the vulnerability of New Orleans and Louisiana should the two become allied against her. A new Spanish foreign minister, Manuel de Godoy, seemed pliable to Thomas Pinckney, who had been sent to Spain to bring about a settlement of difficulties. Pinckney listed the American demands to Godoy without batting an eye: the Florida boundary would be at 31° and the Mississippi must be free to American navigation. Americans should have the right of deposit—the right to store their goods at New Orleans while awaiting transshipment and then to export them without paying anything save a reasonable storage charge. Pinckney obtained all three of these demands in the Treaty of San Lorenzo (1795), which ranks as one of the most successful treaties in American history. In due time—actually almost three years—the Spanish abandoned their forts and retreated to East and West Florida below 31°, New Orleans, and their settlements on the west side of the Mississippi. (The boundary between East and West Florida is usually considered to have been the Suwannee River, though American annexation of "West Florida" in 1810 meant the area west of the Perdido.)

Spain could not afford to give way altogether, however. Her possessions were an economic burden, but Florida and Louisiana did serve useful purposes: the former could be used for bargaining and the latter was an excellent buffer between the Americans and Texas. That vast area was more valuable to the Spanish than Louisiana; and Mexico, Spanish-speaking, heavily populated, and Roman Catholic, was more valuable than either of the other areas. The long-range goal of the Spanish was to keep the Americans away from both Texas and Mexico. They failed because they simply lacked the resources to secure any of their North American possessions. From 1796 on the Spanish frontier from St. Marks (below Tallahassee in Florida) to New Orleans and then up-river to St. Louis was secured by a single regiment of 1,385 effectives, with the aid of a tiny freshwater navy of ten or a dozen boats. This force attempted to police the population of Florida and Louisiana, estimated at 45,000. No Spanish official had any illusions about his country's "ability" to protect the long frontier from another power.

Nor was the threat necessarily military. Americans were crossing the Mississippi and squatting on Louisiana land. Above the mouth of the Red River, which was considered the boundary between upper and lower Louisiana, there may have been 6,000 white inhabitants, French and American. Daniel Boone was one of the Americans on Spanish land that later became the state of Missouri; Moses Austin was another. There was no halting the tide.

Keeping in mind the Spanish concern over the safety of New Spain, it is clear why Manuel de Godoy broached the sale of Louisiana to France late in 1795. Spain could not defend it, her policies had failed, and the revenues derived from that wilderness colony paid hardly a fifth of its administration. The thing to do was sell it, or trade it for some Italian provinces. Although nothing immediately came from this offer, from that time on Louisiana loomed ever more important in French policy. From the American point of view, French control could be disastrous, for while Spain was weak, France was strong. Americans would not have their way so easily in their push into the new country. The Spanish, however, felt that only the strength of Napoleonic France could restrain the Americans and hold Louisiana as a secure buffer between the United States and Mexico.

As the eighteenth century drew to a close the vast Old Southwest was a hotbed of rumor and conspiracy. From settlement to settlement vague French and Spanish plans mingled with the private intrigues of certain Federalist politicians. William Blount of Tennessee, the arch-speculator, was expelled from the Senate when his grandiose scheme for a filibustering expedition (an unauthorized assault against a friendly power) was revealed. He planned to take New Orleans, the Floridas, and, indeed, all of Spain's Louisiana possessions. Alexander Hamilton and General James Wilkinson headed a war party cabal in President Adams' administration. They anticipated a declaration of war on France, and since, at the time of the infamous XYZ Affair in 1797-98, France and Spain were allies, it would have been a justifiable American action to capture Louisiana and the Floridas. But Adams ended the threat of war and retained good relations with Spain. And because Spain was allowing a most liberal use of the Mississippi and the right of deposit at this time, it was hard to get the West riled to the extent of actively advocating war with that declining nation.

By the Treaty of San Ildefonso in 1800, Spain relinquished Louisiana, including New Orleans, to France, though the physical transfer did not take place until late in 1803, when France possessed it for just twenty days before turning it over to the United States. During those years, 1800-1803, the Old Southwest was in turmoil. When Spain in the autumn of 1802 suspended the right of deposit at New Orleans in violation of Pinckney's Treaty the outcry of the Americans was enough to frighten the Spanish into only a half-hearted enforcement of the order; never had it been clearer that the Americans would inevitably take the river and the region to the west for their own uses. Jefferson sent James Monroe to Europe to see what kind of settlement could be made with the French. Congress helped him on his special mission by empowering him to purchase New Orleans and East and West Florida for up to $2 million. Monroe owned lands in the West, and he had opposed the Jay-Gardoqui Treaty in 1785; the West trusted him.

Things changed favorably for the Americans very quickly. In May of 1803, seven months after the right of deposit had been revoked, it was suddenly restored. Then the incredible and unexpected good fortune of the willing sale by Napoleon of all of Louisiana, the city of New Orleans and, as the Americans chose to interpret it, West Florida, for $15 million was successfully transacted. Overnight the young nation more than doubled its holdings, the West remained intact, and twenty years of controversy over the Mississippi, New Orleans, and the right of deposit came to an end. On December 20, 1803, William C. C. Claiborn, the Governor of Mississippi Territory, and General James Wilkinson served as the American commissioners in the transfer of Louisiana to the United States of America.

Most Americans thought of this transfer in terms of unrestricted control of the Mississippi and the end of Spanish or French control of New Orleans. While there was some movement of population into the Louisiana country, it was not at the time extensive. So in 1803 the 828,000 square miles that constituted the Louisiana Purchase were a vast reserve, something to be held for the future.

Jefferson was intensely interested in the West, and the suspicious Spanish knew it. They prevented Sir William Dunbar and George Hunter from exploring up the Red and Arkansas rivers in 1804, as Jefferson had directed; the two men restricted their activities to the Ouachita River in northeastern Louisiana, an area already being settled. In 1806 Thomas Freeman was sent up the Red River but was turned back by a Spanish force before he had reached its source, though his party was more than 600 miles above the mouth of the river. Lieutenant Zebulon Pike traveled first up the Mississippi into present Minnesota in 1805-6, then west from St. Louis in the summer of 1806. He advanced up the Missouri and Osage rivers, overland to the Arkansas, up that river to the Royal Gorge, then over the Sangre de Cristo Mountains until finally he halted and constructed a stockade in the San Luis Valley of southern Colorado. Here he was taken prisoner by a Spanish force and escorted to Santa Fe and the Mexican province of Chihuahua, from whence he was returned to the states by way of Texas and the town of Natchitoches in western Louisiana.

Jefferson was also interested in what lay to the northwest. Was there an all-water route across the continent? And if so, what were its possibilities for use in encouraging trade with the Orient? As early as 1786, while in London, he had urged the Connecticut wanderer John Ledyard to go ahead with plans to walk across Siberia, cross to America, and then walk east to St. Louis. This caper had failed. In 1792 the sage of Monticello had urged André Michaux, a French botanist, to explore up the Missouri, cross the mountains, and advance to the Pacific. Jefferson even obtained funds for him from the American Philosophical Society. But Michaux was a victim of the times. He was involved with the French envoy Citizen Genêt's machinations against the American government, and when Genêt fell from power he dragged Michaux down with him.

As he assumed the presidency, Jefferson took satisfaction in realizing that finally he could launch an expedition overland to the North Pacific. His choice as its leader was Meriwether Lewis, a fellow Virginian and an army officer; he allowed Lewis to choose his partner in command, William Clark. Shortly after sending Monroe to Europe to negotiate in January 1803, the President sent a secret message to Congress requesting funds—all of $2,000—for an expedition up the Missouri and across the "Stony Mountains" (as the Rockies were called) to the Pacific. Congress acquiesced. (The total cost was probably twenty times $2,000 when the expenses of army personnel, supplies, pensions, etc., are included.)

Lewis and Clark had set up a base camp across from the mouth of the Missouri late in 1803; on the ninth of March, 1804, Lewis served as official witness to the overdue transfer of upper Louisiana from Spain to France, followed immediately by its transfer from France to the United States. The Spanish were apprehensive about the expedition, but could not stop it. On Sunday, May 13, 1804, the expedition started up the Missouri. "Up," as they knew, was primarily west for some 300 miles before the wide, surging river swept in a great bend to a north-by-northwest direction. Along those lower reaches—essentially from St. Louis to present-day Kansas City—the land lay fresh as Eden in the springtime, and everything they saw bore promise of good farmland. They also soon discovered that the wilderness already had its exploiters, for they passed several river craft loaded with furs, honey, beeswax, and other wilderness products floating downriver under the control of American and French fur traders.

Lewis and Clark reached the Pacific, at the mouth of the Columbia River, in November 1805. On the Oregon side they spent a miserable winter at an outpost of their own construction which they dubbed Fort Clatsop. Again—as on the lower Missouri and at the Mandan villages where they had wintered in 1804-5—they saw the unmistakable signs of western man. The thieving Indians around the fort possessed all manner of cheap trinkets acquired from trading ships that plied the coast. They had also learned what the white man wanted in trade, such as furs and women. Prostitution was rampant and with it serious venereal disease. Again, on the long journey home in 1806, they encountered on the Missouri above the Mandan villages some trappers from Illinois who were on their way upriver to trap or trade for beaver peltry and who persuaded a member of the expedition, John Colter, to request his release and join them. The request was granted, and Colter turned his face westward into the new country again, to wonders and adventures in the wilderness that would be considered incredible long after his death.

During the three years Lewis and Clark were gone, St. Louis began to change from a sleepy French and Spanish village to a bustling, growing community. It became the center of the fur trade and the jumping-off place for trappers and traders going up the Missouri. Lead mines in the general area added to its prosperity. East of the river in Tennessee and Kentucky, a large population was casting long looks across the Father of Waters, contemplating another move westward. If Daniel Boone could do it, then they could also. Fifteen years after Lewis and Clark returned to St. Louis, Missouri attained statehood.

By that time so had Indiana (1816), Illinois (1818), Mississippi (1817), Alabama (1819), and, to name the first last, Louisiana (1812). In the Old Northwest Jay's Treaty and Wayne's victory in 1795 had initially opened the floodgates to settlement. In the ensuing years, until about 1811, the Indians were pushed back again and again. William Henry Harrison was but one of several officials who at one time or another dictated peace treaties or land purchases to the red men. Only the activities of Tecumseh and his brother, the Prophet, and then the War of 1812 had curtailed the march into the new country.

Tecumseh was a Shawnee chief, a master orator, and one of the truly great Indian leaders. When his father was killed by white men the boy was entrusted to Blackfish, who had at one time captured Daniel Boone. Subsequently Blackfish was killed; indeed, Tecumseh's world was one of violence and defeat. He preached unity and resistance to such distant tribes as the Seminole of Florida and the Osage across the Mississippi. He was helped by his alcoholic, one-eyed brother Tenskwatawa, the Prophet. However, William Henry Harrison delivered a disastrous blow to the Indians in November 1811, by destroying Prophet's Town on the Tippecanoe River. Tecumseh was not there at the time; he continued to incite the Indians until his death on October 5, 1813, at the Battle of the Thames (named for the river in southern Ontario near Detroit, near where the battle took place). This defeat of the British, along with the Indian leader's death, was decisive in ending the Indian menace in the Old Northwest. With the Treaty of Ghent in 1814 ending the War of 1812, and with the issuance of Military Bounty Land Warrants (gifts of land by the government to war veterans), thousands of ex-soldiers who had seen the lay of the land swarmed into the Old Northwest, while the Indians were steadily forced to give way.

The story south of the Ohio in these same years, 1803-20, is similar in its final effects—the settling of the land—but in many ways the proc-

Colonel Johnson's charge and the death of Tecumseh at the Battle of the Thames.

ess was messier and under less control by the federal government. Ever since the first Yazoo land sales in 1789, the area that became Alabama and Mississippi had been under the covetous eyes of land speculators, as were the lands of western Tennessee at Chickasaw Bluffs, now Memphis.

Pinckney's Treaty, by which, it will be recalled, the Spanish relinquished their claim north of the thirty-first parallel, cleared the way for territorial status of the previously disputed region. In 1798 President Adams approved an act of Congress creating Mississippi Territory. Its boundaries were west along the thirty-first parallel from the Chattahoochee to the Mississippi, up that river to the mouth of the Yazoo, east again to the Chattahoochee, and down that river to the thirty-first parallel again—the old Yazoo Strip. In 1804 the northern boundary was moved to the Tennessee line.

Initially there were two concentrations of population. One was at Natchez on the Mississippi, which was growing rapidly, especially after the Louisiana Purchase. The other area was in the black belt, a region with thick, black loam along the Tombigbee River. In 1803 the Tombigbee settlement petitioned Congress for separation from the Natchez area, but not until 1817 was this done by the act creating Alabama Territory; in the same year Mississippi was granted statehood. Two years later Alabama became a state.

The Indian troubles in the Old Southwest were intensified by the Creeks, who occupied much of Alabama and found themselves squeezed by the Georgia settlements to the east of them and the Tombigbee settlement to the west. Even though their great leader, Alexander McGillivray, had died in 1793, the tribe remained strong, and a running struggle, a terrorist border warfare, raged year after year and was accelerated with the arrival of Tecumseh in October of 1811. This "Moses of the Indians" addressed the grand council of the Creeks at Tuckabache, on the Tallapoosa River. In the presence of 5,000 Indians, using his great oratorical skills, he implored the Creeks to take up the hatchet. "You do not believe the Great Spirit has sent me," he said. "You shall know! When I return to Tippecanoe I shall stamp my foot and the very earth will tremble."[1] When the great Mississippi earthquake struck a few weeks later, the Indians were impressed. One red stick per day was broken, from the bundle Tecumseh had left behind, and when the last one was snapped in two, the Creek war broke out.

The Creeks obtained munitions and other provisions from the Spanish at Pensacola. Under the leadership of chiefs William Wetherford, Peter McQueen, High-Headed Jim, Josiah Francis, and other capable warriors, they soon had the settlers cowering in a chain of forts from the Tombigbee southeast across country to Fort Mims on the Tensaw River north of Mobile Bay. There, at high noon on August 30, 1813, the worst massacre of whites by Indians in American history began. The roll of drums announcing lunch and allowing the brief abandonment of sentry posts was the signal for the Indian attack. Led by Wetherford, a thousand painted, howling Indians emerged from the forest and charged through the open gates of the east entrance. So careless had the settlers become that they had allowed sand to wash up against the gate, which prevented its rapid closure. Carnage of the worst kind ensued. Wetherford risked his life attempting to prevent his blood-crazed Indians from slaughtering women and children, but he failed completely and left the scene of the carnage. Over 500 occupants were slaughtered —about 36 escaped—and for weeks afterward thousands of buzzards and packs of wild dogs feasted there.

The massacre stirred the Westerners to action. The Creeks were attacked on all sides, and although they won some of the battles, the end of their marauding became a question not of *if* but of *when*. The tide began to turn in the autumn of 1813, at about the time that their brethren north of the Ohio were defeated at the Battle of the Thames, where

Tecumseh was killed. By February of 1814 General Andrew Jackson had learned that a large force of Creek warriors had fortified themselves at the great bend of the Tallapoosa, known to the whites as Horseshoe Bend. It represented probably the most advanced fortification ever constructed by North American Indians. On a peninsula embracing about eighty acres, surrounded on all sides but the north by the swollen Tallapoosa River, the Creeks dug in. Across the narrow neck on the north side they built breastworks eight feet high, placed in such a manner that attackers would be subject to enfilading fire. Living quarters were at the bottom of the land, where hundreds of canoes were tied up. A thousand warriors were entrenched there.

Jackson sent General Coffee and his men three miles downstream with orders to cross the river and circle around and behind the encampment, thus cutting off the Indians' retreat. Coffee accomplished this by having swimmers cross the river and steal the Creek canoes, which he then requisitioned for his own men's transit across the river. Then Jackson marched with his men toward the breastworks and began bombarding them with two pieces of artillery. With the Indians thus faced with both frontal and rear attacks, the fortifications were soon breached and the Indians, caught in a cross fire, got the worst of it. In a day of intense, no-quarter-asked fighting, the whites killed more than 550 Indians, while quite possibly another 200 drowned trying to escape; Jackson had 49 killed and 154 wounded. Davy Crockett and Sam Houston were participants, Houston being wounded by bullets and an arrow.

Although there was still to be some scalping, burning, and marauding, this battle broke the spirit of the proud Creek nation. In August of 1814 Jackson dictated peace to them in the Treaty of Fort Jackson, by which they ceded 22 million acres in Georgia and Alabama and agreed to allow military posts and roads even in the lands still retained.

In 1802 and 1805 the Choctaw, and in 1805 and 1806 the Chickasaw and the Cherokee had relinquished lands, the former in the Tombigbee Valley and the latter two in the fertile Tennessee Valley. In 1816 the Choctaw, Chickasaw, and Cherokee ceded additional large tracts in Alabama. Beginning in this period more and more of the Indians were called together, and their aging chiefs informed that the remnants of their people were to be transferred by the Great White Father to lands on the other side of the Mississippi.

Into the resultant vacuum came the new country men. In the Old Northwest they came from New England and New York and tended to settle in the northern sections of the new states. The lands close to the Ohio River, on the other hand, were occupied substantially by upland Southerners. Probably those coming across the river were less affluent than those of their neighbors who chose to migrate to the Southwest. They were often people without slaves, who resented the powerful slave-owners. But in their search for lands and their common problems—clearing the land after purchase and building roads, schools, and churches—they were the same.

People came to the Old Southwest from the Carolinas, Virginia and Maryland, and from Tennessee and Kentucky. Soil exhaustion and the decline of tobacco as a profitable staple encouraged movement into the new country. Not only did the lands of western Georgia, Alabama, Mississippi, and northern Florida offer fertile acres for new farms, but a new staple crop promised quick profits. This was cotton, more especially the green-seed short-staple variety that had become economically feasible because of the invention of the cotton gin and the industrial revolution in England. The need for cotton seemed insatiable, and the price in these years increased rapidly.

There were two flush periods east of the Mississippi: 1817-19 and 1832-37. Like swarms of locusts, so numerous that the first comers wondered who was left back home, the settlers came. Over Indian trails that widened through use into wagon roads, down the Federal Road that rounded the south end of the Appalachians, via Old Hickory's military road down from Nashville, or else gliding down the sluggish rivers, the people swarmed out of Kentucky and Tennessee, or out of the soil-exhausted regions to the east. Their fingers of settlement crept first along river bottoms—those of the Tombigbee, Black Warrior, Flint, Coosa, and Alabama. Soon there were communities, many of which no longer exist; others, such as Huntsville, Columbus, Tuscaloosa, Natchez, and Mobile, are still thriving.

South of Georgia, Alabama, and Mississippi lay the Spanish Floridas. For fifty miles below the frontier the terrain was almost identical to that above the line, pine barrens with good soil—prime cotton lands when cleared, plowed, and cultivated. In addition, the Ochlocknee, Apalachicola, Escambia, Pearl, Pascagoula, and Perdido rivers, all deep and sluggish, ended their journeys to the sea by flowing through the Floridas, constituting the natural transportation routes for the flourishing upcountry. Free use of these rivers was an absolute necessity to the Americans settling upriver. Moreover, it was clear that the Spanish were not developing Florida; nor could Spain control the Seminoles, runaway slaves, and renegades who pilfered across the border and then fled to the sanctuary of Spanish lands.

But besides all that, the Spanish had foolishly encouraged American settlement in West Florida, especially in the stretch of land between the Perdido, which flows into the Gulf close to Pensacola, and the Mississippi. In 1810, when Spain, disrupted by the turmoil of the Napoleonic wars, failed to maintain governmental authority there, Americans seized the opportunity to revolt. Encouraged from Washington by agents instructed to show discontent, a certain Philemon Thomas gathered a small force, seized Baton Rouge, and proclaimed West Florida to be free. Two days after President Madison heard of the incident, he claimed West Florida as American land by reason of the Louisiana Purchase. Within a few months the United States had secured West Florida to the Perdido, save for the Spanish stronghold at Mobile, which fell to General James Wilkinson during the War of 1812.

Americans were also interested in East Florida. Amelia Island, at the mouth of the St. Marys River, was retaken in December 1817, not from the Spanish but from freebooters and adventurers who had seized it. In 1818 Andrew Jackson was allowed to lead 3,000 troops into north Florida, taking St. Marks (south of Tallahassee) and Pensacola and executing two Englishmen who traded with the Indians before he returned to Tennessee. Although President Monroe denied he had given Jackson the authority, there is no question that Jackson's actions influenced Spanish policy by making it obvious that the United States could take Florida at will—and probably would.

Meanwhile Monroe's Secretary of State, the brilliant John Quincy Adams, was carrying on discussions with Don Luis de Onís, the Spanish minister. When the Spanish protested Jackson's invasion of Florida, Adams zeroed in on them with blunt language. "The right of the United States can as little compound with impotence as with perfidy," he informed them, adding that Spain must either bolster its forces in the Floridas so as to enforce its commitments, "or cede to the United States a province, of which she retains nothing but the nominal possession, but which is, in fact, a derelict. . . ."[2]

Spain, hard pressed with rebellions throughout her colonial empire, and finding no European nations willing to come to her aid, was determined to gain by the loss of Florida some manner of protection for Mexico. For this reason the negotiations were not based upon monetary purchase (save for an American assumption of claims up to $5 million) but on some kind of an agreement that would fix the western boundaries of the Louisiana Purchase. Faced with this kind of proposition, Adams examined the most recent maps of the continent, especially one drawn by John Melish which was considered the most accurate and up-to-date map of North America. He took into account Captain Robert Gray's discovery of the Columbia River with its rich basin in 1792, Lewis and Clark's 1804-6 journey, and Yankee trade being carried on along the Oregon coast. He also considered the provisions of the Convention of 1818 with England, by which the forty-ninth parallel was accepted as the United States–Canada boundary west to the "Stony Mountains," thus giving the United States the Mesabi Range (though its hidden treasures of iron were not yet known). The convention provided also that the lands from the Rockies to the Pacific, whatever their boundaries north and south might be, were to be jointly owned. This diplomatic parlance meant that a controversy had been set aside until a future time. Adams decided to persuade the Spanish to agree to a fixed Louisiana boundary separating American from Spanish possessions all the way to the "South Sea." By eliminating Spain from Oregon, the United States would be left with only England and Russia as contenders for that distant country.

After weeks of diplomatic haggling about the western boundaries, the treaty was concluded and, fittingly, was signed on Washington's birthday in 1819. The Spanish ardently hoped that in exchange for East and West Florida they had assured the safety of Mexico, and even of Texas, from American land grabbers. Both Monroe and Adams had been willing to exchange the tenuous United States claim to Texas for the strategically important Florida peninsula. The Sabine River, agreed upon as the boundary between Louisiana and Texas, was west of where the Spanish had desired it and east of the Colorado, which the Americans had wanted—a typical diplomatic compromise. The remainder of the line (north along the west bank of the Sabine to the thirty-second parallel, thence due north to the Red River, west up its south bank to 100 west longitude, north again to the south bank of the Arkansas, west to its source, north to 42° north latitude, and finally west to the Pacific) was the result of long negotiations, for the Spanish had hoped to restrict the Americans at most to the Mississippi and at the least to the Front Range of the Rockies as far north as the source of the Missouri.

And the sweep into the new country continued. The years from 1815 to 1846 were times of peaceful activity as the vast, fertile country east of the Mississippi was settled. Save for removals of the Cherokee, Choctaw, Chickasaw and Creek to Indian Territory, the troublesome Seminole in Florida, and Black Hawk's Sauks and Foxes, these were not years of Indian troubles.

Black Hawk was a chieftain of the Sauks, who with the Fox Indians were forced off their lands in northern Illinois and Wisconsin and onto the Iowa side of the Mississippi in 1831. In the late spring of 1832 the elderly chief led a thousand of his people back across the Mississippi and up the Rock River Valley to plant corn. Settlers panicked, war broke out, troops were hastily gathered, and at the "Battle" of Bad Axe, August 2, 1832, the Indians were slaughtered, barely 150 surviving out of the thousand who had crossed the Mississippi a few months before.

The Seminoles of Florida were mostly Creeks and half bloods; they had slaves, many of whom had fled from bondage north of the Florida boundary. In 1823 the Seminoles had been given a huge reservation north of Lake Okeechobee, but in 1832 the whites tried to persuade them to move west. When most of them refused, a ten-year war broke out, in which the Indians, who knew the swamps and hummocks of Florida, frustrated the best efforts of the U.S. Army. After their chief Osceola was captured by treachery in 1837, the war increased in bitterness. Gradually, however, Indian resistance was broken and a treaty of August 5, 1842, granted the few Seminoles left in Florida the right to stay there.

For the whites, the period 1815-46 was a time of filling in, during which Maine (1820), Missouri (1821), Arkansas (1836), Michigan (1837), and Florida and Texas (both 1845) were added to the nation. For the most part these were years of city growth, of the appearance of a permanent look in the eastern half of the Mississippi Valley. Lands left behind in the first sweep were purchased and improved, log cabins gave way to brick or clapboard homes, the crude meeting-houses changed to brick church buildings complete with bells, crossroads settlements became villages, and villages, cities. In these years the National Road, turnpikes, canals, steamboats, and, finally, the coming of the railroad effected a transportation revolution. They were optimistic, lusty years, for the most part. Only two panics marred this period of peaceful growth.

Land purchases were subject to runaway speculative mania. There were not enough actual settlers. From more than a million acres sold in 1814, the number rose to 3,500,000 in both 1818 and 1819. Many a pioneer farmer who speculated in lands—and most of them did—purchased by the government's easy terms. When crops failed or the market fell, that farmer, or eastern businessman or local real estate promoter, defaulted on his payment. A depression swept the country in 1819, and conditions remained sluggish until the mid-1820's. Then for a variety of reasons, including the opening of the Erie Canal in 1825, the economy switched from bearish to bullish. Year by year after 1825 the number of acres sold increased, until in 1835 some 12 million acres were sold, and in 1836, 20 million. This time it was not easy government terms that were to blame, for these had been eliminated by the Land Act of 1820. Instead, it was the inflated paper money issued by unregulated state and local banks—paper money that was accepted as legal tender for payment to the government for lands until Jackson's Specie Circular of 1836. By this executive order only hard specie—federal government coinage—could be accepted in purchase of government land. But the boom had gone too far, and the serious Panic of 1837 sent the economy tumbling again.

As a result speculation was curtailed and there was a breather from land rushes. A "permanent" Indian frontier now extended from the northwestern shores of Lake Michigan west to the Mississippi, southward through Iowa Territory somewhat west of the river to the Missouri, west to the western boundary of the state of Missouri and down that boundary, southward along the Arkansas line, and along the western boundary of Louisiana to the Gulf. Settlement that had first appeared like fingers up the river valleys gradually expanded until settlements from one valley joined hands with those of another; forests fell to the axe and the prairie turf was turned by the plow; crossroads became towns connected by scheduled coaches; and peace, order, and stability settled over the land. Gradually settlement crept west into Iowa, which achieved statehood in 1846, and into Wisconsin, with statehood in 1848. Ten years later Minnesota joined the Union. Settlement approached the land of few trees, short grass, and little rainfall. There was a pause, but only for a while . . . until the great sweep west began again.

Ownership and Order:
Land Legislation and
Provision for Government

The ceding by the states of their western lands to the central government, Pinckney's Treaty settling the Florida boundary, the Louisiana Purchase, and the Adams-Onís Treaty of 1819 giving the United States Florida all resulted in the creation of an enormous public domain. While there were more acquisitions to come, it is time to pause and examine the way the land was disposed of, and what sort of governmental authority was established in the new regions.

Even more than the traders who cheated and debauched the Indians, the white man's lust for the land was responsible for most of the conflict between the races. The extent of this land hunger continually exceeded the anticipations of politicians and administrators, and their shortsightedness, though understandable, was nevertheless one of the causes for the continual Indian unrest.

There were three groups interested in land. First were the pioneers on the cutting edge of the frontier, who were often squatters. They were semi-barbarians living in incredibly humble dwellings, even in lean-tos. Their residence was brief, for the second group soon moved in and shoved them out. This second group was more literate, more law abiding, and had more money. Coming into the new country singly, in small groups almost constituting a clan, or as an entire religious congregation, they took the lay of the land, then assembled at the land auction and made deals with others of their kind so as to keep the price of their lands at a minimum or very close to it. They made their initial deposits and settled on their quarter sections in legitimate style. Often these people were second buyers of the land, purchasing from a speculator for what seemed a reasonable price, even though it was above what it would have cost them from the receiver of the nearby General Land Office.

East of the Mississippi it was this second group that contributed most of all to the substantial, God-fearing stock that inhabits the American heartland to this day. They were the ones who so often flocked in after the battles and treaties, with the "Indian menace" ended and the land lying open and uninhabited.

The third group was the speculators. The word conjures up persons as heartless as a machine, something less than honorable, which many were; but let us also try to humanize them. They were the new country wheeler-dealers. They ranged in wealth from tavern owners or profit-minded farmers on up to the powerful, wealthy eastern plungers, who formed companies and used politics, edge-of-legitimacy methods, and downright bribery to gain ambitious ends. They were sure to know their politicians. It is interesting to note that many land investors were also themselves politicians and often Congressmen. "In securing patents, work on private land claims, and information about the marketing of tracts," writes Land Office historian Malcolm Rohrbaugh, "theirs was a special world, very much as it is today."[1] They were the American pragmatists at work, grabbing everything they could lay their hands on, investing in the future of the country, using the government to further their own ends.

Although there are glaring examples of entrepreneurs who held onto their lands and gloated over their unearned increment, the typical new country speculator was a promoter of rapid settlement, immediate expansion, and quick return. He purchased at minimum cost and often turned right around and sold the land, sometimes for a profit of only twenty-five or fifty cents an acre. Since his capital was tied up in the land, he promoted its sale. When he had returned his investment and earned his profits, he duplicated his success, or tried to, farther west. On the Great Plains such a speculator was likely to be a cattle baron whose company was known as the such-and-such "Land and Cattle Company"; often the speculation was not by an individual, but was rather the policy of a great railroad corporation. In the balance, it is difficult to deny this legion of speculators the accolade of being harbingers of frontier advancement.

This is not to give them a clean bill, however. Many of their activities were unscrupulous, unethical, and, from the point of view of public policy and the public good, outrageous. Certainly they were a deterrent to any steady, regulated, systematic advance of the frontier. The speculator was the one who forced the Indian cession, after first causing the Indian war. He was the one who, with his money, his political connections, and his shrewdness made a mockery of the system of registers and

receivers and land auctions, the procedure first established by the Ordinance of 1785. He was also a waster, for in his desire for quick profits
he did many things that were destructive to the land if not costly to
himself. He purchased timber lands, stripped them, and left nothing
but malarial bogs. He purchased only the best lands, leaving big gaps
of wilderness in the new country. He loved to acquire the land at crossroads or a river ford, lay out a town, divide it into lots, and get rich by
selling them. From mid-century on these were often called "paper
towns" because they only appeared on gaudy lithographs advertising
their virtues; they were speculators' plans that never succeeded. The
pictures showed tree-shaded streets running north and south, east and
west, church steeples, a school, a college or academy, and a bustling
river front with steamboats at various stages of business. In the absence
of a river, the railroad was shown running through the community, and
the lithographed bird's-eye view had the rails appearing out of the horizon, with all the land in between rich farmland. But the reality! A few
weathered stakes in the ground marking out blocks and streets, and
nothing more.

At the same time the speculators must be given credit for their influence upon national legislation. Their forerunners in colonial times had
prevailed upon Whitehall for massive land grants; many a colonial governor had speculated in western lands. So, too, when the new government came into being, did congressmen such as William Blount and
governors such as John Sevier of Tennessee speculate in western lands;
so did Presidents Washington and Jackson. Outside the halls of Congress or the executive offices were the big-time operators; the Reverend
Manasseh Cutler, who represented the Ohio Company Associates out
of Boston, William Duer, a government administrator who founded the
Scioto Company, and John Cleves Symmes of New Jersey are but three
of many who lobbied successfully, though unscrupulously, for beneficial
legislation. From these three men and the interests they represented
came the settlement of much of Ohio and the founding of Marietta,
Gallipolis, and Cincinnati. They were, indeed, among the first of that
callous breed known as influence peddlers. But as well as receiving vast
grants of land at ridiculously low prices (such as a little over eight cents
an acre for good Ohio land, even though it was still a wilderness), they,
or others with similar speculative interests in western lands, were also
promoters of the initial creation of the public domain, of a system of
land survey and sale, and of the establishment of law and order—that is,
government—in the new country. These three requirements were met
substantially because of their lobbying and propagandizing. It is diffi-

cult to imagine how the sweep across the continent would have taken place without the fulfillment by the federal government of these demands.

The land speculators played the major role in the creation of the public domain. When the Revolution broke out, seven of the thirteen states had claims, based upon their English charters, "from sea to sea." All the lands west of the Appalachians were claimed by one state or another, and in a number of instances by more than one state. There was also considerable overlapping of private claims. It was realized that individual states would be hard pressed to protect their western citizens from Indians, and the burden of furnishing them internal improvements would throw a heavy obligation on the tidewater taxpayers. Moreover, since all thirteen states were defending the entire western country, since the Indian knew no state boundaries and would cross them even if he did, and since excessive ownership in western lands could result in all manner of favorable situations for the have-land states, there was a movement by representatives of the landless states for a cession of western claims to the central government. Logic and statesmanship both weighed heavily on the side of such cessions.

But logic and statesmanship cannot always pass legislation. Inertia, lack of interest, and a strong pressure group can defeat logic and statesmanship any day; but in this case the pressure group was on the right side, and the legislation was passed. In fact, it was essentially the lobbying efforts of land speculators that brought about the state cessions to the federal government. Even speculators opposing cession contributed to this result by keeping the controversy before the eyes of Congress.

It was a group of land speculators in the Middle Atlantic states who led the campaign for the state cessions of lands. The groups involved were the Illinois, Wabash, Vandalia, and Indiana land companies, and among their interested investors were Robert Morris, James Wilson, Charles Carroll, Benjamin Franklin, Samuel and Thomas Wharton, and George Morgan. Their land claims were based upon a spurious use of the Camden-Yorke decision of 1757 concerning land policy in British India; it was never intended to be, and was not, applicable to the American colonies. The decision stated that the King's letters patent were not required for transfer of lands acquired by treaty or grant from Indian princes. All the speculators' claims lay within the acknowledged bounds of Virginia's original sea-to-sea grant; so that if they could prevail upon the Virginia authorities, under the Camden-Yorke decision, to accept as legal the treaties made by these private groups with the Indians, then the speculators would have a valid title over the lands thus obtained and could proceed with their colonization plans. (A further complication, though not immediately germane to the problem, was New York's claim over much of the same territory, based upon a transaction with the Iroquois.)

In American politics there is a common belief that a state government is easier to bend to the desires of a vested interest than the federal government, but this was not the case here. Virginians were loyal to Virginians—and the land jobbers of their western lands were for the most part Pennsylvanians, Marylanders, and New Jerseyites: Virginians did not want them to have the lands. Thus, after New York and Connecticut had ceded their western lands to the government by early 1781, Virginia likewise bowed to the patriotic, the logical, and perhaps the inevitable—but, to make sure that the speculators did not get her lands, with a difference, insisting that Congress abide by the specification that private land claims made prior to 1776 were null and void. If Congress did this, then the land companies laying claim to Virginia's western lands would be left out in the cold, which is exactly what the Virginians desired.

This launched a bitter three-year debate in Congress as the land company representatives politicked against congressional acceptance of the Virgina cession, while the Virginians fought to gain it with their anti-land-jobber position intact. Eventually the recognition by the Confederation government that it might obtain much-needed revenue from sale of the public lands, and the recognition of many land-investing congressmen that while Congress haggled the western lands were being squatted upon by settlers, so that if something was not done soon neither government nor private investors could make money, built up to the final acceptance of the cession as specified on March 1, 1784.

The approval of Virginia's land cession is but one chapter in a lengthy volume still unwritten on the western land cessions. A number of states, including Virginia, insisted upon the retention of military bounty lands. The Western Reserve of Connecticut comes to mind, but Massachusetts, North Carolina, and Georgia also reserved lands for their Revolutionary War veterans. Much of this military land was purchased by speculators, who went about the country paying cash for the warrants and then sold the lands at a neat profit.

North Carolina and Georgia, prior to or nearly simultaneously with their land cessions to the central government, passed legislation that enriched the land jobbers and caused litigation for decades to come. In fact, Georgia's cession, which involved the legal technicalities resulting from the Yazoo land frauds, was a financial burden to the United States. North Carolina's policies resulted in land litigation involving that state, Tennessee, the federal government, war veterans and their heirs, and the landowning citizenry; some claims were not settled for more than fifty years. So little actual land was ceded to the federal government by North Carolina that Tennessee—which constituted the cession—has never been considered as a public land state.

To begin with, most of North Carolina's western lands were still held by the Cherokee; but the Carolinians assumed that these tribesmen, having sided with the British, had forfeited their claims save for a relatively small reserve east of the Tennessee and south of the French Broad and Big Pigeon rivers, in present east Tennessee. An act of 1782 provided for a military district in the Cumberland Valley where North Carolina veterans could claim lands ranging from 640 acres for a private to 12,000 acres for a brigadier general; Major General Nathaniel Greene received 25,000 acres. Two hundred thousand acres in Carter's Valley in east Tennessee were given to Judge Richard Henderson and his associates in exchange for claims elsewhere which were thereby repudiated.

Then in the same year as the Treaty of Peace, 1783, the North Carolina legislature pushed through a "land grab" law which encouraged the sale of the remainder of that state's western domain. By April of 1784, when the state ceded its western claims to the central government, nearly four million acres of what now constitutes Tennessee had been sold, at least three-fourths of it to speculators. Much of it had gone for the sum of ten pounds per hundred acres, which at the rate of exchange was barely five dollars. One surveyor alone located 365,000 acres. Two men, John Rice and John Ramsay, staked out 5,000 acres at Chickasaw Bluffs on the Mississippi, the beginnings of the city of Memphis. James White, Robert Love, and Francis A. Ramsay claimed the site at the confluence of the French Broad and Holston rivers. In 1791 White laid out a town there and called it Knoxville in honor of Henry Knox, the Secretary of War. Stockly Donelson claimed 20,000 acres near present Chattanooga. The land speculators of Tennessee were singularly successful in their enterprises, and such names as William Blount, John Sevier, James Robertson, Richard Caswell, and Donelson are proudly displayed on the geneological charts owned by their descendants.

The successful effort of the landholding states to grab their land resource before giving it to the new government can be better understood when one looks at the poverty of some of the states at the end of the Revolution. North Carolinians were in debt to each other, to their state, and their state to them. The members of the state Assembly in 1782 were, in fact, paid for their services in corn. Even the "right people"— those who had been considered wealthy—were impoverished, and they grabbed at a get-rich-quick opportunity. They even provided for the issuance of $100,000 of paper money so that their purchases would not be hampered by a shortage of exchange media.

This 1784 cession of western lands to the central government supplied fuel for the movement toward creation of the ill-fated state of Franklin. Three conventions in the western country in 1784, in August, November, and December, resulted in John Sevier being selected governor, and a constitution being drawn up similar to North Carolina's. Meanwhile on November 20, 1784, the North Carolina legislature rescinded its act of cession. The reasons for this were complex, but the principal one appears to have been resentment at the few speculators—some Easterners and some Westerners—who stood to benefit most from the land grab act if the cession stood. State officials now set out to establish governmental authority out there, creating the district of Washington with a court presided over by David Campbell, a Westerner, and a militia headed by John Sevier. It was hoped that the granting of such authority would placate the western people.

But the Franklinites continued their plans for statehood, prompted, apparently, by a number of land speculation schemes in which many of the western country's leaders were involved. In March 1785, Franklin held its first general assembly, elected John Sevier governor (a continuation of the office given him by the conventions), chose a number of other officials as well, created four counties, and expressed its determination to retain its independence from North Carolina. The assembly also invited the people of southwestern Virginia to join Franklin and indicated a geographical extension of boundaries south and west to include the Muscle Shoals, the head of navigation of the Tennessee.

In the continuing controversy North Carolina found a leader in John Tipton, who soon had a substantial following. Polarization of factions took place; by 1788 the Franklin faction, led by John Sevier, was in retreat. Their failure was hastened by their Indian policy. They had signed the Treaty of Dumplin Creek (June 1785) and had hastily occupied some of the lands ceded by the Indians. In November the Cherokee signed the Treaty of Hopewell with the federal authorities, and shortly thereafter the Chickasaws signed a treaty with the same name with the Confederation agents. Both of these were lenient treaties from the Indian point of view. The one with the Cherokee repudiated the Treaty of Dumplin Creek and nullified North Carolina's claim that by their loyalty to the British the Cherokee had lost title to their lands. The danger in these treaties lay in the weakness of the Confederation government, which was unable to enforce them. When the western men refused to give up lands they had preempted under the Dumplin Creek

Treaty, the Indians retaliated with fagot and tomahawk. There were atrocities committed by both sides and the Franklinites, by their incendiary tactics, lost the allegiance of most of the Westerners. This was also the period in which a number of Westerners, including John Sevier, James Robertson, and Anthony Bledsoe, carried on preliminary negotiations with the Spanish in New Orleans. Nothing came of it.

In 1788 the Sevier-Franklin forces clashed with the Tipton–North Carolina forces, one man was killed, and Sevier was subsequently arrested and taken over the mountains to stand trial for high treason to North Carolina. An old acquaintance signed his bail bond and he was allowed to return home. In November 1789 a North Carolina convention ratified the United States Constitution; in December the legislature again ceded the western lands to the central government with the proviso that all North Carolinian land claims would remain valid. Congress accepted this in 1790 and created the "Territory of the United States South of the River Ohio." This consisted only of Tennessee, which gained statehood in 1796.

Speculative interests were likewise involved in two of the most important acts of the Confederation Congress. These were the Ordinance of 1785 and the Northwest Ordinance of 1787, both basic to the sweep across the continent. They express the conviction, spoken or implied, that Americans were going to rush to the "South Sea" and that regardless of what kind of wilderness lay between the frontier line and the salty waters of that sea they would conquer it all.

The Midwesterner of today, out for a Sunday ride, can see the effects of the Ordinance of 1785. He knows that every country road will be bisected at right angles by another road every mile. If he is a native of the farm areas, including the small towns of the Middle West, he thinks of land and farms in the geographical terms of sections, north forties, base lines, or meridian roads. Anyone who has flown over America's heartland and gazed down upon the geometric checkerboarding of the land; one field plowed, another fallow with cattle grazing, a third green with corn, another darker with soybeans and sorghum; noted the neat, straight-as-an-arrow roads; commented upon the homes, silos, and barns; observed the little towns that follow the same pattern as the land, with east–west and north–south bisecting streets and square blocks, has also been reminded of the manmade survey plan that made it possible. Indeed, the American system of land survey furnished as fine a method for the systematic expansion of a people asserting ownership over a wilderness as the world has ever seen.

The Ordinance of 1785 appears to have corralled the attentions of

This aerial view reveals the effects of the system of land survey set up by the Ordinance of 1785 and later extended west as they still exist today near the Sioux and the Missouri rivers. (State Historical Society of Iowa)

the Confederation Congress because of the need for money. The Confederation was always in financial straits, and the delegates were aware of the potential source of wealth in the sale of lands of the new public domain. They realized, however, that some form of government and a system of survey and sale must be established before any revenues could be forthcoming. Both problems were under discussion simultaneously. Meanwhile, Indian title was being cleared.

Even before Congress accepted Virginia's cession of lands on March 1, 1784, a committee chaired by Thomas Jefferson had been hard at work devising a workable procedure by which wilderness areas could become states and part of the body politic. Now, on March 2, another committee, also chaired by Jefferson, was appointed to develop a system of survey and sale, with Hugh Williamson of North Carolina and David Howell of Rhode Island giving strong support. Elbridge Gerry of Massachusetts and Jacob Read of South Carolina, the other members, voted against the consideration of the committee's report to Congress, and they appear to have given the work only half-hearted support.

The credit for the basic plan of survey belongs to Jefferson, with perhaps a substantial share to Williamson. This fascinating man was, like Jefferson, possessed of many interests. He was not only a public servant but also a physician, mathematics professor, and astronomer. He and Jefferson were friends of long acquaintance. Williamson gave himself the credit for the idea of using parallels and meridians, which was adopted by the committee, and there is little reason to doubt him.

In the new country, in which agriculture was the greatest industry and virgin land the greatest resource, nearly every man outside the seacoast towns knew something about surveying. Two systems had evolved. In Pennsylvania and southward a system of indiscriminate locations merely required that the land hunter obtain a warrant from the land office of the colony (or state after 1776), tramp into the wilderness, determine the land he wanted, describe its boundaries by trees, brooks, springs, gullies, boulders, or other features that would serve, and file the description with the land office: then he was issued a patent for his land. By way of example, General Nathaniel Greene's tract, surveyed in 1783, had its boundaries described as follows:

> Beginning on the south bank of Duck River, on a sycamore, cherry tree and ash, at the mouth of a small branch, running thence along a line of marked trees south seven miles and forty-eight poles to two Spanish oaks, a hicory [sic] and sugar sapling, thence east three miles and ninety poles to a Spanish oak and hackberry tree, north three miles and three hundred poles to a sugar tree sapling and two white oak saplings, under a clift of Duck River whence it comes from the northeast, thence down Duck River, according to its several meanders to the beginning."[2]

The weaknesses of such a system are obvious. Only the best land was claimed, so large acreages were left after general settlement had taken place. Trees and boulders marking a boundary with someone else's adjoining property were apt to disappear. Even a spring could dry up; and there was the "problem of the creeping fence," which inevitably enlarged one piece of property at the expense of another. There was also continual litigation. The southern system did, however, offer the advantage of initial simplicity, and it was a boon to the family unit searching out a home in the wilderness. Its shortcoming, besides the unsystematic physical survey, was that it meant considerable loss of revenue to the new government. And it was a sloppy system, most unbecoming to a government.

Up in New England the township system of survey had been evolved. By this system a given area, preferably one adjacent to a settled region, was surveyed and often granted as a complete township. The grantee would be a religious congregation or a single land jobber or a land company. Colonial governments were especially favorable to petitioners who proposed establishing compact towns on the frontier, where they would act as buffers to the more settled communities in case of Indian disturbances. This system, as it evolved, took care of poor lands as well as the good, for the purchase included them all and left the problem of individual purchase or allotment to the government of the township. It was not as cut-and-dried a procedure as is often pictured, however; although its ideal conditions included survey before the grant of a geometrically perfect township, settlement did in fact often precede survey, for there were always the human mavericks who preferred squatting in the wilderness to residing amongst the church-going, hard-working people of the towns. Furthermore, the township was apt to have uneven boundaries determined by such physical features as lakes, rivers, or mountains.

Jefferson and Williamson began with a compromise between these two forms of survey, then added a number of changes of their own. Jefferson was impressed by the use of the decimal principle in American life, as in the coinage. He advocated a land system based upon the division of the country into decimal units. Each unit would consist of a hundred square miles, divided into a hundred equal parts of a square mile each, resulting in a rectilinear division oriented to the cardinal points of the compass. This was simplicity itself; and to Jefferson it may have had democratic overtones. He stated as one advantage of square measures the fact that "everyone, who has a rule in his pocket" could verify the contents of a square, implying that with rectilinear survey, any settler, using the most rudimentary means of measurement, could verify the contents of his purchase.[3] There were also provisions for registers of land claims, for surveyors, and for the identification of lots.

The initial report was given to another committee, headed by William Grayson of Virginia, which included one delegate from each state, although Grayson and Rufus King of New York were principally responsible for the revised version of the bill. It emerged from the committee in essentially the condition in which it was passed by Congress as the Land Ordinance of 1785, which became the basis for the survey system of the new nation's public lands. Jefferson's hundreds had been changed to townships of six miles square divided into thirty-six sections of one square mile (640 acres). Rectilinear survey and an inner grid were therefore retained. Prior survey—that is, survey of the land before settlement and sale, which had not been mentioned in the Jefferson draft—was required in the ordinance.

The problem of converging meridians was never completely solved,

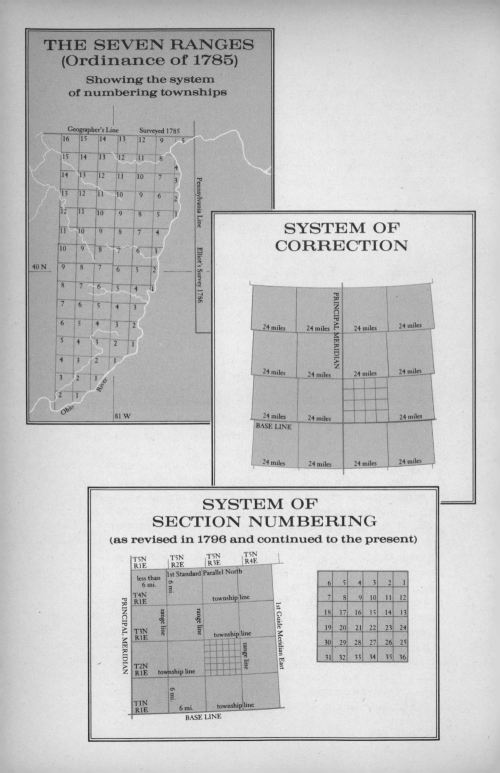

THE SEVEN RANGES
(Ordinance of 1785)
Showing the system of numbering townships

Geographer's Line   Surveyed 1785

16	15	14	13	12	9	5	
15	14	13	12	11	8		
14	13	12	11	10	7	4	
						3	
13	12	11	10	9	6	2	
12	11	10	9	8	5	1	
11	10	9	8	7	4		
10	9	8	7	6	3		
9	8	7	6	5	2		
8	7	6	5	4	1		
7	6	5	4	3			
6	5	4	3	2			
5	4	3	2	1			
4	3	2	1				
3	2	1					
2	1						

Pennsylvania Line

Elliot's Survey 1796

40 N

Ohio   River

81 W

SYSTEM OF CORRECTION

PRINCIPAL MERIDIAN

24 miles	24 miles	24 miles	24 miles
24 miles	24 miles	24 miles	24 miles
24 miles	24 miles	24 miles	24 miles

BASE LINE

| 24 miles | 24 miles | 24 miles | 24 miles |

SYSTEM OF SECTION NUMBERING
(as revised in 1796 and continued to the present)

| T5N R1E | T5N R2E | T5N R3E | T5N R4E |

less than 6 mi.

6 mi.   1st Standard Parallel North

T4N R1E

township line

PRINCIPAL MERIDIAN

range line   range line   range line

1st Guide Meridian East

T3N R1E

township line

T2N R1E   township line

6 mi.

T1N R1E   6 mi.   township line

BASE LINE

6	5	4	3	2	1
7	8	9	10	11	12
18	17	16	15	14	13
19	20	21	22	23	24
30	29	28	27	26	25
31	32	33	34	35	36

and this has always been recognized as a weakness of the system. As one authority has stated, the convergence, which increases with latitude, would mean that "in latitude 33 degrees north, which is near the north boundary of Louisiana, the linear convergence of two range lines six miles apart, in a north and south distance of ten townships, sixty miles, is 311 feet. . . . For latitude 37 degrees, which is near the south edge of Missouri, the convergence is 361 feet; . . . for 45 degrees, near Minneapolis, 479 feet. . . . These distances are theoretical [but are clearly close to the reality]."[4]

The workable solution, not entirely satisfactory but one surveyors have lived with ever since, began with the establishment of arbitrary base lines running east–west, and similarly, arbitrary principal meridians running north–south. These did not adhere to state boundaries, nor were they established with reference to the earth's equator or to the meridian running through Greenwich, England. Indian lands and subsequent Indian cessions cut up the lines so that they appear on a map of the United States as having been determined with no planning. All told, there are thirty-one principal meridians and base lines in the contiguous forty-eight states.

Surveyors next thought in terms of multiples of four townships, which (townships being six miles square) meant blocks of land twenty-four miles square, called "twenty-four-mile tracts." While there were meridional lines and latitudinal township lines every six miles, the line that was twenty-four miles north or south of the base line was called a "correctional line," or a "standard parallel line." Here each six-mile range line (or meridian line) ended and a new one began, but the new one, based upon the fact of convergence, would begin several feet away from where the old one had ended, constituting an adjustment. By this system townships just below a correctional line were deprived of a few hundred feet and those just above got an excess. Somewhere between the two was, theoretically, a perfect six-mile-wide township. Occasionally the planning was not well done, and a "shatter zone" occurred: such a zone exists today in extreme eastern Illinois. The townships there are of odd sizes, and county lines are uneven.

The division of townships into thirty-six sections and the further subdivision into half sections, quarter sections, and quarter quarters (forty acres); the use of numbers to describe each parcel of land; the employment of geometric surveying and the making of descriptive plats—all this began with the Ordinance of 1785 and, bolstered by many improvements such as the use of field books, continues to this very day. Over two and a quarter million square miles have been divided into six-mile squares. The system shows the practical foresight of the concerned delegates to the Confederation Congress. This system of land survey has been admired by geographers and public administrators the world over, and it prevented outright chaos in the process of the sweep across the continent.

The Ordinance of 1785 also provided for the sale of surveyed western lands. One half was to be sold as entire townships, which would appeal to the land jobbers, and the other half was to be sold in sections, implying purchase by individual settlers. Congressmen referred to this as the "wholesale and retail plan." In either case, lot number 16 of every township was reserved for the maintenance of public schools there. The minimum cost was fixed at a dollar an acre, plus the survey cost of a dollar a section. Sales were to be by auction in the eastern states. These provisions were intended to combine two opposing concepts of how to dispose of the public lands: in big parcels to the rich, or in small segments to individual agriculturalists. But the latter did not have $640 to put down on a section, and the place of auction was too distant from their present homes and even more so from the anticipated homes in the new country. In this respect, the Ordinance was a failure. In 1796, 1800, 1820, 1841, and 1862, significant measures were passed which made it cheaper and easier for the actual settler to buy land from the government.

The implementation of the survey began almost at once. The Ordinance stipulated that surveying was to begin "on the river Ohio at a point that shall be found to be due north from the western termination of a line which has been run as the southern boundary of the state of Pennsylvania"—a sop to speculative interests eager to see the Old Northwest opened to settlement. The area constituted a part of the Allegheny Plateau, a hilly country with rugged terrain on the west side of the Ohio where streams flow toward the Muskingum. The greatest north–south distance of the survey was the seventh range, with fifteen townships—ninety miles—extending from the Ohio on the south, north to the east–west geographer's line established by the appointed geographer, Thomas Hutchins. Eastward the number of townships declined until there were just four in the first range.

The boundary commissioners, specified by law as one from each state (and in one year, 1786, twelve of the thirteen states were represented) reached the Ohio on August 20 and began work on September 30, 1785. Hardly had they started when an Indian depredation fifty miles west of their activities brought the year's operations to a halt; just four miles of the base line (the geographer's line) had been surveyed. In 1786, with some protection provided by federal troops, the first four ranges were completed, and the townships within them were put up for sale in the fall of 1787. Less than one-third of the land was sold to a total of thirty purchasers for $176,090, the average price paid being $1.26 an acre. About half the land was sold in large lots, half in small. By the summer of 1788 seven ranges had been surveyed, but no more auctions were held until 1796; for that matter, no more surveying was done for nine years. The new government under the Constitution was being formed, and the Indians of the Old Northwest had to be defeated by General Anthony Wayne before the government could once more turn its attention to surveying activities.

Yet the survey of the Seven Ranges set a precedent. Inefficient and disappointing as the survey and the subsequent land sale turned out to be, they represented the full extent of government land activity as prescribed by the Ordinance of 1785. Three of the boundary commissioners —Israel Ludlow, Absalom Martin, and John Mathews—went from government work to private surveying for land companies in the Ohio country, and from this employment returned to the government survey when it was renewed in 1797. The survey of the Seven Ranges alone spurred land jobbers to promote settlement immediately west of there in the Ohio country. There is, therefore, justification for the emphasis that historians have always given to the first Seven Ranges.

Just as there were precedents dating back 150 years for the system of survey and sale, so were there antecedents to the administrative procedures set up by the Confederation government. In 1641 Maryland created the office of surveyor-general; in 1680 it established a land office with a register in charge, and later it appointed other agents to handle land matters in the back country. In 1774 Virginia was maintaining land offices in its western domain, and in 1779 it established a general land office with a receiver. The auction method of land sale seems to have been a New England development, Connecticut conducting an auction of lands as early as 1736 and Massachusetts doing the same in 1762.

In 1780, anticipating its acquisition of a public domain, the Congress declared its prerogative to settle lands ceded to the central government in such manner as it might determine. By the Ordinance of 1785 land sales were placed in the hands of the board of treasury, which, under the Confederation, had three commissioners; a geographer was likewise provided to conduct surveys and supervise a few surveyors.

Under the Constitution the precedent was followed, the Secretary of the Treasury being given the task of administering land sales. Alexander Hamilton, the first secretary of the treasury, suggested the creation of a General Land Office with a commissioner at its head and a surveyor-general to supervise surveying, all of this to be a part of the Treasury

Department. Although Hamilton's immediate plans did not materialize, the land act of 1796 expanded the secretary's duties vis-à-vis the lands, and also created the office of surveyor-general. In 1800 the Harrison Land Act provided for four land offices in the western country, with a register (to record the deeds) and a receiver (to receive payment) at each. In 1812 an act of Congress finally created the General Land Office with a commissioner at its head, within the Treasury Department (where it would remain until 1849, when it was transferred to the Interior Department).

The commissioner was given funds for clerical help, though never enough, so that the issuance of the final patents—to be signed by him and the president—often ran two or more years behind the date of purchase. Under the encouragement of Albert Gallatin, Madison's first Secretary of the Treasury (he had four in eight years), the first commissioner of the GLO, Edward Tiffin of Ohio, created a bureau that could have functioned very efficiently if there had been no War of 1812, if he had been given more clerks, and if communications had been faster and more reliable. He was a good administrator. Subordinate to the Washington office were the eighteen land districts created by various acts of Congress, with a land office and a register and receiver in each. By Jackson's time the number of land districts had increased to more than sixty.

Until 1820 the GLO followed the provisions of the act of 1800 which established a minimum price of $2 an acre and a minimum parcel at a half section—320 acres. There was a surveyor's fee of $3 per half section ($6 per section). Payment could be on time, one-twentieth ($32) down at the time of purchase, then one-fourth in forty days, which included the initial one-twentieth. The settler had to pay another fourth within two years, another a year later, and the final quarter in the fourth year. Interest on the unpaid balance accrued at 6 per cent a year; an 8 per cent discount was offered for early payment.

But this was the minimum price. Congress liked to think that the public lands should produce enormous revenue. Democracy did not extend to land—all land was not of equal value—and so it was always hoped that an auction system would up the price of good land. Though, under the act of 1800, bidding started at $2 an acre, it was hoped that prime acreage would command many times that figure; but the multifarious deals made by the bidders among themselves prevented this.

In 1820, following the Panic of 1819 and the resulting disruption of the land system, Congress passed a new land act. Since the credit aspects of the Harrison Land Act were primarily blamed for the troubles in the economy, credit was eliminated; cash payment was to be thenceforth required. This hardship (for rare indeed was the settler with $640 in cash) was softened by reducing the minimum amount of land purchasable to 80 acres and reducing the per acre cost to a minimum of $1.25.

For most of the decade of the 1820's business was in the doldrums, there was little money, and much of the new settlement was the work of impoverished but hard-working squatters on the public domain. As for the GLO, the act of 1820 made some helpful changes, for the switch from a credit to a cash system simplified administration. The act did nothing, however, to clear up the $23-million land debt left by the Panic; and politically inspired legal methods by which settlers could "get out from under," such as the Relief Act of 1821, greatly added to the clerical tasks of the Land Office. By this act a debtor could surrender part of his land in payment for the rest, and credit could be extended to debtors for four, six, or even eight years. The rising power of the West, so apparent in relief legislation, was also apparent in the recurring introduction of preemption bills into Congress. Finally in 1841 the Preemption Act was passed, whereby a settler could purchase up to 160 acres of preempted land at the minimum price.

In the decade of the 1830's the land office business began to increase, and from 1834 to 1837 the greatest land sales in American history took place. This was the period known as the "flush times." In 1834 over 4,650,000 acres were sold; in 1836 the number rose to 20,074,870 acres. Parts of Alabama, Mississippi, Louisiana, Illinois, Iowa, Missouri, and Arkansas, and most of the territories of Wisconsin and Michigan, were sold in this period. The General Land Office was maintaining sixty-two land offices in 1837. Then a panic visited the West once again. From 1854 to 1857 there was another land boom, with 1855 the top year when 15,729,525 acres were sold; in 1857 there was another panic.

The question remains: how well did the land policy work? In the context of early-nineteenth-century America, the answer must be, quite well. The founders of the Republic had created a survey system that was about as perfect for American use as could have been made. The Act of 1812 which created the General Land Office was built on decades of experience by colonies, then by the states, and finally by the federal government. By following such precedent Congress created a very workable system, which in spite of incredible problems resulted in a logically satisfactory, eternal registration of land ownership from its first sale by the government right down to the present-day owner, however small a patch it might be. When the United States Government purchases land today, it traces the title all the way back to the original patent on a three-by-eight-inch slip of crisp, crumbling pencil-tablet-quality paper, filed in the Land Office records in the National Archives. At times, as we shall see, Land Office activities did approach chaos, and a total breakdown seemed imminent; but it is to the everlasting credit of the hard-worked and shamefully underpaid employees that they stuck to their jobs and thus insured thousands of landowners a clear title. The excellence of the Land Office "machine" is demonstrated by its persistence in time of speculation and depression. Its failures were caused by Congress, by corruption, or, most often, by the boom-and-bust, speculation-panic-depression-boom cycles of the times.

An administrator can appreciate the plight of a hard-pressed GLO commissioner trying to carry on business in the 1820's and 30's with the register and receiver at, say, Franklin, Missouri; Shawneetown, Illinois; Huntsville, Alabama; or Tallahassee, Florida. Communication was agonizingly slow and highly undependable. Not only were the roads bad and the post offices unreliable, but the land offices were, after all, in new country, where all conditions were primitive. Lack of supervision resulted in loss of money and records—and rats and mice chewed up more than a few land claims.

In the nineteenth century, much more than today, government servants were looked down upon; and the concept that that government governs best which governs least guaranteed parsimonious treatment by Congress of most federal bureaus. Not only was the General Land Office always understaffed, but its employees were overworked and miserably underpaid. Furthermore, this was the pre–Civil Service era, and commissioners, registers and receivers, and even clerks were subject to the winds of political change. Probably the most corrupt appointees were the products of the Jacksonian era. "Old Hickory" removed sixteen out of forty-two registers within seven months after taking office. His own nominees, men such as Samuel Gwin in Mississippi and Richard Keith Call in Florida, virtually made the land offices in their areas into political clubs. Others fell into arrears in submitting funds, and some defaulted, with the government left holding the bag to the tune of—sometimes—fifty or a hundred thousand dollars.

The most serious problem the Land Office had to cope with was boom conditions. The term "doing a land office business" comes straight out of the new country. The land offices had somehow to be established in the midst of the new areas, often on land just ceded by the Indians, and surveyors, their field work done, had to work in offices during the cold, wet winter and spring in order to have the plats ready for examination at the land office prior to the scheduled date of sale. Rumors spread fast, whirling with the winds along the frontier. Well before the posting of the announcements of public sale, the word got out that there was to be a land sale at such and such a place. Possibly there was only a tavern and a general store there, besides the land office. Never mind. In a few weeks—as at Mount Salus, Mississippi, in the autumn of 1833—a tent city appeared. So many men sought private entry—a phrase meaning simply that they planned to purchase at the forthcoming auction—that they could not get in the doors of the office, and stood outside for a week waiting their turns to examine the plats. In 1833 alone, more than a million acres were sold in Mississippi. The register hired additional clerks but still fell behind. In 1836 in Alabama, more than 1,900,000 acres were sold. So many greasy, perspiring hands handled the survey plats that they crumbled to pieces or could scarcely be read. If there was sickness in the area, the bags of asafetida and/or garlic that the men wore around their necks as protection against disease, along with their whiskey breaths and the smoke from cheroots, must have made the atmosphere within the land office almost unbearable. These "flush times" placed a heavy burden on the Land Office, and the issuance of patents fell in arrears. Nevertheless, the office never gave up, and the titles were eventually issued.

Certainly one of the most colorful events in the new country was the first few days of a land office sale. A crier (the auctioneer) called out the description of the tracts, bidding took place, and the lands were either sold or set aside for future private entry, at minimal cost. Yet few lands ever commanded more than the minimum, and if they did, it was just a few cents more; for there was little genuine competitive bidding. This was because the land office business soon had as many "experts" as a race track has touts—shrewd speculators well prepared with money, who sought association with others of their ilk; and deals were made. By the time the auction took place the big buyers all knew each other and had formed into little groups which had made deals with other groups, and so the bidding at auction was strangely sluggish. The various parties had simply agreed not to compete and to honor the lands desired by each. Thus the lands went at the minimum price, not usually to the small pioneer who really wanted to settle down and begin farming, but to the speculators. They were the ones who knew the registers and receivers and surveyors on a first-name basis. They were allowed to examine the plats by candlelight, with shades drawn, and arrange who would bid for what choice parcels, while the innocents encamped outside awaited bidding at auction more or less in ignorance of the deals already made by the speculators, who thus got the choicest lands. Many registers and receivers are known to have done favors for the powerful, and even violated their own trust by themselves speculating in public lands. A sinister type that lurked around the land offices was the loan shark, more than willing to lend the necessary cash payment to the ambitious husbandman—at 28 per cent interest. Possibly that stock villain of nine-teenth-century melodrama, the black-mustached mortgage-holder threat-ening foreclosure—or the hand of the farmer's innocent daughter—was a spinoff from the land office loan shark.

Some of the land laws passed by Congress were so bad, so inviting of fraud, that the suspicion arises that fraud was the whole idea behind such measures. For example, the Preemption Acts of 1830 and 1834 (predecessors of the Preemption Act of 1841, these were temporary acts relating to specific landholders) made it possible for preemptors to swear that they had settled and improved up to 160 acres. If witnesses bore them out, the register could allow them to purchase up to 160 acres at the minimum price. But if two settlers claimed the same land, it could be divided between them, and each would receive eighty addi-tional acres in the land district. By means of these eighty-acre "floats" men laid claims to the choicest lands while selling their earlier acreage at a profit. In the South, overseers or even slaves were sent out to make improvements, swear that they had settled 160 acres, and then purchase the land at the minimum; it was then turned over to the speculator or the plantation owner who had put up the money and sent them there in the first place. In the North friends and especially relatives partici-pated in the same fraudulent practices, so common they were hardly considered illegal. Many of the later land measures, such as the Swamp Lands Acts of 1849-50, Homestead Act of 1862, Timber Culture Act of 1873, Desert Land Act of 1876, and Timber and Stone Act of 1878, were full of loopholes. Though honest entries were made under them, the possibilities of fraud were quickly noticed and so widely practiced that in certain areas, as in Florida, on the high plains, or in the timber-lands of the Pacific Northwest, the fraudulent entry became the norm. The hired hands of cattle barons helped their employers acquire thou-sands of acres of "desert" land, while timber barons paid sailors on shore to fill out fraudulent claims to rich timber lands. Proof of improvements on homesteads was sometimes as ludicrous as tar-paper mobile homes carted by wagon from one claim to another, or houses whose dimensions were actually in inches instead of feet.

In fact, throughout the entire period of the new country, land pur-chasers held the belief that Uncle Sam was against them, that the vir-gin lands were God-given, that they and only they knew best how to make use of them. If they did gain possession, they reasoned that by their improvements they were aiding in building the great country. This attitude toward governmental interference invited them to rationalize fraudulent practices; and, with the apparent naiveté of many congres-sional acts, it led to an amazing record of land-law violations on the frontier by people who hardly thought twice of the illegal aspects of what they were doing.

The land office business, then, though it was chaotic at the place of sale, was never beyond redemption. There were misunderstandings, complexities in the handling of transactions, and the red tape was abominable. Yet a pattern evolved in the sense that amidst the heavy smoke of cheroots, the whiskey breath, and the sweaty, unwashed bodies of men stomping into the frame one-story office of the register and receiver, the business was transacted, the land was sold, and a system operated which ensured that at a quieter and more settled time an accurate record of the sale of the public domain would be in existence.

The years 1784-87 were difficult for the Confederation government. It was without revenue, lacked the confidence of the people, and the Congress was often without the necessary quorum for the transaction of business. A new government was about to be born, but the moves in this direction were of uncertain issue.

Such an unstable condition is made to order for the influence peddler, the speculator, the promoter of grandiose schemes contingent upon some kind of a giveaway from the central government. The result was a temporary change in government policy. Since survey and sale in township or section lots was slow and unprofitable under the conditions stipulated by the Ordinance of 1785, Congress turned to the big-time operators and sold several million acres of land in the public domain to various companies.

It was those interested in the Ohio country who were most successful —men such as the Reverend Manasseh Cutler, John Duer, and John Cleves Symmes, mentioned earlier, along with other investors among whom General Rufus Putnam, Benjamin Tupper, and Samuel Parsons were prominent. The Ohio Company of Associates, the Scioto Company led by John Duer, and the Symmes Tract received in total about 7,500,000 acres. So successful were they that one irritated historian has described them as "an unsavory crew . . . peculiarly shifty and tricky specimens of the genus that throughout the course of American history has sought to reap where it has not sowed and to extract a speculative profit from the man who desires land that he may till it with his own hands."[5]

Ultimately, however, the efforts of these men failed, and the government repossessed most of their lands. Still their enterprises inadvertently accomplished some positive measures for the new country. All government surveying had halted with the completion of the Seven Ranges in 1787, due to Indian difficulties and the instability concomi-

tant with the end of the Confederation and the beginning of the new
government under the Constitution. However, the eastern boundary of
the Ohio Company's grant was the western line of the Seventh Range,
and what surveying was accomplished by the Ohio group was a continuation of the rectilinear township system. They carried the survey
even further, halving and quartering some of the square-mile sections.
In 1796 Congress passed the land act that established the office of surveyor-general and made some changes and improvements in the survey
system. The first surveyor-general, Rufus Putnam, inaugurated a contract system, used until 1910, by which private entrepreneurs surveyed
the public domain. Israel Ludlow, surveyor for the Symmes tract, also
followed the township system.

But the greatest contribution was the part these companies played in
the passage of the famous Northwest Ordinance of 1787. This is the
Ordinance that answered the third of the speculator's demands: law
and order in the new country. It was not statesmanship that led Manasseh Cutler to help in the final drafting of this legislation; it was the need
for an act to provide a government for the lands north of the Ohio. The
Ohio Company was purchasing its tract with money yet to be earned;
and an established government in the Ohio country was a bargaining
point that could aid materially in persuading settlers to move there.
Even in 1787 "law and order" was a powerful phrase. Arthur St. Clair,
a powerful man in the Confederation Congress, worked very hard for
the passage of the Ordinance. He was interested in the Old Northwest
and fostered his own appointment as governor of the Northwest Territory. The Ordinance passed and he assumed the office, inaugurating the
new government at Marietta on July 15, 1788.

Yet the prime mover in the passage of the Northwest Ordinance, just
as of the Ordinance of 1785, was Thomas Jefferson. And in both cases
he authored plans or chaired a committee that submitted plans that
were laid aside. He then went to France, and the final acts were passed
without his being present—but the sure influence of the man was always felt; his initial plans were the basis for the final acts. His proposed
Ordinance of 1784 was a preliminary plan for a system by which territories could become states, a method by which American colonists (and
what were those settlers in the new country beyond state borders if not
colonists?) could retain their American rights and citizenship until such
time as they did enter the Union. He originally envisioned ten states
west of the mountains and north of the Ohio to the Mississippi, each of
which was to have parallels and meridians as its boundaries. He also
made provision for the free males to form their own governments and
stipulated that there would be no slavery in any of the states after 1800.

This initial plan failed for diverse reasons: one was that George Washington believed ten states would result in a serious dispersal of population; another that Southerners rebelled at the anti-slavery provision.

Three years later, with such powerful interests as the investors in the Ohio Company and the Scioto Company backing it, the Northwest Ordinance was passed by the Confederation Congress in its last months of existence. Jefferson's anti-slave wishes were retained for the area north of the Ohio and east of the Mississippi, without mention of the year 1800. Three steps, or phases, toward statehood were described. The move from the initial phase, in which a congressionally appointed governor, secretary, and three judges constituted the government, to the next phase was to take place when the territory had "five thousand free male inhabitants of full age." Then an assembly could be formed consisting of the governor, a legislative council, and a house of representatives. One of its duties was to select a delegate to the national Congress. Phase three began when the area embracing one of the three nor more than five states into which the ordinance stipulated the Old Northwest could be partitioned had "sixty thousand free inhabitants" therein. At that stage the territory could become a state with all the rights and perquisites of the several states, according to a series of steps involving the method for calling a constitutional convention, ratification of the constitution by the voting citizenry of the proposed state, and the approval of the document by Congress.

The ordinance was actually less democratic than Jefferson's 1784 proposal. Control of the territory was in the hands of Congress until the region was ready for statehood. There were no provisions for elections until it had 5,000 inhabitants, and the governor was appointed by Congress right down to the time of statehood. There were rather steep landholding qualifications for members of the assembly, and even voters were required to own a freehold of fifty acres. All these restrictions were placed in the document by the speculators and their congressional cohorts, in an obvious move to control and, if necessary, suppress a citizenry that might become hostile to a money-grubbing land company.

Still, this Northwest Ordinance established a method by which a territory could become a state on a parity with all the states. It was a continental colonial system, solving a problem that had vexed the ancient Greeks. It remains one of the truly notable contributions of this country to the world's slow, anguished, political maturity.

For the new country, it established a highly workable precedent. In 1790 a similar ordinance was passed for the Old Southwest, and the progression from territory to full-fledged statehood was followed for all the new states after Ohio in 1803, excepting Texas, West Virginia, and California. Nevada had fewer inhabitants in 1862 than the stipulated 60,000, and Hawaii and Alaska, when admitted to statehood nearly a century later, had more. Some territories became states due to partisan politics— since they were predominantly Republican, Democrats in Congress kept them out, but when the Republicans did have the power, they were let in. North and South Dakota, Washington, and Montana in 1889 and Wyoming and Idaho in 1890 are examples.

Without this governmental system it is difficult to envision the emergence of a democratic nation extending from coast to coast. At best the settlers still would have followed the democratic heritage of the eastern seaboard, would have formed governments in the essential pattern of the eastern states, would have established land laws and dealt with the Indians in their own way. The habit of the English common law, of a government with executive, legislative, and judicial branches, and elections by the people would have prevailed. But without the public domain, the Ordinance of 1785 and the Northwest Ordinance of 1787, and a federal Indian policy, the advance would have been tragically chaotic. It would have lacked the consistent policies that helped create a single nation from the original thirteen states and all of the new country to the west.

At worst, the Indians would have suffered even more than they did from the frontiersman's open season on the red men; extermination would not have been impossible. Squatters would have defended their lands not only from Indians but from whites contesting their claims. Land ownership would have been precarious, and a form of land baronage could easily have arisen. States would have been established, but without the three-phase system established by the Northwest Ordinance their emergence would have been unsystematic and haphazard; the mere common experience toward statehood gave them a measure of communality. Without it, it is not impossible that they would have warred against each other. Alliance with other nations could have ensued; and in fact Aaron Burr, James Wilkinson, Harman Blennerhassett, John Sevier, James Robertson, William Blount, and William Augustus Bowles did flirt with the Spanish. Intrigue with the French and British was not unknown either. A study of Texas nationalism in the 1830's and Mormon dreams of empire in the 1850's will reveal the precariousness of the federal hold over the new country areas. Surely anything less than these services of Indian policy, land policy, and governmental progression would have made the federal position in the new country tenuous in the extreme. But with these services, sufficient stability was maintained; and when there was a breakdown, it was a Civil War fought between two sections, not a war of frontier factions.

The Sweep Across the
Continent: Final Phase

The pause in the sweep to the Pacific may have been in part the result of a period of filling-in in the new country areas that were virtually secured by 1820. A more significant reason was that the next areas of settlement that appeared attractive were owned by or shared with other peoples. In addition, Oregon and California, if not Texas, were not contiguous with the eastern fringe of settlement. The climate also changed abruptly, and with it the flora and fauna. Men accepted the explorer Stephen H. Long's description of the area from the fringe of settlement to the Rockies as the Great American Desert. Government policy placed the Indian tribes in that region and promised its lands to them forever. Nomadic, mounted tribes of warriors already there hindered American settlement.

Nevertheless, the pause was of short duration. Men in the vanguard of the drive west were already peppered throughout the high plains, the transmontane areas, and the Pacific coast. The energy and restlessness of a free people were already making a mockery of the idea of a forbidding desert, defying the Mexicans in the Southwest and California, and causing some alarm among the British, with whom the U.S. jointly occupied Oregon. The probing and penetration of the westernmost part of the continent began as early as 1792, when Captain Robert Gray in the Yankee trader *Columbia* crossed the sand bar and dropped anchor in the estuary of the Columbia River.

These vanguard elements were characterized by a primitive, often harsh existence which lacked the softening, civilizing influence of white women. Many of the occupations of the age demanded that men be without women for months or years at a time. Fur traders and trappers were without women save for squaws, who—however feminine, submissive, and hard working in their men's behalf they may have been—hardly established Western-type homes and families. Whaling engrossed three

An old-time mountain man with his ponies. (Denver Public Library, Western History Department)

years or more at a time of a man's life without sight of a woman save during a brief watering period at the Sandwich Islands (Hawaii) or at Monterey or Yerba Buena (Spanish San Francisco). The California seal fisheries, which were so heavily raided by Yankee traders that the seals were all but exterminated by 1820, were exploited by men who spent two to five years away from home port. When the seals disappeared, the Boston firm of Bryant, Sturgis and Company, with smaller firms following, picked up a trade in the hide and tallow produced by the Mexicans on their California ranches. In one of the great American classics, Richard Henry Dana's *Two Years Before the Mast*, we are given a vivid description of the long, hard, and lonely voyage of men on a hide-and-tallow boat. Yet, for all their hatred of California and their yearning for home, they acquired a knowledge of the land, and a few remained there, to be met by a horde of their brethren, single men again, Argonauts from overland in 1849.* The China traders, avidly cheating the natives of the Pacific Northwest of their furs, also traveled without women. They learned of Oregon—and met a horde of farmers from the Middle West, coming overland in the 1840's. Most of the farmers had their women and children with them.

Single men for the most part, free as a breeze, searching for the One Big Chance, or just enjoying the free life: such a man was Philip Nolan, who in the 1790's, working out of Spanish Louisiana, had already been to San Antonio and traded there with the Spanish. Later he conferred with Jefferson and then led an expedition into Texas. He pitched camp somewhere along the Brazos River, possibly near Fort Worth, and there was surrounded by the Spanish and killed. Only one man, named Bean, returned to the States. This incident demonstrates the early American interest in the far Southwest.

But Texas was just one of the regions on the crude maps of the time that attracted Americans. The traders who headed into the new country from Natchez, Vicksburg, or New Orleans, who learned about the people across the Sabine and even settled with them at Nacogdoches, had their counterparts all along the fringes of settlement. At the same time that Yankee sea captains were trading or sealing along the California and Oregon coasts, other men were venturing up the Missouri in search of furs. It was two such persons, Joseph Dickson and Forrest Handcock from the Illinois country, who had met Lewis and Clark as they approached the Mandan villages on their way home in 1806. It was with these men that John Colter headed back upstream, trapped for a winter, and then drifted down the Missouri. Near where the Platte comes in, he met the Spanish trader Manuel Lisa with a company of adventurers out of St. Louis, headed upriver for the beaver country. Lisa made Colter an attractive offer, and once again he turned his back on civilization and headed into the great northwest. After several narrow escapes from the Blackfeet and a possible visit to present Yellowstone Park, John Colter returned to Missouri, ventured into marriage and farming, and died in bed of jaundice.

Year by year the fur trade of the Far West increased, until it crested late in the 1820's. Although it functioned in a similar manner to the trade that had flourished in the eastern part of the continent since the

---

* *Argonaut*, the name given California gold seekers, was taken from the Greek name for the men who accompanied Jason in search of the golden fleece.

days of Cartier and Champlain, there were some differences and a few innovations. The role of the free trappers and traders, in competition with company men, was probably greater. It was two St. Louis entrepreneurs, William H. Ashley and his partner Andrew Henry, who developed a method of trading without the cost of maintaining permanent posts. The two men established the trapper's rendezvous, a system whereby the mountain men and Indians met each summer at a chosen place in the wilderness with the traders from St. Louis, who came there with firewater and trinkets, powder and lead. It was sort of a mountain fair, and it soon was attended by representatives of other companies as well.

The search for beaver carried men two thousand miles up the Missouri into the domain of the dreaded Blackfeet. Then they came south into the Grand Tetons, worked over the passes into eastern Idaho, and down the Snake and Columbia rivers toward British Fort Vancouver. Other trappers worked up the Red River, the Ouachita, and the Arkansas. When they reached the Front Range of the Rockies they fanned out across the rushing streams, gathering peltry and looking forward to a return to the settlements or the nearest fort. In the early days this probably meant St. Louis, but later it meant a number of forts along the Missouri, the Platte, the Arkansas, the Snake, the Columbia, and their tributary streams. Fort Union at the junction of the Yellowstone and the Big

The summer rendezvous between trappers and Indians. (Denver Public Library, Western History Department)

Fort Snelling (south of Minneapolis), 1852. (Minnesota Historical Society)

Horn, Fort Pierre on the Missouri, Fort Hall in eastern Idaho, Bent's Fort on the upper Arkansas, are but a few of the 140 forts in the Far West that existed for trading purposes at one time or another. The mountain men learned of Taos and Santa Fe, and some of them took up residence in those places with Spanish or half-blood wives. They were continually violating the ordinances concerning the fur trade, however, and so their peltry was often confiscated; and occasionally a mountain man languished several months in the Santa Fe jail.

St. Louis was the center of the American fur trade. John Jacob Astor, the exploitative miser who came to dominate the business through his American Fur Company, maintained offices and warehouses there, although he resided in New York. Most of the other fur trade entrepreneurs were St. Louisans—men such as William H. Ashley, Andrew Henry, Manual Lisa, Pierre and Auguste Choteau, and William Clark of Lewis and Clark fame. Astor's company, though more stable than its competitors, varied in activities and personnel; at one time it was known as the Upper Missouri Outfit. Among Astor's rivals was the Rocky Mountain Fur Company, first owned by Ashley and Henry. In 1826 they sold out to three veterans of the trade, William Sublette, Jedediah

Smith, and David E. Jackson, who in turn sold out in 1830 to five experienced mountain men: Thomas Fitzpatrick, Jim Bridger, Milton
Sublette, Henry Fraeb, and Jean Gervais. In 1834, at the rendezvous in
the Green River country, the Rocky Mountain Fur Company was dis-
solved; a part of its interests went to the newly formed (Lucien) Fonta-
nelle, Fitzpatrick and Company; in 1836 *they* sold out to Joshua Pilcher
acting in behalf of Pratt, Choteau and Company, which had succeeded to American Fur Company interests after Astor withdrew in
1834. But this represents just a part of the complexities of the trade. In
addition, the great northwest in these years was being trapped out by
the vigorous brigades of the Hudson's Bay Company.

The last rendezvous was in 1840 on the Green River at the mouth of
Horse Creek, in southwestern Wyoming; and with it ended the golden
age of the fur trade, although for another twenty-five years companies
came into existence each spring, financed overland trapper brigades or
boatloads of trade goods bound for the upper Missouri, and, often, dis-
solved in the fall, especially if the season's trade had been poor, or if
catastrophe, such as a successful Indian raid against its brigade or a
snagged and sunken steamboat, had ruined a company's investment.

Of greater interest are the personnel of the trade, and of greater importance was their role as pathfinders. The most notable of these men
were active in the period 1822-40. A number of them got their start when
William H. Ashley, the St. Louis businessman, and Andrew Henry ran
an advertisement in the *Missouri Republican* in 1822 requesting a hundred "enterprising young men . . . to ascend the Missouri River to its
source, there to be employed for one, two, or three years. . . ." Ashley
had made a good choice for his business associate. Andrew Henry had
been to the Three Forks country at the headwaters of the Missouri in
1808. There the Missouri Fur Company, by which he was employed,
met with disaster at the hands of the Blackfeet. Henry and a few followers crossed the continental divide, becoming the first American overland traders on the west side of the Rockies, and established a fur-
trading post on a tributary of the Snake River which still bears his
name, Henry's Fork. He had to abandon this post also, and in 1811 he
was back in Missouri.

Among the "enterprising young men" who answered the notice in the
Republican, or similar notices appearing in the following three or four
years, were Jedediah Smith, David E. Jackson, William M. Sublette,
Milton Sublette, Robert Campbell, James Clyman, Jim Bridger, Jim
Beckwourth (a mulatto), Thomas Fitzpatrick, and Daniel Potts. Every
one of them had tales of high adventure to tell before he breathed his
last.

Jedediah Strong Smith, a Bible-quoting, educated son of a New England farmer, was just twenty-three when he offered his services to Ashley in 1822. Nine years later, in 1831, he died at the hands of the Comanches on the Santa Fe Trail. In the intervening years he came to know the West better than any other man. He rediscovered South Pass (probably first traversed by a party returning from Astoria, John Jacob Astor's failed trading post in Oregon, in October 1812); and he was the first to reach California overland from the East, arriving there after a hot, thirsty trip southwest from Salt Lake in November, 1826. In the spring of 1827 he worked up the great Central Valley of California, crossed the Sierras (another first), and returned due east to Salt Lake and the annual trapper's rendezvous, held at Bear Lake (north of Salt Lake) that year.

Smith had left some of his men and some peltry in California, so in July of 1827, with eighteen men, he set out to return there. He advanced southwest as before, although not by the same trail—credit that to sheer curiosity, or the more mundane search for beaver streams. After losing ten men when the Mojaves attacked his party, he pushed across the desert to California. There he rejoined the men he had left the year before. He was held as an intruder by the Mexicans, sold some peltry to the captain of a ship, the *Franklin*, and had his bond posted by an American businessman, John Rogers Cooper of Monterey. He then started north for the Columbia River, thus once more blazing a new trail for Americans; and was involved next in a massacre. At least eleven in his party, and possibly fifteen, were treacherously murdered by the Umpqua Indians a hundred miles south of Fort Vancouver. Smith and two others survived and arrived nearly destitute at the Hudson's Bay Company post. In time, through the kindness and intervention of George Simpson, a Hudson's Bay Company official, Smith's furs and some of his horses and other supplies were recovered. McLoughlin purchased the furs, and Smith returned with an outfit to the northern Rockies. Not until the summer of 1830 did he finally return to Missouri; less than a year later he started southwest on the Santa Fe Trail, and was killed by Comanches.

Other mountain men forged other trails and went where no white men had been before. Daniel Potts explored into southern and central Utah, along the Sevier River. Jim Bridger first gazed upon the sterile waters of the Great Salt Lake and was ridiculed for his stories about thermal phenomena in the upper Yellowstone country; Warren Ferris and Osborne Russell both witnessed the geyser phenomenon also.

While most American trappers tended to concentrate in an area bounded roughly on the east by the Green River, on the south by the canyons of the Uinta Mountains, on the west by the Salt Lake and Bear

A trapper leading a wagon fur train on the way to the Platte, painting by Frederick Remington. (Denver Public Library, Western History Department)

Lake, and on the north by the southern extremity of the Snake River, there were American trappers active in the Southwest also; these tended to work out of Santa Fe and Taos. William Wolfskill, Ewing Young, Etienne Provost, George Yount, Sylvester and James Ohio Pattie, and Richard Campbell are just a few of these courageous pathfinders. Often they worked north through the Rockies and met with the trappers from the Green River area. Between 1827 and 1831 parties that included the Patties, Campbell, Wolfskill, Young, and Kit Carson (just beginning his adventures) blazed the way across the deserts to California. Wolfskill and Young, with a party of about twenty men, are credited with pioneering the "Old Spanish Trail" from Santa Fe to southern California in 1830. In 1833 a Santa Fe trader named Joseph Reddeford Walker blazed the trail from Salt Lake to the Humboldt River and over the Sierras into California—the first American to cross the Sierras from east to west.

Ultimately the mountain men explored just about every likely beaver stream from the Front Range of the Rockies to the Pacific. They followed buffalo trails and Indian traces and often forged their own trails if none were there. In their wanderings these men suffered greatly; their annual mortality rate has been estimated at 80 per cent. They were killed in Indian fracases, died from accidental gunshot wounds, took sick, froze to death, or starved even after they had killed their horses for food. To slake thirst they cut the veins of their mounts to suck the blood, killed bison and drank the warmish fluid in the stomach, or drank their own urine. Marcus Whitman, the missionary, removed from Jim Bridger's shoulder a three-inch-long spear point acquired in an altercation with the Blackfeet three seasons before. Hugh Glass wore the scars of an infuriated grizzly and lived to tell how his companions, the same Jim Bridger and Thomas "Broken Hand" Fitzpatrick, had left him to die. "Peg-Leg" Smith amputated his own leg after a bullet had shattered it, and lived to tell the story. These legions of single men, contained by no boundaries, restricted by nothing save the inadequacies of the human body and the slowness of horse and boat, inspired primarily by the search for beaver peltry and the material rewards it fetched, solved most of the mysteries of the great West.

But there were as well other Americans active in various parts of the West during these years. Americans were emigrating to Texas, ultimately to assert their independence from Mexico and create a short-lived republic. In 1821 William Becknell, a Missouri entrepreneur, decided to forge southwest from Independence to Santa Fe, far into Mexican territory. Thus began the Santa Fe trade which, though highly successful and lasting until the coming of the railroad, was never a large business; what it accomplished was the dissemination of knowledge about the area which, though much of it was distorted, was favorable to manifest destiny in that it drew an attractive picture of the enchanted Southwest, the land of *poco tempo*. In far-off California Yankee traders in sailing ships were busy purchasing hundreds of thousands of cowhides, while some of their brethren were buying furs along the Oregon coast prior to crossing the Pacific and trading them for items produced in the Orient.

Information about the West was widely disseminated through books, such as Washington Irving's *Astoria*, James Ohio Pattie's *Personal Narrative*, or Josiah Gregg's *Commerce of the Prairies*, or through government reports by such explorers as Zebulon Pike, Stephen H. Long (or his subordinate, Dr. Edwin James), and John C. Frémont. There was a widespread interest in the West, reflected by extensive re-publication of articles on the subject in the nation's newspapers and by lyceum lecturers such as Hall J. Kelley, who proselytized for Oregon. Congress, too, reflected this interest by a prevalence of speeches on the West, speeches

Meeting of the trappers' boats and the inland wagon trains. (Denver Public Library, Western History Department)

which were widely quoted and often published in their entirety in the nation's press.

Thus by the decade of the 1840's the American people were not only acquainted with the border areas of what was to become their country, they were also remarkably aware of the vast interior. Seventeen million strong in 1840, concentrated east of the Mississippi save for Missouri, Arkansas, and Louisiana, they possessed an optimism which in many ways was justified.

The population of the new nation was still of primarily northwest European stock, though by 1840 a substantial percentage were native Americans. English in its American variant was the spoken tongue. Though slavery threatened the unity of the nation, all but a few prophets of gloom believed the problem could be amicably solved. This confidence in peaceful solutions included a blind, simplistic faith in the American system of government, reinforced by a strong, fundamentalist Protestantism. The Declaration of Independence, the Constitution, and the Ten Commandments were the components of the intellectual trinity that the nation's faith was built on. Nearly all Americans were aware of the contrast between the bustling republic in the New World and the unstable countries of continental Europe, where revolts, governmental suppression, imprisonments, executions, and generally unfavorable social and economic conditions seemed to be evidence of decadence.

Even though the country had lost much confidence during the Panic of 1837, optimism was reviving by the beginning of the new decade. Nor had the economic troubles reduced faith in a government that represented the common man, catered to his prejudices, and was run to a great extent by common men. Besides, other internal conditions prompted expansion. The Panic and subsequent depression had slowed down activity for a few years and given the nation a period of consolidation. By the mid-1840's transportation, by way of canals, turnpikes, steamboats, and railroads, was knitting the nation together. The steamboat did not reach its greatest influence until the 1850's, but its improvement was a matter of almost daily comment. It was in 1845 that Asa Whitney, a New York merchant, first suggested a transcontinental railroad. There can be no doubt that these rapid developments in transportation had an influence on attitudes toward expansion.

The assumption that the American people would ultimately rule from sea to sea had always been present in the American mind. What was new as the 1840's got under way was a sudden realization that a single generation might round out the boundaries of a country stretching from sea to sea. Even so, probably no one in 1840 imagined that the nation only eight years later would include Texas, California, and Oregon.

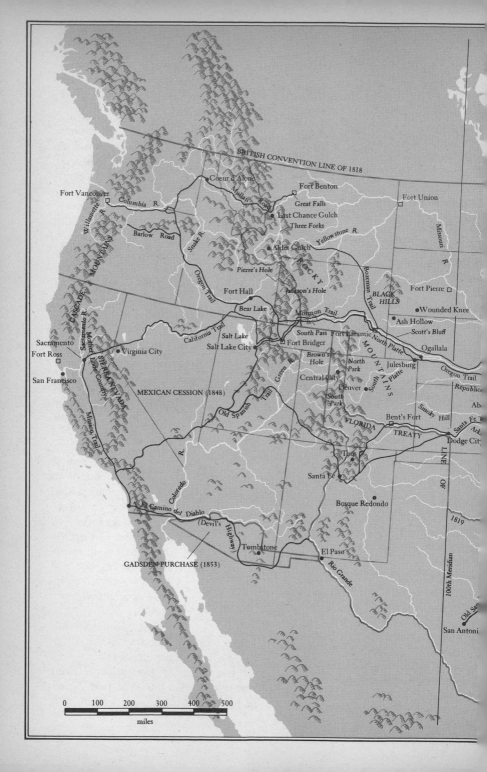

BRITISH CONVENTION LINE OF 1818

Fort Vancouver
Coeur d'Alene
Fort Benton
Fort Union

Columbia R.
Mullah River
Great Falls
Last Chance Gulch
Three Forks

Willamette R.
Barlow Road
Snake R.
Yellowstone R.
Missouri R.

CASCADE MOUNTAINS
Oregon Trail
Alder Gulch
ROCKY
Fort Pierre

Pierre's Hole
Jackson's Hole
BLACK HILLS

Fort Hall
Bear Lake
Mormon Trail
Bozeman Trail
Wounded Knee

California Trail
Salt Lake
South Pass
Fort Laramie
Ash Hollow
Scott's Bluff

Sacramento
Sacramento R.
Virginia City
Salt Lake City
Fort Bridger
North Platte
Ogallala

Fort Ross
MOTHER LODE COUNTRY
Brown's Hole
North Park
Julesburg
Oregon Trail

San Francisco
SIERRA NEVADA
MEXICAN CESSION (1848)
Green R.
Central City
South Platte
MOUNTAINS
Republica

Old Spanish Trail
Denver
South Park
FLORIDA
Smoky Hill
Ab

Missouri Trail
Bent's Fort
TREATY
Santa Fe T
Ark
Dodge Cit

Colorado R.
Taos
Santa Fé
LINE OF

El Camino del Diablo
Bosque Redondo

(Devil's Highway)
1819

Tombstone
El Paso

GADSDEN PURCHASE (1853)
Rio Grande

100th Meridian
Old San
San Antoni

0   100   200   300   400   500
miles

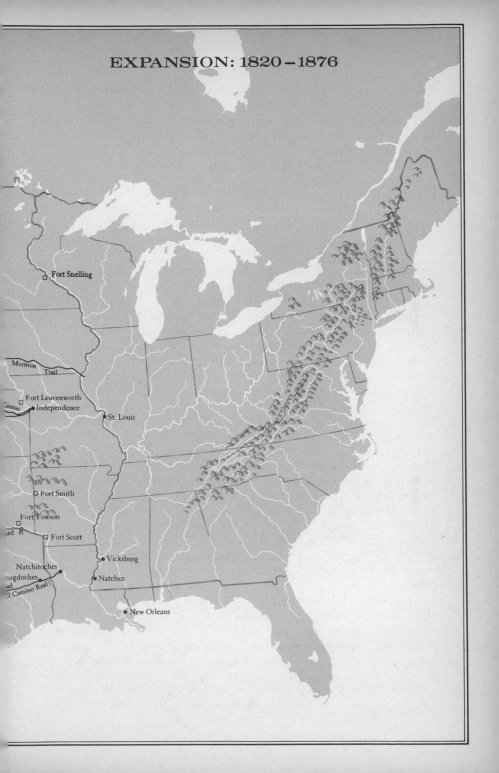

EXPANSION: 1820–1876

n

□ Fort Snelling

Mormon Trail

Fort Leavenworth
Kansas □ ● Independence

● St. Louis

Fort Smith □

Fort Towson □

ed R.

□ Fort Scott

Natchitoches
cogdoches
ad
El Camino Real)

● Vicksburg

● Natchez

● New Orleans

This was movement almost as rapid as the progression of events in our own time.

In one sense, the pattern of settlement was the same as it had been east of the Mississippi, where squatters and speculators had continually run ahead of the government. They had violated Indian treaties, squatted, and then demanded preemption rights. Or, hearing of an impending Indian treaty or creation of a new land district, they would scout the country before the arrival of the surveyors, registers, and receivers, and decide which lands they wanted. By the time government arrived, a crude frontier society was already in existence. This pattern of settlement was to continue.

That another government owned the lands that lay just over the border was more of an irritant than a deterrent to the early settlers of Texas. The pioneers of Louisiana, Mississippi, Alabama, and Georgia had always had a little more hellfire and vinegar in them than their north-of-the-Ohio brethren anyway. Cotton farming was a one-crop, highly speculative investment, appealing to gamblers; it was somewhat less stable and less idyllic than the well-rounded family type of farming north of the Ohio. Moreover the Kentuckians, Tennesseans, and Missourians who chose to migrate southwest instead of northwest of the Ohio were likely to be searching for greater prospects than eighty acres for a self-sufficient family farm.

To these people, Texas was the next logical step. After all, one could stand on the east bank of the Sabine River and view Texas on the other side. Or, after 1819, a man could stand on the north bank of the Red, in Arkansas territory, and gaze south at the new country. It looked just as inviting as the Gulf plains had a decade or two before. There were the same prairies and pines with occasional groves of hardwood; the characteristic deep, sluggish rivers flowing toward the Gulf; the black soil; the humidity; the swarms of insects. The Gulf offered trade outlets to the outside world. The Texas they saw was, geographically, a continuation of the Gulf plains. Its exploitative potential was identical with the already settled lands to the southeast. Few new techniques needed to be mastered. The land called Texas lay there, waiting.

Thus it would have been surprising if the usual pattern of American advancement had *not* been repeated—but it was. There were such traders as Philip Nolan, who was as far west as San Antonio well before 1800. The next arrivals were squatters whose settlements centered upon Nacogdoches, about thirty miles west of the Louisiana border. A departure from the more common process was the Gutierrez-Magee expedition of 1812. Bernardo Gutierrez had participated in the abortive Mexican revolution of 1810-11 and had escaped to the United States; in

New Orleans he became involved in intrigues to free Texas from Spanish control. In 1812, aided by an American adventurer named Augustus Magee, he led an expedition made up of Mexican rebels and American filibusters across the Sabine. After initial successes the expedition met with defeat and rout by Spanish troops near San Antonio. More in the normal pattern were James Long's expedition of 1819, in which a republic centering at Nacogdoches was proclaimed and a flag unfurled before the episode ended in failure, and Haden Edwards' abortive revolt of 1827 (mentioned below). Though Spain (until 1821) and then Mexico claimed possession, the Yankees proposed to insist once more that possession is nine-tenths of the law.

After the squatters came the speculators. The logical thing for them to do was go to the officials armed with ambitious proposals. The man who first succeeded was Moses Austin, who had been dealing with the Spanish since 1797, when he staked an interest in the lead mines of Missouri, took willingly an oath of allegiance, and became a Spanish subject. He had wide-ranging business interests, and as early as 1813 had contemplated establishing trade with Texas. In 1819, when Arkansas became a territory, he and his son Stephen extended their interests to a farm there, overlooking the Red River and Texas beyond. Finally in 1820 Moses, declaring himself a Catholic, a Spanish subject (with his 1797 passport to prove it), and a farmer desiring to settle in Texas, appeared before the officials at Bexar (San Antonio). He also stated that 300 other families desired to settle in Texas, and reminded the Spanish that at the time of the Louisiana Purchase it had been the King's intention to allow his subjects to move to any other part of his dominions. Now Moses Austin was presenting his request.

Austin's wishes were granted, and he made plans for a settlement up the Colorado River of Texas, where he expected to locate the 300 families. He anticipated from fees alone an income of $18,000. However, time ran out on the peripatetic Connecticut Yankee, who was pushing sixty years, although he had told the Spanish he was only fifty-three, and the project fell to his twenty-seven-year-old heir, Stephen, who had spent his childhood among the French and Spanish of Missouri and understood their temperament. After launching his colony successfully he had to travel to Mexico City and wait a year for the final clearance of his Mexican grant. He returned to the states, and found high enthusiasm for his endeavor and no problem in recruiting colonists. Texas was fast becoming a new promised land, and its attractions were heralded all over the South.

Times were hard in the States following the Panic of 1819, and the Land Law of 1820, requiring cash payment of $1.25 an acre on a minimum of eighty acres, had all but dried up the land office business. People simply did not have that kind of money. Compared with these terms, the Texas lands came as a gift. Although there were variations in the terms given the big-time operators who received vast acreages—called *empresarios*—from Mexico, the terms of their grants were always lenient. They in turn sold land to colonists at incredibly low prices, partly because by the terms of their grant they had to settle a certain number of colonists within a given period. Mexican standards of measure were quite different from the American, but the Texans soon learned that a *labor* was somewhere between 174 and 277 acres; and in many cases farmers could receive such a land parcel without charge. For the first six years after settlement there would be no taxes, and, for the following six, taxation was to be at half the normal rate. Cattle raisers could receive a *sitio*, which was 4,338.18 acres, under the same favorable terms. If the settler was both farmer and rancher, then he could receive both *labor* and *sitio*. Most Texans did consider themselves both. The Mexican insistence on Catholicism and prohibition of slavery were so easily ignored in the sparsely settled country that neither was ever to cause real trouble or serve as a deterrent. Soon *El Camino Real*, called by Texans the Old San Antonio Road, was dusty with the wheels of emigrant wagons as colonists to more than a dozen *empresarios* moved into the vast land and established their farms and ranches. Austin's lands were considered prime, however, and early American Texas centered on his grant.

One of the later recipients of an *empresario* was a Virginian, a born loser named Haden Edwards. He received a very favorable grant for an area around Nacogdoches. For each hundred families settled he was to receive five leagues of land, and a Texas league was 4,428.4 acres, about the size of a *labor* plus a *sitio*. But Edwards found settlers with legal Spanish land titles already on his land, which was to be expected, since his *empresario* was in the oldest settled part of east Texas. There were also some Cherokee Indians there. In due time his methods of settling his difficulties aroused animosity. The officials of Texas-Coahuila deprived him of his *empresario*, which jeopardized not only Edwards' fortunes, but also the stakes of the colonists he had persuaded to settle on his grant. Calling his land Fredonia (a play on *freedom*), unfurling a flag with INDEPENDENCE, FREEDOM AND JUSTICE lettered on it, Edwards rebelled—ludicrously, inopportunely, and unsuccessfully. As a result, from 1827, the year of his rebellion, the Mexican government was consciously aware of the Yankee danger threatening Texas; a general tightening of regulations and a new assertion of authority began.

The next seven or eight years, until the outbreak of the Texas Revolution, October 2, 1835, are complex and confusing. There were manipulations by Texans, the United States government, and Mexico, involving such strong-willed men as Sam Houston, Stephen F. Austin, Andrew Jackson, and the Mexican dictator, Santa Anna. There was a "Texas awareness"—if not a "Texas fever"—in the United States; all sorts of lavish claims were made of enormous grants of land to be opened for settlement at a cost that was ridiculously low. And finally, there was knowledge, very distorted but basically correct, about the instability of the Mexican government. The extension of the American domain into Texas came about for essentially the same reasons as its extension elsewhere: land hunger, the excitement of a new start in a new country, and the eternal hope for a better tomorrow—"A great day comin'!"

There is no doubt of Stephen F. Austin's integrity and loyalty toward Mexico. He tried with all the power at his command to work with the Mexicans toward the creation of a democratically run state of Texas, functioning within the framework of the government of Mexico. But what did one do when Santa Anna destroyed the Mexican federal system? Based upon these realities, Mexico lost Texas due to her own failure to maintain a democratic federal form of government.

Andrew Jackson, who had suggested the occupation of Texas as early as 1824, probably reflected the attitude of a majority of Americans, certainly those south of the Mason-Dixon line, plus the New Yorkers and New Englanders who held stock (at the time called scrip) in Texas land companies. Though much of it was fraudulent—and, in any event, it was unlikely that Mexico would honor the claims—the holders sensed lucrative profits if the United States annexed Texas, thus validating the claims of the land companies. Jackson's diplomacy was blundering and a failure, but it left no doubt of American objectives. Sam Houston, a friend of his with a dubious record, appeared in Texas in 1832, settled around Nacogdoches, speculated in land, and became involved in Texas politics; possibly he was there at Jackson's suggestion, though Houston may have gone of his own volition, harboring dreams of a quick fortune and great power as the savior of the Texans. He quickly found plenty of supporters, for in the minds of the many independent frontier types in Texas, independence from Mexico was not only preferable but inevitable.

In April 1830, the Mexicans halted all immigration into Texas, taxes were levied, and a dozen military garrisons were sent into the Anglo-populated parts of Texas. By 1832 insurrection seemed imminent, but a combination of endeavors by Austin plus the political instability in Mexico prevented it at that time; in 1832 the garrisons were removed. The Texans nevertheless held a convention in which they petitioned for repeal of the anti-immigration decree of 1830 and asked for separation from the Mexican state of Coahuila; by the terms of the liberal Mexican constitution of 1824 they could have created Texas as a democratic state within the federal system of Mexico. But the hostile reception of this request by the Mexican authorities tended to polarize Texan feelings; another convention was held in April of 1833, in which a strong anti-Mexican feeling predominated. Sam Houston chaired a committee which framed a state constitution which, along with strong grievances, was delivered personally to the government at Mexico City by Stephen F. Austin. There he was eventually placed in prison, where he remained until July 13, 1835, by which time Santa Anna had come to power. In October 1835, Santa Anna abolished the liberal constitution of 1824: Mexico had become a centralist government under a dictator. In 1835 it also became necessary for Santa Anna to send his brother-in-law, General Martín Perfecto de Cós, to crush opposition in Coahuila.

It was inevitable that a tightening of controls over Texas would follow and indeed, by late 1835 there were skirmishes between Mexicans and Texans. The Mexicans reacted by sending troops across the Rio Grande; in short order they defeated the Texans at the Alamo and Goliad where, on March 27, 1836, they massacred 371 captives. Meanwhile the Texans had chosen a capital, a miserable place among the trees with stumps still sticking up in the single street, though it was a rather attractive setting overlooking the Brazos River. With a total lack of imagination they named it Washington-on-the-Brazos. They drew up a Declaration of Independence and a Constitution which incorporated parts of several eastern state constitutions but was primarily a copy of that of Massachusetts. They chose Sam Houston as their commander in chief, and went knocking on the doors of Washington, D.C., for military aid and quick annexation.

The slavery controversy in the United States forced Jackson, Van Buren, and Tyler to move slowly. Abolitionists feared the creation of several slave states from an annexed Texas. Old Hickory did recognize the Texas Republic as one of his last acts in office, but not until December 29, 1845, by the unusual procedure of a joint resolution of Congress (which requires a mere majority vote in each house), did Texas become a state.

Yet there had been all along an assumption that statehood was inevitable, and Texas from 1837 until the outbreak of the Mexican War was the new country toward which thousands of settlers turned their wagons. A lenient land policy sponsored by the Texas government, which retained its public domain, and an inclination to extend southern culture both legally (by legalizing slavery) and socially made the enormous area extremely attractive to Southerners. Soil exhaustion in the southern states also contributed strongly to the migration. Because another country had owned Texas, the Americans there had to work out their own path from the status of Mexican subjects to that of American citizens. Some leaders advocated going it alone, maintaining a permanent Texas republic. But these people had a democratic heritage, and as they advanced into Texas their premise always was that they would ultimately, and in the not too distant future, join the country from whence they had come.

Men could gaze across the Sabine or the Red and see Texas; even from the Red River it was only a ten days' trudge to Austin's outposts. Those who cast their eyes northwestward toward Oregon, however, saw nothing but prairie and sky, and Oregon could be no more than a gleam in a farmer's eyes. Oregon lay more than two thousand miles away from Westport (present Kansas City), and at twelve miles a day, four to five months must elapse between breakfast at Westport and a supper on the banks of the Willamette. Even so, the 1830's witnessed a rise in interest about Oregon, and by 1843 the annual migration there had become an accepted part of the westward movement. It is easy to understand migration to Texas-across-the-river, but Oregon-on-the-Pacific requires some explanation.

From the published letters of missionaries, the writings of such men as Washington Irving, the government reports of John C. Frémont, and stories that floated on the breeze from general store to livery stable, from town to town, people learned about Oregon. It was said that it was not a howling wilderness, that Fort Vancouver and Fort Walla Walla offered some protection, that there were both Protestant and Catholic missions about, that the Indians of the region had been among whites for years and were peaceable, and that there were Americans already there indulging in agricultural pursuits. Above all they learned about the fertility of that new country. Jason and Daniel Lee, good Methodist missionaries (they had established a temperance society there), could not refrain from boasting of the farming potentialities of the Willamette Valley. In 1837 Ewing Young herded 600 cattle overland from California to Oregon, where they were reported to be flourishing. With all that kind of good news, many a midwestern farmer made the great decision to go to Oregon.

Other conditions made migration to the Pacific Northwest attractive. The depression following the Panic of 1837 continued for a long time in the upper Mississippi Valley. People with a habit in force for two or three generations before them of picking up and heading west for the new country whenever times got bad now looked to Oregon. They looked there rather than to Texas for a variety of reasons. Most Texans were Southerners, and slavery existed in Texas. There were known to be desert conditions on the route there, and the ferocious Comanches threatened along the way. Finally, the unstable relations between the Lone Star Republic and Mexico undoubtedly deterred some potential emigrants.

In the balance, then, Oregon was more attractive. In addition, there appears to have been an abundance of guides offering their services to Oregon travelers. Many of these potential wagon bosses were unemployed mountain men, for after 1840, the last year of the trapper's rendezvous, the fur trade of the far West collapsed. It did not end, but a combination of factors, including the change in style away from beaver hats and the decimation and near extermination of the beaver, changed many a mountain man's status to that of unemployed frontiersman. Acting as a scout for the Army or as a guide or wagon boss for an emigrant train was a natural switch of occupation entailing little change in a fellow's life style. So, the situation was ripe for an outbreak of "Oregon fever."

In terms of the slow pace of life in those days, the enthusiasm came on rapidly. Some knowledge was disseminated through information culled from such fur-trade enterprises as Astoria, Captain Benjamin Bonneville's experiences with the western fur trade, 1832-35, and news items about the adventures of the mountain men. The proselytizing of a weak-eyed, eccentric New Englander, Hall J. Kelley, helped popularize knowledge of Oregon, as did the letters home, articles in the numerous religious periodicals, and lectures of such missionaries as Jason and Daniel Lee, Samuel Parker, and Marcus Whitman. It was Jason Lee's lecture on the virtues of Oregon, delivered in the farm town of Peoria in 1838, that struck a spark in the mind of a Vermont-born young lawyer who had come west for his health. Thomas Jefferson Farnham was fired with enthusiasm; he organized an emigration society and had his wife, a latter-day Betsy Ross, sew a flag for the "Oregon Dragoons," which carried the words OREGON OR THE GRAVE. The party, all nineteen of them, set out for the Far West without sufficient supplies or knowledge. Nevertheless a few, including their leader, made it to the Willamette in 1839. Farnham did not stay long in Oregon; he left on a Hudson's Bay ship for Hawaii; from Honolulu he mailed a petition, signed by about seventy Oregon settlers, which was introduced in the Senate by Senator Lewis Linn of Missouri. Requesting the United States to take the settlers under its protection, the remonstrance also described the Oregon country as "one of the most favored portions of the globe." Yet Farnham also sent home some letters deprecating Oregon: his impression was not entirely favorable. He then sailed to California, crossed Mexico, took a ship across the Gulf of Mexico to New Orleans, took passage on a river boat up the Mississippi and by 1840 was home again.

In 1841 he published his book narrating his western experiences, which was widely read in the States and went through several editions. It was surprisingly frank, suggesting, for example, that for nine-month periods horses and mules had better have their own water supply east of the Cascade Mountains, since no rain fell during three-fourths of the year. His description of their Wallawalla guide Carbo may have enticed emigrants by the very grotesqueness of the Indian: ". . . a jolly oddity of a mortal. The frontal region of his head had been pressed in infancy most aristocratically into the form of the German idiots; his eyes were forced out upon the corners of his head; his nose hugged the face closely like a bunch of affectionate leeches; hair black as a raven, and flowing over a pair of herculean shoulders; and feet—but who can describe that which has not its like under the skies." At the Whitman mission the owners were "desirous to ask how long a balloon line had been running between the States and the Pacific, by which single individuals crossed the continent." And at the falls of the Willamette he passed the night "more to the apparent satisfaction of vermin than for ourselves. These creature comforts," he added, "abound in Oregon."[1]

It must be said that much of the information published about Oregon contained negative as well as positive statements; the writers did not avoid mention of the fog, the constant rain, the fleas, the terrible journey to get there. But the call of the Columbia was stronger than all the negative cries; it was heard by receptive people, and by the mid-1840's the Oregon emigration rose to a flood.

The first emigration party of impressive size left in 1842. The wagon train was assembled through the efforts of Dr. Elijah White, formerly associated with the Lees. About 107 people began the journey from Elm Grove, near Independence; after disgraceful bickering most of them arrived in Oregon in two parties. The next year two trains of sixty wagons each made the journey, carrying around 850 more souls to Oregon as well as a herd of 700 cattle, to say nothing of horses, mules, and oxen that were used en route. Year after year thereafter the big wagon trains assembled at Westport or Elm Grove, and the long journey, the greatest adventure of most of the participants' lives, got under way. By 1845 Oregon had nearly 6,000 inhabitants; and the census of 1850 gave it more than 13,000.

Once again the citizenry had responded to the magnetism of a western area more rapidly than had their government. It is true that both Texas and Oregon had been in the minds of presidents from Jefferson on. Yet it was the actual settlement in those places that aroused the government to take action, and eventually became so important that the presidential campaign of 1844 was waged with expansion as the major issue: "Fifty-four forty or fight!" But in Oregon it was not necessary to fight. Reason prevailed between England and its boisterous offspring, and a treaty of 1846 split the Pacific Northwest between the two countries at 49°.

Unfortunately the Mexicans, justly proud of having thrown off the yoke of Spanish oppression, were not so compromising. Mexico recalled its minister from Washington when Congress by joint resolution annexed Texas. Three days later a Tennessee lawyer named James K. Polk took the oath of office as President of the United States. Rarely is history blessed with such a fine example of a situation wherein the course of events continues inexorably and the leader of the moment passively benefits from the good events and suffers from the bad ones. Texas and the Southwest, and Oregon, were inevitably going to fall to the United States, and Polk, a man whose actions, discussions, diary, speeches, and personality reveal an executive of no more than mediocre stature, has always received the credit.

A caravan of wagons carrying military goods. (The Kansas State Historical Society, Topeka)

He offered the Mexicans a cash purchase; when that failed, and some of General Zachary Taylor's Dragoons were killed on what is now the Texas side of the Rio Grande, war came. Since Mexico too wanted to fight, the emotional, frontier-oriented Americans reached for their guns and looked to the Southwest. Taylor won the battles of Palo Alto and Resaca de la Palma, in northern Mexico, and General Winfield Scott took Mexico City. Most Americans felt they had as much reason to be proud as Mexicans did to be humiliated.

It was General Stephen W. Kearny's "Army of the West" that marched out of Leavenworth on the last day of June, 1846, with 2,700 men, and captured the land that was to remain in American hands. New Mexico was taken without difficulty, without bloodshed, and then the long trek across the southwest desert began. Kearny was headed for California.

Americans had heard of that land from James Ohio Pattie's *Personal Narrative*, from Richard Henry Dana's *Two Years Before the Mast* (although Dana did not particularly like California), from a small section of the *Report* of Commander Charles Wilkes, whose naval exploring expedition was there in 1841, and from Thomas O. Larkin's extensive letters to the eastern press. Thomas Jefferson Farnham, who had gone to Oregon, also visited California and published his *Life and Adventures in California* in 1844. Alfred Robinson, who had represented the tallow and hide firm of Bryant and Sturgis, published his *Life in California* in 1846.

No "great migration" had headed for California by the time of the Mexican War. From 1841 on, however, small parties advanced directly there from Missouri. Best known are the Donners, who in 1846 floundered in the snows of the high Sierras and lost about half their number. Nevertheless there was an increasing interest in California. There were Americans at San Francisco and Monterey, at Sutter's Fort and up the Sacramento River, as well as at lonely ranches in the interior. Jackson and Tyler had both manifested interest in the land, and the British interest there had made them nervous. It was, then, no surprise that Kearny had orders to advance to California after taking New Mexico, at the same time that John C. Frémont was in northern California with sixty men, including Kit Carson, ostensibly on an exploring expedition. But José Castro, the Mexican commander-in-chief of California, had grown suspicious of Frémont's activities and had ordered him out of the country. Frémont moved north to Klamath Lake in southern Oregon. On the evening of May 8, 1846, a rancher named Neal hallooed out of the wilderness and entered Frémont's camp. He said that a Lieutenant Archibald Gillespie of the United States Marines had arrived at his ranch, some forty-five miles south, with dispatches. Because of the Indian danger, Neal had urged Gillespie to wait while he went in pursuit of Frémont.

At dawn the next morning Frémont rode south and met with Gillespie, who gave him some dispatches, letters from home, and his own knowledge of the state of things. "Here," writes Frémont's biographer Allan Nevins, "we are confronted by one of the most baffling problems of Frémont's career. What were the instructions brought by Gillespie which caused Frémont to cut short his explorations, turn south, invade California, and begin in earnest the war which he had threatened a few weeks earlier?"[2] Whatever were the instructions, we know what Frémont did: after repulsing a vicious attack on his sleeping camp by the Klamath Indians he headed south, paused to destroy a Klamath village and kill a dozen or so Indians, and continued south to the vicinity of Sutter's Fort. Here he waited, having obtained arms and ammunition from the warship Portsmouth in San Francisco Bay, and allowed opinion to crystallize among the Americans concentrated in the Sacramento River Valley. On June 14, 1846, having already taken the Mexican village of Sonoma, rebellious elements, primarily Americans, declared the "Republic of California," and one of their number made a flag with a star and a grizzly bear upon it, and the words "Republic of California." Shortly thereafter news arrived of the outbreak of the Mexican War; Frémont enlisted most of the Bear Flaggers in a "California Battalion" and marched south, aided by a naval force. California was taken easily.

The only serious battle took place afterwards, when Mexicans in and around Los Angeles rebelled against American rule and besieged General Stephen W. Kearny and about a hundred dragoons as they marched from Santa Fe into California. At San Pasqual, an Indian village a few miles north-northeast of San Diego, Kearny suffered a number of casualties until Commodore Stockton of the naval squadron sent 140 men to his aid. The siege was raised, and the men marched on to San Diego, then up to Los Angeles, which fell (January 10, 1847) without much bloodshed.

There is a strong element of luck in the lives of men. In the course of events, James K. Polk was one of the lucky ones. He could have experienced the agony of Lyndon Baines Johnson with an unpopular war, but by the greatest piece of luck in any President's career, Nicholas Trist, Polk's executive agent to Mexico, normally chief clerk of the State Department, was able to conclude a treaty with the Mexicans even as Mexican opposition was breaking out and Scott's army in Mexico City was in danger of finding itself cut off from supplies and under siege. The Treaty of Guadaloupe Hidalgo in effect recognized the inevitability of the sweep across the continent. The lower Rio Grande, the boundary west from El Paso to the sea and including the great natural harbor of San Diego, represented in essence the natural southern limits of the westward sweep. In just the same way was the forty-ninth parallel a logical continuation westward of the northern boundary. The slight alterations made later over the San Juan Islands between Washington and British Columbia and the need for a low pass for a railroad that necessitated the Gadsden Purchase of 1853 giving the United States the Gila River Valley, are but footnotes to the larger story of the westward advance. It all worked out very well, with remarkably little trouble in later years. All these developments attest to the inevitability of the westward sweep.

The activity in the Far West in the 1840's was testimony to the youthful energy of the Americans. Bernard De Voto was so impressed with it that he wrote a book about the busiest year of all, 1846. It was in that "Year of Decision," as he called it, that the Vermont-born Mormon leader Brigham Young led his people out of their Illinois capital at Nauvoo and headed them west. By the end of 1847 he had about 1800 "Saints" at Salt Lake City; by 1860 probably 25,000 Mormons were living in the valleys, sloughs, river crossings, and canyons around Salt Lake.

By 1848 some of the trails west had become highways a mile or even several miles wide, as emigrants trudged along the plains and drifted north or south a few hundred yards in search of grass for their horses and oxen. The Oregon Trail was so heavily used that here and there an entrepreneurial-minded mountain man had spotted a damp slough where the grass grew green from which he could harvest hay, built a crude cabin of cottonwood logs with a sod roof, and added a small corral. He thus established himself to trade or sell stock, round up strays or abandoned lame animals and, if they were never claimed, assume possession. He carried a supply of powder and lead, some whiskey and flour, and, thus provisioned, catered to the emigrant trade. Jim Bridger was motivated in this way when he constructed Fort Bridger on Blacks Fork of Green River in extreme southwest Wyoming, where both Oregon- and California-bound people could gain a respite and obtain supplies—for a price.

And as soon as the Mormons were entrenched in Salt Lake City Brigham Young sent some of his Saints out to the river crossings and every wet place where the grass grew tall and green in the desert wilderness. When gentile late-comers arrived, they found lone Mormons manning ferrys across the streams, charging what the market would bear; and when the emigrants found some green pasturage, invariably a bearded Mormon patriarch appeared as out of nowhere, rifle slung across his arms, to inform them that they were trespassing on his property. Yes, they could camp and graze their tired oxen there—for a price.

Up in Oregon new roads were being made for the emigrants. The Barlow Road, hacked out of the forest by a company led by Samuel K. Barlow, passed through the Cascade Range south of Mount Hood, so that after 1846 it was not necessary to float down the Columbia, a journey which included a portage at The Dalles. Another group, the South Road Company, laid out a South Road from Fort Hall southwest by west to the Humboldt, and then north into Oregon, which shortly became the most popular route.

In the Southwest, the Santa Fe Trail, which ran by way of either the Cimarron Cut-off through the arid Staked Plains or Bent's Fort up the Arkansas, and then southward through Raton Pass, experienced increased usage due to the Mexican War. Finally the Old Spanish Trail to California was in constant use by the Army and a few emigrants after Kearny's march in 1846, and was used as well by several thousand forty-niners.

The "Forty-niners"—for it was the search for gold that pulled a hundred thousand Argonauts toward California in that year.

There is something unreal, storybookish, about a gold rush. This greatest one, and the first one in the Far West, puzzles us because of the sudden and overwhelming response that the discovery of gold produced. Long years before, the Mexicans had received reports about gold in California, and the fur-trapping mountain men had known of "color" in some of the cold mountain streams. But the Mexicans ignored the reports, and the mountain men were after beaver. Yet when James Marshall found golden nuggets in the mill race he was digging for a sawmill on John Sutter's land along the Coloma River, that January 19th or 21st, 1848 (the date is disputed), the reception of the news was anything but lackadaisical. Why the change?

The question is perhaps best demonstrated by example. James Marshall, the man credited with the discovery, was not Spanish, nor Mexican, nor a mountain man, nor, as far as we know, had he ever trapped or hunted. Marshall was instead one of those thousands of men, most of them nameless, who drifted west with the times. He and thousands of others were like dust devils, whirling hither and yon in search of a destiny they rarely contemplated and never wholly understood. Probably they sought primarily the One Big Chance, but their restlessness, one suspects, is not wholly explained by the lust for great riches. There must have been present the elements of curiosity and adventure too. Call it some aspect of the human spirit. What else explains James Marshall and his kind? He was a carpenter who had drifted, like many a journey-man of many a trade, first to Iowa; then to Nebraska and the fringe of settlement; then to California and a job with John Sutter, the Swiss ad-venturer who had established a huge estate, Nueva Helvetia, on the American River at its confluence with the Sacramento; then into an ex-periment in cattle raising that failed; then, flat broke, back to John Sut-ter. For such men, opportunities were scarce: the fur trade was gone, and farming or ranching cost money to start; besides, a fellow needed a wife for such an undertaking, and women were at a premium in the new country. Drifting men of James Marshall's type, for whom the en-tire West had become a piece of real estate to hunt over and exploit—these were the kind of people who first felt a faster pulse at the news of gold. By the summer of 1848 settlers, sailors and soldiers, Mexicans—everyone in California, it seemed—was after gold. But it was Marshall's kind who constituted the vanguard.

Then came the deluge from the East. What sparked the men of the settled country?

First, settlement had reached the prairies of eastern Kansas and Ne-braska, and, to a degree, had turned back on itself. It had filled in the vacant spaces, consolidated, been connected by railways, canals, or steamboats. The church graveyards were beginning to display hun-dreds rather than just dozens of tombstones. In short, the great work of settlement east of the hundredth meridian had been accomplished. The greatest danger in life was no longer from Indians or wild animals, or even from a gash in the leg while chopping wood, but from such dis-eases as diphtheria, typhus, malaria, yellow fever, cholera, and tuberculo-sis. By the 1840's everyone east of the Mississippi could pretty well plan on dying miserably in bed. Neither were there so many business oppor-tunities for an ambitious but ordinary man to grab. Quite frankly, life could be rather a bore.

Into this situation came the news of the California gold rush. Even President Polk referred to it in his State of the Union message on De-cember 5, 1848. But this time something of the remoteness of the far West had dissipated, for the news of Oregon, of Frémont and Kearny in California, and the acquisition of that distant place so that it was no longer possessed by a foreign power had made it a topic of household conversation even before the discovery of the yellow metal. Now Cali-fornia and gold simply added up to a great adventure with the added incentive of quick riches. To men whose immediate ancestors had ex-perienced the migration into the new country, this sounded like a great opportunity to live a little of the pioneering life of their fathers and grandfathers.

And so the men left their wives, mothers, or sweethearts, and swept in a great wave to the western foothills of the Sierras. California was suddenly the most heavily populated area west of Missouri, though the population was centered in the Mother Lode country, about 120 miles northwest by southeast and averaging about thirty miles in width. It extended from Sutter's mill southeast to Mariposa, although an area up to fifty miles north of Sutter's mill was rich with "color." From this strip of foothills humanity spilled all over California, and then flowed eastward again. In nearly every subsequent gold or silver rush within American boundaries, the "yondersiders," as the Californians were known, played an important part.

The rush was at its peak when the sectional stalemate in Congress brought on by the victory over Mexico was broken by the Compromise of 1850, making California a state, among other terms. The West had become a region of parts by now, and every newspaper-reading American knew where Texas, New Mexico, California, and Utah lay.

The sweep across the continent was complete as to borders, but now there was a vast interior still to be settled. And there would be many problems; the Indian was one. The Oregonians and Californians did not have much trouble with the red men, who watched the long trains of prairie schooners plodding up the Great Medicine Road (the Platte River Trail), but in the first few years, when the emigrants were simply passing through, did not attack them.

But in the 1850's changes began. Some emigrants chose to stop by the wayside—permanently. Ranch houses began to appear here and there, and domestic cattle spread over thousands of acres of the Great Plains. The buffalo began to decline in numbers. Incidents between red men and whites became more common, and depredations more serious. When the Pike's Peak rush of 1859 brought fifty thousand Argonauts to the Denver area, across the arid heartland of the Cheyenne and Arapaho, things got worse. When other thousands crowded into the Coeur d'Alene district of Idaho, and Alder Gulch (Virginia City) and Last Chance Gulch (Helena) in Montana became filled with bearded, aggressive white men, the Sioux, Blackfeet, Pen d'Oreilles, Flatheads, Nez Percés, and Bannocks became restive. When other prospectors appeared in southern Arizona and New Mexico, the Apache were angered. After prospectors in 1859 discovered the pesky blue stuff which assayed as nearly pure silver up on Mount Davidson in the Washoe Mountains east of the Sierras, and Virginia City and Gold Hill teemed with thousands of miners, the Diggers and Paiutes went on the warpath. Government in the guise of the uniformed soldier or western Indian agent, complete with official papers, always appeared *after* the event; and in any case the protection of the Indians' claims was not a popular vocation in the new country.

Within six months after Custer and his men died on the Little Big Horn in June 1876, the Sioux—all but Sitting Bull and his followers, who took refuge in Canada and did not return until 1881—were ensconced on the Great Sioux reservation in present South Dakota. There were some Indian scares in the next fifteen years: the Nez Percés broke out of their reservation in 1877; the Bannock frightened a lot of people, and killed a few, in 1878; and there was a confrontation between the Sioux and the cavalry as a result of the Ghost Dance craze, resulting in the merciless slaughter at Wounded Knee in 1890. If Nathan Meeker, the Ute Indian agent in 1878-79, had not ordered his Ute wards to farm, he might have died peaceably, instead of on his back in a field with a barrel stave stretching his mouth; all the white male employees of the

A photograph taken of the battlefield of Wounded Knee a few days after the massacre. (Henry E. Huntington Library and Art Gallery)

agency were murdered and the three white women captured and raped. The Apache caused trouble until the mid-1880's. To all intents and purposes, however, the Indian menace, save in one or two areas, was over by 1877. And so the vast new country awaited the herder and the agriculturalist.

But how was it to be settled? In the 1850's the land west of the ninety-eighth or hundredth meridian was still considered a Great American Desert; it was still thought that most of it could belong to the Indian in perpetuity; and the white man's only interference was to cross it along the Oregon and Santa Fe trails. But the proliferation of mining districts from Montana to New Mexico and Arizona resulted in a maze of trails criss-crossing the West. Soon men with agricultural knowledge threw down their miner's shovels, picked up plows, and went out into the valleys watered by snow water rushing down from the mountains; they staked out some land and began farming, knowing there was a ready market in the mining communities nearby. Thus did the Gallatin Valley of Montana, the South Platte Valley around Denver, and the Sacramento Valley in California have their agricultural beginnings.

Without any governmental sanction or planning, the range cattle industry was likewise growing prior to the Civil War. It is a mistake to attribute this to the Texans; it was under way among the Flathead Indians and ambitious white men like the Stuarts of Montana in the 1860's. Similarly, George Iliff was raising cattle for the mining market at Denver and the nearby mining towns of Central City and Blackhawk by 1861. Iliff eventually had an unsurveyed and unfenced range extending 75 miles along the South Platte River and as much as 200 miles south of it.

By the end of the Civil War the concept of the West as a total wasteland was fast disappearing. The ugly, ungainly bison were being killed off, thus starving into submission the mounted, nomadic Indian. The buffalo range was turned into the world's greatest cattle pasture. For twenty years, 1866-86, the 500-mile-wide strip eastward from the Front Range of the Rockies, extending from the Mexican to the Canadian border, was virtually without fences. Trail drives up from Texas, not only to Dodge City, Abilene, Caldwell, and Garden City, but on north to Julesburg, Oglalla, Cheyenne, Laramie, and even to the region around Miles City, Montana, dissected the Great Plains as hundreds of thousands of cattle were driven to new ranges or to the steadily advancing railheads. What had become of the Great American Desert? Not only had the American put the "desert" to good use—he was settling on it, lacing it with steel rails, and finally, farming it.

The farmer was the last one into the dry, high plains of the new country. In 1841 he had received his long-desired general Preemption Act, by which he gained first claim to a quarter section upon which he had squatted. In the years following he settled Iowa, Wisconsin, and Minnesota. Kansas and Nebraska were made territories in 1854; Kansas became a state in 1861, and part of Nebraska Territory achieved statehood in 1867. By then the Civil War was two years past and a new farmer's panacea, the Homestead Act, had been on the statute books since 1862. By this act a citizen, head of a family (which could mean a woman), twenty-one years of age or over, could enter a quarter section (160 acres) of the public domain, improve it for five years, and at the expiration of that time be given a legal patent to the land. He need not have preempted the land to qualify, although the preemption law did remain on the books and land was still purchased under its provisions. But the farmers were more likely to purchase from the land departments of the railroads—the Santa Fe, Kansas Pacific, Missouri Pacific, Union Pacific, Burlington, or Northern Pacific. These roads received extensive land grants from the federal government; if the roads were to be profitable once built, then settlement must exist along their rights-of-way, and so they had a purpose in selling their holdings rapidly and at reasonable prices. There were also great land companies to buy from, many of which purchased their acreages from the new western states. The states in turn had received lands under a number of federal statutes, including the Preemption Act, which had a provision granting half a million acres per state for internal improvements, and the Morrill Act, by which states received 30,000 acres of the public domain for each representative and senator they sent to Congress. The proceeds from its sale were to be used for the establishment of agricultural and mechanical colleges. Such land was likely to be of prime quality and reasonably priced.

Not until the 1870's did the farmer begin to challenge the new country where the timber gave out and the grass grew short. His fingers of settlement ran primarily along the valleys of such rivers as the Platte, the Kansas, or the Arkansas. Occasionally, as we have noted, there was also settlement along the trails. Later homesteaders followed the twin rails of the railroad as they disappeared into the western horizon. Their numbers included Civil War veterans, the children of the first-generation farmers of the Mississippi Valley, and the energetic and restless type that always hankered to be in the vanguard of new settlement.

Civil War, Indians, locusts, parched summers, frigid winters, sickness—none of these stopped the migration into the new country. The white-topped wagons clattered westward towards the fringes of settlement in Dakota, Montana, Idaho, Washington and Oregon, Wyoming and Colorado. Some Mormons still went to the promised land in covered wagons, if not with hand carts. Nevada's mining population enjoyed statehood after 1864, Colorado achieved statehood in the centennial year (1876), North and South Dakota, Montana, and Washington entered the Union in 1889, Idaho and Wyoming in 1890, and Utah in 1896. Settlers were to contest the assignment of Oklahoma as Indian Territory and bring about the establishment of Oklahoma Territory, and then, in 1907, the state of the same name. The sparsely settled southwest would achieve statehood as New Mexico and Arizona in 1912, completing the contiguous forty-eight.

In those same busy post–Civil War years the railroads were laid across the land like steel gossamer, until by 1893 there were five transcontinental lines and branch lines linking virtually every substantial town and village in America. The bison were all but gone, the Indians were on reservations, and the secondary development after initial settlement was everywhere apparent. Large cities were experiencing problems with slums, and a frustrated working class was flirting with socialism, communism, and anarchism. Modern industry ignored state lines and even crossed oceans in pursuit of dollars. The population of the entire country in the census of 1890 was nearly 63 million.

The head of the Bureau of the Census in 1890 was Henry Gannett, who had been a topographer with the old Hayden Survey, a predecessor of the United States Geological Survey, and had spent several years scrambling around the Rockies and the western states in general. To him, the census of 1890 bore statistical information that was unusually meaningful and significant. In his Introduction he summarized his conclusion:

> Up to and including 1880 the country had a frontier of settlement, but at present the unsettled area has been so broken into by isolated bodies of settlement that there can hardly be said to be a frontier line. In the discussion of its extent and its westward movement it can not, therefore, any longer have a place in the census reports. . . .

All of the new country was now settled; the sweep across the continent was over.

II

The People

The Basic Mix

The sweep across the continent" is a phrase that suggests the inevitability of the American rush to the West, implying that the movement was impossible to halt, and carrying a sense of speed, of a swiftness in the advance. Viewed from eight decades after the end of the frontier, the main outlines of the sweep begin to emerge; the numberless pioneer incidents, even the Indian wars, blend into the greater picture as trees blend to make a forest. The people themselves who constituted this movement must also be viewed from a wider perspective. In the years before the American Revolution the settlers who made the frontier advance were mainly English, Scotch-Irish, German, or Negro. In the nineteenth century there were added dozens of additional strains, ranking from Czechs and Slavs to Norwegians and Danes, from Russian Jews to Chinese coolies, from Neapolitans to Finns. And yet—none of them, nor all of them together, caused major changes in the basic characteristics that were "American" in 1776.

Population statistics until the first decennial census in 1790 are unreliable, but it is generally assumed that in 1776 the population of the thirteen American colonies was around 2,500,000, of which 500,000 were Negro slaves concentrated south of Pennsylvania. These poor black chattels were employed in the tobacco, rice, indigo, or sea-island cotton enterprises of the tidewater settlers, most of whom were of English background with some Huguenots and upland Scots among them. The blacks were in the cotton-growing regions from the beginning. Their importance increased following Eli Whitney's invention of the cotton gin in 1793, and again after the opening of the Old Southwest to short-staple cotton culture after 1814.

As for the two million whites, it is estimated that 70 to 80 per cent of them had English antecedents. Of this substantial percentage, the great majority, by the outbreak of the Revolution, were descendents of colonists, for English migration had plummeted after about 1680. These people may be thought of as "native" Americans, for after three to four generations of life on American soil, the way of doing things *as English* had disappeared. There had come to be instead an American way—or at least a Yankee way, a Virginia way, and so on.

In 1776 most Americans were still Atlantic-oriented, still looking toward England for their civilization and their security. Nevertheless there was also a pull toward the West, a subconscious tugging as if some primitive instinct called them there. There has been an impression that only late-comers such as Germans and Scotch-Irish headed for the frontier, but there is no question that the native Americans were attracted to the new country also. They asserted leadership in plans for land acquisition and settlement; the traders from among them knew the lay of the land and the Indian situation within their individual areas of activity. And the native American stock was fecund; many a son married the maid down the lane and headed with her for the new country in hopes of a successful future. In time the Germans and Scotch-Irish were there too: because of their meager fiscal resources they had little choice but to head for the cutting-edge frontier. But it is also undoubtedly correct that many elements of the native stock waited, being better established, biding their time, letting the newcomers from North Ireland or the Rhineland fight the Indians, establish farms, and form settlements. When the forest had been reduced to stumps and the Indian danger had subsided or become nonexistent, then the native stock arrived, cash in hand to purchase the fields and the few improvements made by the "cutting-edge squatter," who left "for the tall timber" while the buyer of his clearing picked up in making improvements where the original pioneer had left off.

The two great branches of native American stock were those called Yankees, of New England, and the Southerners, including the Virginians and the people of Maryland, the Carolinas, and Georgia. Furthermore, it must be acknowledged that there could be substantial differences among Virginians, North Carolinians, South Carolinians, or Georgians; similarly, Connecticut Yankees were a breed apart from Massachusetts Yankees, and Rhode Islanders, as any lantern-jawed, narrow-nosed Congregationalist would inform you, were "beyond the pale" or pretty nearly so. Yet the Yankees had more in common with each other than they had with people outside of New England, just as a Virginian had much more in common with a South Carolinian than with a Yankee.

The question of the relative influence of environment and heredity upon a people is hotly debated by social scientists, and probably always will be. The Puritans of Massachusetts Bay, later of Connecticut and

New Hampshire and still later of Maine and Vermont—and even their dissident elements settling under Roger Williams in what became Rhode Island—were adventurous elements from the vigorous rising middle class of the England of the seventeenth and eighteenth centuries. They were of sturdy stock; they emigrated to an environment that challenged that tough human fiber, and they met the challenge successfully. There is no question that they were aided in confronting the austere New England wilderness by the historical realities of the seventeenth-century Puritan experience. Therein lay the flowering of the Protestant Christian faith inspired by the French theologian of Geneva, John Calvin. And it was from among the followers of this persuasion that the great majority of English emigrants to New England came. Again, the measure of its importance may be debated, but the historical fact remains that the Puritans were a part of the England of post-Elizabethan times, an England torn by religious dissension that had strong economic and political overtones. At the same time, the nation was in the early bloom of greatness, and the Puritans possessed the youthful vitality that was in that very century establishing Britannia's world supremacy. They were a lusty, scrapping, dedicated, hard-working, adventurous people; they were also disciplined, educated, and inspired, possessors of absolute convictions.

Between 1628 and the decade of the 1680's the sailing ships from Liverpool, Falmouth, and Plymouth carried them to the new lands in the western hemisphere. They were not England's poor, nor her rich, nor her nobility; they were not of her "Establishment." They were instead of a rising, ambitious middle class. Many were businessmen and a rather unusual number were lawyers; they were social climbers who were frustrated in their ascent by Stuart hostility. In fact, many either faced or had actually experienced a decline in their social, economic, and political position. Literate and intelligent, they were also, from a religious point of view, positive that they were better than their Anglican brethren. For these rising people in a hostile environment, New England offered more than just the freedom to worship the Puritan way. There was opportunity for economic, social, and political betterment. Led by their own establishment, the Puritans made the most of that opportunity.

There was more system in their settlement, and more successful application of the system, than in any other English emigration to America. Granted that changes took place, and that evolution of their institutions destroyed their undemocratic hierarchy, still the system of religious congregations and geographical townships governed by town meetings gave to New England a stability not present elsewhere, as well as order— a rare ingredient in frontier society.

These good Puritans would have said that God had ordained that His people should settle in New England, and that He was well aware of the rigorous climate, the stony soil, the thick woods, the hills, the freshwater streams rushing towards the Atlantic. They would have acknowledged His infinite wisdom in sending them to a rugged coastline where safe harbors abounded, close to the Grand Banks of Newfoundland teeming with cod and other varieties of edible fish. To civilize such a virgin country and make it fruitful for man was sufficient challenge for His chosen people.

By 1776—or 1783, when the Revolution was over—some of the New Englanders could trace an American ancestry of up to five generations. These people were known as Yankees and were renowned for self-confidence, energy, education and pride in their intellect, stinginess, ingenuity, and reticence. They drove hard bargains and were shrewd horse traders. In the 1820's, 30's, and 40's, the Yankee peddler was to be found everywhere. If there was a potential customer up a hollow in central Tennessee, at a remote plantation on the Black Warrior in Alabama, or up a trail through the woods of Indiana, then the whistling salesman sitting at his leisure, pipe in hand, on the seat of his horse-drawn wagon, would be sure to pay a call. His more successful brethren maintained warehouses at such distant points as Port St. Joe, Florida, and Canton in China. A Yankee was H.A.W. Tabor, running a general store in California Gulch, Colorado; another was Asa Mercer, recruiting New England spinsters to become wives of lonely men in Washington Territory, and chaperoning them on the long voyage there. The Yankee was ingenious: Eli Whitney invented the cotton gin, Samuel Colt the six-shooter, and Lydia Pinkham mixed a concoction called a "Vegetable Compound" that was good for female complaints. Historian Stewart H. Holbrook wrote, "Mr. Estey stopped short in Vermont's Brattleboro, there to make the little sweet organs that went into the covered wagons, to be played in Congregational and Methodist bethels of Oregon and the tented saloons and whorehouses of the Mother Lode."[1] Harriet Beecher Stowe wrote *Uncle Tom's Cabin*, Joseph Smith founded the Church of Jesus Christ of Latter Day Saints, and Brigham Young led the Saints to the Great Salt Lake, Mary Baker G. Eddy founded Christian Science. All were Yankees. Good heredity, tough environment, demanding Puritan faith?—possibly all three combined to create this group that did so much to turn a new country into a settled country.

The Yankee went into the world not only alone, but also systematically, as part of a group. In the early days, a congregation, or simply a group of individuals with a desire to move, had to make formal application to the Bay Colony authorities or to one of their neighboring colonies and specify the boundaries of the land desired and the plans for settlement. Indian title had to be cleared and a survey of the township laid. When permission was granted, the congregation as a unit saw that the lots, the common, the place for church and school, the woodlands and meadowlands were specified. This procedure was quite different from the helter-skelter settlements along other frontiers. It was, in a sense, the planting of "instant civilization" in the wilderness. Attempts were made to make it adjacent to a township already settled to the east, north, or south. Sometimes there was not even a log cabin stage, but immediate construction of New England salt-box houses, two-storied white clapboard dwellings with gables and green shutters. Church services were first held in the unfinished home of a town leader, probably—but not necessarily—the preacher. By the late 1780's, the American Revolution over and the Iroquois menace ended, population pressure in New England pushed the Yankees into central and western New York, into Pennsylvania, and by the 1790's into Ohio. Following General Anthony Wayne's victory at Fallen Timbers and the subsequent Treaty of Greenville on August 3, 1795, Ohio was rapidly settled. After the War of 1812, which cowed the Indians of the Old Northwest, the New Englanders moved westward across northern Indiana and settled heavily in northern Illinois; Indiana became a state in 1816 and Illinois in 1818. In 1825, when the Erie Canal opened, the migration increased; and with the coming of the steamboat in the 1820's nothing was left to deter the ambitious, west-bound Yankees. Now they steamed across Lake Erie from the canal's end at Buffalo and debarked at Detroit. Advance agents of restless groups formed in New England or Yankee-settled areas of New York and Pennsylvania packed provisions on their backs and followed narrow Indian paths into the Michigan wilderness in search of good country for settlement; in 1837 Michigan achieved statehood. The soil, a product of glacial drift similar to that of New England, the streams, the forests, the hills, the springs gushing cold, clear water, all reminded them of "back home." They found their sites, and the next spring, as soon as the ice had broken, the migration began. New Englanders often paid cash for their lands; they established a church and a school at the same meeting at which they settled the boundaries of their town. The forest fell, cabins rose, fields were plowed, a quarry was opened, all while someone was teaching the children and a preacher was quoting Scripture from the King James version—Scripture heavy on the Old Testament and with a strong Calvinist interpretation. If no preacher was handy, a published old sermon read by a deacon would do.

The Yankees in Illinois in the 1840's and 50's looked north to Wisconsin, which achieved statehood in 1848. There, another migration had

Fulton County Court House, Lewistown, Illinois, showing the adaptation of New England architecture and town planning to the Midwest. Abraham Lincoln spoke here in 1858. (Courtesy Chicago Historical Society)

conquered the wilderness. Beloit, Rockford, Troy, Janesville, and a host of other communities bore the New England image—still do today, many of them, if four-lane highways have not destroyed the charm of elm-lined streets, and motels the quiet beauty of white houses with gables and green shutters. Later migrations carried these people to Iowa, Kansas, and Oregon, where the Yankee stamp in names such as Portland, and colleges such as Whitman, originally Congregational, attest to the continued attraction of the new country for the Yankees.

New Englanders even settled in the South; in Colonial times a number of them settled in Guilford County, North Carolina. Perhaps the most interesting settlement, as well as the earliest, was the Phineas Lyman colony in the vicinity of Natchez, which at the time of the colony's being settled (1774-75) was under the jurisdiction of British West Florida, with the government centered at Pensacola. The Lyman colony's origins were rather typical of Yankee expansion, only the remoteness of the spot being unusual. It all began in the mind of a French and Indian War hero, General Phineas Lyman of Connecticut. In 1762 he found himself destitute, "and finding most of his comrades in the same position, they formed an association under the name of 'Military Adventurers.' . . . In December, 1773, with a large party, [the first group] embarked at Stonington [near New London, Connecticut] for New Orleans." Many died, including the General (so that the final grant of 20,000 acres went to his children, his son Thaddeus usually being mentioned as the recipient). Still others came, and many died, but to this day there are descendants in the Natchez area bearing the names of the original Lyman colonists. Among those original settlers possessing a particular ability to survive the southern climate was the Congregational Reverend Smith, a number of whose ten children not only withstood the rigors of the place, but produced a number of hardy offspring. Some of Reverend Smith's descendants are said to be living in the vicinity of Natchez today. Incidentally, his was the first Protestant church in West Florida.[2]

The Yankees exerted an influence out of all proportion to their percentage of the total population. Long after the fields had reverted to wildflowers, weeds, and woods because the Yankees had abandoned their poor soil for better fields of endeavor, and the mill hands had become French Canadians or Catholic Irish, so that much of the flavor of New England was lost—certainly in the cities—the results of the Yankee Calvinist ideals were still being felt in what we might call "New England extended," which stretched all the way across the northern states to Oregon and appeared elsewhere in the most unusual places.

The Yankee had some weaknesses that did not endear him to others, and some that were harmful to his own well-being. He did not always choose the best lands, for like other pioneers he preferred land that reminded him of home. He liked to settle on forest-covered land, though it took months of toil to clear the land for crops. He passed up the prairies, they being rather foreign to him; so it was the Germans who later came along, lifted up clods of rich prairie soil, and settled in the finest agricultural land in the Middle West.

The Yankee's personality tended to be understood and appreciated only by his Yankee neighbors. "If you hear his character from a Virginian, you will believe him a devil," wrote Mrs. Trollope; "if you listen to it from himself, you might fancy him a god—though a tricky one. . . . In acuteness, cautiousness, industry, and perseverance, he resembles the Scotch; in habits of frugal neatness, he resembles the Dutch; in love of lucre he doth greatly resemble the sons of Abraham; but in frank admission, and superlative admiration of his own peculiarities, he is like nothing on earth but himself."[3] Thus did that plump and fortyish Englishwoman describe the Yankees she encountered along the Erie Canal, who cheated and took advantage of the poor, innocent frontiersmen. Yankee peddlers became notorious for their wooden nutmegs and clocks that did not work. (But how long could a clock with wooden wheels and cogs keep good time in the hot, humid South?)

Other people came into the new country, and by the end of the frontier the Yankees were being overwhelmed by sheer numbers of outsiders. But the flood tide of migration was not all that diminished their influence. In the years since 1890, with the frontier ended and the great challenge met, the Yankee Protestant ethic has lost significance. A settled, affluent country has not needed Calvinists with their rigorous standards —or the country has rejected the ethic, whether it could afford it or not. The Yankee has become a character type exemplifying narrow-mindedness, quaint sayings, and rural New England mannerisms. Puritan morality has been twisted to being synonymous with bigotry, and Calvinist emphasis on toil has fallen into disrepute.

The Yankee experience in settling the new country begs comparison with that of those other native Americans, the Southerners. (New York, New Jersey, Delaware, and Pennsylvania people, who had two or three generations of American occupancy behind them, went west too, but, if they did not blend with the New Englanders, their impress was overshadowed in the westward push by Scotch-Irish and Germans, who landed at their ports in such numbers as to soften any tendencies toward strong regional characteristics. We shall deal with these two groups later on.)

The people of tidewater Maryland, Virginia, and South Carolina had an English tradition also. They had migrated to Annapolis, Norfolk, or Charleston in the same years that their New England brethren had landed at Massachusetts Bay. Some had come via the West Indies. South Carolina was especially favored by hard-working French Huguenots. North Carolina had been settled primarily by emigrants from Virginia, and not of the best sort, either.

Georgia's early history is quite different. Initially the land was contested by Spain and England. When James Oglethorpe, John Viscount Perceval, and an organization of humanitarians called "The Associates of the Late Dr. Bray" applied for a charter giving them a trusteeship over the area, it was granted partly because Georgia would provide a buffer between Spanish Florida and English South Carolina. This grant on June 20, 1732, differed in many ways from all others because of the humanitarian goals of its backers: settlers were limited to 500 acres, slavery was forbidden, and strong liquors were prohibited. Hard-working but poor English, Scottish Highlanders, and Germans came in. But the landowners could not compete favorably with the plantation owners of South Carolina who used slaves, nor with the fur traders from other colonies who used rum. Georgia timber merchants could not trade profitably with the West Indies because pay for the timber was in forbidden rum. Opposition to the original charter built up, and by 1751, when Georgia became a royal province, it was rapidly going the way of its neighboring colonies, and prospering.

The settlers of the southern colonies possessed antecedents more similar than dissimilar to those of their New England neighbors. The Southerners came from the same England as did the Puritans; but as there was more than one colony, so there was, in a sense, more than one England. The Puritans represented an aggressive, opinionated minority, while the people who settled the southern tidelands were a part of the English majority, though not of the nobility or the landed gentry. They ranged from poor but honest hard-working folk, peasants especially, to small merchants. To categorize them as the ambitious lower middle class is probably accurate, save that the English middle class was still in the process of developing in the seventeenth century.

They did not come to the New World as religious dissenters or political radicals. Their journey across the Atlantic was a voyage of hope in pursuit of a dream, a testament to the persuasiveness of propagandistic tracts describing the new country across the sea. A remarkable percentage of them found satisfaction, for those who worked and had a little luck found only improvement in their lot in life. If they had been agriculturists, then the taxes, the worked-out land, and the oppressive landlords had made life a struggle. If they had been merchants or artisans, the competition had been intense and only a few met with great success. In the southern colonies there was cheap land in abundance and an incredibly mild tax system, and class lines were far more fluid than in England. Settlers wrote home about the mild climate, warmer than England's but still moist and producing luxuriant vegetation. Some would have considered the live-and-let-live Anglican persuasion that was the official faith an improvement over the solemn and serious religious atmosphere of old England.

Yet there was still much in Virginia, and to a degree in all the southern colonies, to remind the emigrant of rural England. The society was distinctly rural, with few villages, many large estates, and a social life centering in the mansions of the planters. It reminded the newcomer of the social system in England, with the planters the counterpart of the English landed gentry or country gentlemen. The church organization was remarkably similar, and a young man's political career usually started with his election to the local vestry. There was a strong emphasis on noblesse oblige, a paternalism that looked after the small landowner or the white family tilling rented lands.

That white family could have been newcomers recently landed or people who had emigrated down the Great Philadelphia Wagon Road through the Great Valley of Virginia, ultimately into South Carolina. It could have been a redemptioner and the white woman he had taken to wife; he would be working out the cost of his voyage by four to seven years' toil for the man who had paid his passage.

As the decades advanced toward the break with England, the southern society developed its own style and of course differed more and more from the English country counterpart. It had primarily a single-crop economy, mainly tobacco, although rice, indigo, and long-staple sea-island cotton were produced in South Carolina, and naval stores, furs, and a motley array of products were exported. Finally, there was a difference that would mold and then harden the society of the southern colonies and the states that would follow south of Mason and Dixon's line. This was of course Negro slavery.

Southern society in the long years to 1776 tended to stay in the tidewater regions; only Virginians advanced westward into the Great Valley. The life the country squires lived was eminently satisfactory to them, but they paid little attention to their lands, and as a result soil depletion was a factor in the westward movement from early in the seventeenth century on, and it contributed to a declining economy in the eighteenth century, increasing to critical proportions by the time of the American Revolution. Abandoned farms abounded, and from the 1740's on, the more vigorous of the aristocracy looked westward toward land speculation or fur trade investments to maintain their expensive way of life. Even here, however, they were the entrepreneurs, not the original settlers of the western new country; these last were freed redemptioners, Scotch-Irish or German emigrants, or drifters from the settled areas. The landed aristocracy had grandiose land schemes, directed from the comfort of their tidewater mansions; or they staked the Indian traders who went west and harvested the profits when the traders returned.

It was not until the cutting-edge pioneers had destroyed the forest, plowed the fields, and ended the Indian threat that these Americans of two to five generations' duration packed their belongings and left their soil-depleted lands for new country. They moved first in the 1780's and 1790's to the upland Piedmont, then to the other side of the Appalachians. Some, including young men who read law, and others drifting west toward opportunity, were to be found in Kentucky and Tennessee in the decades after 1780. There, if they farmed, corn, hemp, and tobacco were their products. When the War of 1812 ended, the "Black Belt" opened up in the Old Southwest, and, with cotton replacing tobacco as the staple, native Americans were to be found purchasing plantation-size tracts from the pioneer predecessors, bringing in an "instant civilization" with a southern exposure. Overseers, slaves, wagons holding fine china and glistening silver and the white womenfolk clattered along the migratory roads: the Fall Line Road, the Piedmont Road, the Valley Road, the Natchez Trace. Later they used the old Federal Road, Jackson's Military Road, and the Pensacola Road. Within months, if not weeks, after their site had been chosen, the crude beginnings of the same social system as they had known in Virginia or the Carolinas could be seen taking form. True, the manor house might be two cabins with a breezeway between for cooking, but the hillock for the white pillared mansions was already chosen, whether the white pillared mansion ever became a reality or not. (More often than not it did not.) The planter already had his eye on more land and was contemplating the purchase of more slaves in order to raise more cotton, which in the years 1815-37 and 1841-60 fetched excellent prices. Implicit in his actions was a desire to duplicate what he had known, just as the Yankee did on his new lands around the shores of the Great Lakes. But in the South this meant a plantation slave society—which the ruling class was very pleased to preserve. Or—in the majority of cases—such settlement represented the yearnings of another vigorous group that was coming into the new country also. For long before this migration into Tennessee, Kentucky, and the "Black Belt" got under way, the plantation aristocracy had become insignificant in terms of total population. There was simply more land than any aristocracy could control; the growth of a prolific native-born generation or two, plus Scotch-Irish, German, and lesser groups from Europe, resulted in the basic agricultural economic and social unit becoming the small farmer and his family—a stalwart American yeomanry. However, far from hating their aristocratic neighbors, this group allowed itself to be led by them. Their greatest ambition was to achieve planter status themselves. The yeomanry in the South was woefully uneducated, which helped the gentry to control them.

The final group of "original" settlers did not come to America of their own volition; the Africans came, in bondage, from their native land, where slave-trading, by both Arabs and Europeans, was destroying what had once been a fairly stable society. Chained, manacled, sometimes branded, herded naked or nearly so in coffles of both sexes, these most miserable of peoples awaited the coming of the ships to carry them, via the dreaded Middle Passage, to a new world they did not know.

The agonies of the voyage were so awful that thousands died and others were crippled for life. The survivors were sold to masters at many different places in the New World. Those who ended up in Brazil or the sugar islands of the Caribbean were mostly able to retain a modicum

After the sale: slaves going south from Richmond. (Courtesy Chicago Historical Society)

of their heritage. They lived in large slave communities and were worked in gangs; religious ritual and much of their native language would remain.

But most of those who came to the thirteen colonies or, later, the United States had no such good fortune. There were only a few great rice, sugar, or cotton plantations where so many Africans would be assembled as to make possible some retention of their heritage. (One of these areas was lowland South Carolina, where large numbers of blacks speaking the Gulla tongue were concentrated in the fetid rice plantations. In spite of high mortality due to water moccasin bites, malaria, yellow fever, dysentery, and other ailments acquired from standing in the brackish water of the rice fields, many survived and to this day speak a variety of English that includes many Gulla words.) But the usual fate of the slave was to be purchased by a farmer who took his chattel to an isolated farm; the slave might as well have been on another planet. He was reduced to the status of a machine with life in it, the property of a white agriculturalist who probably owned fewer than twenty slaves. Frightened and so miserable that attempts at self-destruction were common, the slave was thrown in with a small group of this kind. Yet blackness and slavery might be all they had in common, for the others might be of the second generation in America, or might have come from areas in Africa so far removed from his own land that they could not communicate in his native language.

The slave had to learn a few basic English words, he had to learn to obey, and he had to grow accustomed to subservient status in a society that was totally different from anything he had known before. The very isolation of the American farm kept him docile; it explains the rarity of slave revolts in the south. Some slaves became house servants, some mastered skills such as carpentry or brick masonry, and some ended up in the new cities, where their masters often let them out to various employers. Although they were concentrated in the South, black people were to be seen in all the colonies and the subsequent states. According to the census of 1790, there were, even at that early date, 59,000 free Negroes in the nation at large.

The slaves' great migration west began after the War of 1812 with the opening of the "Black Belt" across western Georgia, through Alabama, and into Mississippi. (This twenty-to-fifty-mile-wide area of a few trees was so called because of its thick black soil.) By the 1820's slaves were being sold from Virginia, the Carolinas, Kentucky, and Tennessee into the new cotton-growing lands of the Old Southwest. In a very real sense, the Negro slave was a frontiersman; he played a significant role in the taming of the southern wilderness. It was he who swung the axe, forced the plow into the virgin sod, constructed the fences and cabins. And it was the short-sighted system of which he was a part that created that vicious circle: the continual cultivation of new lands with single crops that exhausted the soil in a very few years and the necessity of supporting slaves year in and year out, in good times and bad, resulting in a southern economy based perforce upon continual expansion into new lands. When the central plains of Texas, where rainfall fell below twenty-three inches a year, were reached in the 1850's, the geographical limits of this basically expensive agricultural system had been attained.

His physical ruggedness, sense of decency, and intelligence occasionally brought respect to the black man even in the midst of a racist society. York, William Clark's slave, was such a man. When Sergeant Floyd, the only man to die during the Lewis and Clark expedition, lay ill, probably of a ruptured appendix, it was York who cared for the dying man. Before the expedition was well along, the slave assumed a place very similar to that of the common soldiers; before they returned to St. Louis Captain Clark promised York his freedom at the end of the journey, and Clark held to his promise. A Negro respected for his

A late-nineteenth-century dime novel showing a black cowboy rescuing the white
hero. (Denver Public Library, Western History Department)

agricultural abilities was George W. Bush, who owned a section of
prime wheatland in the Puget Sound country and received a first-place
award for his wheat at the Centennial Exposition in Philadelphia in
1876. Being men who were at the bottom of society, free blacks were
early attracted to the military. More than 5,000 of them fought in the
American Revolution (and Crispus Attucks was one of the men martyred in the Boston Massacre). At least one-sixth of the American navy
during the War of 1812 was black; two battalions of blacks helped
Jackson win the Battle of New Orleans. After the Civil War, during
which 200,000 blacks enlisted in the Union cause, the Ninth and Tenth
Cavalrys and the Twenty-fourth and Twenty-fifth Infantries did excellent
service on the Great Plains and in the Southwest; these were black regi-
ments. A full 25 per cent of the cowboys who rode up the great trails
after the Civil War were Negroes. They were also in the mining camps;
probably the wealthiest Negroes in the United States in the 1850's were
those in the Mother Lode area of California.

The New England Yankees, the tidewater Southerners—both groups
basically English, with a little French Huguenot and some Highland
Scots blood added in the South—and the Negroes in bondage consti-

tuted the major elements of the American people when the Revolution
began. We have seen that these groups later expanded, the Yankees
primarily along the northern half of the states of the Middle West, the
Southerners emigrating as gentry into Kentucky and Tennessee (these
mostly from Maryland and Virginia), or to the new states of the lower
South (these primarily from the Carolinas and eastern Georgia). Like the
New Englanders, they had a strong tendency to follow zones of constant
temperature as they worked west. All the settlers searched for lands that
reminded them of home, except that they expected them to be better, and
hoped to settle close to neighbors from "back home." Even the Southerners occasionally migrated as religious congregations. The slaves, coffles of them chained and marched into the new country, quickly transformed wilderness into southern farm or plantation. After 1815 all
Americans seemed to be on the move, always toward the new country:
Yankees, Southerners, Negroes.

Yet both the Yankees and the Southerners advanced to lands in
which the first rudiments of civilization had probably already been established by white predecessors—the cutting-edge peoples who braved
the Indian tomahawk, the back-breaking work of original clearing of the
land, the construction of the first crude lean-tos or cabins, the first worm
fences, the original wooden bridges. These peoples were newcomers not
only to the frontier (where everyone was a newcomer) but often to
America, the first of many racial or national groups to land at Atlantic
ports and head immediately for the West, for the frontier. The first two
groups, so very important in the story of the new country, were the
Scotch-Irish and the Germans.

Who were the Scotch-Irish? So hybrid a term, the first half biological
and cultural and the second geographical, has led to such confusion that
some historians have refused to grant these people a separate classifica-
tion, and have insisted, simply, that they were basically English. But this
is totally incorrect. Moreover, there are today millions of Americans
with Scotch-Irish blood in their veins, for at the time of the Revolution
there were probably 250,000 Scotch-Irish in the thirteen states, and they
were incredibly fecund. "There is not a cabin but has ten or twelve
children in it," wrote the Anglican itinerant Woodmason. "When the
boys are eighteen and the girls fourteen they marry—so that in many
cabins you will see ten or fifteen children . . . and the mother looking
as young as the daughter."[4] In 1776 from one-tenth to one-fifteenth of
all Americans were Scotch-Irish, and their influence on the frontier,
and ultimately on American life down to and including our own times
has been vitally significant. So important are these people to the story
of the new country that we must study their background in some detail.

Conditions in Scotland in the sixteenth and seventeenth centuries were just the opposite of those in England, which was in the vanguard of whatever material progress was being made. The English had a saying that there was "no law north of the Tweed," a river separating the Scottish Lowlands from English Northumberland. Scotland, both Lowland and Highland, was a land of the most abject poverty, backwardness, ignorance, superstition, and near-anarchy to be found anywhere, not only in the British Isles but in all of Europe. What national government Scotland had (and it did have a king of sorts) was ruled by faction. A Scotch form of feudalism prevailed, with the lairds carrying on Sicilian-like vendettas against each other.

The typical Scotch peasant lived in a stone and turf hovel with a moss or turf roof. There was no fireplace or chimney, merely a hole in the roof directly over the place on the dirt floor where the fire was built. In winter the cattle, chickens, and other farm animals were tethered at one end of the single room, while the whole family slept on a pile of heather used as litter at the other end. Occasional plagues plus a constant run of diseases restricted life expectancy to about thirty-five years. The people were, in brief, dirty, illiterate, and superstitious. But they were also robustly cheerful, a scrapping, swearing, swaggering, swilling people. Life was kept exciting through feuds and cattle stealing. It was notably a man's society; women's status was incredibly low and they were seldom mentioned save in bawdy songs. Even the countryside was forgotten in the high spirits of the peasantry. The Scot appears to have had little love for his land; he exhausted it, left it for Ulster or America, and moved still again with never a sad or nostalgic backward glance.

Yet in 1560 a change took place, bringing about a Reformation. John Knox's successful proselytizing resulted in the Scotch parliament renouncing Catholicism and replacing it with a state kirk, the Presbyterian Church, based upon John Calvin's interpretations of the Bible. Knox had won the people of the Lowlands to the Calvinistic ideals, thus unifying them (though not the Highlanders, who for the most part remained Catholic). As a result of this new unity, they were treated as a greater problem by the English. Moreover, the religious change uplifted the morals of the Lowland Scots; Presbyterians emphasized education, their literacy improved, and with all this their sense of power rose, which in turn brought on more religious and political turmoil.

They were a fecund people living in a barren land. Overpopulation resulted in Scottish mercenaries being found throughout Europe in the sixteenth, seventeenth, and eighteenth centuries, and any nearby area that was depopulated by warfare appealed to the Scots as a place of settlement. Such a land was Ireland, whose long history of civil and religious struggle with the English had left six of the nine northern counties (Ulster) to be populated by English and Scotch Protestants. They settled there heavily under the policies of King James I of England (1603-25); another heavy influx took place after Cromwell had crushed, with merciless brutality, the Irish rebellion of the 1640's; and in the 1690's 50,000 Lowland Scots are said to have settled there, along with Huguenots driven from France by the Edict of Nantes in 1685. For the Scots it was an easy migration: at one point barely twenty miles of sea separates Scotland from Ulster.

Yet life in Ulster in the seventeenth century was one crisis after another. The land remained sparsely settled, and there were many bogs and forests left for hunting—or hiding. The lonely places were the lairs of the Irish woodcairns or widcairns, outcasts from their own land, who pillaged and murdered the Scotch Presbyterians who, with the English, had driven them from their lands—in much the same way as the American Indians were to lose theirs. When there were no woodcairns to hunt, there were wolves to kill. Wolves were a constant menace, and their presence attests to the wildness of the land. Yet the Scots, and the people who intermingled with them during the three to five generations they spent in Ulster before migrating to the New World, appear to have thrived in such an atmosphere. They were in every sense frontiersmen, bulwarks of Protestantism against the Irish papists. They even held emotional revivals on occasions, not unlike the camp meetings held by their descendants on the American frontier; and one form of their protection from the Irish, the bawn, was similar to the American frontier station.

But the good fortune of settling the fertile northern counties of Ireland did not last for long. The Presbyterian Scotch-Irish proved to be excellent agriculturalists and husbandmen—and by the mid-1660's protests were being heard in both the Scotch and the English parliaments against the competition from Scotch-Irish products. In both houses laws were passed prohibiting the import of these products. To offset this blow the Scotch-Irish turned especially to woolens; the same protests were heard, and in 1699 the English Parliament prohibited exports of wool, raw or as cloth, to any country. These were harsh times. The destruction of Ulster's economy and the impoverishment of its people was simply an application of the mercantile theories of the time. To add to this, an act of 1704 excluded Presbyterians from legal and military offices, while in 1717-18, when leases came up for renewal, the absentee landlords doubled or more than doubled their rents. The Scotch-Irish by this time had had enough; the American colonies beckoned.

They could have gone to New England, which was Calvinist, and some did. But the habits of the Scots did not meet with the approval of Yankees, who soon discovered that a common religious origin (from John Calvin) and a similar language did not necessarily make for a harmonious meeting of peoples. People who churned milk into butter by throwing frogs into the tubs, and who spread their butter on bread with their thumbs did not quite fit into the New England scheme of things. At Worcester, Massachusetts, the Yankees burnt the Scotch-Irish meeting-house; New York was rather hard on dissenters; Maryland was Catholic; and the southern colonies were Anglican and slave-holding. William Penn's colony, on the other hand, not only promised complete religious toleration, but his agents actually encouraged the Scots to come to Pennsylvania. So they sailed to the Delaware River ports of Philadelphia, Chester, and Newcastle, and then headed into frontier areas forty miles or so north or west of Philadelphia. The quiet-mannered Quakers were shortly to be rather concerned over what they had allowed in, for the Scots were soon squatting rather than buying, they were touchy, dirty, and arrogant, and they seemed to have landed on America's shores with a hatred of the Indians already well developed.

Geography affected their migration. The so-called Great Valley of the Appalachians is actually a trough up to sixty miles wide, running northeast and southwest from Pennsylvania; there are ridges and hills in the trough, so that it embraces many smaller valleys within it. The Scotch-Irish soon discovered that they could enter the valley by way of the Delaware River in eastern Pennsylvania and follow it as it curved for a few miles like a scythe southeastward, then extended southward and a little west into the Carolinas; they could also make their way into its northern parts in Pennsylvania and New York. It was a natural highway and the land was rich and well-watered, inviting settlement along the way. By the 1730's immigrants from Ulster were landing at the Delaware River ports and heading directly into the valley. So inviting was it that one of the principal arteries of colonial America, the Great Philadelphia Wagon Road, ran all the way down the valley, ending 700 miles south of Philadelphia at the Savannah River in Georgia. By the 1740's and 50's these Bible-quoting frontiersmen were settling the Carolina Piedmont; by the late 1760's they were pushing over the mountains into eastern Tennessee; and by the 1770's, into Kentucky.

They were the stock frontier type. Protestant, English-speaking, and numerous (probably between two and three hundred thousand came over between 1717 and 1776), they landed as virtually ready-made frontiersmen, and came to where their friends and relatives had already settled. Used to a violent frontier-type existence in Ulster, they more or less transplanted their way of life to the new country. In Ulster, for example, they had wrested the land from its rightful owners, the Irish; and as a result they had hated the Irish and taken pleasure in ferreting out Irish revolutionaries or woodcairns—in essence, guerrilla warriors—and punishing them brutally. In America the counterpart of the Irishman whose land was stolen or taken by force was the Indian—the new guerrilla fighter was the Indian brave. It was a simple matter to replace the Irish as objects of their hatred with the Indians, and the Scotch-Irish achieved this transfer with great success.

They were in the vanguard of the advance westward, notably along the cutting edge of the frontier. Here the men could abandon all self-discipline and become addicts of drink, for they early learned how to make corn into a potent liquid; peach brandy was a common product also. A second addiction was the hunt. To many a man, the wilderness, his gun, his dogs, and the unrestrained freedom to hunt equaled the closest approach he knew to heaven on earth.

They were a restless people, these Scotch-Irish, caring little for their farms, content to live in lean-tos—cabins still open to the world on one side—or completed cabins with earthen floors and few improvements. It was this restlessness that took them into Tennessee and Kentucky, on across the Mississippi into Missouri and Arkansas, onto the plains of Texas; as Pike County illiterates they made their way along the Oregon Trail toward the Pacific coast. These people were, some say, overwhelmed by the frontier and reduced to little above the savagery of the Indians. There is no doubt that this was true of many of them. Charles Woodmason, the Anglican itinerant in the Carolina back country just prior to the Revolution, was appalled at their indolence: "They delight in their present, low, lazy, sluttish, heathenish, hellish life, and seem not desirous of changing it," he wrote caustically in his *Journal*. He found that "these People despise Knowledge, and instead of honoring a Learned Person . . . they despise and Ill treat them [sic]. . . ." He found them sensual and promiscuous. It is hot in the Carolina Piedmont in the summer, but still the parson was shocked at the young women who wore nothing but a thin shift and a thin petticoat underneath. "They draw their Shift as tight as possible to the Body, and pin it close, to shew the roundness of their Breasts, and slender Waists (for they are generally finely shaped) and draw their Petticoat close to their Hips to show the fineness of their Limbs—so that they might as well be in Puri Naturalibus," he complained.

With emphasis let us add that this Anglican preacher was hardly an impartial observer. Nevertheless there is a ring of authenticity about his writings, the probable inaccuracy being his exaggeration of condi-

tions. He accused the back country folk of "swopping wives as cattle"
and estimated that 95 per cent of the young women he married were already pregnant. He concluded that nine-tenths of the settlers had venereal disease.[5]

It should be added, first, that the cutting edge, even in the Carolina
back country, was filled with people other than Scotch-Irish—drifters
and ne'er-do-wells from the tidewater settlements and people of other
nationalities. Any frontier area would be rough, but the Scotch-Irish
areas were especially so. An educated Presbyterian pastor would have
his work cut out for him, but in general the restraining influence of such
a man was lacking, for there were very few of the kind on any frontier.
Until they did arrive, and the forces of law and order were established
with the aid of the settled areas to the east, conditions remained raw.
Time, the maturing of the society, the natural social distinctions that
were bound to arise, and the eventual presence of learned men were what
made the new country into an orderly, settled society.

The Scotch-Irish seem to have been notably successful in resisting
outside authority. Resentment of the more settled elements who were
accused of levying unfair taxes, of being reluctant to establish counties
in the new country, of refusing reapportionment so that the eastern
counties always held the upper hand in the colonial legislature, and of a
failure to protect the inhabitants from the Indians, all fostered a backwoods hatred of the Easterners on the one hand, of the Indians on the
other.

There are four notable cases in frontier history when the frontiersmen
raised the standard of revolt, and in each incident the Scotch-Irish contingent was predominant. The first was the uprising of the Paxton Boys
in what was then western Pennsylvania. Elements from the little town
of Paxton, on the east bank of the Susquehanna River, which had suffered much from Indian depredations during the French and Indian
War, rose up in December 1763 and murderously butchered the Conestoga Indians located about fifty miles from there. That these Indians
were peaceable made little difference. The Paxtons, representing their
brethren in Pennsylvania's back country, nearly 2,000 of whom were
said to have died by fagot or tomahawk or been taken into captivity
during the French and Indian War, then rode toward Philadelphia,
where they threatened to slaughter 125 Christianized Indians who were
being protected there. Six miles outside the city, at the village of Germantown, they were met by a delegation headed by Benjamin Franklin,
who accepted a declaration of grievances from them; later the Paxton
Boys issued a remonstrance, a document listing nine of their complaints.
Although Franklin succeeded in preventing the Paxtons from invading

Philadelphia, the colonial legislature pigeonholed their declaration of grievances and their later remonstrance; nothing came of their pleas. Yet their discontent was understandable and based upon essentially the same conditions as were found among Westerners in North and South Carolina. It was not only the failure of the eastern "establishment" to offer them protection from the Indians that these people protested. Usually they wanted reapportionment: in the case of Pennsylvania, the eastern counties plus Philadelphia had twenty-six members in the legislature, while the western counties were represented by only ten. There was always the sensitive subject of the indebtedness of the Westerners to the Easterners, and often a clash of religions also; there was the matter of inequitable taxation, and controversy over social services such as schools and churches and legal services such as judges, justices of the peace, and courts.

In North Carolina the colonial government had established a system of courts in the back country, but they were corrupt and the judges and sheriffs were arrogant appointees of the authorities down in the lowlands. So much dissatisfaction did this engender that the back country people took matters into their own hands. They stormed jails, coerced colonial officials, burned the homes and barns of their enemies. Calling themselves Regulators, they fomented a rebellion that ended with the Battle of Alamance on May 16, 1771, in which they were put to rout. The most significant outcome was a movement of these frontiersmen over the mountains into the headwater areas of the Tennessee River system.

The South Carolina affair was a reaction to the failure of the tidewater people to provide law and order for the new country men. That colony's back country had been ravaged by a bloody Cherokee war in 1760-61, the aftermath of which was a deterioration of society, even a brutalizing of the people. Law-abiding farmers, storekeepers, and the like were hindered in their efforts to establish law and order because the influence of neither counties, courts, nor churches reached their settlements, which were 150 to 200 miles west of Charleston—a good week's ride by horseback.

By 1767 conditions in the back country had become intolerable. There were entire settlements of outlaws, including women, children, and elderly relatives. Gangs numbered up to 300 members, and had connections with criminal elements down in Georgia and northward across North Carolina into Virginia; their confederates were often unwilling but coerced wagoners and merchants. Horses and Negro slaves were prime items of theft, but the thieves also entered farmhouses, tortured the occupants into confessing the hiding places of their valuables, and then often set fire to the house after robbing and killing the occupants. Young girls were kidnaped and raped.

The law-abiding elements did two things: they banded together calling themselves Regulators and, much like the vigilance committees of early California and Montana, tracked down the outlaws and delivered harsh frontier justice to them. Nineteen were hanged at one place, while others were flogged, branded with a hot iron, or otherwise punished. Vagrants were told to work or be flogged.

The second action the Regulators took was to send remonstrances—documents justifying their actions and explaining their grievances—to the authorities in Charleston. But distances were so great that there was a lack of understanding on the part of the governor. Their taking of the law into their own hands smelled of rebellion, and the Regulators were peremptorily ordered to disperse. They at first refused, and South Carolina came within a hair's breadth of civil war. Cooler heads prevailed, however; a Circuit Court act of 1769 went far toward alleviating the new country men's grievances. Yet fair representation in the South Carolina Assembly, fair and equitable taxation, and the establishment of a school system had to await statehood and the period after the American Revolution.

About twenty years later in western Pennsylvania and Virginia there occurred the fourth such incident, the first serious defiance of the new government under the Constitution. In these semi-settled areas the Scotch farmers predominated. Not all of them were first generation, however; many had been born on the other side of the mountains, where their fathers had fought Indians in the 1760's and 70's. "They are a religious as well as a warlike race," wrote Henry Marie Brackenridge, who resided amongst them, "qualities inherited from their ancestors as well as their dislike to excises and excise officers. The names of the M'Farlanes, the Crawfords, the Hamiltons, the Bradys, the Butlers and the Calhouns, show their origin . . . they neither considered it immoral nor unpatriotic, to oppose the execution of bad law."[6]

The Scotch-Irish of western Virginia and western Pennsylvania had a tradition of opposition to this form of taxation. When Alexander Hamilton pushed through an excise tax on whiskey in 1791 there were rumblings of discontent in the West. The new tax applied to the commodity most used for purposes of trade in the new country; it was high, taking about 25 per cent of the net price of a gallon of whiskey; and it had to be paid in cash—and specie was in short supply. To collect the tax the collector had to gather information on a man's still, the number of barrels of whiskey he possessed, and so forth—information which Westerners considered their private possession. The Ohio River was closed to through trade in the early 1790's because of the Indian menace and Spanish policy down the Mississippi, while roads over the mountains were so bad as to make the transportation of grain uneconomic. But a farmer could distil his corn into a potent liquid, place it in eight-gallon barrels, one on each side of a pack horse, and in that manner carry it to market, doubling its value by crossing the mountains. So lucrative was the trade, and so popular was "Monongahela rye," that amongst every twenty or thirty farms there was bound to be a distillery run by the inhabitants of one of them.

Although dissatisfaction with the tax was widespread, it was concentrated around Pittsburgh (but not in the town itself, which was considered a Federalist stronghold) and down the Monongahela River Valley. More than one tax collector had his wig singed "accidentally," or red-hot coals secretly placed in his boots just as he was about to put them on. But the real trouble did not begin until July 1794, a time of saturnalia, as Henry Brackenridge called it, when the farmers gathered in neighborly groups to help each other with the harvest, and the whiskey flowed free. This was the wrong time for excise men to be about. John Neville, the excise inspector for western Pennsylvania, soon found himself besieged inside his home by a mob, shots were fired, and some of the whiskey rebels were wounded, one fatally. The mob increased to 2,000 or so, tarred and feathered some of its victims, some homes were burned, and federal authority was defied. When a militia army of about 13,000 commanded by "Light Horse Harry" Lee and accompanied by Alexander Hamilton crossed the mountains and arrived on the shores of the Monongahela, the rebels simply melted away. Meanwhile, "Mad Anthony" Wayne's victory at Fallen Timbers opened the country to the west, prosperity returned, and the economic difficulties that had contributed to the disturbance came to an end. The tax continued to be collected.

In all four of these incidents of backwoods action, the Scotch-Irish people constituted the majority in the areas of disturbance, but more than this, the disturbance itself was due to their nature. They were a fiercely independent people, touchy about their religion and their rights. They leaned toward direct, impetuous group action and in fact contributed the tendency toward emotionalism and mob action to the American character. They were distinctly anti-intellectual, yet proud of their insistence upon education for their children. They were a mobile people, moving again and again and yet again. They were despoilers, creating farms without beauty, cutting or burning the forests without foresight, and planting fields over and over again until the land was leached and barren. They were a people who could work unceasingly for a time, then lapse into a long period of lethargy—in glaring contrast to the steadiness of the New Englanders. Eventually the shortage of Presbyterian ministers brought on their adherence to other sects, the Baptists being most successful with them.

The blending of the Scotch-Irish into the American population at large was well under way by the early years of the nineteenth century. Yet the impetuousness of the Tennesseeans, marching off to free Florida in 1813 or Texas in 1846, bore the marks of the strong Scotch-Irish strain in their character; and the lynch law justice of the southern states from Georgia to Texas is partly due to the heavy preponderance in much of those parts of Scotch-Irish blood. It has been said that without the Scotch-Irish the West could never have been conquered so rapidly. This is probably true, but it would have been conquered with less injustice to the Indians and less damage to the land if they had not been around.

Somewhere around the turn of the nineteenth century a journalist named James Hall remembered his first sight of a frontiersman. Hall was a lad in Philadelphia at the time, and the stranger with "brawny limbs and sun-burnt features" was described to him as a Kentuckian.

> The rough, hardy air of the stranger, the jaded paces of his nag, the blanket, bear-skin, and saddle-bags . . . bespoke him to be of distant regions, to have been reared among dangers, and to be familiar with fatigues. He strode among us with the step of Achilles . . . I thought I could see in that man, one of the progenitors of an unconquerable race; his face presented the traces of a spirit quick to resent—he had the will to dare, and the power to execute; there was a something in his look which bespoke a disdain of control, and an absence of constraint in all his movements, indicating an habitual independence of thought and action.[7]

Such a man was probably Scotch-Irish, and indeed could be a marvelous warrior, a great conqueror of the wilderness. But he could also be something else; Appalachia today attests in some degree to his weaknesses.

The English and Scotch-Irish, who have thus far been our concern, constituted well over 60 per cent of the whites in the thirteen states at the beginning of the Revolution. There was one other substantial immigrant group, however: the Germans. Quieter, more methodical, more peaceful, and more inclined to find one good spot and settle there for generations, these people, and the Germans who followed them throughout the nineteenth century in a wave that crested after 1848, brought to the frontier intelligence, stability, ingenuity, and hard work, and proved an excellent balance to the wilder Scotch-Irish.

The first arrivals were refugees from several generations of warfare. Although they were (and still are) often called "Dutch," this term is an English corruption of "Deutsch." These people were actually Germans from the Rhine Valley, especially the Palatinate, an extremely fertile area embracing both sides of the Rhine that was one of the principal regions of contention in the Thirty Year's War (1618-48), which was followed by the Wars of Louis XIV. The eighteenth century was well under way before all the devastation ended.

After generations of calamity the people of the lower Rhine reached a condition of wretched near-hopelessness. In addition to the sufferings caused by almost constant warfare, the princes of the German states, totally lacking in compassion, the better aspects of statecraft, or foresight, overspent and overtaxed in order to live in lavish opulence. Wherever the poor people turned, they met abuse. Their reaction is understandable; they retreated into pietistic or mystical religious sects from which they gained the courage to face a world of horrors. The region, although mostly Lutheran, was soon sprinkled with Mennonites, Moravians, Anabaptists, Dunkers, Amish, and finally Quakers, all of whom suffered persecution, since, in the age of absolutism, they were expected to adhere to the faith of their prince. It was small wonder, then, that these peoples welcomed the opportunity to migrate to the new country.

They first heard of it from occasional letters home from a sprinkling of their number who had emigrated to America. When shippers saw the possibility of profit in carrying the Germans overseas they used pamphlets and hired individuals called *Neuländers* to go from village to village boasting of the wonders of America and explaining how the Germans could get there. By the second decade of the eighteenth century a substantial migration had begun. It was encouraged by the British, who even furnished some naval vessels to help in the transportation, because, it was hoped, the Germans would settle in New York and work in the forests along the Hudson to produce naval stores. This did not work out; the Germans spread elsewhere, and by the 1720's they were to be found along the Mohawk and southward into the Wyoming and Cherry valleys of Pennsylvania.

Other Germans, attracted to Pennsylvania by Penn's advertising and even his personal appearance in the Rhineland, arrived at Philadelphia and were soon congregating at such places as Germantown, founded in 1683 and incorporated in 1689. They settled heavily in the Susquehanna Valley and by the 1720's were advancing down the Great Valley. Frederick, Maryland, was settled by them in 1745, Winchester, Virginia, in 1732, and by 1751 they were on the Yadkin River in North Carolina.

The Germans developed their farms as if the farm buildings and the hills upon which they were built would remain together forever. They were very good farmers, putting the Scotch-Irish and English to shame; they were also skilled artisans and lovers of good music and painting. On the other hand many did not believe in education, and possibly 25 per cent of them or their children were illiterate. The German farmer also revealed a lack of balance in his priorities. His barn was a two-story husbandman's castle, while his home was often a dirty cottage. Clannish as they were (and still are in some places), the Germans constituted an important addition to the basic American stock by the time of the American Revolution.

Something must also be said of the Swiss and Huguenots. Probably at least twelve thousand Swiss came to the colonies prior to 1776, mostly to Pennsylvania and South Carolina. They were *Landsassen*, the very poor and landless, or else, like many of the emigrants from neighboring principalities along the Rhine, they were members of despised and persecuted sects, such as Baptists, Anabaptists, Mennonites. It should be pointed out that many of the Rhenish and Swiss migrated in the face of opposition, for the princes considered a good population as an index of success and a guarantee of continued wealth and levied all kinds of legal devices against would-be migrants, who yet continued to come to America.

The Huguenots were far more important than their numbers would indicate. These French Calvinists, most from the area of western France between the Loire and Gironde rivers centered at the seaport of La Rochelle, represented the rising middle class of France. The revocation of the Edict of Nantes in 1685 dispersed thousands of them to Prussia, England, and the American colonies. Huguenots founded New Rochelle in Westchester County just to the north of New York City. They also settled in Boston and Salem, and especially in and about Charleston, South Carolina. It is through their names, soon anglicized, that their influence in the new country is realized: John Sevier, Peter Faneuil, Paul Revere, John Jay are some of the well-known ones.

The basic elements of the new country population were, then, well established by the outbreak of the Revolution. They all had become Americans very rapidly. Even the redemptioners, people who took ship for America and paid for their passage with four to seven years' service to whoever should purchase them, had fulfilled their obligations, married, and set up housekeeping and farming with astonishing alacrity.

Basic Traits and
New Ingredients

It was these people or their progeny who carried out the initial settlement of the trans-Appalachian region as far west as Missouri and Arkansas. During the Revolution there was practically no migration from Europe, save that some ten to twenty thousand Hessian mercenaries remained in America; and from 1790 until 1820 the total immigration into the United States has been estimated at just under 250,000, a negligible figure. The population of about four million in 1790 increased to over 9,600,000 in 1820, an indication of the wealth and productivity of the new nation; during this period no new elements were added.

This generation-long respite in migration is of extreme importance in American history, for it gave the colonial peoples the opportunity to mix, blend, and accept in near totality a basic language and the "American way" of looking at things—social life, religion, politics, land ownership, and government. The basic mix, once blended, was so strong that never was the foreigner, no matter how great his numbers or how concentrated in time was his migration, ever able to impress his ways to any serious degree upon more than a region or a state. Even in the areas of greatest concentration, the second generation witnessed the beginnings of a break away from the old ways and the old customs. Occasionally the process seemed slow, and the tenacity of Greeks, Italians, Irish, Poles, Scandinavians, Jews, and others in retaining traditions has resisted assimilation. But this is a narrow view. A more long-range view of change, by centuries rather than decades, would hold that, in general, the mixture of peoples blended with remarkable rapidity.

This was also the period when the move to the Gulf Plains region and the Appalachian plateau (which embraces western Pennsylvania, most of Ohio, western Virginia, and much of Kentucky and Tennessee) took place, as well as extensions into Indiana, Illinois, and Missouri. This migration has been described as a mighty stream of people in covered wagons, moving along the unimproved roads from Philadelphia to Pittsburgh, from New England across the Hudson between Albany and Newburgh, then through Cayuga and down to Pittsburgh, or from Baltimore to Wheeling. John Bradbury was told in April of 1816 that more than 15,000 wagons had passed over the bridge at Cayuga in the past eighteen months, "containing emigrants to the western country." In the same year he visited upper Virginia and noticed "a great number of farms that had been abandoned" by people heading West.[1]

"Old America seems to be breaking up, and moving westward," the British traveler Morris Birkbeck observed in 1817. Between Baltimore and Pittsburgh he was "seldom out of sight . . . of family groups behind and before us." He described a typical emigrant wagon ("so light that you might almost carry it, yet strong enough to bear a good load of bedding, utensils and provisions, and a swarm of young citizens,—and to sustain marvellous shocks in its passage over these rocky heights") pulled by two small horses, a cow or two following; this, save for a small amount of cash for the land office, was all their possessions. The wagon was covered, sometimes just by a blanket, and the family traveled before, in, and behind the vehicle, depending on the weather and the spirits of the party. As for the women, the saying was that the New England damsels were cheerful, and walked in front of the vehicle, the women of Jersey origin rode in the wagon, while the Pennsylvania women lingered behind, "as though regretting the homes they have left." Sometimes the conveyance was a cart and a single horse, sometimes "the back of the poor pilgrim bears all his effects, and his wife follows, naked-footed, bending under the hopes of the family."[2]

At Pittsburgh or Wheeling the emigrants would probably separate, or regroup on the basis of ultimate destination. Some held onto their wagons and pierced the timbered wilderness with them until they found the spot which they wanted to call home. There, so said one observer, they proceeded to prostrate the forest and deposit the seeds of art and refinements. Others, possibly with more money, embarked on steamboats, which became ever more common after 1815. And many purchased flatboats, three or four families sometimes joining in the purchase of the $35 to $75 conveyance that could take them down the river to their destinations.

Indeed, the flatboat was the true emigrant ark. It was flat-bottomed, of course, and squared at both ends; and all flatboats had remarkably similar dimensions: about fifty feet long by fourteen feet wide, the latter explained by the Indian Chutes at the Falls of the Ohio, opposite

Louisville, which were just fifteen feet across. The "flats" carried twenty-five or thirty tons, which pretty well took care of the horses, cows, pigs, chickens, wagon, wife, children, and assorted truck the pioneer needed for his new home, wherever it might be. In later years the boats grew longer—ninety or a hundred feet or more.

Most of the pioneers were farm people, a little frightened by it all but used to hardship and heartache and physical exertion. They knew that their journey into the new country was full of chance. There were the risks of travel, such as sickness, snake bites, broken limbs, the danger of thieves stealing the small bag of specie. And they were aware that once the decision to move had been made, the two moments of greatest crisis would be the times of purchase of the flatboat and of their new homestead. Once the first purchase was made they were still nervous and uneasy, for, since they were unaccustomed to it, that part of the journey that consisted of flatboating down the Ohio was the riskiest segment of their journey. In a "flat" of good, bad, or indifferent quality, they trusted to God and set out down the mighty Ohio.

If they were prudent, they also wanted to learn all they could about flatboating and would have purchased a river guide, of which the most informational, and overall probably the most accurate, was Zadoc Cramer's *The Navigator: Containing Directions for Navigating the Monongahela, Allegheny, Ohio and Mississippi Rivers*. Within a quarter century after it was first published in 1801, it had run through twelve editions. At a dollar a copy, even in 1801, it was considered a good buy. When Cramer added maps of the Ohio and Mississippi, segment by segment, to accompany his running description and advice as to what to look for and how to manipulate the "wicked river" (as the Ohio was sometimes called), it was a bargain. After purchasing boat and book and shoving off into the current, there was plenty of time to read what Cramer had to say.

His little volume radiated the conscious, visible good feelings of the new country Americans. Not only was "no country perhaps in the world . . . better watered with limpid streams and navigable rivers than the United States of America," he wrote, but moreover "no people better deserve these advantages, or are better calculated to make proper use of them than her industrious and adventurous citizens." This feeling about their worthiness under God and their privilege of assuming the task of settling the vast Mississippi Valley is one of the characteristics of the American people in the nineteenth century. They were, said Cramer, "a people worthy of all the advantages that nature and art can give them, a people the more meritorious, because they know how to sustain peace and live independent, among the crushing empires, the falling of kings, the slaughter and bloodshed of millions, and the tumult and corruption and tyranny of all the world beside."[3]

Such eloquent writing was not merely the result of a democratic political climate. The Americans looked down upon the wide Ohio and the still wider Mississippi, the waters still fresh and, even if muddy, hardly noxious or polluted, and saw only nature and beauty. On either side stretched the great forest, with butternut, tulip tree, black willow, cherry, mulberry, and plum growing along the banks. Occasionally the woods thinned out; in these "wood pastures," as the pioneers called them, deer could be seen peacefully grazing. Farther up on the hillsides grew red, white, and black oak, hickory, walnut, ash, poplar, and sycamore.

Those who came to the new country by flatboat would sometimes pole and pull their loaded arks up a small tributary stream until they found their homestead site, but were more likely to pull into a riverside community, such as Cincinnati or Marietta, or Limestone or Louisville, sell their boat for lumber, and then make their way inland. Their flatboat had contained the paraphernalia of a farm, after all, with dismantled wagon, horse, family cow, pigs, chickens, and dogs. When the ark was sold, the wheels were attached to the wagon, the box loaded with the pioneer's truck, and again the party was on its way inland.

Excitement over the "great day coming" was equated with a pride in America that enveloped the emigrant when he got off the boat from the old country and remained with him and his descendants to the third and fourth generations. "The rapid progress of the American empire," the traveler James Hall observed in 1828, "[is] a constant theme of exultation. . . . Foreigners may call this *national vanity*: so let it be: we *are* proud of our country, and are not ashamed to proclaim that pride."[4]

Going into the new country was the most thrilling thing an American could do in the nineteenth century. It was the attainable challenge; it was an investment in one's life with nominal risk and high return. It touched the young and the old, the middle-aged with numerous progeny, and those whose children were grown. James Hall described such a gray-haired couple migrating down the Ohio in a small boat: "The primitive couple looked as if they might have been *pulling together* down the stream of life for half a century without having grown tired of each other's company, for while their oars preserved a regular cadence, they were chatting socially together. . . ." When he learned that they sought a new home, he expected to hear from them a tale of woe. But no—their children were grown, and as for the neighbors, " 'a good many of em's gone *out back*, and so the old woman and me felt *sort o' lonesome*, and thought *we'd* go too, and try our luck.' " Confidently, they spoke of clearing new lands in the wilderness.[5]

The new country was a land of strangers, yet common problems and common experiences melded them together. For a brief moment there was in each new area an approach to true egalitarianism, a wonderful faith in the inherent goodness of man, both in the abstract and in reality. The warm hospitality of the settlers was based in part upon this faith and in part had been built up through decades of the continuing frontier experience. John Bradbury, who was in America from 1809 to 1811, said that he had traveled through two thousand miles of wilderness where there had been no taverns, but he had always received a welcome from the inhabitants. He acknowledged that the furnishings were rustic, but then no remuneration had been accepted. So moral were the people that few houses were even equipped with locks and bolts, and the town jail, if there was one, was usually empty.

The taverns were a shock to European travelers, for these American public houses followed what one writer called "the gregarious plan: everything is public by day and night," he wrote, "—for even night in an American inn affords no privacy." The guests, whatever their number, received their entertainment *en masse*, slept *en masse*, and ate *en masse*. Sleeping was particularly rustic. After the evening meal they repaired to "rooms crowded with beds, something like the wards of a hospital; where, after undressing in public, you are fortunate if you escape a partner in your bed, in addition to the myriads of bugs, which you need not hope to escape."[6]

From the very first the Americans bore in common a number of pronounced character traits that were noted by nearly all travelers. The class-conscious Englishman was warned to watch his conversation to be sure that he never spoke down to anyone in America. Everyone in the new country considered himself as good as the next fellow; he was discharging a duty to society and deserved respect for it. Among themselves the Americans carried mutual esteem to the extent of addressing one another as Captain, Major, Colonel, or General, a habit that rather fooled Mrs. Trollope, who soon discovered that these "officers" were hardly even "gentlemen" in the British sense.

There was something about the obvious crudeness of civilization in the new country that bred a touchiness in Americans. The Virginian's "When you call me that, *smile*" (in Owen Wister's famous cowboy novel) had an earlier counterpart in a statement made by James Hall in 1828: "You may make remarks freely, in the West, if you do it pleasantly." Thus the tavern guest who said "he had been obliged to eat *bacon* until he was ashamed to look a pig in the face" was greeted with a smile; "but if he had used any coarse language in regard to that popular and respectable dish," said Hall, "the affront might have been swallowed as reluctantly as the bacon." It all depended on the stranger. If he smiled he was well treated, if he was testy he was teased, if he was impudent, he was flogged.[7]

The American was proud of his hospitality. Hall once accepted a bowl of milk from a pioneer, and tried to pay him for it. "I never sell milk," his host replied. "But . . . I have money enough," pleaded Hall. "Well," said the host, "I have milk enough, so we're even; I have as good a right to give you milk, as you have to give me money."[8]

The pioneer was also inquisitive to the point of discourtesy, by European standards. Yet his questions were never meant to be bold or rude. An intelligent and vigorous citizen in new, sparsely settled country was eager for news. Occasionally his ignorance of the world about him seemed childlike, and certainly his progeny, born and raised in the new country, were as innocent of the outside world as children of Eden. (But sin found its way into the Biblical garden; so too in America.)

It was a happy, simple society. In a day when an artisan or skilled laborer was but a short cut above the jack-of-all-trades, when family background or formal education was unnecessary, the world was indeed an oyster for the man of health and reasonable abilities. The new country people could do everything necessary for a comfortable existence. They could chop, shoot, plow, sow, harvest, distil corn, butcher a pig, tan a hide, build a cabin, construct a fireplace, dig a well; the women could spin yarn, sew, knit, cook, preserve, make soap, administer backwoods nostrums to sick husbands and children. Cabin raisings, corn huskings, and sewing bees were as much occasions for socializing as they were necessary events.

Such people were active and optimistic. Young men married and then thought about supporting their brides. Tall, loose-jointed, and lean, the American stood well-adjusted to an exciting world. If he lived in a town —and the new country had plenty of them—he was a speculator of some kind, investing in a salt mine or a tannery, building a grist mill or a toll bridge, or doing whatever looked profitable, providing it suited his whim. He was imbued with the pleasure of business, something every Rotarian understands. If he lived on a farm the continued challenge to improve his property or expand his holdings kept him busy, and the completion of his plans gave him deep satisfaction. His greatest sport was hunting—either alone, save for his dog, or with companions. In his leisure he walked about with his hands in his pockets, or sat in front of the hearth, tilting back in his chair, and chewed and spat; or he whit-tled. Whittling was a relaxation throughout the new country, and many a piece of "store-bought" furniture succumbed to a whittler's constant activity.

He was wasteful. Even emigrants from Europe and the British Isles overcame in a short while their reluctance to chop down trees and burn endless cords of wood, while native Americans never had been bothered with such qualms. When the Germans began arriving in large numbers they were aghast at the waste, and their criticism of it was a barrier between them and their non-German neighbors. It was not just the destruction of timber that shocked them, but the abuse of the land, the loose control over livestock, the willingness to speculate and the shrug of the shoulders and "oh, well" when speculation failed. There can be no secret about the source of such profligacy—it was the abundance of all the good nature-given things.

The man of the new country was interested in politics; in his day one met that charismatic extrovert, the American politico, at the local crossroads, drank his corn liquor, and questioned his word. Within less than a decade after 1820 the new country men would bring about universal white male suffrage, elect Andrew Jackson president, and the West would come into its own as a political power.

As for the women—well, it was very much a man's society. How unhappy was a woman with a good provider for a husband and a passel of children? She hardly had time to consider. When she did, she probably decided that she was lonely, and she had a deep hankering for such frills of civilization as store-purchased cloth, windows, better cooking and eating utensils, an improved house, a new rocking chair. Women were segregated on steamboats, in taverns, and even at religious gatherings. Loneliness, ill health, and the mystery of God's ways resulted in a wife less well-adjusted than her husband. Yet many a woman was just as strong in spirit as her man. She wrapped a shawl around her shoulders, tied on her sunbonnet, cradled the youngest babe in her arms, and pointed her face West. She shared her husband's pride in the achievement.

To more cultured and genteel Easterners or foreign travelers, the speech of these men and women seemed uncouth and profane. "Profanity and strange curses," Timothy Flint commented, "is ordinarily an unpleasant element in their conversation." They spoke more rapidly, with "an appearance of earnestness and abruptness." They overused some words—*elegant* was one of them, *country* (as in "the Alabama country," "the new country," etc.) another. They made up new words: *combobbolate, absquatulate, exflunctify*. Yet, if one took passage on a riverboat from Louisville to New Orleans, he found them more open, friendly, and interested than he could ever expect of fellow passengers on a trans-Atlantic packet.[9]

Finally, the Westerner was a traveler. "Time to an American is everything and space he attempts to reduce to a mere nothing," wrote the Englishman Captain Frederick Marryat in 1837.[10] Timothy Flint stated, with some exaggeration, that the majority of the males in the western country had flatboated or keelboated to New Orleans—a journey of up to fifty days, filled with new sights and experiences—and then had returned upstream on glittering, garish steamboats, tiny cosmopolitan centers on the western waters. The western people did appear to know the country's geography in a way which belied the traditional impression of them as hayseeds and country bumpkins.

Until the end of the 1820's this movement was by and large, an emigration by native-born Americans. But in the 1830's and 40's new elements were arriving and heading west.

Starting in 1816 the cotton and timber ships returning from ports in the British Isles had begun to debark a noticeably increasing number of passengers from Ireland. They generally appeared wearing tattered corduroy breeches, tight short waistcoats, and plug hats perched saucily on their heads. They hailed not from the northern counties of Ulster but from the Irish Catholic part of the island. The Irishman came seeking escape from hopelessness; at home he was taxed oppressively for the maintenance of a church to which he did not belong, and an absentee landlord gathered rent on his meager farm in order to maintain himself in luxury. If there had ever existed an incentive to build up his farm, it had disappeared long ago. Furthermore, the country had become dependent upon the potato, which could not be kept from spoiling for long, so that a crop failure could bring on famine and death. In general, the quality of life of the Irish in the early nineteenth century represented no improvement over that of their Celtic ancestors of 1500 years before.

Until about 1830 most of the Irish migrants were able to come to America with a little money and plans for betterment. The Panic of 1819 and the resulting depression curtailed immigration for the first half of the 1820's, but of those who did come, many were Irish. Serious potato famines in 1821 and 1822 prompted many to head for America in spite of the depression. Then after 1830, the Irish began to swarm in. In the famine years 1845-48 a veritable flood of humanity fled from an island that represented starvation, and death. New York and the cities of New England soon had their Irish shantytowns. All told, some four and a half million Irish are estimated to have left home for the United States between 1820 and 1920.

Most of the histories written of the Irish in America emphasize their clannishness, pugnacity, and excessive drinking. It is said that they chose to remain in the slums of the cities, that they were encouraged to remain there by the church, and that their blending into the American stream was accomplished as unskilled labor and within the framework of political bossism. Although census statistics will bolster these claims, there is another facet to the Irish people's Americanization: the part they played in the settling of the new country—the frontier West—and, in turn, what the frontier West did to them.

For the Irish were the canal and railroad builders of America. Their reputation advanced down the right-of-way with them; a Norwegian immigrant, for example, wrote,

> When these roughnecks get together it is a pretty dull party unless there are a couple of fights and someone gets a good hiding. As you go along a railway under construction it is easy to detect the places where they have had their frolics by the torn-up sod, the tufts of hair, the broken bottles, pipes, pants buttons, blood, and so forth, which they have left behind them. I imagine that if the most brutish hog in the world could express himself he would do it something like these fellows.[11]

When the job was done, the Irish did not all drop their shovels and head for the big city—or at least, not for the big cities of the East. Many stayed along the canals or the western railroads and worked in those transportation industries, or they drifted into mining camps, or became farmers, or worked for "the city" as road builders, sewer diggers, and maintenance men in the western communities.

In sheer numbers the Irish had their greatest representation in New York City and Boston. But percentages indicate that they were influential in the frontier West also. In round numbers, California in 1870 had more than 54,000 Irish and 29,000 Germans, out of a total population of 560,000; Nevada more than 5,000 Irish and 2,000 Germans out of a total of 42,000; Montana more than 1,600 Irish and 1,233 Germans out of 20,000; and Colorado, 1,685 Irish and 1,456 Germans out of 40,000. Of the 149,000 inhabitants of San Francisco, more than 25,000 were Irish, more than 13,000 German. The population of Virginia City, Nevada, was almost 50 per cent foreign born. From a third to a half of the troops stationed at such lonely forts as Fetterman, D. A. Russell, and Fred Steele in Wyoming were foreign born, and again, a third to a half of that number were sons of Erin. More than a third of the population of

Helena was foreign born, a fourth of Denver, nearly two-thirds of Tucson, half of the gold town of Grass Valley in California's Sierras, and in all cases, a third to a half of those immigrants were certainly Irish.

The virtues of settlement outside the big cities were known and publicized by some of the Irish, even if others encouraged concentration. In 1873 the Catholic Reverend Stephen Byrne published a book for Irish immigrants in which he stated that the Irish had made "a very fatal mistake in crowding into the large cities . . . ," that "it would have been far better for the majority of them to have sought employment and homes on the vacant or semivacant lands of the United States."[12] The church, with administrative divisions covering the entire West, indicated a willingness to give succour to all who came.

The Irish were not isolated newcomers amongst the old-line Americans. The Germans were flocking to the United States in nearly equal numbers, especially after 1848, as were the Scandinavians. Somewhere between five and seven million Germans came in the century after 1814, most of them in the years 1840-60, and 1880-90. Some two million Scandinavians (Swedes, Norwegians and Danes) came, mostly after the Civil War. Prior to the 1880's, these peoples had almost exclusively agricultural backgrounds, and large numbers of them therefore headed for the prairies and forests of the West. The agents sent to Europe by railroad companies and western states with lands to sell and above all the letters home from friends, relatives, and neighbors who had gone before had prepared a distorted view of what would soon become for them a reality.

This was the most tremendous folk movement of modern times. It took place primarily in the same period as and was part of the sweep to the Pacific, and in the enormity of the process, we can mention only the most important and widespread experiences most of these people shared in common. For the most part, they were poor, or, as has been said by others, they were the respectable and ambitious poor. Their odyssey had three parts: the trip from the ancestral home to the seaport; the terrible voyage, lasting eight or ten weeks; and the journey from the port of debarkation into the interior, to where their new home would be. The terrible apprehension so many of them experienced was usually softened somewhat by the knowledge that others they knew had gone before and were waiting for them somewhere far to the west. Most of them landed at New York—at Castle Garden in lower Manhattan from 1848 until 1892. Some came in via Quebec—especially the Irish—and a good many Irish and Germans also entered the country at New Orleans and then worked their way up the Mississippi Valley. There is no question that

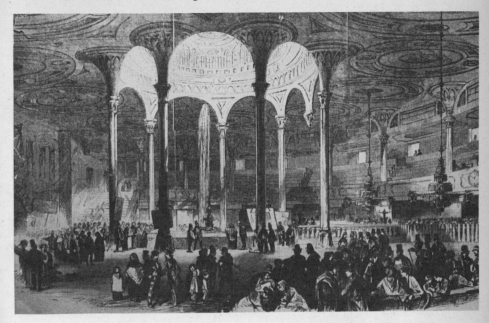

A sketch of Castle Garden, where American immigrants first landed before Ellis Island was opened, from *Frank Leslie's Illustrated Weekly*.

land was the cynosure that beckoned these people, with the possible exception of the Irish. Owning their own land was for them a lifelong ambition, the meaning of which can perhaps only be appreciated by those who have lived on a farm and made a living from it.

The journey west for many of the new people began with a steamer or railroad trip up the Hudson to Albany. There followed a dreadfully slow journey to Buffalo along the Erie Canal. This great artery, constructed between 1817 and 1825, was the scene of many an Irishman's first gainful employment in America, and employment on the canal or alongside it led many of them to settle along its route. From Buffalo a steamer journey along the Great Lakes awaited the emigrant, who by now, several weeks into his American residency and several hundred miles inland, was beginning to experience a revival of courage. Indeed, he had met many others who had the "western fever"; he no longer felt so completely alone.

Although the descendants of neither Irish nor German immigrants would like to admit it, these groups had a great deal in common, as well as wide divergencies, in their adjustments to the new country. Many Germans, as well as Irish, tended to settle in the cities. The Germans were prevalent in the Ohio cities of Cincinnati, Columbus, and Cleveland, in St. Louis, Missouri, and in Milwaukee. The Irish, of course, centered in New York, Boston, and the mill towns of New England. Yet, as has been pointed out, the two groups constituted equal percentages of total population in such cities as Denver, San Francisco, Tucson, Laramie, Virginia City, and other towns or cities of the Far West. Some of each nationality came over as groups or settled out West in group undertakings. Fredericksburg and New Braunfels, Texas, were settled by the Mainzer Adelsverein in the decade of the Texas Republic, while O'Neil, Nebraska, was the first of half a dozen Irish communities in that state alone.

Outside the cities, Germans did concentrate on farming more than did the Irish. In Wisconsin, and in Missouri from St. Louis west along the river until "Big Muddy" bent to the north, these enterprising people built their new farms and villages. Even today the marks of heavy German settlement in Wisconsin, Missouri, or Texas are unmistakable: farms with buildings as neat as a picture postcard, farm machinery aging gracefully with tender loving care. Those who came with families to the new country tended to settle at various German centers; even in the Great Plains, the mining regions, or the far western cities, they still sought out their own. Yet there were always the lone, unattached men, accepting the hardship of pioneer life; typically, their beginnings in America might consist of life in a one-room cabin, shared with five or six bachelors. Their basic food that first year might be a thick corn soup. Some precious musical instrument or some other memento of cultural Germany was meanwhile being warped, perhaps beyond salvage, by the rain that fell on it from the leaky roof of the barn. Floods and cholera added to the destitution of the German settlers in the Mississippi Valley.

In spite of their growing love for the new country, the Germans nevertheless tried desperately to retain their cultural heritage. In this they had the advantage of a language of their own. In addition they were very literate, and a goodly number of them were trained in the arts and professions. All over the West there were German *Liederkrantz* clubs and Schiller societies; in St. Louis a "shabbily dressed, bewhiskered, and demonic-looking" German emigrant named Henry C. Brokmeyer was a leader in establishing an influential Hegelian society which among other accomplishments, established the *Journal of Speculative Philosophy*.[13] *Turnverein*—societies combining gymnastics and physical fitness with liberal, even free-thinking ideals—flourished in most American cities. There were breweries bearing German names (though usually called "Dutch" by the Americans), and occasional mining engineers and metallurgists who had graduated from the School of Mines at Freiburg. There were numerous German-language newspapers. Yet the power of the predominant American culture was such that the Germans were overwhelmed, as were the other groups coming. Islands of German people still holding on today merely emphasize the blending of millions of others.

The German language; the challenge of German intellectualism, which was democratically inclined, politically active, and often hostile to established religion; the spread of radicalism by some German revolutionists who had escaped from the Germanies following the abortive uprisings of 1848, and the clash created by German customs, such as Sunday picnics or Sunday afternoon festivals in which good beer flowed copiously, brought on much of the Know-Nothingism of the 1850's. But this nativism does not appear to have been strong on the frontier, where there were many educated refugees of the 1848 revolutions who were commonly called "Latin farmers." Natives needed to be jealous only of their intellectual training, since most of these learned Germans made miserable farmers. In fact, most gave up tilling the soil and became schoolteachers, music instructors, or German-language newspaper editors. In Texas their log cabins had madonnas hanging on the walls, coffee was drunk out of tin cups placed on precious Dresden china saucers, and both the Germans and their native American neighbors could gather round for a songfest. Everywhere they settled, their failures were the subject of many a tall tale, but they constituted, as Carl Wittke has said, "a cultural leaven for the American frontier."[14]

There were also several attempts at German communal settlements, of which the best known in the Middle West was the one at New Ulm, Minnesota, established in the mid-1850's. At first the residents, all of them members of a *Settlement Society of the Socialist Turner League*, nearly starved, eking out their existence by eating their seed potatoes. Then in 1862, just as they had sent most of their fighting men off to the Civil War, the Minnesota Sioux went on the warpath. New Ulm was twice attacked, and the survivors were temporarily removed to safer areas 150 miles to the east. When hostilities ended they returned but, like most utopian communities in the United States, they soon abandoned their communal plans for the free enterprise system. Yet New Ulm is to this day an enlightened community enjoying an afterglow of Turner League liberalism. The public library, the public school system, and a

A diorama enacting the battle of New Ulm, showing not only the Indian massacre but also the neatly laid out houses of the German settlement. (Minnesota Historical Society)

tradition that the six-member school board will always consist of two free-thinkers, two Catholics, and two Protestants, all stem from the Turner League background.

Although canal and railroad construction employed an incredibly motley array of male humanity, German and Irish almost always predominated among the foreign laborers; these two nationalities were also to be found fighting Indians or doing guard duty—or sobering up in the guard house—with the frontier army. So, too, were members of both groups present in the mining camps of the West. It was a couple of Germans whom H. A. W. Tabor, a Vermont-born Yankee, grubstaked who made the first silver strike in Leadville, Colorado. It was a couple of Irishmen, Peter O'Riley and Patrick McLaughlin, who made the initial strike of the Comstock Lode in western Nevada. Adolph Sutro, the builder of the Sutro Tunnel under Mount Davidson near Virginia City, Nevada, was a German Jew. Adolph Coors founded a Colorado brewing dynasty.

In spite of their rapid Americanization, the Irish, like the Germans, attempted to retain their ethnic identity. For the Irish, concentration in the cities helped, but the mastic that most kept them together was the Catholic Church. A second cementing influence was a cherished love for oppressed Ireland, with commensurate hatred for Britain. When a Catholic father appeared on the prairies or in the mining camps they flocked to church, be it in an abandoned general store or in a barn, knelt before the improvised altar, listened to the chant of the priest as he said mass in Latin, and partook of the Sacrament. Up in Virginia City, Montana, as Christmas of 1865 approached, the Italian Jesuit Father Giorda, himself an emigrant with a most rudimentary command of the English language, searched unsuccessfully for a building in which to conduct mass. At one of the local saloons his plight was discussed, "and various of its customers, raising their glasses high, vowed to contact the forceful Irishman who was acting governor of Montana, General Thomas Francis Meagher." This energetic son of Erin raised enough gold to rent an already engaged local theater for two weeks. The gaudy pictures were removed, a cross erected over the entrance, and evergreens brought in as decorations. The midnight mass was so crowded that many persons knelt outside in the frigid air. Later a Delft plate was passed, complete with a spoon with which the miners could scoop out their gold dust of-

Mottagningshus.

A meeting house for Scandinavian immigrants provided by the Northern Pacific Railroad. (Minnesota Historical Society)

ferings from leather pouches. Father Giorda went on to establish the first urban church in Montana.[15]

The emigration of the Scandinavians was at its heaviest in the 1850's and 80's. They settled in Missouri, Illinois, Iowa, Michigan, Wisconsin, Minnesota, and across Dakota into Montana; many followed the Northern Pacific construction, working as laborers at $1.50 a day and saving enough from it to make a down payment on a parcel of land. The lone Swede, Dane, or Norwegian took his place on the railroad work gang alongside the Irishman, the "Dutchman," the Italian, the Yankee, the Southerner. He found the northern prairies cheap to buy, productive of crops, cold like northern Europe, but for the most part treeless. He was accustomed to town living and found the American custom, necessary because of the extent of the land, of living on one's own acres in an isolated soddy or wood frame farm house, difficult to adjust to, as attested by the novels of Ole Rölvaag.

To this day there are areas of almost total Swedish or Norwegian settlement in Minnesota and North Dakota. Danes and Finns added to the emigrant tide in the areas northwest of the Great Lakes. For the most part these peoples blended with the Yankees already there but retained their Lutheran faith, their tradition of hard work, love of the land, insistence upon education for their children, and loyalty to the new country. They were a law-abiding, moral folk who made good neighbors, intelligent and community-minded.

Just as the first-generation Irish never forgot the Emerald Isle, nor the Germans their *Vaterland*, neither did the Scandinavians forget their homelands. Yet their "American Letters"[16] for the most part are optimistic and American-centered, rather than breathing nostalgia about the old country. These letters shed much light on the thoughts the Scandinavians, and by implication other emigrant peoples also, had about the new country.

Their first reaction, after they had reached a geographical anchor (or if not a permanent one, then at least a "home" for a few months or a year), had to do with work. The American concept of work was different from that of the European tradition. One had to do three days' work in one day in America, the immigrants reported back. One could live without want in America, but one must work for it, as anywhere else in the world; only here the work was better rewarded. Deer were plentiful in the forests for hunting, but they were mostly hunted by the Indians, for others did not have time for such things. Here you were not asked what or who was your father, but what are you? The old and infirm should not come, but healthy young men, with families or in the single state, should come to America, for through hard work they would be

A Scandinavian family in front of their extended log cabin house. (State Historical Society of Wisconsin)

better off in a year than in a decade at home. Here, the immigrants said, there is no tax gatherer to take your earnings from you, no road laws to force you to give so many days a year in labor on their maintenance or construction. Here a healthy farm maid can earn ten dollars a month plus bed and board, and need do no outside labor. Here a hard-working man's reward is not only monetary; as soon as he is known as honest, sober, and dependable, he is just as much respected as anyone else. Just don't expect to find roast suckling pig on the table with knives and forks ready for you to start eating. It takes hard work to get ahead in America.

The lack of police and other manifestations of government and authority was a striking contrast to the old country situation. The only tax was a land tax, and, compared with old country taxation, it was negligible. The lack of police was justified by the absence of beggars and the rarity of theft in the farm communities where so many of the Scandinavians settled. (The American "tramp" or "hobo" was different from the European beggar.) People were good, kind, and accommodating; however, one could be swindled by sharpies.

A subject of continual concern in the new country was health. Asiatic cholera, malaria, typhus, diphtheria, smallpox, scarlet fever, pneumonia, tuberculosis, and blood poisoning—all these and many more caused early death. "If I only stay healthy," or words to that effect, are found all through the immigrants' letters. As long as he had his health, as long as he could sweep grain with a scythe, strike trees with an axe, work behind a plow, milk a cow, or build a fence, the future looked good. But if his health failed him, destitution faced the emigrant, and all his grandiose plans were shattered.

Land was a subject of equal interest. Its price and, more to the point, the amounts of money (in old world currencies) that would be necessary to purchase land, cows, pigs, chickens, seeds, etc., was mentioned over and over again. The beauties of the prairies, carpeted with colorful wildflowers, the soil so fertile it needed no manuring, the trees—or lack of them—the streams and springs, the heat of the summers, the cold of the winters, all of these characteristics were elaborated upon in the letters home.

There was some nostalgia, of course, a feeling common to all immigrants, most of it not for the native land but for the food and customs of the old country. Settlements where there were large groups of emigrants tried to continue these. The German and Scandinavian to-do over Christmas undoubtedly did much toward breaking down the austere Yankee tradition which, in its most extreme cases, even refused to acknowledge the validity of a Christmas celebration of any kind. Swedish and German pastries and tempting dishes added to the bland American diet.

Although the Scandinavians came into the new country in droves during the 1880's, it was clear to immigration officials and nativist alarmists that the "old migration," made up primarily of people from northwestern Europe and the British Isles, was coming to an end, and a "new migration" of southern and eastern European peoples was getting under way. By the time the waves of this migration were sweeping over America, the frontier had been declared at an end and the new country had become settled country.

There is, of course, much more in the American blend than the major groups discussed so far. The list of peoples who helped settle the new country is nearly equal to a list of the peoples of the world, and a discussion of them all is impossible. A few brief statements should be made, however, about the Jews, Italians, and Chinese.

Although the Jews have always been a minority group, their influence has been great. In 1820 there were probably about 4,000 of them in the United States. By 1850 there were probably 50,000 out of the total population of 23,000,000; but by 1860, following a decade of revolution, rebellion, and persecution in Europe, their numbers probably reached 150,000. Of the 2,000,000 immigrants in that decade, 3 to 5 per cent

were Jewish. Most of them were young men and women (for many
European states actually restricted the number of Jewish marriages); and
some of these young people headed west for the new country. They
were "an integral part of the great American tide that rose and flowed
west," writes Rufus Learsi, a historian of the Jews in America. "With remarkable speed they threw off the yoke which the ghettos of Europe
had laid upon their bodies and souls and joined in the American
adventure."[17]

Others of their race had come to the new country before them. In
1785 Abram Mordecai founded Montgomery, the capital of Alabama.
He lived for fifty years in the Creek nation, married a squaw, and was
convinced to his own satisfaction that the Indians were descended
from the Jews. In 1801 Georgia elected as its governor David Emanuel,
a Revolutionary War veteran, who was probably Jewish. In New
Orleans Jewish communal life began in the 1820's; prior to the Civil
War there were established Jewish congregations in Houston, Galveston, and San Antonio, Texas.

Cincinnati had its first Jewish organization, the Sons of Israel, in
1824; after receiving aid from their gentile neighbors, they erected the
first synagogue there. In St. Louis the Jews first worshiped as a group
in 1836. Others had been there before, but had intermarried with gentiles and left their faith. Up in Illinois the first Jewish pioneer was John
Hays, who served as county sheriff and collector of internal revenue before Illinois achieved statehood in 1818. Wisconsin had a congregation
in 1848, Michigan in 1850. On the Day of Atonement in 1849 there
were enough Jews in San Francisco to hold services in a tent; by 1860
that city had ten Jewish congregations; and there was another one at
Sacramento. Oregon had its first congregation in 1858, a year before
statehood. A number of Jews were prominent in early California and
Oregon politics. One of them, Adolph Sutro, is remembered not only
for the tunnel under Mount Davidson, which drained the mines of the
Comstock Lode, but also for his notable book collection, the nucleus of
the Sutro Library which still exists in the city by the Golden Gate.

In the great westward push the centripetal force of Jewish custom
and faith was retained when there were sufficient Jews present to form
and support a synagogue, or, on occasion, a loosely knit organization
which was a predecessor to a religious establishment. Where there were
several Jewish families there was the magnetism to draw still more.
These people, concerned with educational and community affairs, and
consciously, vigorously aware of American freedom compared with a
European intolerance that they knew only too well, became hard-
working citizens, defending American ideals.

Temple Emanu-El, a Jewish synagogue erected on Sutter Street in San Francisco in the 1860's but destroyed by the earthquake and fire, 1906. (California Historical Society, San Francisco)

Often there was not a number of Jewish families, however, nor even any women, but just a lone wanderer, far away from a "home" that had hardly been a place of peace. Such a single man was common in the new country. Sometimes he was a peddler; later on he was likely to be a drummer, working the emporiums along the main lines of the Northern Pacific, Union Pacific, or Santa Fe; sometimes he ran a general store or a saloon. For him there was the choice of bachelorhood or marriage to an available gentile girl. Often he left his faith, and his progeny blended into the American stream. Yet America was never completely free of intolerance and anti-Semitism. Out on the frontier it could be as volatile as anywhere else, bearing all the usual marks of racial prejudice and, like smoldering coals, contained a latent heat that could burst into the flame of persecution. "Jew Levy's Saloon" was a name for his establishment that Mr. Levy would have preferred to be cut from three words to two.

The Italians went west to the new country also. Some 20 per cent of the Italian immigrants ignored the teeming eastern centers. In the last third of the nineteenth century these adventurers signed on with a countryman called *patrone*—a sort of labor contractor—and worked on the western railroads or in the mines, or settled in little agricultural clusters here and there. As aggressive conquerors of the new country they lifted their heads higher than ever they had in Italy. They worked hard, and sang to the strains of flute and accordion when evening came on. From the mines or the railroads some of them drifted to other pursuits. One saw the need for decent food out West, and so Adolf Rossi became a restauranteur in Denver. Others who began by working the California mines—there was an "Italian Bar" just as there was a "Mexican Bar" and a "Mormon Bar"—saw the need for hostelries. "The ruins of stores and hotels run by Italians named Bruschi, Trabucco, Brunetti, Vignali, Noce Marre, and Ginochio still dot the Mother Lode country," writes Andrew Rolle. "In 1858 some three hundred lonesome [Italian] miners, loaded with gifts, walked nine miles to welcome the first Italian woman ever to travel into the California mines."[18]

Some became stonemasons or opened rock quarries. Still others sought out the land, for Italian farmers had a particular love for the good earth; they knew how to make it productive. Soon the West was dotted with Italian farms. When they discovered California, with its Mediterranean-type climate, the new Italian heaven on earth had indeed been located. The popularity of Del Monte brand foods attests to their success. Viniculture was begun, and by 1897 the production of wine was so great that one of the founders of California's Italian Swiss Agricultural Colony had a half-million-gallon wine reservoir cut out of solid rock; their wines are still sold.

Still other Italians found other occupations. There were priests, painters, singers, and there was opera. Domenico Ghiradelli's candies were early tidbits for the miners and their women. He began his chocolate factory in 1851; the site has now been turned into a shopping center. Two leading California bankers of the 1850's were Felix Argenti and Andrea Sbarboro, fitting predecessors to the twentieth-century California banking genius A. P. Giannini.

Another element in the new country, especially in the hard-rock mining areas of the Rocky Mountains, was the Cornish miners, with their wives and children. It is difficult to determine their numbers, for the census included them with the English, but they were numerous enough to have been given the identifying phrases "Cousin Jacks" and "Cousin Jennies," for, as A. L. Rowse has written, "When men were wanted for the mines, or a job was going, they always knew somebody at home for it: Cousin Jack. So they became known all over the world as 'Cousin Jacks'; 'Cousin Jennies' for the womenfolk seems to be a later addition."[19] Many of the men had worked in the tin mines of Cornwall, where they had mastered the techniques of sinking shafts into the earth. In Colorado and other parts of the West where hard-rock, or lode, mining was common, this knowledge made the Cornishmen welcome additions to the labor force. They were independent people, often contracting with the mine owner to work a given portion of a vein in return for a percentage of the profit.

The Cornish people were rugged, broad-chested, friendly, and individualistic. Though they were from the British Isles, their lingo readily identified them, for they misused pronouns and verb forms. When one of them was thrown from a horse, his explanation was: "Damme she I would ride she if it warn't for damme dinner pail." The women liked to dress up for special occasions in purple velvet dresses and big hats with yellow plumes, while the men wore loose-fitting suits and bowlers—a kind of stiff hat. They loved to sing and eat, and their yellow saffron cakes, made without eggs, were so typical that they were sometimes dubbed "saffron cake eaters." Protestant—usually Methodist—they clashed with fellow Tyrolese and Irish miners who were Catholic. For the most part, however, the Cornish people acculturated rapidly.[20]

There were, in addition, Rumanians, Russians, Poles, Greeks, Chinese, and Slavs who helped settle the new country. Some were from such remote places that they must have passed long periods of their life in America without seeing a compatriot or hearing their mother tongue. Yet they made their mark in the new country. In 1815 a young Serb arrived in Philadelphia, fresh from the disorders of southeastern Europe. He abandoned his Serbian name, Djordje Šagić, and began calling himself George Fisher. In his long and active career Fisher was a successful Mississippi planter, a customs agent for Mexico, an active Mason, an intriguer with Joel Poinsett, the American minister to Mexico, in behalf of the federalist faction there, an internationally active political journalist, an early justice of the peace and alderman of Houston, Texas, and a close friend of Stephen Austin. Later Fisher was in Panama, where he met the archeologist John Lloyd Stephens; from there he moved to California, where he became Secretary to the California Land Commission. In time he gave his papers to several Texas depositories. He ended his days as an honored citizen of San Francisco, the founder of a Pan-Slavic society, and the Greek Consul in that city. Fisher was of course atypical, and yet he merely represented in his own life the potential destiny of every man who came to the new country.

The more alien their culture, the greater their difficulties. Yet the emigrants still came. The magnetism of quick riches, adventure, a better life pulled even non-Caucasians to American shores. In the balance, they probably fared better in the new country than they would have in their homelands, where famine, political turmoil, and heartless landlords made life a constant struggle for survival.

At some time during the decade of the 1850's San Francisco had thirty-six newspapers, published in French, German, Spanish, Jewish, Italian, and Chinese. Just as the Chinese papers were most intriguing to the other settlers because of their Chinese characters, so did the Chinese themselves seem more exotic than all the other nationalities put together. Ranging from 25,000 in the mid 1850's to more than 50,000 in the 1860's, they added charm, mystery, and some turmoil to the unstable population of the new State of California. By the 1870's they were spreading to the Rockies, to the industrial East where they were occasionally used as scab labor, and even to the South for railroad construction and gang labor on cotton and sugar plantations. The hostility and occasional violence they suffered was only partly because of their race; some of it was due to the conditions under which they came to America. For the Chinese came only as sojourners; they planned to return to China.

The area of the Celestial Empire (the source of a common name for them, Celestials) from which most came was the Pearl River Delta. This is that hilly, humid country with bays and inlets, harbors and teeming cities in southeast China. Canton is its hub, but Hong Kong and Macao are also a part of it. For many decades prior to the California gold rush thousands of Chinese, unable to maintain their hallowed family ties under the unstable conditions in the Delta, had set sail for Malaya, Siam, Burma, Indochina, even Borneo and the Philippines. They went under a credit-ticket system whereby they obtained passage from merchants who were either reimbursed by the family or by future employers in those countries. The Chinese in effect went as indentured servants, but often ended as virtual slaves in permanent debt bondage. Their families or their wives and daughters constituted their collateral, the guarantee that they would not renege on their contracts.

Into the mines and plantations of the humid lands stretching like a great fan southeast to southwest of the Pearl River Delta the Chinese went, not as emigrants but as sojourners. If they succeeded in paying off their debt, then they remained as employees, sending money home and saving a little, dreaming of a final return with sufficient savings to live out the remainder of their lives with the comforts of a concubine and the respect granted an elder in the extended Chinese family.

When news about Mei Kwok (beautiful land) or Gum San (land of the golden mountains) reached the Pearl River Delta, a new area was opened to the indentured-servant contract-labor system. The first Chinese in California are believed to have arrived on the brig *Eagle* from Hong Kong in February 1848: two men and a woman. The numbers increased with surprising rapidity. Concentrated in San Francisco and

the mines of the Mother Lode, they constituted as much as one-tenth
of the population of California. As historian Gunther Barth has pointed
out, most Chinese came on the credit-ticket system, whereby Chinese
businessmen in San Francisco or Hong Kong paid the expenses of the
traders—a matter of forty to sixty dollars—and retained the emigrants
under their control until the debt (which was usually run up to about
$200) was paid. In California the Chinese worked for Chinese entrepre-
neurs or else their lien was sold to other employers. As with the sojourners in southeast Asia, kinship furnished an extra-legal control over the
Chinese emigrant. "During their sojourn," writes Barth, "the majority of
the emigrants never left the narrow confines of the Chinese world
which demanded their allegiance from the moment they turned their
back on their villages."[21]

Typically the Chinese landed from an American ship which had taken
two months or more to make the journey if by sail, a month or more if
by steam. They were led to a crowded dormitory until the conditions of
their future labor were settled. Then, if they were going to the Mother
Lode country, they sailed up the Sacramento or San Joaquin river and
debarked at Sacramento, Stockton, Marysville, or some other streamside
settlement. Carrying a roll of bedding and a basket containing clothing
and private belongings, they debarked under the watchful eyes of agents
of the Chinese creditors. Eventually, under the control of a Chinese
or an American headman, they reached their destination. In gangs
typically of ten to thirty the Chinese usually took over an abandoned
placer. Here they were employed in reworking the abandoned diggings,
using rockers and long toms. For housing they occupied crowded tents,
brush huts, or deserted miner's cabins where twenty could sleep in space
two white men had considered crowded. (Once $3,000 in gold dust was
collected from the dirt floor of such a cabin—dust that had accumulated
in the course of the previous miner's activities.)

Americans got used to the sight of gangs of Chinese dressed in wide-
bottomed, blackish trousers, a loose blouse of the same material, and in
cold weather, a sleeveless, quilted coat. They also wore a wide umbrella-
shaped hat made of split bamboo or grass. In addition, they often carried baskets with the aid of a pole set across their shoulders. All would
have shaven heads and queues—long braids sometimes reaching to the
knees, of which they were very possessive. Nearby would be a Chinese
store that sold the fish, rice, and tea they consumed, the clothing they
wore, and anything else they might need.

This is what the Americans in the mining districts observed. They
were not aware of the evils of Chinese debt bondage. They did not know
that perhaps 97 per cent of the Chinese were under the control of the Six

Placer mining in California in early 1850's, including Chinese miners. (Wells Fargo Bank, History Room, San Francisco)

Companies, as they came to be called—six companies of Chinese entrepreneurs in San Francisco who exerted total control over the debt-ridden sojourners. What most Americans did dislike was the sight of several dozen Chinese being herded and worked like beasts. This violated concepts of democracy, muddied the California dream of a great western center of free men, and savored of the evils of black slavery in the American South.

Yet many a Yankee entrepreneur saw nothing wrong with contracting for gangs of Chinese laborers. The builders of the Central Pacific Railroad sent recruiters to the mountain districts of the Pearl River Delta country who paid for outfit and passage and exacted from each Chinese a promissory note for $75 in United States gold coin, secured by the endorsement of friends or relatives. Repayment was to be by installments, with payment completed within seven months after the laborer began working on the railroad. Between nine and ten thousand Chinese were brought in for work on the Central Pacific. They were especially used as "gandy dancers" (a gandy was an iron bar used to tamp ballast under

A festival in San Francisco's Chinatown prior to 1890. (California Historical Society, San Francisco)

ties), but they also cleared sagebrush, dug tunnels, and, after the line was built, stayed on as maintenance men.

City dwellers observed the Chinese in Chinatown. Here they were concentrated in quarters that reeked with filth, vice, and disease, much of which was not noticed by the nineteenth-century tourist, who only saw the veneer—merchants dressed in exotic silks, a plethora of strange oriental goods for sale, or perhaps a Chinese holiday celebration. But beneath the surface was prostitution—for Chinese girls were imported under a bondage system as vicious as that of the men—extensive gambling, and opium dens. There were also secret societies, the Tongs, which carried on warfare for control of vice and thus added to the bad reputation of Chinatown. The fact that white men became frequenters of the opium dens, gambling houses, and brothels there further enhanced the opinions of reformers that Chinatown must go.

Although the Chinese were liable to persecution and mob violence at any time, the periods of greatest distress were during depressions, such as in the mid-1850's, when mining was in the doldrums and many unemployed white miners drifted to San Francisco, and in the 1870's, another depressed period. Demagogues such as Denis Kearney campaigned for an end to Chinese emigration and competition, and in 1882 Congress passed the Chinese Exclusion Act.

By that time, however, the Chinese, still under the contract-ticket system, had spread throughout the West, and even into the South and East. In Colorado they worked the abandoned placers as they had in California, and when they had time off they flocked to Denver's Chinatown—Hop Alley—on Wazee Street. There they could eat Chinese rice, tea, and fish for twenty cents a day, purchase Chinese clothing, and dream away their troubles in one of that city's seventeen opium dens (as of 1880), twelve of which were concentrated in Hop Alley. But troubles arose, and a mob burned Hop Alley in October 1880. It was never rebuilt.

Gradually some Chinese abandoned their intention to return to China. They paid off their indebtedness and found themselves independent in a white man's land. There were legitimate occupations open to them: they hired out as domestics, became fishermen, freighters, wood choppers, gardeners, and railroad maintenance workers; they went into business for themselves as restauranteurs and laundrymen, or maintained Chinatown retail stores selling silk and fans to miners for their hard-working mining-country wives. Some Celestials found Chinese wives or married emigrant girls of Irish or German origin; many lived out lonely lives as bachelors.

Most especially the Chinese became laundrymen. Whereas whites had charged up to twenty dollars for a dozen items, the Chinese would charge just a tenth of that—two dollars. The washhouse was usually a shack in the back of which John Chinaman (as he was often dubbed) did the washing; he dried his laundry on the roof and then did his ironing up front where the public could watch him. Making use of his Chinese iron, which was kept hot by an iron saucepan in which burned a charcoal fire, the Chinese washee man ironed: "With his mouth filled with water from a mug nearby and the saucepan in hand, the laundryman would seize a garment, commence to eject a water spray from his mouth over the garment and with his iron would press whatever he had dampened."[22] The quality of his work was undisputed.

Many Chinese never abandoned the dream of returning to China with riches, and more than a few did return with modest sums of two or three hundred dollars—substantial wealth by Chinese standards.

Others contracted with certain Chinese concerns which, upon death of the subscriber, had his bones dipped in brandy, polished brightly, packed carefully, and shipped back home for burial.

Yet for still more Chinese, the commitment to America was permanent. Persecuted to the extent that they never knew whether their entrance into a new country community would result in a welcome or a beating, they still, like other ethnic groups in the new country, eventually became a part of an alien land.

The people who settled the new country did not all share in a covered-wagon migration; in fact, most of them did not. They landed at New Orleans, San Diego, Monterey, San Francisco, Portland, or Seattle and came across the land on a railroad train. But whatever their past, whatever their race or nationality, however exotic their dress, customs, and language, they had thrown in their lot with the new country. Here was their new home. Here, in the face of *some* prejudice, *some* hostility, and *some* hardship, was an attainable goal. With a little luck and a lot of hard work, a man could rise to the limit of his abilities; and he could sense this, breathe it in the air. Here one's past was irrelevant, his future was exciting in its promise.

The emigrant's life was initially simple. In the nineteenth century a substantial amount of all the work done could be accomplished by a muscular male in good health. This included not only virtually everything on the farm save tanning and blacksmithing, but also the skills by which men earned their livings in town. Even the work of a railroad trainman, telegrapher, blacksmith, tanner, miller, miner, local butcher, itinerant printer, sign painter, or general storekeeper could be mastered by most men in a short period of time. This is why many a man who rose to prominence in the nineteenth century listed so many callings in his checkered career. Even reading law or learning medicine involved only a few months of formal training.

Phrases and mottoes suffer from overuse and lose their effect, but "the land of opportunity" was a beautiful phrase because of its validity. Because America needed the services, devices, symbols, institutions, and professions that would make it a settled country, it presented a challenge to ambitious men such as the world had seldom if ever before offered. So numerous were the possibilities that some men never really mastered one and remained jacks of all trades their lives through. So great was the country geographically that many a restless itinerant wandered constantly, east to west, north to south. Known as bums, tramps, or hoboes, these drifting men were so numerous that they became a cause for concern after the Civil War; crimes of all kinds were attributed to them.

Those men most likely to succeed were the family men, who encouraged, persuaded, threatened, cajoled, pleaded, or forced their wives and children to pull up stakes and come with them to the new country. Especially on a farm, but in young cities and towns also, the family was a protective enclave; sons worked to further the family fortune, and all united as an island of peace and strength. In spite of fiction, memoirs, and biographies which portray a tyrannical, if not sadistic, patriarch, European travelers were so struck by the warmth, love, and tenderness in typical American families that they mentioned it again and again. Moreover, because the family usually succeeded, and because the work was so hard and the accomplishment so real, there was apparently a minimum of psychological trouble. And in vast areas of the Middle and the Far West, there was much less crime than has been pictured since in the entertainment media. Men were too busy, opportunity too widespread for all who would engage in honest endeavor to earn respect. Of course, not all succeeded. Some did turn to crime; there was considerable alcoholism; and whole families that failed.

The geologist Clarence King once camped in the western foothills of California's Sierras, near a family of pig farmers, the Newtys, Pike County folk. This term originally applied to people from Pike County, Missouri, but came to be used loosely for people from the general areas of Arkansas, Missouri, and northeast Texas, who were crude and illiterate Anglo-Saxons. So it was with the Newtys. King found them all in a disheveled old bed, their big, bare feet to the fire, pa on one side of the bed, ma at the other, the children all sleeping in a mass between them, and the stars for their roof. The oldest daughter was waving a bare, size-eleven foot in front of the fire as she tried to hide the bright flames from her eyes. The sole property of the family was a herd of three thousand pigs.

Fascinated by such a family, King determined to get their story. "It was," he wrote, "one of those histories common enough through this wide West, yet never failing to startle me with its horrible lesson of social disintegration, of human retrograde." Most people aimed at betterment as they headed into the new country, but for some, he said, the westward push "degenerates into mere weak-minded restlessness, killing the power of growth, the ideal of home, the faculty of repose; it results in that race of perpetual emigrants who roam as dreary waifs over the West, losing possessions, love of life, love of God. . . . The Newtys were of this dreary brotherhood." They had left Pike County in 1850 and gone to Oregon. From there they had drifted southward with their pigs to California, and when King saw them, Mr. Newty was contemplating a migration to Montana.

Mr. Newty would have liked to have seen gangling Susan, his eldest daughter, married and no longer supping at the family mess. Would King be interested? "Thet—thet—thet man what gits Susan *has half the hogs!*" he assured the brilliant young geologist. But King was not.[23]

They were, indeed, of all kinds, these people of the new country. But most of them—Serb or Chinese, Irish or Scotch, German or Swede, old-line Yankee or impetuous Southerner—were happy, hard-working, God-fearing, law-abiding, and initially, at least, egalitarian.

III

Agriculture:
The Basic Endeavor

Farming the
Appalachian Plateau

Actually a very small percentage of American frontiersmen ever faced the realities of Indian warfare; slightly more lived through an Indian scare or two but never actually saw an Indian painted for battle or fired a shot at one. The great majority of people moving into the new country went as part of a deluge of migration *after* the Indians had been defeated and, by forced treaty, had been summarily removed. Even for those who did forge ahead into Indian lands, the period of guerrilla warfare rarely lasted more than a decade.

Most of the frontier was empty as far as human life went—a splendid temperate-zone wilderness awaiting the assault of the white man. Sickness, accidents, and old age were what took the toll of the frontier people. For most of them, "Injun stories" were for telling around the hearth on frosty autumn nights.

The cutting edge of the frontier has been stressed altogether too much by novelists and most American historians. It was romantic and adventurous out there beyond law and order, beyond the school and the church, but it was not the real new country people spoke of. The real new country was the area behind the cutting edge, cleared of Indians and awaiting the settlers. It was this vacuum into which the newcomers swept like a wave, cutting, slashing, and burning the forest, grubbing out the stumps, erecting cabins, worm fences, and, at the crossroads or the ford of a river, stores, smithys, schools, and churches. Within five years of the initial settlement, cabins were in the minority and brick or clapboard houses, some two stories high, were preponderant.

Thus the land itself was domesticated, occupied, changed. It was trod over and plowed and cultivated and its crops were harvested. The system of land survey checkerboarded it, provided for crossroads every six miles, and invited the growth of towns every twelve to twenty miles—the distance a horse-drawn vehicle could traverse in three or four hours. A start right after chores and breakfast on Saturday morning brought the farmer to town by ten o'clock; the shopping could be done, a packed lunch consumed, a couple of drinks belted down at a saloon, and the family would be homeward bound, arriving at sundown in time to do the evening chores and still have lamps snuffed out by eight or nine o'clock. This pattern was in contrast to other parts of the world, where people all lived in villages and trekked out to their fields by dawn, returning by the setting sun.

The farmer's acquisition of land was an essentially simple matter. A residue in the original colonies of feudal obligations, holdovers from European customs, had never worked well in America and was washed away completely by the Revolution. Primogeniture (the exclusive right of inheritance of the first-born son), entail (restriction of inheritance to a certain class of descendants), and quitrent (the discharge of a feudal obligation by the payment of a fixed rent), all ceased to exist in the new states between 1776 and 1800. As Judge Richard Henderson discovered when he tried to levy a quitrent of two shillings per hundred acres upon the Kentuckians, feudal dues and obligations were quite impossible to collect or enforce. The consensus of the new country people was that the land lay there for whoever would take it, defend it, and improve it. Since fully nine-tenths of all Americans were agriculturalists in 1776— and even in 1910, twenty years after the close of the frontier, more than 54 per cent lived in towns of 2,500 or less—this "sense of the people" carried weight. So they came to the new country and took up the land.

They came, however, from a civilized area and carried with them into the virgin land the knowledge of farming acquired through generations. Crude as their beginnings were, most new country folk were advanced far beyond the Indian with his tiny patch in the woods and were armed with better tools.

No farmer, not even a prairie or, farther west, a Great Plains farmer, ever went far without an axe. It was his most basic tool, the sine qua non of his existence. He needed it to hew out the clearing, to cut the logs for his cabin, the rails for his fences, and the first crude pieces of furniture, and to make the rudimentary beginnings of the moldboard on his plow. While the rifle gave him protection and fresh meat, the axe gave him his farm.

Both these tools underwent many changes as the pioneers gradually adapted them to the needs of the new country. The European axe of the seventeenth and eighteenth centuries was light, weighing about three pounds, and thin, not only at the bit (the cutting edge) but at the poll (the other end). The bit was about eight inches long, looking rather like the headsman's axe seen in gory old prints. The handle of this axe was simply a straight round pole attached at the extreme poll end. Such a light axe, swung with a vengeance at an oak or a sycamore, wobbled as it moved through the air, and its incision into the hardwood was shallow. It would be a long, sweaty task to down these common American trees with such an impractical instrument.

The frontiersmen in America began to experiment, and by about 1740, according to Richard G. Lillard, an "American axe" had developed in the colonies. The poll had been widened, so that it was considerably heavier than the narrow bit; a side benefit was the usefulness of the poll as a pounding tool. The bit remained broad, but the old crescent shape gave way to a blade considerably straighter. The handle was set into the head an inch or two forward of the pounding edge, achieving a better balance. The head now weighed close to seven pounds, and when it struck a tree the wood chips flew.

The handle changed too, for it was the component which, in the hands of an expert, almost became an extension of the man. Nearly every pioneer community had a craftsman whose specialty was the axe handle. He designed it especially for the user, balanced it perfectly, and fitted the grip to the customer's hands. If the purchaser was satisfied, he was very proud of it, and as touchy about its use by others as a golfer is about a favorite putting iron or a baseball player about a favorite bat. By mid-nineteenth century the hickory handle had become gracefully curved, so tremulous in the delicacy of its balance that it seemed almost fragile. What an experienced woodsman could accomplish with such a handle attached to a well-honed broadaxe was simply incredible. Even before the final perfection of the curved hickory handle, observers were amazed at the skill and progress of the axeman. Benjamin Franklin once timed two axemen from first whack to "TIMBER!" on a pine tree fourteen inches in diameter: six minutes.

Of equal importance in the new country was the rifle. It is nearly impossible to envision the pioneer going west without a Kentucky or Pennsylvania rifle or, in later decades, without a coveted Henry's, Sharp's, Smith and Wesson, or Winchester; a Colt revolver likewise equalized a man's status. Certainly most of the European emigrants arrived in the new country without these arms; and in fact, in much of new country America, where settlement was surrounded by a large area devoid of human habitation, where the Indian had been driven out and the white man was just coming in, the actual need of firearms for defense is open to question. Yet we may also assume that a fowling piece (ancestor of the shotgun), a rifle, or more rarely a pistol—was one of the first purchases of emigrants in the new country. Hunting meant sport as well as

Broadaxes used in farm work and in turpentining operations. The extremely wide axes were used for stripping bark from or squaring the logs.

A mallet or froe-club and a froe. The long metal piece was placed across a piece of wood and the club used to pound it in, thus splitting the wood to make shingles or shakes. It served much the same purpose as an adze.

(Photos by author from collection at Tallahassee Junior Museum)

food in an area where there were relatively few amusements. Furthermore, there were still such varmints about as coyotes, wolves, bobcats,
and painters (mountain lions), and, if the presence of Indians and ban-
dits has been overemphasized, there were always tramps who had to be
chased off down the lane. Occasionally a warm-blooded daughter was
wed to a new country swain with the aid of a shotgun in her angered
father's hands. Thus was the tradition of firearms ownership established;
its afterglow remains in the heated debate over firearms in mid-twentieth-
century America.

There were some other tools that the early farmer would almost certainly carry along to his new homesite. He would have a mattock, often
called a grubbing hoe, still widely used. Typically (for it has not changed
much), it has two blades, one for digging or grubbing out roots, stones,
etc., and one for cutting or hacking. It did a good job and was often
used in the laborious process of removing stumps. Somewhat similar to
the mattock, with a handle about the same length of 36 to 40 inches,
was the adze. It was (and is) a cutting instrument, the blade set at right
angles to the handle. The adze was used for squaring logs, smoothing
puncheon floors, and for a variety of other purposes involving wood. Later
emigrants into the Middle West and Far West had regular hoes, spades,
and hand rakes along, three basic instruments that were considered important enough to occupy a safe place in the wagon bed or be securely
attached to the outside.

Examples of the crude agricultural tools used in the 1790's. (Secretary of Agriculture,
The National Archives)

Add a sheath knife, a wedge, a mallet, homespun clothing—or, in the earlier era, the deerskin hunting shirt, leggins, and moccasins; add some seeds of corn, squash, pumpkins, beans, and gourds in the early years, furniture in the later years, and a Bible; include some pigs and chickens, a cow or a yoke of oxen, a horse, the family dog or dogs and cat, and the pioneer had all the truck he needed in the new country.

When we consider the brevity of the frontier period along the Appalachian plateau, the emphasis that several generations of American historians have placed upon the backwoods system practiced there appears excessive. In terms of accomplishment, clearing and planting a field of two or three acres was all that was humanly possible there, whereas the new country man in Ohio, Indiana, Illinois, and Iowa, or in western Georgia, Alabama, or Mississippi certainly thought in terms of an initial clearing of twenty, thirty, or forty acres. When the plains of Dakota, Nebraska, Kansas, and Texas were reached, some six to eight decades later than the early period of the Appalachian plateau, the initial clearing could consist of a quarter section of 160 acres without causing undue comment.

Perhaps historians detail those little Kentucky and Tennessee settlements because they were the first; or possibly because so many of the romantic aspects of new country existence were concentrated there. Certainly Theodore Roosevelt concentrated on that area in his *Winning of the West*; and so did Lyman Draper in his great collection of western records.[1] But a far better explanation seems to be that, however much they were altered by time and distance, the farmer's basic problems of settlement remained essentially the same: choice and purchase of land, clearing of timber and brush followed by breaking the primeval sod, and thus the domesticating, we might say, of the very earth itself. Then there was the construction of a habitation and the building of fences, followed by an increase in farm size, the problems caused by both man and nature inherent in horticultural pursuits, and the necessity of feeding the family while crops were growing or in time of adversity brought on by drought, grasshopper invasion, or blight. These were universal problems, and though climate, distance, and the change in area altered them somewhat, they remained basically the same.

In those first few months, usually late spring and summer, life was certainly basic. If he settled in timber, the farmer might build only a crude lean-to, completely open on one side, probably facing south. In front of it was the fire, with pots and pans hanging over it, suspended by hooks from a rustic frame or tripod, with more truck piled close by and clothing, powderhorn, and rifle hung on nearby trees. Sometimes the lean-to was nothing more than a brush shelter; at other times and places it was made of small logs and could be used to shelter animals after the humans had abandoned it. The father was invariably a hunter, so some venison, squirrel, turkey, or duck was available. Probably chickens or pigs, taken along from "back East," could be killed occasionally for food. As for corn, salt, beans, and so forth, the family depended on a supply carried along or borrowed from neighbors, until a first crop was gathered in.

Before the farmer could erect a more elaborate dwelling, he had to make the beginnings of a field. The trans-Appalachian frontiersman determined the boundaries for an enclosure of perhaps three to five acres. (A convenient frame of reference for visualizing acres is this: a typical city block is considered to contain about six and four-tenths acres.) With his axe he then slashed a circular strip of bark from the trees— "girdled" them, as the saying went, to kill them. In a few weeks or months the leaves fell, leaving gaunt tree limbs and branches through which the sun could sift through to the ground.

The pioneer knew that corn, squash, and beans could grow in just such a "deadening." With axe and grubbing hoe he cleared his small patch of brush and weeds. He planted corn Indian style, by hand, covering it with the aid of the mattock, and leaving it in a small earthen mound. It was the most certain of all crops to grow the first season, planted along with a few beans and squash, thus giving the family corn meal, hominy, and johnnycake, as well as corn on the cob. It gave his pigs, rooting out in the forest, something sufficiently delectable to attract them to the homestead feeding lot every day. And if he could find the time, some good corn carried to a neighboring distillery resulted in a barrel of fiery liquid that could warm a man's innards on a cold day or relax his tired muscles after long hours of hard labor.

At this stage the pioneer was but a subsistence farmer; possibly not quite even that. But each day was satisfying to him because he made a little more progress in the creation, by his own hands, of his new country domain. He could envision the results of the fields he had created from the forest: the crops he had grown, the orchard that arose so slowly those first few years. The time would come—that great day— when he could sit under his own apple or peach tree. If he lived to an old age and his sons and daughters became stalwart citizens, then indeed he would sit there in contentment in his old age. By this time his farm would consist of 50 to 400 acres.

By the time the first corn had ripened the deadened trees were crackling dry. They were not easier to chop down, and if he did not hanker after such sweaty toil, he might set fire to them and trust that the green timber outside his clearing could withstand the heat. There were times in the new country when the full circle of the horizon was dotted with black clouds of smoke wafting upwards from where farmers were clearing the forest. Assuming he did not start a forest holocaust, the farmer's deadening would soon be a scene of blackened desolation, a sore on the face of the green wilderness. Now, with his yoke of oxen and chain, his axe and mattock, he still had to grub out those stumps. He might haul the wood away on a wooden sledge pulled by oxen; in New England these were called "stone boats." Or he might choose to leave the stumps, for nature would rot all but the hardest woods in a few years, and in the meantime corn and other crops could be raised amongst them. Meanwhile his wife, as well as the nip in the air and the V's of ducks winging south, reminded him that a better dwelling than that miserable lean-to was needed. The time had come to raise the cabin.

Understand we are generalizing here. Sometimes there was no lean-to stage; the pioneer lived in his wagon or slept in the open while he built his cabin. Or neighbors came from the surrounding area, often part of a river valley, and helped in a "cabin raising." If the pioneer was out on the cutting edge, he would have to do all the work himself, with the aid of his sons. The point is that a log cabin could be built by a solitary man, but he usually did have some family or neighborhood help. Above all, it should be realized that all the materials were available within fifteen minutes' walk of the site he had chosen, and the entire cabin could, if necessary, be constructed with just one axe.

The initial dwelling was often set four-square with the points of the compass; it might face south, or east, or overlook a river valley, or be hidden in the forest. It would be very small, roughly fifteen by eighteen or sixteen by twenty feet. If plans included a slab floor, then at the four corners would be foundation logs set upright with their smoothed tops just inches above the level of the smoothed earth (which had been purposely so prepared). Upon these the mudsills, or base logs, would be placed. Cinder blocks or concrete pilings serve much the same purpose today. If the cabin were crude, however, pounded earth constituted the floor, and the mudsills were simply placed flat on the ground.

But before the raising, the farmer quite likely had taken a number of preliminary steps. In the course of slashing and burning or otherwise clearing his field, he had kept an eye out for logs of the correct circumference, length, and kind, for there was an unwritten but well-established understanding that all the logs should be of the same kind of wood. He wanted about eighty logs, twenty per side; half of them, say, fifteen feet, half twenty feet long. In New England and the upper Ohio Valley, his logs, preferably of white pine, might be ten to twelve inches wide, and he would need only about fifty of them. These prime building logs he had chained and snaked along the forest floor, pulled by his horse or oxen, to the site of his proposed abode, arranged them in two groups, and cut them to an approximate consistent size. He would have stripped them of limbs and knots, but would probably have left the bark on, for it protected the wood from dampness and decay. In addition, with his froe he had split some prime logs and broken the slabs into pieces for the shakes, or shingles for the roof. (This was not absolutely necessary; sod or branches and logs would do if the froe was missing or the time was short.) He would also have available a number of timbers graded into smaller lengths; these were placed at the top of the walls at each end, pyramiding to a high point upon which was laid the central ridge pole. Similar poles were placed in succession down the pyramid or triangle to the eaves, and upon these the shakes were placed, to be anchored snugly by other poles placed on top of them and held down by heavy stones.

With no blueprints or instructions but plenty of woods know-how, the erection of the dwelling got under way. If it was a neighborly raising, an expert notcher was stationed at each corner who, with his trained eye and dexterity with an axe, notched the logs just so. The logs were hoisted ever higher until about twenty, one above the other, had been raised on each of the four sides. (Actually, some more sophisticated chopping took place on one side, where a doorway thirty-six to forty inches wide and five and a half or six feet high had been provided, as well as a window eighteen or twenty-four inches square, though sometimes just a loophole or two sufficed.) On one side space was cut in the wall for the fireplace, which in Appalachia took up almost the entire back wall. Most neighborhoods could boast someone known for his skill in making this vital element. The fireplace and chimney, made of mud mixed with sticks, straw, or hog bristles as a mastic, was molded into shape; with luck it would be completed at about the same time the final roof timbers were laid on. All the while others, including the children, were "caulking"—daubing clay, moss, mud mixed with animal hair or straw, even stones and wood chips, between the logs, hoping thereby to keep out the cold winds and drifting snows of winter. Finally a slab door with an inside wooden latch and crossbar was added; its hinges were of wood or tough animal hide. A leather thong was attached to the latch and threaded through a small hole in the door, so that the end hung outside. All one had to do to enter was pull the latchstring, and the door would open, usually outward. "The latchstring," so the saying went, "is always out"—a mark of welcome, an invitation to come in and be sociable for awhile. As for the window, a primitive cabin would have a slab covering that could be slid over it, shutters, a piece of thin deer-

A Mormon family in the Great Salt Lake Valley in front of their log cabin. (De-Golyer Library, Dallas)

skin, or an old newspaper dipped in bear grease to stretch across it, letting in light but keeping out some of the cold and helping maintain privacy.

If there were neighbors to help, the entire cabin took no more than a day or two to build; and even if it was all done by a man and his twelve-year-old son, it was a matter of only a few weeks, with the work done between hunting, planting, and other chores. It was a dwelling that could last out the builder's lifetime, be made snug in winter, and, with its thick log walls, be relatively comfortable in summer. Suitably caulked and roofed, it was dry and comfortable. Unbeknownst to its builders, the mathematical principles behind log cabin structure, with each log held in place by its own weight, supported by the log below and reinforced by the log above, represented an excellent system of construction.

Proudly the pioneer farmer entered his new home. If he had ante-cedents within his memory of homes in Scotland or Ireland, or the peasant hovels of the English countryside, he felt that he had advanced considerably toward affluence. Here was a home with a fireplace rather than a hole in the roof, made of wood logs, something already rare and precious in the old country, and which was *his*. Even if his memory was restricted to the American experience—and until 1840 we can assume that he probably was native born—it still represented a step up the lad-der to success. The fire sent out a warmth that enveloped the small room, rather than being lost to the elements like the one in front of the lean-to, and the chimney drew well. Wooden pegs held the rifle, powder horn, and clothing. His wife could store seeds in gourds that hung by cords from the roof. She had some cherished petunia, morning glory, or nas-turtium seeds from back home which she could plant in the dooryard alongside the log walls. The wind whistled about the new dwelling, moaning as if it had not known the cabin was there and had run into it and hurt itself. The wolves howled as usual, but the fear was less than it had been when they had slept in the lean-to. The children sat on the dirt floor and gazed at the flames; the husband sat on a stump he had dug out, smoothed over, and brought inside to use as a chair, and puffed on his pipe; the wife, having arranged the kettles properly on the hooks, sat with the children and knitted.

Their bed, that night or soon thereafter, would be attached to two sides and a corner of the cabin, with just one leg resting on the floor. The mattress might crackle from dried corn husks or straw, or it might be full of feathers. Eventually the children would have beds, also, but for now they slept by the hearth; their youthful suppleness, combined with fatigue after an active day, led them to accept such primitive bed-ding without a second thought or a physical protest.

A wooden floor would come next if it had not been laid at first. The typical kind to begin with was a puncheon floor, made of split logs laid rounded half down, so that the floor had at least a semblance of smooth-ness. Another kind of floor consisted of dowels an inch and a half to two or three inches in diameter, pounded into the earth so that they felt fairly even to walk on. If there was a slate or stone quarry nearby that produced flagstones, these could be laid out on the bare ground and made a better floor. Wild animal skins could be used as rugs or stretched over particularly drafty places on the walls.

Later, when more children came, the wife would want her husband to construct a loft covering a third to a half of the upper space of the cabin, with a permanent ladder or pegs in the cabin wall leading to it. There was no "outhouse" or privy at this early time. The nearby woods offered privacy for the women, and the men tended to "let water" just about as freely and promiscuously as the farm animals. Yet as soon as shelter and sustenance were reasonably secure, the privy was built.

When the cock crowed at dawn the farmer rose from his bed, and his wife cooked some pork and made some cornmeal mush. His planted field was only three to five acres; but he had probably already extended the deadening and anticipated ten or fifteen acres of cleared land as a realistic goal within a short time. But for now he and his son went out to the deadening and chose logs for splitting. Deer, as well as his own oxen, had invaded his small field and he needed some kind of fencing to keep them out. Here the rail-splitter tradition of the vast trans-Appalachian frontier began, for wood was the logical fencing material where trees were in abundance. The farmer probably constructed a Virginia worm fence which zig-zagged its way down the four fringes of his field. He also made small corrals with his rails and erected rough timber shelters, covered with straw or sod, in which the livestock could get some protection from the elements. As time went on, he built corn cribs, a smokehouse, perhaps a root cellar, and, finally contemplated building a barn.

How long had he been there by then? Quite possibly not more than three to five years, so rapidly did the new country change, so fast did the pioneer's wealth, in terms of his physical "plant," accumulate. In his second year, with eight or ten acres cleared for cultivation, the farmer planted fully half his field with wheat. Almost certainly this area included all of the first year's field, for wheat did not do well on virgin soil. The remainder he had put to corn and vegetables. And at the harvest, he took another step towards affluence: he sold his wheat for cash. Thus from a purely subsistence enterprise, he had already risen to a state in which he possessed a marketable surplus. Moreover, there was a market for it. There were years between 1800 and 1850 when it looked as if all the men of the Ohio River Valley and its tributaries, north and south, had built flatboats and were carrying their produce all the way downriver to New Orleans. Or, in upper New York and Ohio, they loaded produce on canal boats and headed them east. If the farmer did not make the trip himself, he sold his produce to a speculating middleman, or contracted with a neighbor making the trip. In one way or another, his wheat, corn liquor, apples, cider, peaches, pork (salted or pickled down in barrels), honey, and some peltry made its way to a market. Or, there may have been a military post nearby, a fortuitous circumstance providing a cash customer as well as security for the countryside.

Meager as his cash income was, even in prosperous years, hard specie

gave the new country settler purchasing power, and he found many ways
to spend it. He had an insatiable lust for land and was willing to borrow
at 12 to 20 per cent interest if he did not have cash on hand. He bought
land for a number of reasons, so he said: for his sons who were growing
up, for meadowland, more timberland, or more fields to plant with
grain. And he bought for another reason that he did not quite so often
specify—speculation. For the new country settler was a capitalist in
spirit and design. He raised his crops in hopes of profitable sale, and he
grabbed all the land he could buy because the country was filling up
and land values were rising. Many a farmer overdid it, of course, and
brought hard times down on his head in 1819, 1837, and the late 1850's;
so too did settlers in the Middle Border (which consisted of parts of
Minnesota and Iowa, the Dakotas, Nebraska, and Kansas) mortgage
themselves into difficulties in the 1880's and 1890's.

Meanwhile, as the new country filled up, as trails became roads, and
crossroads became towns, so too did the farmer's family grow. His wife
desired better housing, and he tried to satisfy her. They shortly outgrew
the original little log cabin, and in a period of prosperity, changes were
made. The wife got her floor and the loft, and glass panes filled the window. But she still complained because the cabin was basically too crude
and too small.

For example, the logs had been left rounded, with the bark still on
them, and the simplest kind of notch, known as the saddle and rider,
had been used. But down the lane a half mile, perhaps, the neighbors
had raised a cabin in which the top and bottom of the logs had been
roughly hewn flat, so that it was far more snug—tighter and free of the

A typical style of log cabin. (The Kansas State Historical Society, Topeka)

need of constant caulking. And a mile and a half farther might be the home of a farmer already identifying himself as a community leader and a man of wealth, whose log house was constructed of timbers completely hewn or "squared." Moreover, the builder had used the mortis method of notching and fitting the logs, which was more difficult but resulted in a tighter fit and kept the rain from working in and rotting the ends. Our farmer's wife let him know that she liked that kind of a house, which, by the way, was a story and a half high.

Then news came that a sawmill had been set up less than a half day's wagon drive from home. Slab lumber was available in quantity, and now it was possible to have a house like those they had known back east. And so, five years after the initial cabin had been constructed, the farmer moved his family into a new house. Probably the cabin was left where it was and used as a storehouse, a place for harness and farm tools, a woodshed, or for other purposes. But as a visitor traveled the country— Kentucky in the 1790's, western Pennsylvania or Ohio in the early 1800's, or Indiana and Illinois in the 1830's—he was struck by the progress that a few short years could make. So extensively had the cabins given way to frame houses that folk still occupying the former were a subject for critical comment.

This idyllic picture is historically accurate; but there were, of course, all manner of variations. In the South the cabin might initially be larger, and when the opportunity for expansion arose, a breezeway was made and a second cabin, remarkably like the first, was added. The family lived in both, and in the breezeway was built a fireplace-stove where the cooking was done. Sometimes in Appalachia the settler built one identical cabin after another, sometimes forming a U. Or, rather than abandon his cabin as the area developed, he attached clapboards to the outside of the logs and added on a new clapboard section. If he plastered over the logs in the interior, future occupants of the house might never realize that they were living, at least partially, in a log cabin. Many such old houses still stand today.

Although there remained substantial stands of virgin forest in the region, we may assume that the real backwoods period was on the wane within a decade of our farmer's initial settlement. Ohio and much of Indiana was certainly settled by 1820, and Illinois, Iowa, southern Michigan, and southern Wisconsin by 1830. The deep South was a settled country by 1850, but settlement there, with the lack of industrialization in the towns and the tendency toward large agricultural units, resulted in the persistence of a frontier mentality that is rampant in the backwash areas of north Florida and parts of rural Georgia, Alabama, Mississippi, Louisiana, and Arkansas even today.

Farming the Middle
West and the South

Although many pioneers moved several times during their lives, let us assume our first farmer remained wherever his farm was—Tennessee, western New York, western Pennsylvania, or eastern Ohio. But his sons, on attaining age twenty-one, headed for Indiana, for the Sangamon or the Rock River country of Illinois, for Michigania (Michigan) or other areas to the west. Like their father they purchased their lands, at $1.25 an acre from the federal government, from a state government, from a land company, or from a neighborhood entrepreneur who had somehow acquired a lion's share of the good land. Similar purchases were made by pioneers' sons below the Mason and Dixon line. Soon the young men were slashing and burning the pine barrens of Alabama and Mississippi just as their brethren in the Old Northwest were repeating the same backwoods patterns that their fathers had practiced before them. But there were differences. The pioneers of the 1820's and 30's probably purchased a minimum of eighty acres, which cost at least one hundred dollars in the years following the Land Act of 1820. They may even have purchased a generous quarter section of 160 acres, or a half section of 320. The point is that the initial purchase was probably larger than the father's had been farther east.

Moreover, the arrival of the young man and his bride in the new country was a little more propitious than the journey over the mountains that his parents had made with a couple of pack horses when he was a baby. This young man came in a farm wagon with a canvas cover over it, drawn by a team of horses that vouched for his being at least relatively well off, even though they were a far cry from being prime horseflesh.

By now, if this was the early 1820's, there were two generations of pioneers behind him, since the first crossings of the Appalachians had been made in the 1770's. Now there was a "back-up" population west of the mountains that was increasingly impressive in number. Ohio, for example, had 937,903 residents in 1830 and 1,519,467 in 1840. The total population of the United States in 1830 was 12,860,020, of whom 2,456,162 lived west of the Appalachians and north of the Ohio; in 1840 that number had increased to 4,628,936, out of a total population of 17,069,453. Indiana increased from 343,021 inhabitants in 1830 to 685,866 a decade later, while Illinois jumped from 157,445 in 1830 to 476,183 a decade later. Michigan grew tremendously, from 31,639 in 1830, to 212,267 in 1840.

It has been said that pioneers tended to work west along isothermal lines—that is, remaining in familiar climatic zones—and it is clear that the New Englander and New Yorker stuck to the upper reaches of the developing Middle West, hugged the Great Lakes, and worked up their shores. Cold winters in those areas simply reminded the newcomers of the frigid Decembers, Januarys, and Februarys back home. Kentuckians went across the Ohio to Indiana, whose "Hoosier" population included so many Virginians as to give its people a characteristic rustic yet charming intellectuality quite unlike that of any other. Or they headed for southern Illinois—"Egypt," as it was called—an area which still possesses something of a southern attitude. Other Virginians and Carolinians headed for western Georgia, Alabama, and Mississippi, crossed the great river, and continued into Louisiana, Arkansas, and Texas. Wherever they went, they had to purchase land, build a house (often a log cabin), cut the timber, clear the land, and do the "breaking," as they called it, of the virgin soil.

The settlers in the Middle West, which was fast becoming the nation's breadbasket, still cherished the conviction that timberland had the finest soil. Many a midwestern farmer and his sons spent hundreds, even thousands, of hours clearing timbered land, grubbing out the stumps, and making it fit for cultivation. Of a summer's evening they would sit outside their cabin (which may very well have had a porch by this time) and survey their little field gradually taking shape among the trees. Yet just a bit farther, beyond the forest fringe, its wild grasses waving gracefully in the evening breeze, lay the unplowed treeless prairie. There were flat prairies and rolling prairies, wet ones and dry ones. One authority has named 271 kinds of plants that grew wild on the Iowa prairie. Some who viewed it were moved to poetry. Others, crossing it, felt like lost souls amidst its billowing grasses.

The prairies were left in their virgin state, therefore, long after the timbered areas had been settled, although cattle, hogs, and occasionally sheep were driven out in the grassland to graze. It was a common pasture and, in autumn, a common meadowland from which hay could be cut, originally for the livestock in the winter; though as towns grew in the area, baled hay to feed the towndwellers' horses became a source of income.

Then one day the timbered lands were all privately owned, and their going price was too high for a German or Swedish emigrant to swing even a down payment. But there were the prairie lands, often still in government hands, for sale at the $1.25 minimum or for little more than that from a private owner-speculator. The foreigner pulled up a prairie plant and examined the black, waxy soil clinging to the roots. Then he dropped to his knees and with his fingers dug deeper; still the soil was black. While his American neighbors shook their heads in disbelief, the latecomer attacked the prairie sod, with its thickly interwoven mat of roots. His success was not immediate, for the first crop of corn or flax had to vie with the tenacious prairie grasses. But by the second or third planting the crop of corn, wheat, rye, flax, barley, buckwheat, or oats was excellent. The native farmer acquired a new respect for the prairie lands, and when he thought of the backbreaking toil he had gone through to make his field out of the timber, he felt very close to a damned fool.

By the 1840's the myth that the prairie could not produce crops had been destroyed. The prairies were succumbing to the plow, while farmers of the new country looked toward the vibrant, energetic, volatile, crop-consuming eastern populace.

To help him break sod, plow, and harvest, the new country man needed beasts of burden. Farming implied the raising of domesticated animals for slaughter and for products ranging from wool to hog chittlings, animals as new to the new country as were the farmers.

Ordinarily his animals were of farmyard quality, although occasionally an intelligent farmer had a blooded bull, stallion, ram, or boar to aid him in establishing a productive new farm. Until at least the 1820's, however, there was almost no real attempt at selective breeding. A scrubby bull which should have been butchered was instead allowed to run free with the cows; good and poor milch cows alike received his services. The swine grubbed in the forest and were so wild that sometimes they had to be shot. Sheep did fall into a somewhat different category, as we shall see; but horses, in general, were not scientifically bred either.

Swine were basic to the new country economy, at least as far west as the Mississippi River; Missouri, Arkansas, and Texas were also hog-raising states. Porkers were extremely fecund: a good sow produced two litters a year, each containing eight to twelve little pigs. By contrast, a cow produced a single calf in nine months. Furthermore, the swine were unbelievably simple to raise. The pioneer notched their ears in such a way as to identify his own, and let them run. On the Appalachian plateau they foraged in the woods, feeding upon forest mast. Unless a few million passenger pigeons had been through recently, the hogs would flourish, fatten, and multiply rapidly. To bring them home the farmer offered them some corn, opened his cornfield to them after he had removed the ears, or put out salt. Then he called them—"Sowe-e-e-e-e-e!!!"—and pretty soon they appeared out of the forest, snorting and grunting, the little pigs squealing, and all running in that way pigs do, as if they have no shock absorbers in their anatomy.

As hogs became a marketable commodity, and an increasingly high percentage of his income was derived from them, the farmer began to manifest an interest in upgrading the stock. Improvements had begun late in the eighteenth century when east coast farmers imported breeds from England, China, and Spain. Woburn or Bedford hogs from England, with short legs, small bones, light offal (that is, which constituted only a small percentage of the total weight), and good quality flesh infused improvements into New England hogs, so that a fat, indolent, fairly gentle "grass-fed hog" had emerged there and in New York by about 1820.

Then the Old Northwest became acutely interested in swine improvement. A variety of fine boars were brought into the grain states, literally from all over the world, and it was a certainty that before many years some new breed would emerge, possessing a high percentage of the choice qualities the farmer desired. Eventually, along with the Berkshire and the successful Chester White, two other breeds emerged, the Duroc Jersey and the Poland China, the latter having blood strains from about every country *but* Poland.

Hog raising was extremely profitable in the Old Northwest, and it was a boon particularly to small farmers. It gave them some cash, put storebought clothes on their children, and paid for occasional sorely needed commodities, such as new farm machinery. From barely 2 million swine in Illinois in 1850 the number increased to nearly 6 million in 1890; from just 323,000 (in round numbers) in 1850, Iowa's hog population increased to 8,266,000 in 1890. Of all domestic animals, swine were the first in the new country to profit widely from scientific work in controlled breeding and in care and feeding.

Cattle were scrubby and small and gave little milk. They fell into the category "native breed"; only an expert could see in them signs of their ancestry of English breeds before those breeds had been scientifically improved. However, men such as Isaac Funk, "Long John" Wentworth of Illinois, and several dozen others, both east and west, who set up as gentleman farmers and raised blooded stock which they stood at stud, brought about the improvement of some herds. By way of country fairs and the agricultural press, farmers were also made aware of improved varieties. By the 1840's short-horned Lancashires, Bakewells, and Herefords, North Devons, Alderneys, and Guernseys were being shown, and their obvious merits began to register with the farmer. Yet the Middle West became settled country before substantial improvement, both in breeding and in care, took place.

On the prairies the farmers in the 1830's began to develop a cattle-feeding routine, making use of range cattle imported from elsewhere (even from Texas as early as 1854, and possibly as early as 1842), fattening them on corn and then driving them to packing houses in larger cities. Some 51,606 cattle were processed in Chicago as early as 1851. Good corn-fed beef was growing in popularity; and thus was created another saleable and profitable commodity for the prairie farmer.

Sheep profited from the introduction of new strains such as Spanish Merinos, Saxonys, and New Leicesters. A mixed type called the Bakewell developed. As with pigs and cattle, the concentration of production moved westward from New England, western New York, and Pennsylvania. Sheep could be grazed on the lush prairies and their wool, which did not spoil, was easily transported to the East. In the early 1840's the full realization of the profit potential of sheep raising on the prairies struck not only western farmers but eastern sheepmen also; a common sight along the roads leading west from Ohio in those years was the sheep drover with five hundred or a thousand sheep, bound for a new prairie home. In 1844, "the great sheep year," Illinois, Wisconsin, and Missouri received large flocks of the docile animals. As time went on and prices of farm goods rose again in the 1840's following the lean years after the Panic of 1837, the Midwesterners reduced their flocks, which were less profitable than other farm products, and only kept a few for the livestock menagerie that was part of the well-stocked farm. Between 1850 and 1860, Ohio, Indiana, and Illinois showed a decrease and the other midwestern states showed very little increase. In the 1860's there was a resurgence due to the demand for wool by the Union Army, but after the war the market fell, and with it the interest in sheep declined again. But farther west in the still newer country, in the decade 1850-60, New Mexico's sheep population increased from 377,000 to 830,000; that of Texas from 100,000 to 750,000; and California's from 20,000 to over a million! In fact, from the earliest times in the new country, violent fluctuations in the market have hampered the emergence of a stable sheep industry.

Besides hogs, cattle, and sheep, the new country farmer in the period 1830-60 had horses and oxen. Until the 1840's the horses of the Middle West were nondescript. They were small, indicating a preponderance of Spanish horse blood. Often, however, the horse trader noted some finer points indicating the presence, somewhere along the way, of the Morgan. Many of these new country horses were raised for sale to the eastern market. They also satisfied the local people, who enjoyed their swift and spirited gait. With the coming of heavy agricultural machinery, however, the demand arose for heavier animals. In the 1850's Percheron, Norman, Clydesdale, and English Shire horses were introduced into the Midwest, and by the 1870's powerful work horses weighing 1,300, 1,500, and even 2,000 pounds were common throughout the area. Men who owned good stallions traveled from village to village announcing that their horse "stood" at the local livery stable. The farmers bred their best brood mares to such studs, and thus improved the work stock. In time, many of these heavy, powerful horses were sold westward to freighters on the Great Plains. Many of the lighter horses were sold through the years into the South.

The horse swept the oxen out of the picture in the 1860's, 1870's, and 1880's. Yet the patient brutes, their necks encumbered by the heavy wooden yoke, are usually envisioned as the very embodiment of the pioneer experience. And they should be, for during the first half of the nineteenth century in the new country there were more of them around than there were horses; they were less expensive; the yoke was cheaper than a harness; they worked better at such laborious tasks as grubbing out stumps and boulders or hauling logs; and when exhausted from years of such activity, they could be, and usually were, butchered and eaten. They were indispensable to pioneering in New England and the entire Appalachian plateau region.

The finest oxen were raised and trained in New England. The most spirited, spritely, light-footed, and intelligent beasts were castrated young bulls of the Devon breed, but it should be kept in mind that any young steer could be trained to the yoke if it was started early enough. Texans, for example, became attached to their oxen which, if not altered, would have matured to big ill-tempered longhorns. Between 1850 and 1860 the number of oxen nationwide increased from 1,700,000 (in round numbers) to over 2,255,000. Yet the horse was catching up, even in New England, and in the Middle West horses were far outnumbering the placid beasts. It was not just the introduction of heavy farm machinery, which did not work well unless pulled at a faster speed than that of oxen; it was also that, with the coming of the railroads, the pace of life was stepped up. Men simply did not want to wait for a slow-moving ox. They could get to town with a load of grain faster with a horse-drawn than with an ox-drawn vehicle.

In general, domestic beasts in the new country were raised by a trial and error method, until the men knew how much of the cold winters their stock could stand, learned how much shelter they needed and how long they could thrive on certain types of forage. At first there was a tendency to be neglectful of livestock, but soon breeders learned how to protect them and have more of them alive and healthy when spring arrived, when the time came for killing them, shearing them, or using them as beasts of burden.

The new country was originally devoid not only of domestic animals but also of domestic plants. It was more than just a problem of breaking the soil. What grains would grow in the soil and in the climate? Wheat, corn, barley, rye, oats, sorghum, flax, and hay, to say nothing of the farm wife's vegetable garden, had to be planted as they had been "back east," but whether they would thrive, and whether certain new considerations had to be taken into account, were questions that only time and experience could answer.

Corn was basic to new country agriculture. The story of the steady improvement of this miracle grain that originated in the mists of pre-history in Central America continues even today. Corn demanded proportionally little seed for planting and was planted easily over a period of up to two months. It then proceeded to grow with a minimum of care, and could be harvested almost at leisure; and every part of the plant was useful.

In Ohio, Indiana, Illinois, and Iowa the settlers began to improve their corn almost as soon as they arrived. They experimented first with planting methods in fields of new-broken sod, and then with varieties of corn. Since they were learning about the idiosyncrasies of climate and soil and plant behavior all at once, it was common practice to exchange information about farming methods. With plants, this meant discussion about resistance of strains to blight, resistance to frost, rapidity of growth, and many other traits. The farmer probably saved some of the best ears of his corn crop for the next season's planting; possibly he borrowed some seed from a neighbor whose strain showed qualities he admired. Hybrids might appear among his stalks, the result of wind-blown pollenization from a neighbor's acreage. By the 1830's the farm journals were mentioning improvements in corn; and at the Paris Exposition of 1867 some 115 varieties were included in the United States exhibition. There was corn that was especially good for cattle, for hogs, for human consumption, and for grinding into meal. From his earliest settlement in the new country, the farmer was aware of the relative merits of the various strains.

Corn was not, however, a subsistence crop nor even the principal crop in some parts of the new country. Wheat, that golden grain gently waving in the breeze of a hot day in late summer, was the cash crop of New York's Genesee Valley, of much of the Ohio Valley, and of Indiana, Illinois, and Iowa. For while corn was eminently useful, and very quickly entered into a corn-hog economy or could be adapted for commercial, large-scale cattle feeding, it had certain shortcomings in the early days prior to the coming of the railroad. Corn might produce up to sixty bushels an acre compared with but half or a third that amount of wheat, but corn (which was sold cob, kernels, husk, and all) was bulky and, bushel for bushel, was always of less value than wheat. A bushel of wheat weighed 50 to 60 pounds, far more than a bushel of corn. Furthermore, when forty miles, or two days' travel, constituted the economically feasible limit of carrying grain to market, the more valuable commodity, wheat, obviously prevailed.

Corn was, however, simpler to grow than wheat. In the 1830's and 40's farmers experimented with winter wheat—a wheat planted in the fall and harvested in the spring—but results were discouraging. Freezes and thaws cracked the ground and left the new wheat exposed to the elements. If it escaped freezing, then the Hessian fly, rust, blight, and chinch bugs attacked it. Farmers engaged in heated controversy over the merits of soils, some insisting that wheat did best in fields that were formerly stands of timber, others on fields with a southern exposure, or others that wheat could only flourish in new-broken ground. In the 1840's and 50's they were already experimenting with exotic varieties, such as Black Sea, Canada Flint, and Yellow Lamas. Finally, by general unwritten and unofficial consensus, the new country farmers decided that spring wheat would do better, and in this switch they proceeded to experiment with still other varieties, including some strains produced locally.

Oats were raised because of livestock demands; barley, rye, sorghum and flax (for the linseed oil) likewise constituted at given places and times part of the farmer's plantings. So too was grass a product of some value in the days of horse-drawn power. The prairie grasses were originally harvested in their wild condition. It took up to thirty years after initial settlement in the 1820's for all the prairie lands to succumb to private ownership and domestication. The taming of the wild prairie into meadowland consisted in simply scattering bluegrass or timothy seed, and later clover, onto the prairie after first burning off the wild grasses. (Incidentally, Kentucky's bluegrass was not a native grass, but

New country farm houses could be spacious, but they could also be chillingly cold in winter. (State Historical Society of Iowa)

an importation from Europe which flourished and spread in the new country.)

Livestock, grains, and vegetables were three of the farmer's areas of interest, and fruit growing was a fourth. Every farmer was expected to have an orchard. Here again experimentation took place as the climatic limitations were fixed by trial and error in raising apples, peaches, pears, figs, apricots, cherries, and plums, as well as grapes and berries. Typically, then, the new country eighty-acre farm, included fields of corn and wheat, and some oats, barley, rye, or sorghum; it had pig pens, pastureland for cattle and horses, a vegetable garden, and an orchard.

Within an incredibly short period the differences in ability, or at least in ambition and "drive," could be noticed by any banker or mortgage dealer as he clattered around the countryside in his one-horse buggy. One farmer's fields were fenced, the furrows plowed straight, and the fields kept harrowed, and he had a house and outbuildings. Another new country man on equally good land still sheltered his family in a log cabin, his fields were unfenced, and his crops competed with weeds. Between the two extremes were the other farmers.

The challenge, in living and earning a livelihood in the new country, to accomplish a multiplicity of tasks all at once and right away, plus the challenge to inventors to meet the demands of farmers who wanted to make large tracts of land—quarter, half, and even full sections—productive and profitable, provided the necessary incentives for a rapid development of agricultural technology. Indeed, it is one of the fortunate occurrences of history that the industrial revolution was sufficiently advanced at the very moment in time when the westward movement would have been perceptibly slowed without revolutionary technological developments in agricultural machinery.

Still, with so basic an endeavor as agriculture, one wonders why technology was so late in coming; the industrial revolution was well under way before agriculture began to profit from technological advances. Possibly it was due to the traditional worldwide conservatism of the husbandman; but the experimentation of the new country farmer with corn hybrids and various grains as described above rather tends to refute this thesis. A better answer is that not one machine, but several—a machine for every step from plowing through harvesting—were necessary, and a single new labor-saver for just one of the four or five steps was useless. Why a better plow when the seeding process restricted cultivation to ten acres at most? Why a rapid seed drill when not more than ten or twenty acres of wheat could be harvested within the ten-day period when the kernels were at their peak of quality? Yet farmers gazed upon their fallow acres, heard the toot of a nearby railroad locomotive, and knew that with the machinery to handle the acreage, and the means already near at hand for the transportation of the produce to burgeoning markets, great profits could be made.

A brief discussion of farm machinery is essential to our story; but the urban-oriented American of today tends to be so ignorant of agricultural processes that a bit of explanation (which few people a century ago, save for city slum dwellers or the very rich, would have needed) is advisable here. What does a plow do, or a harrow? What is a sulky plow, or a harvester, or a thresher? It is exasperating to note that high school and college history texts all assume basic knowledge of farm machinery which probably less than a tenth of their readers possess. A field of grain must be plowed, harrowed, cultivated, harvested, and, if it is wheat, rye, oats, or barley, threshed; each stage entails a different operation and the use of a different tool.

Plowing consists basically of sinking a prong into the soil and moving it along the field in as straight a line as possible, making a furrow. The prong is called a share; behind it is a curved board called a moldboard. As the share cuts into the soil the moldboard guides the turned-up earth over and away from the furrow. This sounds simple enough, but placing the share into the soil at just the right depth, and angling the moldboard at just the right tilt so that the soil will fall away from the furrow and land upside down to the side of it is a feat that defied generations of rather unimaginative farmers. Dirt stuck to the moldboard, the angle was wrong and the soil fell back in the furrow, the share broke—all of these were problems that went back to Roman times.

The plow used by the Kentucky pioneer in the 1770's and 80's was likely to be nothing more than a crooked tree branch with, perhaps, an iron share crudely attached, or a wooden share enforced by some sheet iron nailed around it. Two to four oxen were needed to help the farmer drag it through the soil, and it broke frequently. Then towards the turn of the century several men, among them Thomas Jefferson, began applying mathematical calculations to the problems of angles, stresses, and strains of shares and moldboards. In 1797 Charles Newbold patented a cast-iron plow which farmers promptly rejected on the ground that so much iron poisoned the soil and promoted the growth of weeds. Jethro Wood picked up the challenge and designed a plow with interchangeable parts; its share and moldboard could be replaced if broken without replacing the entire instrument. The farmer eventually accepted it. Thus the manufactured plow with cast-iron share and moldboard, or at least iron sheeting, became a reality. Such a plow was a great improvement over its primitive predecessor; still by the 1830's more improvements were in the offing.

Once the field was plowed, the soil lay exposed to the elements, and the atmosphere plus rain did much toward pulverizing it and preparing it for seeding. Big clods of dirt ordinarily remained, however, and so the farmer resorted to harrowing, a process of breaking down the clumps of soil and in general smoothing the field. At first a heavy log or just a brushy tree limb was dragged along broadside behind the oxen, accomplishing the task to the relative satisfaction of the farmer. Later a simple A-frame with iron teeth on the bottom, dragged along behind the horses or oxen, did the job more satisfactorily and with fewer breakdowns.

Then came the seeding. In the early years the process was to sow broadside, but by the 1840's there were seed drills and endgate seeders, with improvements coming rapidly and acceptance being widespread. For corn, however, the inventions came later; even into the 1850's, the method of hand planting the corn in mounds was still in wide use in the Middle West. If the crop was corn, weeding—cultivating—had to be done several times during a growing season. Not until the 1850's were practical horse-drawn cultivators in production. Other cereals, once planted, grew without interference.

The great cash-crop cereal was wheat, of course, and the peculiar problem of wheat was that it had to be harvested within a short span

The scythe, a companion tool to the sickle or reaping hook, was used for mowing grass and sometimes for cutting oats and barley as well. (International Harvester)

The cradle was the most efficient means of cutting grain before McCormick invented the reaper. (International Harvester)

of time. Even with the help of women and children and able-bodied neighbors, not much more than fifty acres could be harvested with all hands using the scythe, the sickle, or the cradle. At first thought, cutting swaths of wheat seems so simple that we wonder that some inventor did not come up with a horse-drawn machine hundreds of years ago. But despite their simplicity, the hand-operated tools accomplished more than mere cutting: in the hands of a good reaper they cut the wheat so gently that the kernels did not fall off the ear, and the swath left the stalks so neatly arranged that the binder could gather them in a single motion of his arms and have them assembled in sheafs in jig time. The grain was next winnowed into the air or horses flailed it on a treadmill to separate the wheat from the chaff. The whole process was slow, wasteful of time and grain, and laborious, even if it was picturesque.

By the 1830's Ohio, Indiana, Illinois, Iowa, and Missouri were the big agriculture states. The large farms of 80, 160, 320, and 640 acres were there, as were the farmers who sought implements that were labor-saving, speedy, and space-shrinking. They wanted technological improvements to make it possible for a one-family farm to produce a bigger and bigger surplus that could sell for more and more money. Farming was leaving the subsistence stage, although the farm that produced 80 per cent or more of a family's needs would still be around into the twentieth century. But the fertility of the soil, the large acreage he contemplated planting, the growing cities which were expanding markets, and the railroads, canals, and riverways which could transport the produce all created an intense desire on the part of the traditionally conservative farmer for new and better machinery. The fact that the land was new and the people were all newcomers who had to work from and adapt a basic knowledge gained on smaller farmsteads to the east seemed to encourage widespread experimentation, with a consequent receptiveness to the new implements.

This is why the first great era of technological improvement on the American farm is usually considered to be the generation from 1830 to 1860. In this period the corn and hog belt lands of the Middle West fall to the breaking plow, the railroad comes, and the farmer can, generally speaking, sell everything he grows. It is the era of the settling of the midwestern new country and its adjustment to its own problems and challenges, and, after experimentation, to its own cycles, techniques, and methodology. Agricultural machinery had begun its development prior to the 1830's, but it was in the three decades down to the Civil War that the demand created a supply that was explosive in its impact upon agricultural productivity.

And the new country posed some real challenges. It was tough

One of the three original plows made by John Deere in 1838. (Deere & Co.)

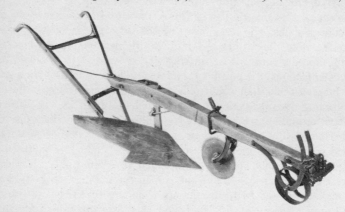

John Deere Prairie Queen walking plow with wood beam. (Deere & Co.)

Deere sulky plow. (Deere & Co.)

enough back east breaking a field in which the stumps remained, but breaking the prairie sod was a task no eastern plow, not even the most modern and expensive one, could accomplish satisfactorily. The prairie contained an interwoven mat of roots that for rankness and toughness defied any other sod anywhere on earth. It was the task of the new country man to break the prairie sod and make tame fields of it. Plows to accomplish such a task were constructed by local handymen, and in time evolved into something no one in Kentucky or New England had ever seen. These "breaking plows" grew to be as long as twelve feet, with the front end resting on little wheels; way back at the rear was a ponderous share, a big moldboard, and the handles for the determined plowman. It was hitched up to six yoke of oxen, the share was inserted, and while one man drove the team another guided the plow, hoping to make a furrow across the virgin turf as much as thirty inches wide. When was the best time for breaking? And how deep should the furrow be? And what should be planted first in the new field? And where was the money coming from to use this massive plow, half a dozen yoke of oxen, and an extra man—for several days, since only two and a half to three acres could be broken per day? All these questions had to be answered through trial and error and innovation. Late spring was the best time, two and a half inches the best depth (though many a farmer had strained a breaking plow into making a five-inch furrow). The question of the best crop to sow remained a point of controversy for many years. The money problem was solved by hiring professional breakers who owned their plows, or by a group of neighbors pooling interests, purchasing a plow in common and, in a neighborly way, pitching in to help one another with the breaking. Neighborliness in the new country was actually an economic necessity.

Once the breaking had been accomplished, the farmer turned to light plows, many of which were made at home or by the local blacksmith. These plows had many faults, possibly the most common being the tendency of the prairie sod to stick to the moldboard. The farmer often carried a wooden paddle with which to bang on the moldboard or scrape it clean, a messy, time-consuming, annoying process. Then, so one story goes, the proverbial Yankee showed up. He was thirty-three years old, fresh out of Vermont, a blacksmith by trade, and with his tools to prove it. In 1837 he settled at Grand Detour, a prairie village of about three hundred souls on the Rock River in northwestern Illinois. It was here that he designed and assembled his first steel plow. (A controversy exists over who built the first ones—it seems probable that there were several plow builders who did this, and John Deere—for that was his name— was just one of them; but he followed through in manufacturing them.)

His plow had a moldboard and share made of sheet steel ordinarily used for saws that he had obtained from a nearby sawmill. He appears to have made ten or a dozen such plows in 1839 and 1840, each one representing a new experiment in the curvature of the steel moldboard, each one hopefully throwing off the sticky loam better than the previous ones. By 1846 he was turning out a thousand plows a year. At about that time he moved to Moline, contracted with Hones and Quigg Steel Works for a special cast plow steel, and was soon an implement tycoon, manufacturing ten thousand or more plows a year by the late 1850's. In the next two decades, James Oliver's chilled-iron plow, whose hard moldboard could outlast three steel ones, and the sulky plow, whereby a farmer could sit down while he plowed an ever-increasing acreage, became common sights in the agricultural areas.

Now that the new country farmer could plow forty or eighty acres or more, he needed the machinery to harvest it. And along came an imaginative Virginian of Scotch-Irish antecedents to furnish the machine. Cyrus McCormick was born of a substantial Virginia family whose acres in Rockbridge County in the Great Valley, called Walnut Grove, were among the finest farmlands around, which was unusual for the Scotch-Irish; the family had established its roots there. The other unusual thing about the McCormicks was their tinkering. Robert McCormick, the father, was widely known for his inventiveness in his blacksmith shed, and Cyrus was known to take after his father in that respect. Apparently the father had tested a reaper, or possibly two or three of them, in 1831, but they had not worked.

Remember that reaping only seemed simple; the wheat had to fall just so, and so gently that the rich ripe kernels stayed on the ear. The inventor of a workable reaper was confronted with a whole series of problems, each of which had to be solved at least in part before the whole machine could satisfactorily reap a field. There had been experimenters in England and Europe; one authority has counted forty-seven reaper patents prior to McCormick's, of which twenty-three were American. Cyrus McCormick appears to have done the best job of combining the seven essential parts so that they worked harmoniously. Such a delicate balance of working parts would take time to perfect, and McCormick tinkered with his machine each year through 1838. Not until 1839 did he publicly state that his reaper was finally ready for general use, and that orders would be taken; and not until 1841 did he achieve such a perfection in his machine as to justify warranting it completely. In 1847 he moved to Chicago, a bustling city of seventeen thousand, and began manufacturing reapers and mowers for a receptive clientele that was literally just a few steps beyond the factory doors. By 1851 he was

Cyrus McCormick's original reaper, invented in 1831. This machine with two-man crew would cut as much grain in a day as four or five men with cradles or twelve to sixteen men with reaping hooks. (International Harvester)

sole owner of the McCormick Reaper Works and was selling his machines by the thousands.

With the reaper two men could work ten to twelve acres a day, whereas one man with a sickle could harvest a half acre a day. Good sales promotion and customer relations encouraged its acceptance. The fine attributes of the machine were widely advertised in the agricultural press, complete with lengthy testimonial letters. Moreover, the price of McCormick's machine was right: from $100 up to $115 or $120 in the early years. Dealing with a penny-pinching farmer was no easier then than it is now, but McCormick knew how to inveigle him into buying, keep him satisfied, and finally he even trusted him and sold the reaper on time. (Time payments were, of course, as American as speculation—the public domain had been sold on a time basis from 1800 until 1820.) The farmer found detailed instructions included with his reaper, for in those days, when both men and horses were unused to machinery, they tended to abuse the instruments through ignorance. With its turning blades and rattling parts, the reaper needed steady oiling, and the blades needed sharpening every fifty acres. The methods of doing this and other suggestions for making the reaper last ten years were clearly explained.

By the 1850's implement manufacturing was big business, with Oliver, Deere, Manny, McCormick, Hussey, and many others competing for the farmer's dollars. With competition came the necessity for more in-

ventiveness and innovation if a company was going to prosper. Mowing
machines were in demand both east and west, so McCormick developed
a reaper that could also serve as a hay mower. Finally the thresher
entered the scene. It had first been developed by a couple of Maine
Yankees in the 1830's, but with the coming of the reaper the need of a
practical machine to thresh the grain from the straw spurred others to
experiment, and by the 1860's threshers were upping the output from
seven bushels per man per hour flailing the grain to thirty bushels with
a threshing machine. Cultivators, corn planters, wheat drills, horse rakes,
horse forks for hay, cornstalk cutters, along with sulky plows, seed drills,
reapers, harvesters, combines (of the two), and mowers, were revolu-
tionizing agriculture by the 1850's. Binders, headers (which cut only the
head of the wheat), and silos and other improvements in the 1870's and
80's continued to make farming both more expensive and more efficient.
And yet, farming remained a gamble, for weather, diseases, international
markets, and plain bad luck all figured in the odds.

With the end of the Civil War, the Old Northwest had become
settled country. There were, it is true, stretches of virgin prairie and
virgin woods, but by now the roads were a single span rather than two
wheel tracks across the prairies, the crossroads were towns, and railroads
connected the farmlands with the growing cities. Young Americans
dreamed—of going west again, to new country again—to central and
western Kansas and Nebraska, Dakota, Colorado, Wyoming, Montana,
or possibly to California and Oregon. When they got beyond the ninety-
eighth meridian, new problems arose which had never bothered their
parents. But before we discuss agriculture in that new country, in the
Middle Border and on the high plains, let us glance south, at Alabama,
Mississippi, Louisiana, Arkansas, and even Texas. For in those states,
in these same years of the 1820's until the outbreak of the Civil War,
the new country was put to the plow also, but for a different crop.

Much of the story of the settlement, the development of the land, and
the beginnings of society in the Old Southwest is similar to the story
in the region north of the Ohio. Soil exhaustion was more important
as a cause of emigration in Virginia and the Carolinas than in New England, New York, and Pennsylvania. While all American farmers, lulled
by the abundance of virgin land, abused the good earth mercilessly, the
Southerner's depredations were worse because, among other things, his
crops—tobacco and cotton especially—were more enervating to the soil.
When his lands gave out he had always sought new fields. Now, with
Eli Whitney's invention in 1793 of the cotton gin (which, like McCormick's reaper later, was the subject of incessant tinkerers who were not

as lucky as Whitney), the Southerner knew that short-staple cotton was economically feasible. The clearing of Indians from much of the Old Southwest during the War of 1812 opened the lands of the Black Belt, that strip of black loam stretching westward across the Gulf Plains from Georgia to Mississippi. Northeast of Vicksburg in northern Mississippi was the so-called "Delta country,"* occupied by the Chickasaws and the Choctaws until they were forced out by Indian removal treaties of 1830 and 1832. This vast area was the site of a primeval swamp, and the rich black loam extended downward as much as thirty feet in some places.

There were two great tides of migration, from 1815 until 1819 and from the late 1820's until the Panic of 1837; then a gradual recovery from the panic, with a steadily expanding movement southwestward, and a filling-in of vacant pockets until the Civil War. In this period the Southerners created a plantation cotton economy and a culture in the new country of the Old Southwest. Cotton was King in this new South, and the desire to raise it in ever greater quantities smacked more of a profitable business than of an agricultural pursuit. Purely and simply, the Southern planter was so dominated by the lust for profits that he neglected raising sufficient corn, vegetables, and orchard products such as peaches for his own family and slaves. "Ante-bellum Southerners," wrote the agricultural historian Weymouth T. Jordan, "not only glorified agriculture, but they made a ritual of their homage to cotton."[1] This adulation is no textbook myth. When prices were high, the Southerners did indeed believe cotton was King. "We have the only soil and climate adapted to its cultivation," editorialized the *Southern Cultivator* (a leading farm journal). "The raising of cereals, usually the prime end and aim of Agriculture, with us, is merely secondary or rather auxiliary. Their main value to us grows out of the question: How much cotton do they enable us to raise?"[2]

Nevertheless in the new country of Alabama, Mississippi, Louisiana, Arkansas, and east Texas, there were the usual problems of beginning agriculture. What variety of cotton did best in virgin soil? Which varieties were most resistant to fungus? What kind could best retain lint in the pods in severe weather? Every cotton farmer searched for acclimatized seeds which produced long staples, but the danger of being duped by shady dealers was always present. While there were at least fifty different types of seeds, there was no standardization, and some identical types bore two or more different names. One type known as Sugar Loaf

* The Delta country is the rich floodplain between the Yazoo and the Mississippi rivers, extending 200 miles from Memphis southwest to Vicksburg. It has unusually rich soil. It is *not* the delta of the Mississippi.

was noted for its productivity in virgin soil with a rich and moist texture. Vick's Handfed Seed was good for either rich or poor soil, and Mastodon was good for keeping lint in the pods in severe weather. As in the Old Northwest, there were some advanced farmers who became seed experts. Mississippi's Martin W. Philips was the great ante-bellum expert on cotton seeds.

Most southerners were guilty of wasteful cultivation; they rather seem to have generally expected virgin cotton land to be always available to the west. Indeed, the desire for new lands, especially in the 1850's when cotton prices rose and seemed to be permanently increasing, resulted in the spread of cotton culture over a thousand-mile expanse from South Carolina to Texas, some 400,000 square miles in all. Yet there were prophets crying in the disappearing wilderness, pleading with their fellow agriculturalists to cultivate their lands so as to preserve the soil. Dr. Noah B. Cloud of Alabama was well aware of the widespread soil exhaustion in the older Southern states. He advocated heavy manuring, deep plowing, and great distance between plantings. He was in essence advocating a method of producing a high yield of cotton and at the same time building up the soil. His method was by and large ignored; that of his rival, Martin W. Philips, a simple but more enervating method involving horizontal plowing, seeding along the furrow, and then covering it was more widely used throughout the South. Erosion was a serious consequence. Crop rotation was also advocated in enlightened agricultural journals; a four-year sequence of cotton, corn, a grain such as rye or oats, and finally a year of rest, in which clover, cowpeas, or some other enriching legume was planted, was deemed the best method. Yet in the desire for quick profits, few Southerners adopted this routine.

When cotton prices were depressed, as they were in the 1840's, Southerners paid more attention to the raising of corn, which fed man and livestock and grew easily. Actually, as late as 1859 the South produced 52 per cent of the corn crop of the United States, although the per capita production there declined during the 1850's. The usefulness of the crop was never doubted, however, and there were farmers who planted on a careful and scientific basis and were as concerned over seed types and methods of cultivation as were their counterparts in the North.

The rapid expansion into the new country by a section possessing half the population of the North prompted some Southerners to advocate a reopening of the African slave trade. They felt that the South's ills were caused primarily by a shortage of labor, and that only the labor of the black man could break new ground or be economically feasible in restoring exhausted lands. The blacks were good frontiersmen, and the South, ever expanding and with an increasing market price for its staple, desperately needed them.

Livestock was also essential to any kind of agriculture in the nineteenth century, and the South was likewise a leader in livestock production. When the Civil War began—and the Old Southwest, Arkansas, and east Texas may be said to have ceased to be new country by then —the South contained more than half the neat cattle in the United States, 60 per cent of the swine, 45 per cent of the horses, 52 per cent of the oxen, 90 per cent of the mules, a third of the sheep, and half the poultry.[3] Yet in the midst of this abundance the South lacked draught and meat animals.

The change from oxen to other animals, already noted in reference to the North, took place at about the same time in the South and for the same reason. The new agricultural implements, including corn crushers, cane grinders, cotton gins, cotton presses, reapers, and threshing machines, were all geared to a faster pace of operation. The ox in the South gave way not to the horse, however, but to the mule.

A mule is a hybrid between a male jackass and a female horse, and the breeding of such animals, who are for all practical purposes sterile, is a highly developed art. (A jenny mule can be made pregnant by a stallion or a jackass, but the foal will nearly always be born dead.) The breeder of mules must be an expert on the bloodlines and desirable qualities of both the jackass and the mares to which he proposes to breed them. Kentucky and Tennessee were the principal producers of mules, and good Spanish and Maltese jacks were imported to improve the quality. The offspring of these jacks and spirited horse mares were sold into the Old Southwest, until by 1860 there were more mules than horses in the South. Mules were simply the cheaper animal: cheaper to buy and keep; healthier, enduring the Southern heat and humidity better; longer lived; and quicker to recover from excessive work. The mules used by the plains army and those developed in Missouri and Kansas for freighting were much larger than the ones that strained at the plow on the little plots of the southern poor whites, the larger fields of the middle-class or yeoman farmers and on the great acreages of the big planters; these were descended from small Spanish jacks and the small "native" American horses. Despite the practical virtues of the mule, however, the plantation aristocrat always demanded good-blooded riding horses, and New England Morgans fetched absurdly high prices in the new country of the Old Southwest.

The best breeds of cattle were a subject of considerable interest among those few who cared, but a true picture of the ante-bellum

South, including the western parts, had to include scrawny cattle grazing in the dismal landscape of exhausted fields. Most owners let the livestock fend for themselves in fields and woods. There was virtually no planned selection, almost no planting of timothy or other proven "tame" grasses, and no shelter was provided. A cold winter's day could find them huddled together at the corner of a pasture shivering, their lowing sounds pleading for someone to take better care of them. Only an occasional farmer in the South showed real interest in his cattle. Among such individuals, the Devon, so widely used in the North as oxen, was the most popular breed.

As for smaller animals, the hog was, of course, of great importance in the South, but there appears to have been less interest in types and improvements of the breed than in the North. A farmer was likely to choose his swine on the basis of local needs. If he lived far from market or a navigable river, then he wanted long-legged hogs with thin bodies which could be easily herded some distance to market. If he lived close to market or a navigable river, then he wanted short-legged, fat hogs with plenty of meat on their bones. Sheep raising was somewhat more widespread in the South than it is usually credited with being, but most of the sheep were a scrawny native variety. Some farmers bred Merinos with their own natives, however, and the result was a well-acclimated beast. But Southerners were the nation's greatest dog lovers, and the dogs they kept were primarily hounds, used for hunting. Canine packs made serious inroads on sheep, sometimes killing half a flock in a single night.

For all the knowledge that was disseminated throughout the South in the ante-bellum period in agricultural journals, by schools, and by means of agricultural fairs, Southerners coveted their cash crops and resisted the admonitions of book-learned experts. Diversification and a well-balanced agricultural economy would have stood the Southerner well in 1861, but this he did not have. Besides the psychology of "Cotton is King," Southern plantation owners, as well as the yeomanry, feared that diversification might destroy the existing social structure. There was also a labor problem, for new skills and tasks were required to care for improved livestock, new crops, and fruits and vegetables. How, they asked, can diversification be accomplished with ignorant slave labor? And rice, sugar, tobacco, and especially cotton, offered too much cash incentive in the 1850's for a change to be possible.

When the Civil War began in 1861, the Southerner was only vaguely uneasy over the growing awareness that perhaps all the good cotton land in the country was taken up. The existence of cotton country to the west (or southward into north Florida, which was new country in the 1840's and 50's) had led him to neglect his lands, exploit them, and be aware of a smaller return per acre year after year, without being sufficiently apprehensive of the future. He had always looked forward to new lands elsewhere; and until he reached the Brazos River in Texas, new lands, in hot, humid climates, with rich soil, and close to deep, navigable rivers, were always available. The very wealth of the new country created a false sense of security in the Southerner, which he was only just beginning to lose when the War Between the States began.

Far Western Farmers and Cattlemen

By 1861 there were still areas in or close by Mississippi's Delta country and in Arkansas and east Texas where pockets of virgin land remained. Northwest Iowa was virgin country into the late 1880's; most settled states, in fact, still possessed large tracts of virgin land. But these tracts were surrounded by settled country where towns were well established, pastures were being fenced, and graveyards were beginning to receive their second generation of corpses.

There was at this time a slowing down of emigration westward, for the new country now was different: lands where the timber gave out, the rainfall diminished, and the wind blew wild and free. During the decade of the 1860's men gazed out upon the treeless, rolling prairies, noted the short grasses that seemed always dry and rustling in the incessant wind, and hesitated. They had reached western Minnesota, Nebraska, and Kansas; they were facing westward beyond the ninety-eighth or hundredth meridian, where new methods of farming would have to be learned by trial and error. Still, they only paused: between 1860 and 1900 over four hundred million acres were added to the farmlands of the country, and most of those acres were west of the Mississippi, and even west of the Missouri. The number of farms increased from two million to six million.

Much of the settlement was in the "Middle Border" country of Dakota, western Minnesota, most of Nebraska and Kansas, and parts of east, north, and west Texas. There was also agricultural activity on the lands hugging the Rockies, where water was easily available. Farmers settled the high mountain valleys like the Gallatin Valley of Montana or the Yampa Valley in Colorado. They irrigated the lands around Greeley, Colorado, and in Mormon Utah. They developed massive bonanza farms along Dakota's Red River and they tapped the fertility of California's great Inland Valley; they settled the Palouse hills of Idaho.

Each of these areas possesses the pride of its own history, but the basic aspects of the breaking of new land gave a common beginning to all. The glaring difference among them is that the dry, treeless Great Plains posed problems of trial-and-error adjustment and radical departures from what had always been the way of doing things farther eastward. Some experts today say that much of the land should never have been put to the plow and that the economic disruptions which gave rise to the Populists were partly caused by overproduction, human suffering, crop failure due to faulty farming methods, and such natural disasters as locust plagues, bitterly cold winters, hail, and cloudbursts that brought the needed moisture too fast and at the wrong time. The settlers were misled by the circumstance that the late 1860's and 70's were wet years (relatively speaking, for this was a dry area) of a climatic cycle which they did not even know existed; they were not prepared for the drought years—the other side of the climatic cycle—of 1886-96.

To a degree the pattern of settlement was different also. East of the ninety-eighth or the hundredth, the tendency had been for the pioneers to locate first in the river valleys, only later up in the forests, and finally on the prairies. In the Middle Border country where there were fewer rivers; and although the Red River of the north, the Platte, the Kansas, and the Arkansas, to mention a few, were all sites of settlement, the farmers also risked their fortunes in crude sod houses or slab board shacks that stood exposed on the treeless plains. There they were subject to the beating rays of a merciless summer sun, the whiplash gusts of prairie thunderstorms, the bone-chilling cold of winter northers, and strong winds that blew the calcareous soil into great dust clouds. Settlements also occurred around military posts, and, since the railroads advanced with the pioneers, along their rights-of-way also.

In the more humid regions of the East experimentation had usually meant a better crop if successful and a poorer one if the new idea failed, but in the arid lands failure was total. For this reason farmers did not experiment a great deal, but stayed close to plowing, planting, and cultivating methods they had known in the East. Only after many had been reduced to stark poverty, even starvation, and others had given up and gone "back east," did experts come forth, men such as Willard D. Johnson, Frank Hiram King, Hardy W. Campbell, John Wesley Powell, and E. W. Hilgard, to point out the more sophisticated differences between the soils, climate, nature of runoff, and the grasses of the arid lands compared with those of the humid climates. The plainsmen began giving the land the respect that was required if farming was to be successful in this hostile environment. By this time, with just a few exceptions, the farmer had entered the twentieth century, and the arid plains were experiencing a second-stage attack by farmers who benefited by the errors of their predecessors and profited from the information of the experts.

The truth is, nature played the Middle Border man a dirty trick by being in the wet phase of the climatic cycle during those early years of settlement. Land was cheap; it could even be acquired for nothing— or at least virtually for nothing—from the government. Under the Pre-emption Act of 1841, still in force, it could be purchased for $1.25 an acre; and under the Homestead Act of 1862 the original cash outlay could be as little as $10. In addition, for from $2 to $10 an acre, with up to five years to pay, better land could be purchased from railroads, land speculators, or states with school lands at their disposal. Federal legislation such as the Timber Culture Act, the Desert Land Act, and the Mineral Lands Act helped increase the acreage of shrewd farmers who sensed the potential for fraud written into them (possibly consciously and purposely). Railroad promoters as well as state emigration offices and large speculative land companies advertised hundreds of thousands of acres that were up for sale. They encouraged farmers in the East to come "out of the woods into Kansas"; "Jay Cooke's Banana Belt" was the phrase given to the Northern Pacific route because of Cooke's exaggerated boasts about the country through which his railroad was being built. Colonies of emigrants were encouraged to come from Europe, with acreage donated for their churches and schools. So great was the migration in the 1870's and 80's that it looked as if all America was pulling up stakes and moving west—a repeat performance of at least three other great movements into the new country, from 1815 to 1819, from the late 1820's to 1837, and from the late 1840's to 1857.

While many thousands of Scandinavians, Germans, and scatterings of other northwest European peoples migrated into the plains country, the great majority of the pioneers were from the nearest states to the east— Illinois, Iowa, and Missouri. A preponderance of them, as always, were the honest, hard-working poor; but therein lay much of the problem.

For this new country was deceptive. Since it was mostly devoid of timber, the hard work of destroying a forest and rooting out stumps was not necessary; settlement and planting a field looked incredibly simple. Just erect a dwelling (but of what material?), plow the prairie, plant the corn, wheat, and potatoes, and let nature do the rest! But nature did not follow through, and the farmer, if he had crop failure that first year, faced ruin. There were few if any of the vegetables that would have been produced by the farm wife in the forested areas. There were few wild animals to kill and help fill the larder. There was no quickly available fuel, and what was used—cow chips, corn cobs, straw —hardly offered the cheerfulness of flaming logs crackling in the fireplace. For that matter, there was no fireplace. Life was immeasurably more rigorous, less "civilized"; the sawed-wood and tar paper shack and the sod house lacked the coziness of the log cabin; the wind blew colder around the eaves and the jagged corners; and, when she stepped outside, the pioneer woman gazed upon a world of grass stretching to the horizon. There was only the cold wind, the rustle of dry grass, and the gaunt, ugly shack and outbuildings that defied the elements by daring to stick up out of the sod. Life was reduced to an elemental struggle for existence, and the risk of failure carried with it the risk of insanity or death.

Even boastful railroad pamphlets suggested that the newcomer would need $800 to $1,000 to get started on his 80, 120, or 160 acres. And it was expected that he would already possess a yoke of oxen or team of horses, a cow, a rickety wagon, a plow, and household truk; but most settlers did not. Yet they came, hoped for the best, and set to work to achieve their dreams. And they innovated.

Their houses were most likely to be shacks of rough lumber, carried in farm wagons from a sawmill that was busy denuding the sparse forest cover along a nearby stream or, occasionally, from a lumber yard at the sprouting village by the nearest railroad. After a house—all eighteen by twenty-four feet of it—had been erected, it was covered with tar paper and battened down with thin wood strips; a small stove whose chimney stuck up through the roof was installed, and thus shelter for a year or so was provided. Sometimes a man and a woman, wed by clergy or by common law, would each erect this kind of "claims shack" in such a manner that the structures had a common wall on the boundary of adjoining 160-acre tracts and would each file for a homestead. Thus they conveniently lived on and improved separate tracts, yet lived conveniently in wedlock and on a total of 320 acres.

By comparison the sod house was often a distinct improvement. And there were plenty of them out there, even though the simple frame dwellings were more numerous. Sometimes, as in the case of line camps maintained by ranchers for itinerant cowboys, they were little more than crude dugouts cut into the side of a prairie hillside. On occasion, destitute but hopeful homesteaders, often called "nesters" or "scissorbills" by the ranchers, constructed these one-room hovels as their first type of shelter. Anyone who could not afford such a dwelling was destitute indeed.

For example, the construction of a fourteen-by-fourteen-foot dugout consisted of digging into the side of a hill and excavating to the approxi-

A pioneer dugout. Note the horse and wagon in the field above. (The Nebraska State Historical Society)

mate size of the room, then building a front wall of sod bricks, leaving space for a window and a door. The total cost, not counting labor, was less than $3.00, as follows:

one window	$1.25
18 feet of lumber for a door	.54
one latch and pair of hinges	.50
one stovepipe joint to go through the roof	.30
3 pounds of nails	. 19
	$2.78

Such a primitive "soddy," with its roof of grass, dripped from the ceiling when spring arrived, making it almost impossible to keep things dry. An occasional intruder might come crashing through the ceiling— a stray horse or cow.

A more substantial, four-walled home would warrant calling an old-fashioned house-raising bee, but, whether done with neighbors' help or with the muscle of the men of the "house," the technique was the same. The prime time for cutting the sod was when it was still heavy and damp from rain and snow. Its thickness was considered ideal at two and a half inches. The best sod would be permeated throughout that thickness with grass roots, which when dry became small wiry outcroppings on the underside of the sod, keeping it together and preventing it from crumbling and disintegrating.

The high plains farmer cut his sod as straight as possible in pieces a foot wide and a foot and a half long, after having prepared the foundation for his home and erected a door frame. Quite simply, the sod was placed flat, one piece on top of another. Here space was made for a window, there for the door and the corners were set with care. The sod was heavy, and it was hard work, especially by the time the sides reached five or six feet, with three more to go to the ideal height of nine feet.

Most likely the pioneer would have sacrificed some of his cash reserves in order to purchase some two-by-fours or four-by-fours, plus additional timber to form a crotch at the top. These he would raise at either end and in the center of the sod house; then a cross beam, or ridge pole, also purchased, would be lifted awkwardly by the men across

A family in front of its sodhouse near Norton, Kansas, 1878. (DeGolyer Library, Dallas)

the length of the house, to be supported by the beams. Then poles from the cottonwood and willows of the nearest creek bed—and anything else that would work for that matter—would be laid across to support the sod roof.

There was the house. It was going to settle some, and there might not be a truly straight wall in it, or a true right-angle corner. Snow could sift through small holes that extended to daylight, but these would be plugged when noticed. Vermin and dried sod seemed to go together; bed bugs and mice thrived in the walls. So, too, would rattlesnakes on occasion find their lairs there. The story is told of the boy who complained to his parents, one night, that his brother, in bed with him, had pinched him hard—an accusation the brother vigorously denied. This warranted a tongue-lashing from the parents, and a warning to quiet down—or else! The next morning the lad was cold and dead in bed—the bad pinch had been the lethal bite of a rattler, which had then crawled back into the sod.

Many an American today still remembers life in a sod house, and he is quick to remind us that this did not identify him as born in poverty. As farmers experienced successful years, they added wings to their soddies, roofed them with regular wooden shingles, built partitions inside so that the house was divided into parlor, kitchen, hallways, and bedrooms. From somewhere close by they obtained clay and ashes, which were mixed with water to just the right consistency and spread on the inner walls, resulting in a surface not unlike plaster. Then they whitewashed it. To a considerable degree this eliminated the vermin, and the house became snug, warm, and aesthetically acceptable.

Such houses were still common in parts of Kansas and Nebraska as late as the 1930's. A generation or two of Americans were born and raised in them; and those sod houses bore all the nostalgic memories that any family in a brick or frame house could possess. When the latter became a kind of plains country status symbol, and the family moved fifty or a hundred feet away to a new house, their first hot summer's evening brought yearnings for the cool of the old sod house, and the first blizzard of the winter brought memories of its warmth and snugness.

All this was, of course, an adjustment from what had been known and accepted back east. Since coal and wood were missing, the pioneers made use of twisted hay, corn cobs, and of course cow chips—"prairie lignite." Stoves were even designed for these fuels. Unfortunately all three burned hot, burned rapidly, and left a lot of ashes. No one would call a cow chip fire a luxury—it smelled, there were vermin, and heaven knows it was dirty. But it was also available and it was free. As late as

Windmill used for power on the plains. (The Kansas State Historical Society, Topeka)

the depression years of the 1930's cow chips and corn cobs were being used as fuel on the Great Plains; more than one rural school district saved money by having its members stack cow chip fuel up the back wall of the schoolhouse, as high as the rafters, to provide fuel for winter days.

Three other developments of life on the plains involved wells, fencing, and irrigation. At first the farmers dug their wells and prayed for water at thirty or forty feet, although in many places fifty feet may have been more common. If they lived in poverty, a bucket on a windlass would do; but as time went on, hand pumps or the windmill became the accepted means of bringing well water to the surface. The merits of the windmill were noticed early, and that useful device became almost a symbol of the plains environment.

There was nothing new about the windmill, which had been used for centuries in Europe and was not unknown in the American east—in Pennsylvania, for example. But the wind in the western country was stronger and steadier than elsewhere, the wells were deeper, and the reliability of the machine almost a matter of life and death; so adjustments were made. The propeller was reduced in size, the rudder changed so that it would not break in the gusts but swing the propeller rapidly into the eye of the wind. A governor was needed, so that the propeller would not be whirled to the breaking point; a clutch was needed to sever automatically the power from the pump when the cattle drinking-tank was full of water. Bearings and cogs and housing were designed to last without servicing for long periods of time. The entire machine, including the tower, was being manufactured of steel and marketed by the big mail-order companies by the 1890's.

So necessary were the wells that professional well diggers and windmill builders were to be found in the plains region, much as there had been specialized prairie sod breakers farther east. Costs rapidly came down, so that by the late 1880's the twenty-five-dollar windmill was a reality. And so practical was it that it remains a concomitant of high plains rural life into our day—although now it costs a good deal more than twenty-five dollars, and rural electrification is making it obsolete.

There was also the need for fencing. On the Illinois and Iowa prairies, where timber was a valuable commodity, all manner of other fencing had been tried. Osage orange was the most successful of the many varieties of hedge plant that were experimented with for fencing, but sheep, hogs, and heifers often went through it—especially hogs. Hedgerows, actually ditches between fields, used along with hedges, were also tried as fencing substitutes, but nothing was completely satisfactory. Joseph Glidden, a Yankee-born Illinoisan, experimented with barbed wire and

Two cowboys fixing a break in a barbed wire fence, from a drawing by Frederick Remington. (Denver Public Library, Western History Department)

brought out a practicable, marketable product in the 1870's. There are some myths involved in the history of barbed wire: Joseph Glidden has been given credit for its invention, and the impression has been spread that the West was dissected by miles of barbed wire fencing in an incredibly short period of time. But Glidden was in fact not its inventor, since two Frenchmen in their native land had developed a barbed wire in the 1860's. And Gilbert Fite, an agricultural historian who was raised on a South Dakota farm, questions the emphasis that has been placed upon "bobbed wire." In his part of the country, children herded the cattle and kept them from the corn and wheat, while fencing advanced gradually, year by year, as the farmer progressed in the development of his farm. Barbed wire did not splice up the Great Plains all at once.

In the lands adjoining the mountains the cold, rippling creeks that carried water to the Platte, the Arkansas, or, on the western slope, to the

Colorado—or to the sterile Great Salt Lake—caught the eyes of the settlers and led to experiments in irrigation. The Mormons became masters of the art—and good irrigation practice *is* an art. On cold winter evenings when the wind whistled around the gaunt cabins at Winter Quarters on the bluffs overlooking the Missouri on the Nebraska side—where the Mormons halted for the winter of 1846-47 on their trek to the Great Salt Lake—Brigham Young had had men learned in the art give lectures to his bearded husbandmen. Having impressed upon them point number one—that water can *not* flow uphill—they went on to the more technical aspects. There was the size and depth and shape of main ditches and lateral outlets, the measurement of water allotments in acre-feet, the construction of locks, the elements of what every farmer should know about irrigation law. The pioneer band—a party of artisans that advanced ahead of the main migration—cut the first irrigation ditch down onto the parched desert from Cottonwood Canyon in the Wasatch, and as the hard-working Saints watched the sparkling, cold waters, their spirits rose, for in the waters lay the promise of future abundance. The water softened the soil so that it could be plowed and planted, and from the planting would come the grain.

And just as there were men who made a business of breaking the prairie with a special kind of plow, and men who became professional well diggers, so there were shrewd pioneers who sensed the importance of irrigation; ditch companies sprang up all along the front ranges. Years before the Newlands Act of 1902, which set up the Bureau of Reclamation, irrigation systems based on damming high country lakes, digging ditches, and the construction of aqueducts serpentining down Rocky Mountain canyons to small lakes on the plains (some of the lakes manmade) were being developed by pioneer entrepreneurs or by mutual companies. From these reservoirs more ditches led to the farms, which, when water was accessible, were almost immediately of premium value; for miners had to eat, and David K. Wall, who had been a farmer "back east," anticipated more gold in his pockets from diverting the waters of Cherry Creek into a plowed and planted field than from hard-rock mines or messy sluices. And indeed, he turned a neat profit. So did the early farmers of the Sacramento Valley in California and the Gallatin Valley of Montana.

Thus it happened that the pioneers spread over the new country and domesticated the land. Nature still reacted with her usual fare of tornadoes, droughts, blizzards, hailstorms, blight, bugs, days too hot and nights too cool; but still and all the earth produced in abundance. There was a beauty in the land's youthful fertility, a promise in the rich, earthy-smelling furrow plowed in the spring, and fulfillment in the wav-

Bottling champagne at the Buena Vista vineyard, Sonoma, California, in the early 1870's. (U.S. Office of War Information, National Archives)

Threshing by steam in the great wheat fields in the Red River Valley, Dakota Territory, 1878, from *Frank Leslie's Illustrated Weekly*.

ing golden grain, fresh and rich, in the autumn. Love for the new country was strong, for it sustained its promise.

There still remains a sub-chapter to this story. Historically, pastoralism existed prior to agriculture; the herder preceded the peasant. Even in Biblical times, the herders represented an earlier stage of civilization than the farmer and the village or city dweller. Herders were usually nomads, they ranged far, and loneliness and physical hardship were basic to their lives. There was little social intercourse and nothing of the "finer things of life" in their existence.

Surely herding and the new country went together. Colonial Massachusetts had a cattlemen's frontier in the western part of the Commonwealth, and cattle herders were so dispersed throughout the Carolina piedmont as to give a center of their activities the name Cowpens. The term "Old South" conjures up an image of white-pillared plantation mansions and slaves picking cotton, but it has been documented that the cattle business was of substantial importance to the ante-bellum economy. Davy Crockett had herded cattle across the Tennessee mountains. Like many another pioneer, he grazed cattle on a "range," as it was called, erected a cabin, and grew truck such as corn, cabbages, beans, and potatoes. When the range was overgrazed—to his way of thinking—he moved on. More sedentary agriculturalists took his place.

"Tara"-type plantation houses, lovely southern belles in hoop-skirted dresses, and happy slaves working the cotton make up the stereotyped image of the Old South. Yet the barefooted herder, with his crude cabin and truck patch and his swine and cows, was far more common, and was important to southern culture and economy. In the southern climate cattle could graze the year round without being fed hay and oats and other stored fodder. The forested hills were cleared by years of being fired by the Indians, so that wild oats, pea vines, and innumerable strains of wild grasses provided fodder; canebrakes and pine and brush clumps furnished protection from colder winter winds. Cowpen keepers, as they were called, moved their herds from grove to grove, pasture to pasture, always moving into public domain lands as former pasturage areas were surveyed and taken up by agriculturalists. Along the Mississippi in Louisiana and Arkansas, and in north and central Florida in the ante-bellum period, cattle grazed by the tens of thousands. When cotton pushed the herders out, they moved to the piney woods and sand barrens scattered over the southern terrain. Because they were adept at cracking their long snaky black whips, they were sometimes called Crackers. Casual travelers were not aware of the pigs and cattle they owned, hidden amongst thousands of acres of pine and mountains.

What is surprising is the extent of the grazing industry. The southern historian Frank L. Owsley estimates the number of cattle in the South as of 1850 at 650,000, "and a proportionate number of sheep and swine." The Georgia pine barrens in the same year (1850) produced 400,000 head of cattle, 85,000 sheep, 365,000 swine, and 36,000 horses and mules. "Grazing," writes Owsley, "as distinct from livestock feeding was of greater relative importance in the ante-bellum South than in any other part of the United States." Some owners ran 3,000 to 5,000 cattle, and branding was required by law.[2]

There is no question that herding was an important facet of the southern economy in the ante-bellum period, with the cities above the Ohio, along the Mississippi south of St. Louis, the plantations of the inland South, and the towns of the South Atlantic seaboard consuming the products. Yet history barely touches upon the subject. We ask why.

There are several reasons. In the South many of the grazing lands became cotton lands as soon as the public domain was surveyed and put up for sale. Eventually the herders were pushed into the infertile piney woods and sand barrens or swampy lowlands. Cattle did fine in those areas—the common belief that cattle only thrive on treeless plains is a fallacy, the result of two generations of "horse opera" movies and radio and television shows. (Actually, cattle take to brush, open woods, and canebrakes; they are whimsical brutes, canny in a stupid way, purposely hiding from man if at all possible.) The herders who lived in such areas did not compete with the agriculturalists. Semi-literate at best, neither politically nor socially did they carry weight in state or national politics. Most did not ride "high in the saddle" either; their herding, at least much of it, was done on foot. To their illiteracy and backwardness add the hookworm and occasional cases of pellagra, goitre, and other deficiency diseases, and the disappearance of this southern herding society, without leaving a heritage or even a trace, is readily understandable.

Yet after the Civil War a range-cattle industry arose which left a deep imprint upon American life. The industry still thrives. Besides its blooded Brahmas, white-faced Herefords, Shorthorns, jet-black Aberdeen Angus, and garish Santa Gertrudas, it has produced leading figures in business and politics.

There is a common belief that the range-cattle industry began deep in the southern heart of Texas. In a great diamond bounded on the north by San Antonio, east by Old Indianola, south by Brownsville and west by Laredo, the western cattle business is said to have had its beginnings; but this is, in fact, a historical half-truth. There were indeed millions of gaunt, horned, mealy-nosed, reddish and brownish longhorns on the southern plains of Texas, descendants of Spanish cattle. To "work" them, the Texans adopted Spanish words, methods, and paraphernalia such as the riata, chaps, and the cowboy boot, with its high heel and hard toe. The business expanded with remarkable swiftness after the Civil War, although in the 1840's herds had been driven to New Orleans or loaded on boats at Galveston and shipped there. After 1850 they were driven to California, where hungry miners, who had already decimated the California herds, provided a lucrative market for Texas beef.

What is not too well realized is the existence of a cattle-ranching business north of the South Platte River, dating at least from the late 1840's and the time of the heavy use of the Great Medicine Road—the Oregon Trail. Among the half million people who went up the trail were thousands who possessed oxen and milch cows, calves, and certainly an occasional bull. The stereotyped image of a close-knit wagon train, its members staying together until the destination was attained, is wrong in many respects, one of its most glaring omissions being the total absence of the cow column straggling in the rear; this consisted of the extra oxen and cattle being driven to the new homes. There, it was hoped, and with good reason, the cows and occasional bull would constitute the seed stock for healthy, fat, lowing herds.

But cattle and oxen developed sore hooves, they took sick, they occasionally died. They also needed fresh grass or succulent hay, both rare on the broad trail. In peak years, it must be remembered, the lead wagon of one train was rarely out of sight of the last wagon of the train up ahead. If there was only someone to trade tired oxen for fresh stock, some place along the trail where hay could be purchased or stock grazed, even for a price, in a well-watered meadow!

The demand created the supply. The Oregonians and the Forty-niners discovered shortly after they left the Missouri that the great trail was already enlivened with crude entrepreneurial establishments owned by ex-mountain men, ex-freight handlers, ex-soldiers, and other flotsam of the frontier. For one reason or another they had now settled down to sell, trade, and often build cattle and horse herds from the strays, mavericks, or sick or lame stock they acquired by fair means or foul.

From the Oregon Trail the cattle industry expanded both north and south. In the search for protected valleys in which to winter their cattle, as well as out of fear of the Mormons, cattlemen in northern Utah or southern Idaho worked northward to the Beaverhead, Ruby, and Deer Lodge valleys; thus began the cattle industry of western Montana. The Flathead Indians of western Montana and northeastern Idaho were already herding cattle when these white ranchers arrived.

By the mid-1850's the feasibility of wintering cattle in the northern valleys had been proven; all that awaited the emergence of a thriving industry was demand for the product. The gold discoveries of 1862 and after, which brought stampedes of miners to Coeur d'Alene, Virginia City, and Helena, provided the market. So lucrative was it that in 1866 Nelson Story trailed six hundred head of Texas longhorns across the Bozeman Trail, which in that year was under constant siege by Indians, and got them—or most of them—safely to the lush Gallatin Valley, where by the end of the 1860's the cattle industry was thriving. However, it was another decade before other ranchers dared advance above the North Platte in central and southern Wyoming, the hunting lands of the Sioux and Cheyenne. But the practicality of cattle grazing south of the Platte was demonstrated when the firm of Russell, Majors, and Waddell, the great freighters of the plains, wintered some fifteen thousand head of oxen over an area extending two hundred miles south of the river. When the Pike's Peak gold rush began small ranchers and a few large ones emerged almost at once to supply beef to the gold seekers.

Just as a form of government materialized almost magically in the gold camps, so too did a system, a *modus vivendi*, appear among these early cattlemen. Since water was the single absolute necessity which was not in abundance, an implicit understanding about land ownership arose. A cattleman had so many yards or acres along a stream, which gave him his water and his hay, and his cattle ranged outward from the stream, at least to the next water divide (a high point of land from which water would flow to a different gulch, canyon, or valley), this much land being considered that cattleman's property, though it was actually a part of the public domain.

Almost at once there were great ranchers. One was J. W. Iliff, whose ranch home was on the South Platte near the present town of Fort Morgan; by 1872 he was said to have 25,000 cattle grazing between present Greeley and Julesburg, Colorado Territory, in an area bounded on the north by the Union Pacific Railroad and on the south by the South Platte River. By 1868 or 1869 virtually all the good cattlelands in this area south of the Union Pacific had been taken up; and at this juncture "Hack" Reel of Cheyenne brought 148 head of cattle up from Texas and placed them on Pole Creek, north of the Union Pacific. The cattle wintered well and sold in Chicago as prime beeves. Knowledge of Reel's success led others to settle north of the UP, and after the Custer fight—and, within six months thereafter, the subjection of the Indians—cattle were being driven onto the ranges north of the North Platte. By the mid-1870's the ranges of Montana all the way to the Canadian border were being grazed.

The answer to questions about Indian troubles or trespass in this new country is that the cowboys and cattle barons defied the red men, grazed the lands where the rapidly disappearing buffalo had roamed, allowed cattle onto Indian reservations, got waylaid and scalped while herding, and murdered the Indians in return. Iliff's men were killed, his ranch buildings burned, his cattle wantonly slain; but he prevailed over all such adversity, while his Indian adversaries were subjected to increased restriction and control. In the 1870's and early 80's the business was so profitable that wealthy Easterners and Europeans, especially the English and the Scots, entered the business and ultimately controlled much of the western range.

It was in the late 1860's that the inevitable connection between the Texas range-cattle industry and all the rest of the western range was made. Texas had the stock; it was cheap and could be purchased easily. Contracts could be let for delivery of hundreds, a thousand, or fifteen hundred head to a northern range. Soon some Texans came north themselves. John Hittson's ranch in southern Colorado, for example, was the new home of a man whose first ranch had been along the Brazos.

Over all the vast spaces the Texas cattle were spread, and with them, up the Chisholm, the Goodnight-Loving, the Great Western, and other trails, came the most romantic of all American folk heroes, the cowboys. Though the word had been used in Texas prior to the Civil War, it did not achieve national usage until after President Arthur, in his State of the Union message in 1881, used it in speaking of some troublesome American renegades and desperadoes along the Mexican border. Previously, in common parlance, the cattle workers had been "herders," but to the public the word "cowboy" seemed to fit the new breed better. Now they became dime novel heroes. They were mounted, they were free, they were fighters. The mystique was complete.

Actually much of their life was sheer drudgery, their work dirty, tedious, and dangerous. Sometimes the only water they had to drink was so alkaline that, in order to drink it without unpleasant effects, they would add a small amount of vinegar to neutralize the alkali, then a teaspoonful of soda, which gave them a refreshing soft drink. Far from being a handsome lover, the typical cowboy was apt to have a crooked nose that had been broken at least once, a game leg, a hernia, a finger or two that had never mended satisfactorily after a fracture, and a couple of teeth missing, with the rest yellowed from tobacco juice and full of cavities. Save for a very few, whom we can thank for chronicling their way of life, the cowboys were non-readers, non-writers, and non-capitalists. Like sailors who lived most of the time at sea and caroused in port, the cowboys worked on the range and raised hell when they came to town, which was not very often. They were a group distinct from their employers, who were always called ranchers or ranchmen.

Yet by the 1890's the cowboy at his best had become a living myth. In such cattle country areas as the expanse along the North Fork of the Gunnison River in Colorado, they were "the recognized blue-bloods . . . the aristocrats of Louix XV's Versailles court," wrote an historian of the area, "were no more particular about their attire than these colorful, hard-riding inhabitants of the cattle range."[3] Above their high-heeled boots and jingling spurs they wore woolen pants and smooth leather chaps; and they actually did wear six-shooters. Their shirts were likely to be blue and double-breasted, with large pearl buttons down the sides. They wore a gaudy handkerchief around the neck and a big sombrero or ten-gallon hat. Indeed, there was a glaring contrast between their flamboyance and the dirt and drudgery of their day-to-day chores.

Never mind. The cowboy had worked his way into dime novels; Stephen Crane published his short story "The Blue Hotel" in 1899; and Owen Wister's *The Virginian*, replete with good guys, bad guys, a pretty schoolmarm from the effete East, and a lynching, appeared in 1902. But by the time the romanticism began, most of the romantic elements, such as they were—the long drive, a limitless range, and the roundup—had disappeared from the range-cattle industry; all but the roundup had pretty well ended by 1887.

Although the long drive is associated with the Texans, it must be remembered that cattle had been driven up through Tennessee and Kentucky to Cincinnati and other markets in the eastern Midwest in the 1820's and 1830's. Texans in the 1840's had shipped cattle to New Orleans, Vicksburg, Natchez, and St. Louis by boat, and after 1849 had herded them along the hot trails to California. Thus the idea of driving cattle to the railhead at Sedalia, Missouri, was new only as regards destination. From there, since the idea seemed successful, it was natural that the point where buyer and seller met would advance westward with the iron rails. Joseph G. McCoy, an Illinois livestock trader, was instrumental in making Abilene a great cattle town; Newton and Wichita, on the Santa Fe, and finally Dodge City by 1875, were later centers of the trade. Then, as the Texans expanded and had business dealings with the northern ranchers, Ogallala, Nebraska; Casper, Wyoming; and cold, windswept Miles City, Montana, all had their days as cattlemen's centers (which, to a degree, they still are). It can be said that by 1880 the western range-cattle industry had expanded to its limits. Not only the high plains but the mountain pastures of the Rockies, the mountain parks such as North, Middle, and South Parks in Colorado, the mountain encircled "holes," such as Brown's Hole, Jackson's Hole, and

Texas cattle in a Kansas corn corral, from a Frederick Remington engraving. (The Kansas State Historical Society, Topeka)

Cattle drive on the trail. (The Kansas State Historical Society, Topeka)

A typical cattle town, Lawrence, Kansas, 1867. Note cattle in the street. (The Kansas
State Historical Society, Topeka)

An early Montana ranch. (Geological Survey, The National Archives)

Pierre's Hole (now known as the Teton Basin), the sage flats of Idaho, and the watered parts of Arizona were all part of the land of prairie and sky that constituted the cattleman's new country—the last new country. The wide-ranging nature of the cattle-raising process, the vast area of public domain in which the critters could run, the quick potential profits, and finally, the coming of the railroads, all explain the rapid spread of the industry.

And as was so often the case in the new country, settlement was ahead of society. In the cattle business, settlement meant a ranch house, a corral, and outbuildings down in a cottonwood grove alongside a stream, on a parcel of 160, 320, or 640 acres that was eventually claimed, surveyed, and legally purchased (with the aid of the Timber Culture, Desert Land, Preemption, and Homestead acts, all of which had township-sized loopholes). From the home ranch the cattle grazed free on public domain rangeland that extended for thousands of square miles in all directions; a cow could easily stray over a hundred miles from the home range.

Like the California gold seekers, all of whom staked out claims on lands that never belonged to any of them, the cattle kings asserted range rights and evolved their own system of control over land they did not own. At best, as with the Wyoming Stock Grower's Association, they created an organization that managed the roundups, provided for the registration of brands (by 1891 there were more than five thousand in Wyoming alone), maintained itself with revenue from the sale of mavericks, exerted itself as a lobby, hired detectives and inspectors, and took concerted action to keep pleuro-pneumonia and Texas fever from the Wyoming herds. At worst (and again the Wyoming Stock Grower's Association is the example) these extra-legal "governments" protected the ranges and the herds of those who were already there, attempted to keep out or squeeze out the small rancher, and fought the government when attempts were made to enforce land laws. Finally, their members, or a substantial minority of them, forgot that the frontier was ended. The association used murder-by-ambush and hired thugs imported from Texas or Denver via a special train to frighten off the farmers and small ranchers—"nesters"—who were settling on the range. If the big ranchers had waited a generation or two, the course of events would have forced most of the small operators out of business anyway, and the lynching of Cattle Kate, the damning evidence that resulted in the legal execution of the hired gunman Tom Horn, and the Johnson County Range War would not be to this day dark marks on the association's record.

In essence, the initial range-cattle industry was based upon the rapid exploitation of a vast new country owned but barely managed by the

United States Government. The land was temporarily free, and as soon as the Indians were forced onto reservations and the buffalo were gone, the nutritious grass cover lay waiting for the white man's herds. These cattle were very cheap, too, so that a winter's losses of 10 or 15 per cent was considered normal shrinkage and was easily absorbed into the few costs that did exist. The cowboy was cheap labor at forty dollars a month and room and board. In the early 1880's the dividends of some companies were as high as 20 per cent.

It could not last. Some of the worst offenders in overstocking the ranges were the very cattle companies that were titans in the associations. Homesteaders, known as grangers, nesters, honyockers, or scissorbills, staked out quarter sections, and their stock mingled with the vast herds of the big companies—and somehow the little fellow's herd grew. Courts in the cow towns championed the small ranchers. Rustling became endemic, and the victims were the big ranchers. Meanwhile cattlemen had begun building up their herds with Hereford bulls; they lost money every time a scrawny but virile old Texan horned in on the cows, or when the blue northers of winter took the lives of their expensive but softened-by-civilization bulls. A man could afford to lose 10 or 15 per cent of a herd of scrubby Texas steers, but imported "pilgrims" (as they were called) from the Middle West were something else again. Ranchers began using barbed wire to fence ranges they did not own. In winter storms the cattle drifted southward with the prevailing wind, struck the fences, and piled up and froze. Up to 85 per cent of some herds were thus destroyed. Yet, as nearly always happens, the "system" was too massive to be broken save by catastrophe. The acrid odor of prairie fires in the hot, dry summer of 1886 warned that the herds would be thin and in bad shape as winter came on. The terrible winter of 1886-87 is still remembered. Charles Russell, the artist, used to tell of the cowboy who left a saloon for home in a blizzard, and froze stiff down at the crossroads. Since the ground was frozen and burial would have to wait until spring, his drinking buddies hung a lantern on him to guide others to safety.

That terrible winter was the trauma that ended the first phase of the range-cattle industry. From then on, the cattle country could be lonely and desolate, as it still is in many parts, but it became settled country within the limit of the sparse population such country can maintain. Men purchased lands all along the streams, then learned about irrigation canals, lateral ditches, locks, and reservoirs. They planted timothy, bluegrass, alfalfa, and lucerne. The cowboy had to get off his horse and ride a hay mower, operate a haylift, work on barbed-wire fencing. Blooded livestock, given loving care, chomped hay in a barn while the blue northers whistled outside. Only in the summer did the cattle go out on the open range, leased now from the government under terms that remain a source of hot dispute to this day.

The cowboys still wear Stetsons and cowboy boots, but now they drive air-conditioned pickups and heat their branding irons with Skelly butane gas flame. In both farm country and cow country today, corporations purchase the acreage that until recently had remained in the hands of one family for generations. The old homesteads are burned up, dismantled, or bulldozed to the ground. Consolidation takes place. Expensive machinery such as $30,000 gleaners, operated by hired laborers, works the consolidated corporate farms and cattle ranches and produces more food than ever before for a population that is greater than ever before. Computers determine a steer's sojourn on the plains, the feed lot to which it is later sent, the time necessary to fatten it, and the slaughterhouse to which it will be sent. Even the cattle country is settled country now.

IV

Despoilment: The Rape of the New Country

Destruction and Construction by Nature and Man

The frontiersman's life-style involved only simple things; he lived at first almost entirely off the land. Civilization decreed that he have a shelter, and so he built a log cabin; that he have fields and raise grain, so he girdled the trees and burnt them when they dried. To the pioneer the sound of a good, clean lick of the axe in a two-hundred-year-old oak was but the pleasant staccato assurance of civilization's advance. Fields of waving grain, meadows in which cattle grazed, crossroads settlements —these were sure signs of the march of civilization. The existence somewhere of a virgin forest meant that man had not yet arrived.

Availability of wood in the new country meant that a civilization could be built. Wood is easily worked; much can be done with it using a minimum of tools. Coachmakers, cabinet makers, furniture makers, coopers, boat builders, coffin makers, gunsmiths, and housebuilding carpenters came to know the good and poor qualities of a dozen or more kinds of wood. They knew how to season it, how to cut it, how to use it. In the early days live oak, red cedar, and cypress were chosen for ships; black walnut made excellent furniture, supplied the framework for Singer's sewing machines, and provided the material for coffins fit to bury the affluent and the gunstocks for rifles. There were certain kinds of wood for blocks and pulleys, mallets and buggy whip handles, yokes for oxen, wagon and coach frames, felloes and hubs for wheels, for all but the springs of Connecticut-made wooden clocks, and for the floors of covered bridges whose sides and roofs were of a cheaper, softer, and less lasting variety.

The balloon frame house, an American innovation, housed much of the nation, and it was made entirely of wood. Sidewalks and corduroy and plank roads were constructed of wood. All river boats were of wood. Save for the running gear and the little pot-bellied stove, the railroad car was of wood, as were the water tanks, station buildings, platforms, and warehouses. Millions of ties were used to cushion and hold fast the rails that criss-crossed the nation. Wooden trestles reminiscent of some kind of gargantuan Chinese puzzle carried the trains across gorges. Wood fired the steamboats, each of which consumed about a cord of hardwood an hour—and a cord is a pile eight feet long, four feet high, and four feet wide. Locomotives continued to use wood long after the trend had turned towards coal burners. Both the Union Pacific's No. 119 and the Central Pacific's No. 60 (also called the Jupiter), which touched cowcatchers at Promontory Point on May 10, 1869, were wood burners. Here, then, is part of the explanation for the plunder of the forests. The nation could not exist without lumber. It wanted it in all kinds and in great quantities, it demanded steady, reliable supply, and it wanted it delivered to the door at a reasonable price.

Originally about 40 per cent of the contiguous forty-eight states were covered with forests, nearly all of which were in the public domain. Save for a minor exception or two, that forest cover was considered by the government to be like any other acreage. It was sold at a base price of $2 an acre, later reduced to $1.25, just like prairie lands, mountain lands, bottomlands, and even desert and swamp lands. At this point, in theory, the auction system was supposed to correct the obvious differences in value of lands. In theory prime timberland would command a much higher price than would scrub or farm land at auction time.

It did not work that way. In the "up for grabs" climate of opinion that prevailed during most of the nineteenth century, the government was a weak, far-off landlord, the new country was a vacuum, and the general attitude sanctified the right of possession and exploitation as a part of the scheme of things, as a part of natural law. The people were in a frenzy to build a civilization; and no one considered the terrible cost to the environment. That frenzy is only partially explained by the profit system. It was that, and something more, something connected with the spirit of western man that demanded an end to the Garden of Eden.

Furthermore the plundering was done in illegal ways. Granted that government should have come up with a workable system, it is nonetheless true that fraud, deception, bribery, and other forms of chicanery were used to seize the forests which legally belonged to the government. The goal of the lumbermen was the acquisition as cheaply as possible (and often for nothing at all) of hundreds of thousands of acres of timber. There *did* exist a seemingly inexhaustible supply that was very weakly secured, and an insatiable demand for lumber; and thus opportunity for great profit. A corollary was the creation of a great and powerful industry employing thousands of people who became specialists—the lumberjacks; from it arose songs and stories, including the legendary figures of Paul Bunyan and his Great Blue Ox. Not just communities but entire regions flourished from the lumber business. Thus there existed a pressure group that possessed potentially great political power which it could guide in the direction of favorable timber policy. Political power in the nineteenth century, as in our own day, could accomplish much that was basically dishonest, immoral, and unethical. It is from this situation that the word *plunder* attains validity as a description of what happened to America's Great Forest.

Timber stealing began very early in American history, antedating by many years the American Revolution. The pine forests of New England offered choice mast trees, the pine forests of the Carolinas produced turpentine and tar—"naval stores"—and deep in Florida and along the sluggish rivers flowing into the Gulf, all the way into Louisiana, were the live oaks, red cedars, and cypresses so useful in shipbuilding. His Majesty's government had sent timbermen through the forests, who, when they came upon fine trees for naval uses, branded them with a Broad Arrow, a sort of large crow's foot. This signified that a tree was to be retained for the King's navy, and no one was to disturb it.

Of course such a simple evidence of ownership in thinly populated country did little or no good. By numerous subterfuges the natives checked the King's intentions and cut promiscuously; and many a felled tree was a forest giant bearing the Broad Arrow.

Little was done by the new nation to protect the forests until 1799. Trouble with warring European nations and the Barbary pirates made Congress aware of the need for naval timber reserves. Stories were bandied about telling of widespread stealing of hardwood from the public domain, especially in Florida and along the Gulf Coast. Congress provided up to $200,000 for President John Adams to purchase such lands to be used as naval timber reserves, but the country was not yet really conscious of the threat, and so only Grover's Island and Blackbeard's Island off the coast of Georgia were purchased. In separate actions in 1817, 1822, and 1827, the president was authorized to set aside live oak lands along the Gulf Coast, and John Quincy Adams at least saw that this was done; Santa Rosa Island off Pensacola was one of the reserves he established. He was the first President to manifest any real interest in conservation and was ahead of his time in comprehension of the problem. His term of office was just four years, however, and his successor, Andrew Jackson, cancelled nearly everything Adams had tried to do. An act of 1831 decreed that it was unlawful to cut timber from the public lands, but, with Jackson in the White House, the act was virtually a dead measure from the first.

By the 1840's the forests of New England and New York had been sadly depleted, and the lumber trade began to shift to the Great Lakes states. An enormous timberland was opened at the same time that the prairie and plains states and the rapidly expanding railroads needed millions of feet of lumber. In 1842 some two million shingles were delivered in Galena, Illinois; in 1850 Wisconsin and Michigan alone produced about nine million feet of lumber. Long before 1860 Chicago had become the lumber center of the nation, replacing Bangor, Maine, and Albany, New York. The building of the Illinois Central contributed materially to this boom. Even the Pacific Coast enjoyed an early timber business, and in the 1850's was exporting lumber to the Orient.

Timber barons had by now emerged with prestige, political power, and great plans. They coveted the forest covering the public domain, but they did not desire to pay a minimum of $1.25 an acre for it or to compete for it with others at auction, nor even to wait until the federal government had surveyed it and formally opened it to purchasers; and they did not want it for settlements. One of their practices was the "round forty." By this subterfuge they actually did purchase forty acres of land, but it was often land poorly surveyed—very useful for legal defense if questions were asked. Upon this piece of private property they set up a saw mill, barracks, cook house, and field office. Then the owner cut to the horizon on the adjoining public domain, on land he described as being "captured."

They had also found ways of obtaining legal possession of lands by questionable means. The Preemption Act of 1841 permitted bona fide settlers to squat on public lands and then have first rights to the acreage at $1.25 an acre when the land was opened for sale. There was nothing to prevent the sale of such lands to timber barons as soon as the purchase had been made, and fraudulent preemption claims were widespread. Military bounty land script, issued to veterans of the War of 1812 and numerous Indian wars, was purchased in great quantities by lumbermen.

Perhaps the greatest windfall of all for the timber barons was the Swamplands Act of 1850. This well-intentioned act was based on the growing awareness that millions of acres along the new country rivers had not been purchased because of the danger of flooding. The idea was to give such lands to the states, which would use the revenue from their sale for reclamation projects. But soon the federal government was giving lands to the states without examining the plats to make sure the lands *were* swamplands. It was the greatest land grab in the country's history; some 63 million acres were transferred to the states which, easily manipulated by the timber barons, turned around and sold such prime land for as little as 25 cents an acre, less than the value of the lumber in a single harvestable tree. Or the states gave land grants to wagon road, railroad, or canal companies, which in turn certainly knew what to do with them. Florida did both: it sold 4 million acres for 25 cents an acre and disposed of 16 million acres of land grants to wagon road, canal, and railroad companies. Much of that state's total domination by special interests, nearly as powerful today as they were more than a hundred years ago, stems from these seamy beginnings. Louisiana sold prime cedar stands for 50 cents an acre. And what about all those funds for reclamation? Almost none of the revenue went for the avowed purpose.

The famous Morrill Act, by which states were given 30,000 acres of the public domain for each representative and senator they had in Congress, the revenue from which was to fund agricultural and mechanical colleges, resulted in the issuance by many states of land script, a substantial portion of which fell into private hands at much less than $1.25 an acre. Some of the best pinelands in the southeastern states were sold to a very few men for about 50 cents an acre.

When the government reduced the size of Indian reservations, much of the freed land fell into the hands of timber barons, who received in this way some of the best timberlands in the Wisconsin and Minnesota north woods. Loopholes were found in the Homestead Act, and lumberjacks gladly took up homesteads and claimed settlement and improvements that were ludicrous as well as fraudulent (such as construction of a cabin eighteen by thirty *inches*). After fourteen months at most, the lands could be purchased for $1.25 an acre. Thousands of such fraudulent homestead entries were filed.

Many a Victorian wooden mansion, with its gingerbread scrollwork, iron deer on extensive lawns, and dainty gazebo in the garden, was the property of a local timber baron, much as the state road contractor's mansion graces so many small towns and cities today. Government's share of the guilt lies in its failure to provide sensible legislation. Incredibly, it was not until 1878 that measures were passed specifically to provide for the acquisition of timber from the public domain: the Timber Cutting Act (also called the Free Timber Act) and the Timber and Stone Act.

The former granted citizens of certain areas the privilege of cutting timber from mineral lands. But what *were* mineral lands? This was never clearly specified, so the exploiters chose the most liberal interpretation and cut at will. The latter act at first applied only to the Pacific states of

A group of loggers who have just felled a mighty redwood in the Pacific Northwest.
(Culver Pictures)

California and Oregon, plus Washington Territory and Nevada; in 1892 it was extended to all states still possessing a public domain. It provided that non-mineral, unoccupied land that was considered unfit for cultivation but was valuable because of its timber cover or deposits of stone was open to entry; and it prohibited both preemption and homestead. No one was to be allowed to purchase over 160 acres, and the purchaser signed an affidavit certifying that he bought for his own uses and did not purchase the land for speculative purposes. For a score of years after its passage the price per acre, $2.50, remained the same.

Little land was purchased under the Timber and Stone Act in the five years after 1878. Then timber barons let it be known that they would purchase forest lands from anyone who entered an acreage under the act. They used sailors, hoboes, their own employees, and whole railroad carloads of people to stake out claims, even giving them the funds to buy. At all stages of the transaction the lumber company handled the formalities of publishing the proper notices, hiring men to swear to the validity of settlement, paying for the lands and receiving the receipts. Obviously the local register and receiver had to be in collusion. In one case, over 14,000 acres in California went to one man under this act; in a Washington case, a company gained control of 100,000 acres, attempted to bribe the investigating government agent for $5,000, and prevailed upon the government to have him dismissed. Local feeling, it should be added, was almost always in favor of the company; the government men were considered snooping pests. All told, some 13,500,000 acres were disposed of under the Timber and Stone Act; the record for the Timber Cutting Act is equally dismal.

Two Italian companies, one in Florida and one in Alabama, were charged with receiving, by way of fraudulent homestead entry, in the case of the former, 4,512,000 feet of timber from the public lands, and in the latter 17 million feet. Turpentine distillers brazenly hacked at the trunks of pines and took the sap; after a few years this killed the pines, but what matter? They were on the public domain. There was one case in which the turpentiners worked along the line of a southern railroad, destroying the trees of the public domain sections, but leaving the alternate sections belonging to the railroad strictly alone. Turpentiners, incidentally, were among the most vicious subscribers to the barbaric convict lease system which lasted well into the twentieth century in a few southern states.

The railroads quite understandably took a liberal view of the right granted them of using raw materials from the public domain "adjacent to the line of the road" for construction purposes. President Chester Arthur's secretary of the interior, Henry M. Teller (1881-85), interpreted this as meaning timber growing anywhere within fifty miles of the track. By the turn of the century some four-fifths of the timber in the United States had fallen into private hands. The Southern Pacific and the Northern Pacific railroads were the two largest owners, with the Weyerhauser lumber company third. At one time that timber baron purchased over 600,000 acres of prime forest land from the Northern Pacific. Most lumber men, however, were small operators who had control over relatively small acreages of forested lands.

Besides the lumbermen there was another forest destroyer that wreaked havoc in the new country: the forest fire. It is clear evidence of the absence of concern that terrible fires raged out of control and destroyed millions of acres in the nineteenth century with hardly a warning from officials. Timber thieves set fire to land from which they had taken—to the brush and stumps and young trees—to destroy the evidence of their thievery. Settlers in piney woods areas of the South set the forest on fire to kill off snakes and insects. Fires raged out of control because hunters and campers never took such simple precautions as dousing their campfires when they left them; the big smokestacks of railroad locomotives shot sparks and cinders out into the dry fields and forests adjacent to the rails; and it was not at all unusual for entire regions to live in a late summer haze caused by the smoke of raging fires, with no attempt being made to control them.

In 1871, the same year as the famous Chicago fire, a blaze cut across the state of Michigan from Lake Michigan to Lake Huron; in that same year the terrible Peshtigo fire occurred, burning a million and a quarter acres and killing more than a thousand people. In 1881 a fire east of Saginaw, Michigan, killed 125 people and destroyed 1,800 square miles of forest. The fury of a forest fire is difficult to convey in words. The heat becomes so intense that whole trees burst into flame at once, and fire tops from one tree to another. The earth cover is destroyed, and six

Scene of the kind of panic and disaster that a raging forest fire could create, from *Harper's Weekly*, 1871. (Chicago Historical Society)

or eight inches of ashes may cover the ground where fertile humus once lay.

There were some prophets in the declining wilderness who brought about the nation's first wave of conservation activity. The names of Carl Schurz, Hayes' secretary of the interior, Bernard E. Fernow, head of the Department of Agriculture's Forestry Division, and George Perkins Marsh, a philosopher of conservation, loom large in the story. The growth of the conservation idea is evident in resolutions of the National Academy of Sciences and of the American Forestry Association which called attention to the depletion of the nation's forests and suggested measures to halt the destruction. Arbor Day was probably originated in Nebraska, April 27, 1872, and the Timber Culture Act, passed by Congress in 1873, provided land in exchange for the planting of a portion of it with trees. Arnold Hague of the United States Geological Survey grasped the need of forest cover as a means of controlling stream flow to prevent floods. Others saw the demise of the forests as ending the prevalence of game animals, and therefore the thrills of the hunt.

The first great victory for the conservationists was in 1891 when Arnold Hague manipulated John W. Noble, President Harrison's secretary of the interior, into setting aside 13 million acres as forest reserves in which lumbering was forbidden. By 1909, when Theodore Roosevelt left office, over 150,000,000 acres had been set aside, including much of that part of the original forest—about 20 per cent—that, as of 1920, was still uncut, virgin forest.

But the story of conservation, though its beginnings are in the nineteenth century, belongs essentially to the twentieth. In the century of the new country the Great Forest was all but destroyed as a great nation was built. We are fortunate that an age of youthful maturity arrived while there was still enough forest to make it worth saving—and that it was rescued.

Change, of course, is the very essence of life, and of nature. Long before the white man came, or the Indian roamed at will, nature itself was making alterations in the landscape. Forest and prairie fires, started by lightning, reduced millions of acres to ashes and desolation. Man had nothing to do with the climatic cycle that included long periods of drought, when prairie and forest became tinder dry, as ready to burst into fire as an open bucket of gasoline, and then wet periods resulting in prairies inundated with water, such as George Rogers Clark encountered on his winter expedition to Vincennes in 1778. Long before the white man there were swollen rivers that carried off everything in the way of their rushing waters. The mighty Missouri, by way of example, was always muddy—so much so that its waters permanently changed the appearance of the Mississippi into which it flowed.

The Missouri was so boisterous, swift, and tree-strewn that the phrase "new country" takes on a very literal meaning when it refers to the vast area drained by that river. The Missouri flows through many hundreds of miles of bluffs, which the river, as it twists and turns, undercuts, weakens, and thus brings down upon itself with thousands of tons of sand and marls. Any willow or cottonwood, bison or, today, cattle which may be standing on top tumbles into the mighty river. As snags and sawyers or as free-floating hulks the great trees began a long watery journey. Just how far any of these Missouri River cottonwoods came toward the Mississippi delta is conjectural. Those that did make it were mere additions to others that had fallen in along the Mississippi's own banks. In the delta country this river driftwood stacked up and was used as perches and nesting places by pelicans and herons; the great piles reminded some travelers of palisades. Yet much of the time the Mississippi was wide and placid, whereas the Missouri was a river in haste and turmoil, a stream that belonged in a geologically active terrain where sea level was thousands of feet down and maddeningly far away.

Basically man has done two things with the Missouri River country. In his haste to tear up the soil for farms and cut off the forest cover for lumber, he hurried the runoff from thousands of ditches, creeks, and rivers tributary to the Missouri, and so increased the big river's latent destructiveness. Then came those myopic twentieth-century beavers with bulldozers, the Army Engineers, who built dam after dam (and, if not restrained, will continue to do so). In a precarious and tenuous way, the mighty Missouri is today under control; it is less destructive than it was before the coming of the white man. But—let three or four heavy rains occur at just the right time and at just the right places—then, watch out! Moreover, the dams themselves upset the spawning of fish and the nesting of wildfowl where marshes once lay; and they inundate prime ranch and farm land.

Usually, man has made things worse. For example, in the 1840's and 50's there was much malaria in the Ohio and Mississippi valleys. Probably the disease was carried there initially by white men who had it in their systems and had then been bitten by New World mosquitoes. Settlers in the valleys made things worse by cutting timber, often leaving a wasteland full of pools in which stagnant water collected, providing breeding places for clouds of the humming pests. In Indiana reservoirs were constructed to hold and control the waters for canals; these too became breeding places for malarial mosquitoes.

Today civilized man has drained swamps, reforested, and in other ways taken measures to make the land more liveable—for himself, at least. A rare example of man improving on nature is his final destruction of the so-called Red River Raft above Natchitoches, Louisiana. First noted by French explorers as early at 1721; this was an amazing tangle of old logs, brush, limbs, branches, silt, leaves, and anything else that came floating down the twisting stream. The material was caught at the upstream limit as by a dam. By about 1800 it was at least fifty miles long, and by the 1830's nearly 140 miles. It rose and fell with the river that gurgled under it; in places it gave sustenance to trees rooted in its tangled floor that grew to heights equal to trees on land. Where soil collected amongst the vines, trunks, branches, and detritus, the vegetation was like a jungle. There were a few spaces in this 140-mile span where the river was clear, but within a mile or two the Raft began again. It was, of course, a hindrance to navigation and settlement. As the front end tore away, the rear picked up new flotsam, so that the massive encumbrance worked upstream like a serpent. The Army Engineers, led initially by Captain Henry W. Shreve of steamboat fame, began clearing the river in the 1820's; not until 1880 was the Raft finally eliminated.

So it is true that the land was not all perfect when the white man arrived, and that he sometimes did succeed in improving the Garden of Eden he found here. We hear much of the bluegrass region of Kentucky; but few realize that bluegrass is not native to Kentucky's sylvan glades and meadows. It is an Old World grass, its date of introduction into this country unknown. It probably came in with an early colonist who carried a bag of grass seed which contained, among others, the type *Poa pratensis*. Climate and soil in the new country were just right for it, and this nourishing pasture grass (not blue but a rich green) added to the natural attraction of the limestone regions of Kentucky and Tennessee. However, the Canada thistle, the Yellow Star thistle, and the European herb known as the Russian thistle (the "tumbling tumbleweed") did not prove so beneficial.

So too did the white man bring the European honeybee to this country. Its exact date of entrance is not definitely known (one authority places it in 1638 in New England), nor are we sure how a colony of bees, or at least a queen and a dozen workers, were kept alive through the long voyage. Once here, however, the honeybee found many a flower for nectar. By the 1770's the bees were busy in the Ohio Valley and down in Kentucky, and they seem to have advanced ahead of the pioneers all the way across the continent.

Still another white man's importation was the horse, which came with the Spaniards, was raised on ranches in the high central plain of

Mexico, was in New Mexico at the time of the founding of Jamestown, broke out to freedom or was stolen by Indians, and advanced into the Great Plains. Here was the most perfect home for the horse save, perhaps, for the steppes of Asia. Texas, from the Palo Duro Canyon southward to the Salt Fork of the Brazos, and between the Nueces River and the Rio Grande, was the most idyllic area of all. In this "Wild Horse Desert" the mustangs—coyote duns, grays, pintos, coppers, milk-whites, midnight blacks, and just about every combination of the above—flourished with few dangerous enemies. Over time they multiplied, until they ranged from the prairies and river bottoms east of the Mississippi to the high plains and valleys on both sides of the Rockies and into the Pacific Northwest and California. What these horses, which were descended from excellent Spanish stock, lost in attractiveness, they made up in endurance, agility, and ability to survive in the feral state. These were the horses acquired by the plains Indians, making them the freest and most mobile of the red men, and the most formidable opponents to the white man's advance into the new country.

In the balance, man probably brought more flora and fauna that was detrimental than was beneficial to the new country. Sometime around the end of the nineteenth century someone imported some Chinese chestnut trees. They carried a fungus, *Endothia parasitica*, to which the Chinese chestnut was immune, but not the American chestnut. Today about nine million acres of chestnut trees have been killed by this fungus, which has defied all the scientific expertise of America's best parasitologists. The "spreading chestnut tree" is as rare in America today as the village smithy who once worked under it.

Or take birds: the house sparrow was imported into Brooklyn in 1850 and 1852 to feast on the pestiferous cankerworms that were attacking the shade trees there. Until about 1900 these blandly colored little chirpsters were seen mostly in the larger cities. Then a population explosion took place, and they spread throughout the land. They now number in the millions and have pushed out many prettier birds with pleasant songs. Or again, no one who has cringed as he walked away from some of the big public buildings, such as the National Archives, in Washington, D.C., has not cursed the presence of the ugly crow-like starlings there. These too were introduced—in New York in 1890—and, being without natural enemies, have multiplied until they number in the millions. They too have displaced other more pleasurable birds but have given the new country very little in return.

Of more interest, but more tragic, is the story of what man did to the birds and animals that were already here. Perhaps nowhere in history is there a better example of man's destruction of entire species of bird and

Route of a proposed ship canal in Illinois, from *Frank Leslie's Illustrated Weekly.*
Note the flocks of birds in the sky.

animal life. The bird life of the new country was rich almost beyond imagination in both numbers and varieties. Tanagers and swifts, owls and
swallows, eagles and hawks, vultures and turkeys, parakeets and hum-
mingbirds, ospreys and terns, swans and egrets, ducks and geese, flickers
and chickadees, all flourished on the land and in the clear air above it.
Hardly was there a pen-and-ink sketch or an etching made of scenes in
nineteenth-century America that did not have little flocks of birds dap-
pling the sky. Such flocks are no longer commonplace, and what was the
normal scene then now strikes us as somewhat unusual. Men did not
comprehend the human ability to destroy, just as a half century ago
they could not comprehend automobiles so numerous as to cause smog;
so there was no effort whatsoever made either to understand or to protect bird life. Not until 1918, with the passage of the Federal Migratory
Bird Treaty Act signed by the United States and Canada, was spring
shooting of game species forbidden, although the Lacey Act of 1909 and
the McClean Law of 1913 (also known as the Migratory Bird Act) were
the beginning steps in placing migratory birds under federal protection.
Of what good was a protective law in one state when the birds flew next
over a state without such legislation?

And so, as was inevitable, several species were destroyed. The great auk was already all but extinct by 1776, although the last one was not taken until July 3, 1844, off the coast of Iceland. These penguin-like birds, whose breeding place was Funk Island off the far northeastern side of Newfoundland, could be bopped on the head or otherwise killed easily. Their feathers were useful for mattresses and their meat edible and also good for fish bait. It is true that many species have become extinct due to natural selection, and that about 97 per cent of the birds that have become extinct in the past two hundred years have been island birds which were anomalies in the modern world. However, although it exhibited great stupidity and helplessness before man, the great auk was in no way endangered with extinction until man appeared.

Then there was that rather odd-looking bird, the Labrador duck, of which the last one ever seen was killed in New York in 1878. And there was the heath hen, resembling a small chicken or the still-flourishing great prairie chicken. Probably never abundant, the heath hen was known to have lived from New Hampshire to Chesapeake Bay. Active attempts were made to save this attractive bird: some 200 of them were coddled and protected at Martha's Vineyard, and their numbers grew to about 2,000 before fire, disease, an influx of their natural enemies the goshawks, and a poor sex ratio of about two females to ten males, reduced the heath hen to extinction by 1931.

A far more prevalent bird, and a beautiful species, therefore a more tragic loss, was the Carolina parakeet. Of some 500 species of parrots, this was the only one that lived and bred in the United States. Colored in beautiful yellows, oranges, and greens, a foot long overall, it lived in flocks and was found from the Atlantic coastal plain inland to the Mississippi and then south to the Gulf Coast. The factors in the bird's undoing were its taste for the farmer's fruits and seeds, its plumage, which was saleable, and its tendency to flock, so that large numbers were easily killed with a scattergun. It was a chattering species, and if caught was easily tamed. The last of these beautiful birds was taken in Florida in 1912.

But the greatest loss of bird life has yet to be mentioned. This was the destruction of the passenger pigeon. Sometimes new country farmers who lived along the Great Lakes or in Ohio or Pennsylvania, Kentucky or Tennessee, Missouri or Iowa, would pause in amazement at the sheer numbers of these birds. How many? A horde of them sometimes took twelve or fourteen hours to pass a given point, each flock at least a mile wide, one flock so close behind another as to be almost indistinguishable from the one ahead. And they were several layers deep. Anywhere from two to ten pigeons filled every square yard of space. This means that a

Sometimes the bag was limited only by the capacity of the wagon to carry it home.
Duck hunters with a morning's bag. (State Historical Society of Iowa)

single flyover of a day's duration involved hundreds of millions of pigeons—and the incredible part of it is that these statistics are almost certainly correct. Conservative estimates put the passenger pigeon population within the United States—essentially east of the Mississippi and northward to Canada—at three to five billion, 25 to 40 per cent of the total bird population of America at the time. Yet the last wild passenger pigeon was killed probably in 1899, the last one in captivity died in 1914.

It was an aristocratic, beautiful bird; it had a small head and neck, but red eyes so bright as to suggest flame, a proud, robust breast, a graceful body, and a long tail. Its wings were long and pointed. The male had a slate-blue head, a hindneck of a metallic iridescence of bronze, green, or purple (it changed with the light); its back was slate gray, and its lower back and rump grayish purple. The throat was a rich, wine-colored russet, changing gradually to white on the abdomen; the wings were grayish brown, grayish blue, or even purple. In length the male averaged over sixteen inches; the female was about an inch smaller and duller in color. From a short distance the birds seemed blue—and were so fast they were sometimes called "blue meteors."

From the earliest time of white habitation these pigeons were killed and sold commercially. The settlers soon learned how to preserve the flesh, even before ice was available. They roasted the birds, then packed them in casks and covered them with molten fat, which kept out the air; or they salted the meat down and stored it in barrels, as with fish; or they pickled the birds, especially the breasts; breast of pigeon pickled in spiced apple cider was a delicacy. Down in Virginia they put up the fat of the birds in tubs. It would last for months, and was described as being as sweet as butter. What seems worst of all, they even fed the carcasses to the hogs.

The precipitous decline in the passenger pigeon population began in 1871. Throughout the next three decades more pigeons were killed every year than were hatched. This decline was noted, but, save for a very few voices in the narrowing wilderness, little was suggested to stem it; instead the talk was all about bolstering the efforts to find and kill the diminishing supply of birds. No matter how small the nesting or the roosting, the pigeoners headed for it, sometimes two or three hundred strong, determined to kill every squab and adult with nets, stool pigeons, corn soaked in alcohol, axes, fire, and shotguns. The ice and the barrels were forthcoming in the freight cars arriving on the nearest tracks, and the buyers were there too, with instant cash. When the birds had become so rare that the commerce in pigeons had come to an end, "sportsmen" were always around, ready to pick up their shotguns and head for the rumored nesting or roosting on the double. If they discovered a score of lonesome passenger pigeons, they killed every one they could find. Could the pigeon have survived for just one or two more decades after the last wild pigeon was killed in 1899, the climate of opinion would have changed, and steps would have been taken which would probably have saved it; for one more decade would have placed the birds in the middle of the first great conservation movement in America. But this is a bitter afterthought: the pigeon is no more.

Far Western
Spoliation

Thus far our concern has been primarily with the well-watered, heavily timbered lands east of the Mississippi. This is where settlement first occurred, and it is in this vast region that perceptive people first began to note the reduction in number of deer, bear, bison, wolves, bobcats, panthers, and other wild animals. The Southeast had abounded in deer, and as early as the beginning of the eighteenth century, long before our story opens in 1776, well over a hundred thousand deerskins a year were being shipped out of Charleston. Two hundred bearskins were shipped out of the Ohio Valley on an early steamboat. The last buffalo south of the Ohio was seen in 1810; north of that river but south of the Great Lakes in the same year; and east of the upper Mississippi country in 1830.

But the trans-Mississippi West still retained the fresh breath of nature, and while wildlife was becoming rare or extinct east of the Mississippi, it remained, for a little while longer, wild, unrestrained, and vigorous on the other side of the river. In the spring of 1805 Lewis and Clark observed hundreds of bloated buffalo carcasses bobbling downstream amongst the ice flows, the victims of the ice cover breaking up in the spring thaw. Below Great Falls the explorers also found many dead bison, the victims of pressure from the back of the herd which pushed the leaders out into the river too far as the beasts came down to the banks to drink. Those in the lead lost their footing in the swift current and were carried over the falls to destruction. The explorers noted that the pesky prickly pear was rampant at one of the principal fords used by the bison to cross the Missouri on their annual migrations; the bison had destroyed the grass cover and the prickly pear had grown up in the breach. They noticed, too, that the Indians occasionally fired the prairie, and at least once Lewis and Clark did it themselves, to signal the Indians to come in for a conference.

Buffalo were so numerous in places that the explorers had to fire their guns to prevent the top-heavy-looking beasts from inundating their camp, and one time as the party floated downstream they were held up an hour while buffalo crossed the river. There were mule deer and elk, too, and that strange little beast of the western plains, the pronghorn, better known as the antelope. It is estimated that there may have been thirty million buffalo in pre-white man's North America,[1] and there may have been just as many antelope.

Lewis and Clark were also intrigued by the prairie dogs, those little rodents that live in "towns," sometimes of ten or twenty square miles in size. (They are not dogs at all, and would be better known by the Indian name of "wishtonwish.") Today, although they are apparently not in danger of extinction, there are few left. They are considered destructive, and have been heavily poisoned in most places.

Wherever there were prairie dogs, jackrabbits (really hares), bison and deer, antelope and elk, the lobo—the prairie gray wolf—was sure to be seen skulking along the fringes of their habitat. This intelligent but deadly predator made short shrift of the sick, weak and diseased animals, and thus helped nature maintain a balance. Lobo and his sneaky cousin, the coyote, fared well until the coming of the cattlemen. For years rare was the cowboy who did not carry a pouch of strychnine in his pack. Whenever he came upon a cow dead by disease, freezing, locoweed, lightning, or attack by a predator, he planted strychnine on the carcass. It was not long before the wolf and the coyote—more especially the wolf population—as well as grizzlies, bobcats, mountain lions, vultures, bald eagles, and other devourers of carrion, began to diminish materially. Few are left.

Lewis and Clark also saw the beaver, their signs on the trees—or tree stumps—and the dams and ponds they had built. The beaver is a big rodent, weighing thirty to fifty pounds; he measures from two and a half to three feet from tip of nose to butt of tail, and that wide, flattish, useful muscular appendage adds another ten inches.

Beaver have always been good citizens in the animal world, minding their own business, killing no fish or animals, choosing one mate, and raising four to six kits a year. When the country was new, no one ever thought of those sixty to a hundred million beaver as water conservationists, but in constructing their dams they did—and do, where allowed—control the water level of streams.

Man soon discovered, however, that the beaver's pelt was soft and thick, with, closer to the skin, a velvety, downy buff that could be worked into attractive, stylish, long-lasting hats, coat collars, and even shoes. No other readily available animal had a pelt with such characteristics, and so the beaver was trapped nearly to extinction.

Centuries before the white man splashed ashore in North America the European beaver had been in demand, and by the sixteenth century it had become almost extinct. Peltry had been the prime reason for the demand, but something else produced by the rodents had also been used, as it was in the New World: the granular, yellowish substance taken from two large glands in front of the rectum of both sexes. Castoreum, as it was called, has a sweetish, musky, but not offensive odor. Indians sometimes sweetened their tobacco or kinnickinnik with it. In the Old World, even in classical times, this substance had been considered a nostrum, a cure-all for just about everything. In America it was used as a medicine, but primarily it was valued as a beaver bait. A stick dipped in castoreum was too tempting for the beaver to pass by. So he went to sniff the stick, stepped in the trap and, if an expert had set the instrument correctly, splashed around in water so deep that he soon drowned.

Peltry and castoreum had made him nearly extinct in Europe, but until the white man came, *Castor canadensis* held his own in America. The sparse Indian population trapped or otherwise killed him, used the castoreum for medicine, kept warm with the peltry, or ate the roasted flesh, sweetish and succulent, prepared over the fire while still unskinned; the tail was especially good. There were plenty of beaver for the Indians, but things changed with the coming of the white man. Understanding the quest for beaver does, in fact, reduce admiration for the trading or trapping frontiersman. He may have been curious about what lay on the other side of a mountain or a pass, but there was a mercenary purpose even more prominent in his mind. Were there beaver over there?

By the time of the American phase of the fur trade the beaver had been exterminated or so reduced in number from the Mississippi east that the companies and their men had to move west. The phase Americans know best began about 1800, with St. Louis the center. There, Spanish traders were working the rivers southwest of the Mississippi, trading peltry with tribes inhabiting banks of the Red, the lower Arkansas, the Kaw, and the rivers shortly named the Republican and the Smoky Hill. Then they began working the Missouri, hesitantly at first, but heavily by the 1820's.

Extending westward on a line with the mouth of the Platte, to the south, and the great bend, to the north, the initial Missouri River fur trade flourished westward into the northern Rockies, covering the Tetons and the Green River, the country west of South Pass, and up into Oregon, as the vast northwest was called in those days. By the 1830's the mountain men ranged from New Mexico, Arizona, and California north-ward in a great sweep extending to British Columbia and Alberta.

These men softened up the Far West for the Oregonians, the Forty-niners, and the Fifty-niners who came later. They were also ravishers. They "worked out" beaver stream after stream, until only the change of fashion in Europe and the East saved that hard-working rodent from ex-tinction. They exposed the Indians to smallpox, measles, and venereal diseases, corrupted them with alcohol, and made them dependent on firearms, ammunition, and even blankets. When beaver peltry became scarce they turned to the buffalo, the very basis of the plains Indians' way of life, and killed them by the hundreds of thousands for their hides and tongues—this prior to the terrible slaughter of the bison after the Civil War.

It is difficult to find a more ideal subject for a case study of unregu-lated, unrestricted business than this far western fur trade. It was tied to the time-honored rule that the greater the risk, the greater the profit. One authority has pointed out that a keg of gunpowder worth $2 in London could be traded for a gross profit of $140, and of this John Jacob Astor himself realized a minimum net profit of $50.02. William H. Ashley was able to return to civilization with a minor fortune after only two or three years in the fur trade. Others fared not nearly so well, for while the potential riches were clearly there—and the accumulation of wealth was seemingly simple—the realization was rare. The imponder-ables were simply too numerous.

Mere distance was one of the problems of the far western fur trade. The principal source of peltry was the vast, uncharted area of the north-ern Rockies, which lay 2,000 miles up the Missouri or over 900 miles overland just to South Pass from Independence. Either route required two to three months each way, during which time men and livestock could take sick and die, be defeated or massacred by Indians, carried off by floods, or wiped out by prairie fires. Even if their goal was a trading post, there was no communication with St. Louis from the time of their departure in the spring to their return in the autumn, save for intelli-gence carried by travelers floating downriver or trekking across the plains from the west, for there was constant movement in and out of the wild country. That an Indian tribe was friendly to traders last season was no assurance that their greeting would be friendly again.

The instability of the fur trade makes it difficult to generalize about its personnel. Much of the custom and lore of the business was a con-tinuation of the procedures of the eastern trade, which had flourished around the Great Lakes for 150 years and whose members included the French-Canadian halfbloods, so happy and carefree as they poled or cordelled their heavy boats up the Missouri. The western trappers included French halfbloods plus such an assortment of American adventurers as defies description: runaway youths who joined the trapper brigades, educated men who lusted for adventure and exploration, businessmen who saw in the trade great profits, and more than enough rogues.

Originally trading, not trapping, had been the interest of the St. Louis capitalists who, save for John Jacob Astor of New York, by and large dominated the business. Such men were the Spaniard Manuel Lisa and the French Choteaus, a large family dominated in the years 1800-60 by Auguste and then his son Pierre; many descendants of both the Lisas and the Choteaus are living today. Other investors were William H. Ashley and Andrew Henry; even William Clark of the Lewis and Clark Expedition was not averse to investing in fur-trading schemes. Initially many of these men with their employees went upriver, established fur-trading posts, and there traded with the Indians; between 1807 and 1809 both Lisa and the Choteaus were thus established up the Missouri or into the northern Rockies.

All fur-trading posts had some similarities based upon earlier French-Canadian developments. At the head, a virtual dictator over all the personnel at the trading post, was the licensed company agent. He was known as the "bourgeois"; in English, the "bushway." He usually knew the Indian language thereabouts and was a career man. Below him in rank was the commis, or partisan. He fixed the conditions of trade and assumed authority in the event of the death, illness, or absence of the bushway. Also present at the post would be various employees—carpenters, a blacksmith-gunsmith, various sub-clerks and laborers. Other employees worked out of the post, going into the field to trade with the Indians wherever they found them. All of these employees had taken an oath of allegiance to the company. Some lived there the year round and took Indian wives—became squaw men.

Soon, however, trapper brigades set out from St. Louis with no destination save the trading-trapping country. These so-called "trapper brigades" included in their ranks some of the best-known of all the mountain men: Jim Bridger, Jedediah Smith, Thomas "Broken-Hand" Fitzpatrick, Hugh Glass, "Old Bill" Williams, Jim Clyman, Osborne Russell, and others. Such brigades would have hired out to a company— or the brigade itself consisted of such a company—and its personnel, in exchange for an outfit, food, and transportation, promised to turn over all their peltry to the company; they were "company men." Others loved the wilderness so much that they purchased Indian wives and became wandering trappers, selling their peltry at the various forts that dotted the Rockies; they were "free trappers."

By 1825 the instability amidst great potential profits had brought several newcomers into the field with new ways of doing things, and had also brought the return of another, John Jacob Astor. The failure of his Pacific Fur Company and the loss of Astoria in the Oregon Country in 1813 had soured the German-born schemer on the western fur trade temporarily, but in 1823 he re-entered it. In time Astor's fur empire included thirty posts, and his business acumen brought him to the point of dominating the commerce. Not only did he own most of the forts; he also sent out his own trapper brigades. Already fabulously wealthy, he sold out in 1834; his successors dominated the trade for several more years.

For a time his chief rival was the Rocky Mountain Fur Company, led by Andrew Henry and William Ashley. To checkmate their competition they hit upon the idea of a mountain meeting where furs and "store-bought" goods could be exchanged. Twenty miles up Henry's Fork from its junction with the Green (just north of the Colorado-Wyoming line, still a lonely and remote area), the site was chosen for the first of these trappers' rendezvous, in the summer of 1825. Until 1840 these fairs provided competition for Astor and his successors. In fact, Astor's American Fur Company men even participated. To these mountain fairs came a wagon train of falderal, whiskey, powder and lead, beads and trinkets and bells to weaken the resistance of Indian women; and from all points of the compass came the mountain men and the Indians, to some well-watered, grassy setting where the fair was held.

Probably the best attended one, at least by the whites, was the rendezvous of 1832, at Pierre's Hole in eastern Idaho. There were several brigades of free trappers, as well as elements of the Rocky Mountain Fur Company; probably a thousand persons, whites and Indians, in all. It was considered a successful rendezvous, although it ended with the largest pitched battle ever fought between mountain men and Indians. Eventually the attackers dispersed under cover of darkness; subsequently the white brigades likewise left the site. Only in terms of the numbers involved was the rendezvous or the battle different from any other. The trapper's West was a land of anarchy, ambush, and death.

By the 1830's the competition was intense; the number of trappers and traders involved, though never large (less than a thousand and probably never over five or six hundred), was such as to make the trade unprofitable for many of the participants. Moreover, the American Fur Company and its successors, with their stationary posts, simply held onto what proved in the long run to be a better system than mobile trapper brigades and annual rendezvous. Towards the end of the decade the demise of the rendezvous era was in sight; in 1840 the last one was

Buffalo left dead in the snow after they had been shot. (Public Health Service, The National Archives)

held where Horse Creek joins the Green, in southwest-central Wyoming. So too did the trade in the Southwest out of Santa Fe and Taos decline; it had never been as large as the Missouri trade. Although the fur trade did not end completely until the Civil War (and, in a minute way, it continues today), it did cease to be an energetic, important industry after about 1840. The depletion of beaver and the change in men's styles to silk hats brought it to an end.

The fading paths along the river banks were but one manifestation of the end of an era. Where once large beaver dams and lodges had dotted mountain canyons, controlling the waters in flood time and releasing

pent-up waters in the dry seasons, there were now few signs of life. The
dams were rotting and giving way, and the beaver lodges looked like
masses of indiscriminately placed driftwood. Rarely did one see beaver
any more.

By 1840 the main Indian paths, long used by the trappers and traders,
were well known and clearly marked throughout the Far West. And the
bleaching bones to be seen along the trails and at the campsites already
confirmed the hunch some of the hunters had that even the countless
numbers of bison were on the decline. Sir William Drummond Stewart,
a Scottish sportsman who was in the Rockies in 1833 and several times
more in the following decade, was an observer of the change. What he
witnessed in 1844 led him to insert a nostalgic note as a preface to *Edward Warren*, a mediocre novel he had written. The "Scotsman in Buck-
skin" found himself comparing the Rockies, especially the country of
the upper North Platte, South Pass, and up towards the Tetons, as they
had been in 1833 to the way they looked ten or eleven years later. Even
1833 had been, he said, "the evening of the roving life of the Far
West. . . . The plains around [the rendezvous, held at Green River
and Horse Creek, about fifteen miles west of present Pinedale, Wyo-
ming] were black with bison then, and the tyro . . . killed a bull, as he
[the bull] passed with his herd within shot of camp." Then Sir William
lamented, "There are a few bones bleaching there now, but no living
thing, . . . there are marks of many a trail to the south and west, and
broken wagons and horse bones, ox bones, and the graves of men." He
found it "a scene of desolation, improvidence, and famine." The whole
Platte Valley, along which ran the Great Medicine Road, was that way.
"There was a noble poplar which bore the name of the 'Lone Tree,' near
Scott's Bluffs, on the North Platte; it had been respected alike by the
caravan and the hunter, but fell under the knife of one of the first Yankee invasions. . . . Such," he wrote with finality, "had been the gradual
steps of alteration preparatory to the wholesale immigration which has
partly peopled and partly desolated (but everywhere changed) the western plains."[2]

"Partly peopled and partly desolated . . ." Already, in the 1840's and
50's, the signs of wanton destruction were apparent to the discerning observer. By 1840 there were no bison left west of South Pass; by the end
of the decade, buffalo were becoming rare along the Platte River Trail.

For the white man, the hide and tongue of the bison were all that were
worth taking; these constituted a marketable product that was so cheap
to obtain that the selling price and the profit were very nearly identical.
For food out on the range the hunters might also roast a hump rib.
Mountain men occasionally wrapped the fatty lower intestines around a

A buffalo hunters' camp. (The Kansas State Historical Society, Topeka)

Some of the two hundred thousand buffalo hides at Dodge City, 1874. (The Kansas
State Historical Society, Topeka)

stick, roasted them and consumed them with gusto (today we still eat crunchy hog chitlings with cold beer).

The immensity of the hide and tongue trade, even prior to the Civil War and the coming of the railroads to the prairies, is startling. The first systematic hunt appears to have been out of the Red River settlements in Manitoba. The year was 1820; it is recorded that 540 squeaky, two-wheeled Red River carts carried the hides to the place of sale. This was just the beginning. By the 1840's the average number of hides per year arriving in St. Louis was 90,000, and in the 1850's and 1860's it went up to at least 100,000. By the mid-1840's buffalo tongues had become a gourmet delicacy. More tongues than robes appear to have been sent down the Missouri, meaning that more buffalo were slaughtered than the statistics in hides indicate. After the Civil War, the hide trade reached massive proportions. The ten million bison that existed in 1865 were reduced to approximately one thousand by 1890, all of which were captives in private hands. Although a few states had passed laws to protect the bison, these were virtually unenforceable. Not until the 1890's were voices raised against the slaughter, voices that were heeded because of the intelligence and position of such men as William T. Hornaday, a zoologist and first director of the New York Zoological Park, who made the public realize that the bison had become nearly extinct.

What did the new country men think of all this slaughter? It is unreasonable to expect that they should have thought as we do. For them there was no question but that nature's system must be destroyed. Just as the hardwood forests of the East had been cut down or burned to make way for an agrarian society, so must the millions of bison, antelope, wolves and coyotes, jackrabbits, and prairie dogs be destroyed. When the buffalo were gone they would be replaced by kine. When antelope, deer, and elk were destroyed, the hay men cultivated in the stream bottoms and the wild grasses elsewhere could be used to feed cattle. And where prairie dogs and jackrabbits had lived, dry land farming could produce wheat and corn. Where there had been worn buffalo trails, two gleaming lines of rails could be laid, and a black, belching monster could whiz along faster than any buffalo. Where Indians had pitched tepees, sod houses and dugouts, then white frame houses, then water tanks, grain elevators, cattle pens, railroad sidings, a public school, and a white frame church could rise; ash and elms planted by the townspeople could provide a heavy shade on hot days when the prairie that surrounded the village like desert around an oasis shimmered in the blazing, silvery summer sun.

One rarely finds evidence that the new country man was concerned about what was being done to the Great Plains. The pioneer carried

with him the vision of western man, and, as he surveyed the treeless sea
of grass with bison grazing on it as far as the eye could see, he contemplated nothing but improvement resulting from the changes he proposed to make. Cattle were a step above the undomesticated and un-
breakable bison; to remove the bison and replace those ugly, prehistoric
beasts with manageable bovines was nothing but improvement. Once in
a while a sensitive newspaper editor, a far-sighted member of a state legislature, or an eastern sportsman might lament the passing of the buffalo, but this was usually in the nature of a sigh and a shrug. The pioneer, far from regretting the extermination of the buffalo, helped in
every way to hasten its demise.

Mining is an extractive process; whether it involves bituminous or lignite
coal, copper, silver, gold, or other metallic ores, it is a dangerous, dirty,
exploitive industry. It not only damages the land through cave-ins, slag
dumps, settling ponds, or smelting with its attendant discharge of noxious gases—it also exploits the human beings who work at it. Miners
work under bad conditions today, but they are treated with loving care
compared to those they endured, for example, in the 1880's and 90's,
three and four thousand feet into the earth, in some of the 3,000 miles of
tunnels under Butte's great hill of copper. Wild, boisterous Butte, killing or maiming a man a day in her mines, crippling with silicosis those
whose arms and legs stayed secure, was the ultimate of nineteenth-
century new country laissez-faire industrialism.

Shortly after the Utah Northern Railroad reached it in 1881, making
the transfer of ore economically feasible, Butte was a hustling, masculine, twenty-four-hour-a-day city. It came to cover about five of the drab-
best square miles in existence, sitting on top of "the richest hill on
earth." Sterile yellow and gray slag dumps stretched out across gulches
like lava from the mines, and noxious fumes from the great smelters
killed all the vegetation in Butte and for miles around, to say nothing
of its effect upon the populace. The land and the people were exploited.
Even the tycoons in their affluence—Marcus Daly, William Clark, and
F. Augustus Heinze—somehow fitted into the drabness. Everything
about Butte reeked of the worst of nineteenth-century despoilment;
and people put up with it without ever asking why.

This was a predominantly male society, made up of Cousin Jacks
from Cornwall, Irish, Welsh, Chinese, Jews, Finns, and men from the
Balkans. In 1898 William Clark, one of the "copper kings," possibly affected by the hideousness from which he had profited so splendidly,
spent a million dollars on an outdoor amusement park nearby. Columbia
Gardens, as it was called, once boasted a mammoth pansy bed contain-

Although every hut, tent, or false-fronted building was constructed to individual tastes, mining towns all looked strikingly similar. This one is Deadwood, Dakota Territory, in 1876. (U.S. War Department General Staff, The National Archives)

The crudeness of a miner's existence is well portrayed in this photo of the inside of a miner's cabin in Colorado. (State Historical Society of Colorado)

ing 85,000 plants; children of the miners were allowed to pick them. These were, needless to say, the only pansies in or near Butte.

There were hundreds of lesser Buttes in the new country. Virginia City in Nevada and Montana; Helena, Deadwood, Lead, Cripple Creek, Leadville, Nevada City, Grass Valley, Tombstone; Galena, Illinois, with its lead mines; the coal camps of southern Colorado such as Ludlow, remembered for its labor unrest; the squalid coal camps of the Wyoming Valley of Pennsylvania, are just a few examples of many.

Possibly the best case study of the new country mentality is, however, the situation in California's Sacramento River system, including its tributary streams, the Yuba, Bear, American, and Feather rivers. Within the area drained by these arteries and their up-country watersheds lay a substantial segment of the fabulous Mother Lode, which was worked from the very beginnings of the gold discoveries of 1848. Gold was, of course, the beginning of modern California, and was the principal source of her wealth for at least a generation after 1848.

The gold seekers came in just after the treaty of Guadaloupe Hidalgo, and for the first score of months after the great rush of 1849 there was hardly the shadow of governmental control there. Political scientists and sociologists have always been intrigued at the remarkable way in which mining communities, exploiting streams and digging up lands and constructing jerry-built hovels, liveries, saloons, assay offices, and hotels where they had no legal ownership, ran their affairs by means of buckskin-and-flannel governments that had evolved of themselves. Surely a part of their success lay in the general prosperity of the thousands who flocked in. It was equality to begin with, or very nearly so, and every man for himself; and for a time, almost any hard-working man could make a living.

In such a free society the man with ingenuity could greatly enhance his chances by applying his resourcefulness to the conditions at hand. Soon the washing pan gave way to the cradle, and the cradle gave way to the long toms, sluice boxes sometimes fifty feet long, with up to a dozen men shoveling in the Tertiary gravels that contained the gold. This enlargement of the placer-mining process required more water than was usually available, so water companies were formed to construct aqueducts and flumes from water sources higher up in the Sierras.

But shoveling the gravel into the sluice boxes was time-consuming, enervating, and inefficient. And "coyoting"—digging down to bedrock to get at the richest pay dirt, shoveling it into buckets while one's "pard" slowly cranked it up with a windless—proved not only inefficient but dangerous. By 1853, with the stream beds and their embankments rather

Panning for gold near Virginia City, Montana Territory, 1871. The devastation wrought by mining is apparent. (U.S. Geological Survey, The National Archives)

Hydraulic mining in Northern California, circa 1880. (Wells Fargo Bank, San
Francisco)

thoroughly "worked," decline set in, for there seemed no way to make
the operation economical enough to pay.

Then in the spring of 1852 Anthony Chabot built a series of penstocks
to hold water and added a canvas hose at the lower end. When he released the water it gushed out with sufficient energy to wash away the
soil into a ditch of the stream's own creation. At intervals he would shut
off the water and collect the gold that had settled in the ditch, which
had become a natural sluice; hence the term "ground sluicing." This
was done as follows: at intervals of a week, a month, six months, or a
year the water was diverted from where it was washing earth and gravel

into the ditch—diverted directly into the ditch—where it washed out the heavy material. Then it was diverted away from the ditch entirely, and the miners collected the gold amongst the rocks and gravels in the now-dried ditch and poured rich ore into buckets of quicksilver to extract still more gold by amalgamation. Later long wooden sluices were constructed into which the ditch led. In these long sluices were cleats and even heavy stones to act as obstructions to catch the heavier gold particles. Again, every so often the water was diverted and the gold taken from the sluices. It sounds wasteful, and it was—extremely so, estimates of the gold that was lost ranging from one-fourth to three-fifths of the total that passed down the stream and the sluices. Even when far more sophisticated methods of hydraulicking were developed, the waste was still great.

The canvas hose was obviously crude, and Chabot, with another man named Matteson and a partner of theirs named Miller, began experiments with a similar contraption, but this time using a sheet-iron nozzle upon the gravels in a hillside embankment. The contraption worked; the gravels became thin, watery mud that was carried into the sluices, where the gold was dropped. The remaining mud and water was carried out of the canyon via the tributary river into the Sacramento. Thus, in the spring of 1853, hydraulic mining, or "hydraulicking," was born. It was to flourish in Nevada, El Dorado, Placer, Yuba, and other counties containing tributary streams running into the Sacramento.

Once the idea proved practical, improvements were made until the gushing, guided streams of four or five hundred feet could be dashed against hillsides, so forcefully that boulders two feet thick were washed and batted down like so many marbles. Some preliminary blasting of the hillside loosened the earth and speeded the process. In 1870 a final, supremely efficient nozzle, called the "Little Giant," was introduced. It was basically the same as a Civil War cannon; it had a six- to ten-inch bore and could be pointed in various directions. To feed these monsters enormous quantities of water were needed. By 1857 more than 700 miles of ditches, along with dams and aqueducts, had been constructed in Nevada county, the center of the hydraulicking industry.

San Franciscan, eastern, and even British capital entered this new, lucrative mining field. A typical operation was that of the North Bloomfield Gravel Mining Company, which used more than a million gallons of water a day. In its first years of round-the-clock operation, beginning about 1876, great pine pitch fires were lit so that the miners could sweep the hillsides all night long as well as all day; in 1879 an electric lighting system was installed. In 1878 the operators strung California's first long-distance telephone line, sixty miles of it connecting various stages of the operation. By the late 1870's nine companies owned more than a thousand miles of ditches which fed the huge monitor nozzles.

Not only was the timber and grass cover carried off, one way or another, by these massive operations, but entire hillsides were cut away, leaving, somewhat as in the strip-mining of coal today, nothing but bleached sands or gravelly marls. At no time was any strong voice raised about the destruction of the mountains. No one asked what would hold the winter snows and prevent spring thaws from releasing the millions of gallons of snow and rainwater that would accumulate and come roaring down the canyons to wreak vengeance upon mankind, animals, and ground cover. For nothing was left to hold it: no forest, no thick humus on the ground.

Meanwhile, between 1849 and the 1870's, another industry, more basic to mankind than mining, had taken hold in the beautiful valleys of the Sacramento watershed. This was farming: it included peach orchards, wheat, and some livestock. The land was fertile, the climate ideal, and from the earliest time of the white man's presence there had been a market for the husbandman's products in San Francisco and up in the Mother Lode country. Among the many towns which arose in the valleys, Marysville, Wheatland, and Yuba City were particularly vulnerable to flooding. They profited from agriculture and were primarily agrarian in outlook, but among their merchants were a few key mining outfitters whose primary consideration was the well-being of their customers up in the hills. The devastating monitors, for example, were manufactured right in Marysville. And so even in the towns that suffered most there was a fierce political struggle between pro-mining and pro-agricultural elements.

At first the troubles concomitant with hydraulic mining affected only the miners themselves. As the great jets of water washed away thousands of cubic yards of hillside, the slow-moving creeks proved incapable of carrying away the debris, or tailings, as the miners called it. The logical answer to this problem was to construct tunnels or flumes down which the muck would pour at great speed into the river canyons. This was a satisfactory solution for the miners, but it was a different story down the valleys. The rivers carried the tailings downstream, where they raised the beds of the streams and made any small rise in the water level the signal for a flood. Soon the broad, gradually sloping valleys were deluged by brownish flood waters sweeping over lush farmland, inundating meadows, orchards, fences, buildings, and homes. Shoals formed in the rivers by the slowly descending tailings brought much of the steamboat river traffic to an end. Marysville and other communities began building dikes to protect themselves; eventually Marysville's dikes were above the roofs of her houses, and the town acquired the epithet "the walled city."

So new was the country that neither the federal government nor the state had contemplated any regulatory machinery to fix policy and oversee the conditions of rivers. The miners were there first; they provided California with her first great source of riches, and they had built up a great extractive industry that represented millions of dollars in investment, thousands of employees, and several thriving towns, such as Grass Valley, Dutch Flat, You Bet, and Red Dog. Much of the prosperity of the valley towns lay in doing business with the mining people. Caught in an impasse of conflicting interests and feelings, not the least of which was the laissez-faire attitude of the times, the valley people did little but complain until 1872.

In that year, up in Dry Creek Valley, a single big operation was clearly responsible for extensive inundation of farm land. The farmers sued the culprit, the Spring Valley mine. The jury decided in favor of the miners. Then in 1875 and 1876 Marysville was inundated in spite of the town's raised and greatly strengthened levees. By this time, however, the bed of the Yuba River where it passed Marysville was more than sixteen feet higher than it had been twenty years before! By 1880 the Army Engineers reported that some 33,000 acres of farmland had been destroyed and another 14,000 acres damaged.

The farmers' anger grew, an Anti-Debris Association, among others, was formed, and the great interests of mining and agriculture clashed in the legislature at Sacramento, in the courts, both state and federal, and in Congress. The emphasis everywhere was on the harm that would be done, one way or another, to the economic interests of one of the two industries. Miners insisted that the deposits enriched the soil (look at the Nile River through the ages!), that they were merely hastening nature's own sure actions; they offered other rationales, too, but above all towered the argument of economics. California needed the wealth the mines brought her. Thousands of miners would be laid off if hydraulicking was declared illegal; mining communities would become ghost towns. But, replied the farmers, a man does not have the right to use his property to destroy another man's property.

It is a long and complicated story, this struggle of two clashing economic forces, in which saving one certainly meant ruining the other. Dams were built, injunctions issued, newspapers took sides and published strong editorials, and lawyers pled long and convincingly before the courts. The final decision, favoring the farmers and ending hydraulic mining, at least as a serious threat to the valleys, was handed down by Judge Lorenzo Sawyer of the Ninth United States Circuit Court in San Francisco on January 7, 1884. By this time the farming element had become of far greater importance to the general welfare and economy of California, and mining had declined. But the scars left from hydraulicking will be there as long as there is a Sierra range, as long as there are rivers and valleys in northern California.

The spoliation of the northern Sierras and the Sacramento Valley system is a particularly poignant example of new country rapacity. Whole hillsides were flushed away by the gushing, roaring, hissing monitors, while nature's own water system was twisted and reconstructed with dams, flumes, and aqueducts to the needs of the miners. A magnificent farming country was ruined, and the rivers were never the same again.

Who was to blame? No one, or everyone. The time in history, the total disregard for conservation because few sensed the need for it, the unknown and uncontemplated ecological results, the widely accepted concept of economic laissez-faire, the suddenness of the problem in a region where the state government was new, the people new to the land and totally wanting in aesthetic considerations, especially since California was not yet "home" to them: these were the conditions that brought on spoliation.

Have we made progress? The answer is a measured yes. We are far more aware of the problems, and there are organizations to alert us when harm is being done. Yet the mercenary spirit is still strong among us, and modern technology can do much more harm in a shorter period than was possible a hundred years ago. For money still talks: just let the price of gold rise to a level where it is again profitable to extract it, and watch the hydraulickers rise from the dead, out there in California, and make another effort to ravish the earth.[3]

V
Transportation

Travel by Road

In the new country freedom meant mobility, the freedom to roam. It was this implicitly understood aspect of American life, assumed to be in the nature of things, that led a man to go whither his whims or his hopes led him to better his life. Mobility was, and is, an integral part of freedom; without it the whole concept, as Americans know it, would collapse.

The freedom of mobility was total in the American colonies (save for slaves and indentured servants), but we know that until the Revolution there was little use made of it. Even after America became a nation there was not a great deal of north–south intercourse. The real movement was in an arc from north to south but with its emphasis at center west: Ohio, Kentucky, Tennessee; Indiana, Illinois, Missouri. This freedom extended also to the sea; a coastal trade flourished from Maine to Florida, down around the Keys, and illegally along the Spanish Gulf Coast. Ocean-going ships flying the Stars and Stripes cruised up the coast of California and Oregon, then crossed the great watery expanse to the ports of China, the East Indies, India, around the Cape of Good Hope and on to the ports of Europe.

The story of transportation in the new country involves not simply a progression from footpath to pack trail to wagon road to railroad, or canoe to flatboat and keelboat to steamboat. Whatever the means of transportation, geography had its effects, both positive and negative. A first problem was the Appalachian barrier, as much as 1,300 miles long from Vermont to Alabama, and extending for up to 300 miles or more of ridges, valleys, and mountain crests from east slope to western flatlands. Westward, across the Mississippi and Missouri, were prairies and deserts, the high Rockies, the Great Basin, the Sierras; there were river gorges and swamps, seasonal droughts and spring freshets. There was unpredictable nature, creating an unseasonal blizzard, a cloudburst, a forest fire, a locust plague, a devastating hailstorm, a hurricane, or a tornado. Whether he trudged over an Indian trace, floated down a river in a canoe, cannonballed a steam locomotive over the ridges, or piloted a quarter-million-dollar steamboat down the changeable Mississippi, the American had to be prepared for the whims of nature.

The solution, by no means always followed, was to discover the natural highways. When the new country man used Indian traces, waterways, and portages he was taking advantage of nature's terrain. The traces led to the best fords of the streams, avoided swamps and bogs, and led to green pastures where stock could graze. The gradients of the

The Wilderness Road, 1774. From a Bureau of Public Roads diorama. (National Youth Administration, The National Archives)

The National Pike (or Road). From a Bureau of Public Roads diorama. (National Youth Administration, The National Archives)

The Natchez Trace. From a Bureau of Public Roads diorama. (National Youth Administration, The National Archives)

trails were seldom steep, they kept to the ridges, and so were known as ridge roads. They followed along water divides. If there were gaps, or gently rising hills towards a pass, the traces led to them. Small wonder, then, that these paths later became railroad rights-of-way and automobile highways.

The success of the Philadelphia-Lancaster Turnpike, completed in 1794, served as an incentive to the building of similar roads in New England and the middle states. Its initial cost was about a half million dollars, which was raised by stock companies incorporated by the state, with the state usually subscribing to some of the stock. Road maintenance and dividends to the stockholders were paid for by tolls. It was the popularity of the National Road (built by the federal government but usually maintained with revenue from tolls imposed by the states), completed from Harper's Ferry to Wheeling in 1818, to Columbus by 1833, and to Vandalia by 1850, that helped usher in an era in which states, localities, and private interests invested large sums into this kind of transportation artery. The boom lasted from about 1815 until 1830. Outstanding among the many turnpikes were the James River and Kanawha, completed to Guyandot (in present West Virginia) in 1831, and the Northwestern Turnpike connecting Winchester, Virginia and Parkersburg (in present West Virginia), completed in the same year.

Southwest of the National Road was "the Devil's Backbone"—the Natchez Trace. Specifically, it ran north-northeast from Natchez to Nashville, a distance via the zigzagging trail of about 500 miles. It passed through Choctaw and Chickasaw lands; much of it had been an Indian trace long before the coming of the white man. For miles and miles it was a narrow artery beneath a canopy of willow, ash, water maple, cypress, sweet-bay, magnolia, paw-paw, pecan, persimmon, locust, dogwood, tulip tree, pine, wild cherry, beech, chestnut, and such vines as sumac and trumpet flower. From Nashville one could take a road to Maysville, Kentucky, via Lexington. Crossing the Ohio at Maysville, one advanced to the National Road which he could then take eastward to Washington, D.C. This was the principal link of the nation's capital with the Old Southwest.

The trip from Natchez to Nashville alone could take three weeks, and until 1800 there were spans of 120 miles between "stands"—the Natchez Strip word for a hostelry. The humid, still air reminded travelers of the grave and the devil, but mosquitoes, gnats, and horseflies reminded them that they were alive. Big and Little Harpe, John Murrell, Samuel Mason, and Joseph Thompson Hare were criminals who robbed and killed along the path.

Passengers expected accidents to occur. This is Charles Russell's *Coach Overturned*.
(Wells Fargo Bank, San Francisco)

Corduroy Road by Charles Russell. This type of construction was used to cross boggy places. (Wells Fargo Bank, San Francisco)

There were many other traces: from the Wilderness Road to Nashville; from the southern fringe of the Appalachians across Georgia and Alabama; Gaines' Trace and Jackson's Military Road, both army built, across Tennessee and Alabama; and a trace in Florida from St. Augustine to Pensacola.

The number of failures of turnpike companies ran high. Good roads not only cost money to build, they were also expensive to maintain, and the loss of revenue due to dishonest tollkeepers was enormous. Moreover, the independent American traveler was always on the lookout for ways to evade paying tolls. He would cross farmland at night and climb onto the pike after the tollkeeper had gone home, or he would take a back-country lane, known as a "shunpike," instead.

By no means were all highways in the new country turnpikes, although a traveler did best to have a small amount of specie in his possession, for one never knew when a stretch of pike, a toll bridge, a ferry, or a toll plank or corduroy road would lie in his path and be open to him only at a price.

Only by contrast with the usual back-country roads were such turnpikes as the National Road something to look forward to. There were even stretches on "Uncle Sam's Highway" where the stumps had not been grubbed out, or where it was a boggy morass during much of the year. Yet the other roads were worse. Improved, if at all, from the original Indian or animal trace only by the tight-fisted taxpaying citizens of a community, these country roads were the sorriest means of communication imaginable. If they were new roads originating with the white man, they were likely to show less judgement than had been manifested by animals and red men when they made their trails through the wilderness. Rather than take to the ridge, which meant climbing hills, the white man meandered around the base, and received the runoff water. He tried to bridge streams, he built plank or corduroy roads through the bogs, and he complained and complained, but he continued to use them.

By 1821, when Missouri entered the Union and the new country was expanding west of the Mississippi, the states to the east of that river may be said to have possessed a network of roads, although few of them were constructed along the scientific principles of Telford and Macadam. Many still had stumps sticking up in the roadway; big boulders had been conveniently left where the glaciers had dropped them; chuckholes made detours necessary; and often bridges were yet to be constructed, or consisted of as little as a big log or two for a rider to cross upon while he urged his mount to swim; or the road crossed the stream at a shallow ford. Government units were reluctant to finance repairs. Obviously, by modern standards the roads were hideous. Yet apparently they were no worse than the pikes of England and the Continent in the same era.

The people who traveled such routes were emigrants, politicians, land speculators, businessmen, army officers, and foreign visitors, most probably on horseback or in their own buggies or carriages. Neither the time factor nor the inconveniences appear to have prevented travel; for the point is that such journeys could be accomplished. Everyone in the new country assumed this; true, the trip might be difficult, but no government, federal, state, or local, could prevent it from being made.

This was a point of great psychological significance; for when men began to cast long covetous looks across the Sabine into Texas; gazed thoughtfully southwest from St. Louis toward the exotic town of Santa Fe; or stood on the river bank at Westport and stared dreamily across the rolling Kansas prairie toward Fort Laramie, South Pass, and beyond, their dreams were bolstered by the confidence engendered by the American experience in the eastern third of the continent.

Many of the western trails, like the eastern, were originally Indian traces. In addition, the Spanish had created several arteries between points of settlement. *El Camino Real,* "the King's Highway" between Natchitoches and Bexar (San Antonio) was 150 years old by the early 1800's when Americans dubbed it "the Road to San Antone." *El Camino del Diablo,* "the Devil's Highway," headed across Arizona and connected with the Mission Trail of California. The Spanish also had trails leading into the upper Rio Grande area to Santa Fe and Taos. Pedro Vial, a Frenchman in Spanish employ, had traveled from Santa Fe to St. Louis in the years 1792-93. By 1821, when William Becknell, a Missouri trader, set out for Santa Fe, the general direction and character of the Santa Fe Trail was known; it was more for commerce, however, than for emigration.

The great migration roads were, of course, the Oregon and California trails. From the Missouri River departure towns to South Pass or a little beyond, the two trails were the same. In 1812 Robert Stuart, who had been a member of the party that had come to the mouth of the Columbia River aboard Astor's sailing vessel *Tonquin* to land and establish the fort named Astoria, led a party eastward overland. Stuart is often credited with the discovery of South Pass, although he may have crossed the Continental Divide somewhat south of that low (about 7,550 feet) eighteen-mile-wide area strewn not with trees but with sagebrush just south of the Wind River Mountains, which constitutes a

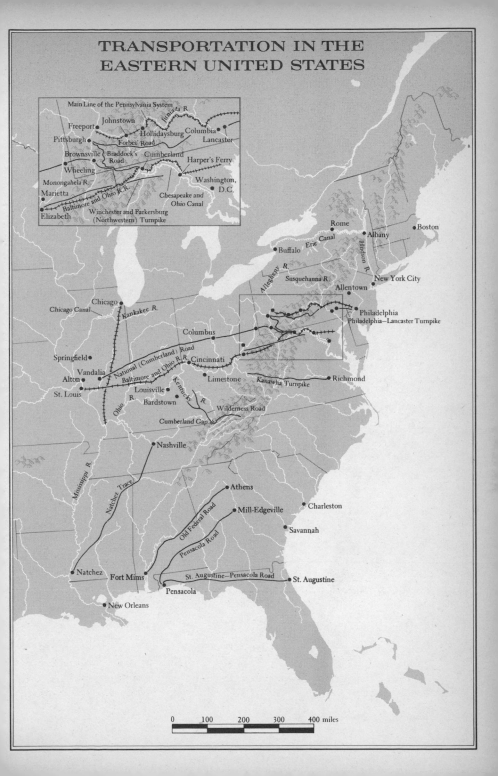

TRANSPORTATION IN THE EASTERN UNITED STATES

Main Line of the Pennsylvania System
Johnstown
Juniata R.
Freeport
Hollidaysburg
Columbia
Pittsburgh
Forbes' Road
Lancaster
Brownsville
Braddock's
Cumberland
Road
Harper's Ferry
Wheeling
Washington,
D.C.
Monongahela R.
Marietta
Baltimore and Ohio R.R.
Chesapeake and
Ohio Canal
Elizabeth
Winchester and Parkersburg
(Northwestern) Turnpike

Rome
Boston
Albany
Erie Canal
Buffalo
Hudson R.
Allegheny R.
New York City
Susquehanna R.
Allentown
Chicago
Philadelphia
Chicago Canal
Kankakee R.
Philadelphia–Lancaster Turnpike
Columbus
Springfield
National (Cumberland) Road
Cincinnati
Alton
Vandalia
Baltimore and Ohio R.R.
St. Louis
Limestone
Kanawha Turnpike
Richmond
Louisville
Ohio R.
Kentucky R.
Bardstown
Wilderness Road
Cumberland Gap
Nashville
Mississippi R.
Natchez Trace
Athens
Mill-Edgeville
Charleston
Old Federal Road
Savannah
Pensacola Road
Natchez
Fort Mims
St. Augustine–Pensacola Road
St. Augustine
Pensacola
New Orleans

0   100   200   300   400 miles

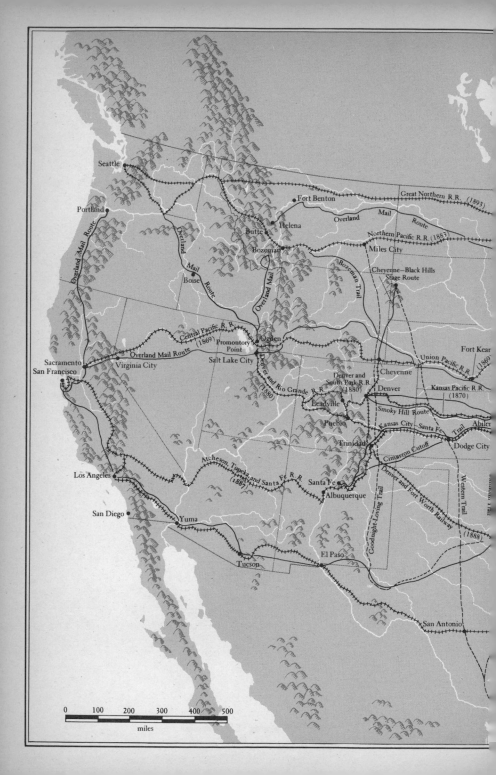

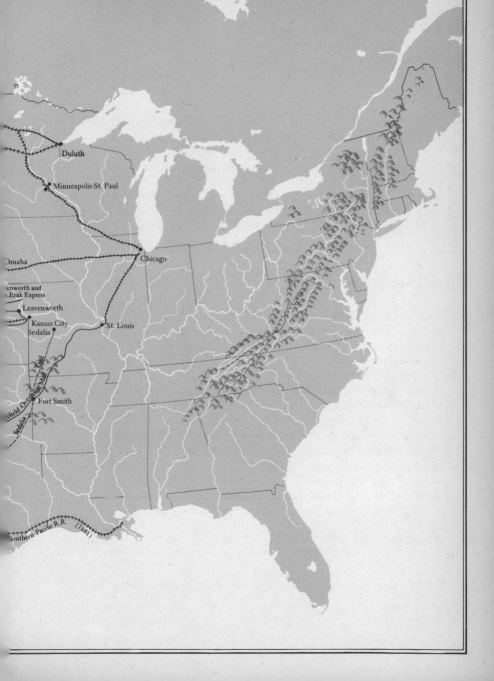

TRANSPORTATION IN THE
WESTERN UNITED STATES

Duluth

Minneapolis-St. Paul

Chicago

Omaha

enworth and
Peak Express

Leavenworth

Kansas City

Sedalia

St. Louis

Sedalia Trail

Fort Smith

tfield Overland Mail

Southern Pacific R.R. (1881)

wide pass over the divide.* Stuart subsequently struck the Sweetwater, then the North Platte; via that river he came to the Missouri and finally arrived in St. Louis in April of 1813.

This route was used by the fur trappers, so that by the time people began going to Oregon (the first farmer-emigrants went as the Palmer party of 1841), the trail was fairly well known. Thus when the California Forty-niners came along there was already a well-marked trail west as far as Soda Springs or Fort Hall to the north, and Fort Bridger or Salt Lake City to the south. The Mormon migration of 1847 and 1848 (with small beginnings in 1846) had added a well-worn trail along the north side of the Platte. (There is considerable misunderstanding about this Mormon trail. Authorities generally agree that the Mormons concentrated on the opposite side of the river from the trail used by the "gentiles"—this would place Mormons on the north side—and of course, they turned southwest at Fort Bridger in order to reach the Great Salt Lake. Yet in fact the Great Medicine Road was wide and deviating; both sides were used, as the result of a democratic concept of "every man his own trail maker.")

To the person who drives Interstate 80 today from Salt Lake City across the desert lands of Utah and Nevada, it must seem nearly incomprehensible that anyone could traverse such sterile country in an animal-drawn wagon. Yet it is estimated that 45,000 gold seekers reached California in 1849 via this wasteland. How did they do it? The answer lies in their understanding of that land of changing pastel colors, shimmering under a cloudless sky. Those who had to learn the country or die soon discovered that water, usually in springs, lay at the base of the mountain ranges, and that these north–south-running ranges occur every fifteen to thirty or forty miles. They were dry trips, sometimes thirty-five miles at a time of tormenting struggle with emaciated, thirsty stock that at best could average not more than twelve or fifteen miles a day. But they could and did also travel in the cool of the night. Knowledgeable pioneers came to look upon *jornadas* (dry drives) with respect, but not with cringing fear. And by the late 1840's the trail was sufficiently trodden to eliminate the apprehension of getting lost.

For the Oregonians the mountains toward the end of the journey, or

* South Pass is peculiar in that it is a much wider depression than is common across mountains. It is a wide, low place in southwestern Wyoming; the Continental Divide crosses it from approximately south to north. Because of its unusual width, the railroad, the automobile highways, and the crossing of the old Oregon Trail are at different places, yet all cross the Continental Divide at South Pass. It was called South Pass because it was south of the passes used by Lewis and Clark. There are, of course, many passes to the south of South Pass, all the way to the Mexican border. See Marshall Sprague, *The Great Gates* (Boston, 1964), especially pp. 88-89.

the frightening trip on a raft down the Columbia from The Dalles, was the worst part of the trip. For the Californians it was the crossing of the Sierras. Many an emigrant came through four months of danger and tedium, only to have his wagon reduced to kindling wood when its brakes gave way, or ropes used to lower it broke free in the mountains of Oregon or California and the vehicle crashed far down into a canyon.

In time there were other trails through the West: the Bozeman Trail, from Fort Laramie to Bozeman, Helena, and Virginia City; the Smoky Hill Trail to the Pike's Peak country; the Old Spanish Trail from Santa Fe to California; the gold rush trail, also known as the Gila Trail or Cooke's Wagon Road, across northern Mexico (until 1853, when it was a part of the Gadsden Purchase); and the Sidney-Black Hills Trail into the sacred country of the Sioux.

Finally, wagon roads appeared, with the aid of the federal government. Federal funding had been supplied for the National Road, as well as for various military roads. In 1830 the Corps of Topographical Engineers and the Corps of Engineers were being employed increasingly to survey possible routes and then construct them. These were always, theoretically at least, considered military roads, or post roads, or in some instances territorial roads, thus justifying the federal funds used for their survey and construction.

On the west side of the Mississippi the first major federal road project was a north–south artery joining Fort Snelling (south of Minneapolis) and Fort Towson (in present southeastern Oklahoma). The distance involved was about 850 miles, via Fort Leavenworth and Fort Smith, Arkansas. It has been said that by 1840 one could travel from Louisiana to the Great Lakes along federally constructed roads. Arkansas and Iowa especially benefited from such federal military construction.

All of this was, however, a prelude to a much more energetic federal policy that materialized after the Mexican War. Wherever the army was out West in the years 1848-60, it manifested much of its energy in the survey and construction of roads. In New Mexico the principal link today between Taos and Santa Fe is along the old military road; the old Fort Union Road to Santa Fe is today the main line of the Santa Fe Railroad, and its route from Albuquerque down the Rio Grande Valley and across to El Paso likewise follows a road constructed by the army. In much of this activity Edward Fitzgerald Beale was involved. He was the man who administered for the army the experiment of using camels in the southwest desert, while at the same time he superintended wagon road construction in that vast area. From El Paso to Fort Yuma at the crossing of the Colorado River into California—the route of the Southern Pacific—the Department of the Interior was delegated by Congress to construct a road; this was accomplished, in the years 1857-59, by James B. Leach and N. Henry Hutton. Whether under the auspices of the army or of the Department of the Interior, the work crews built bridges, dug wells, constructed reservoirs, and did side-hill digging. By 1859 there was a remarkably good wagon road from Fort Smith, Arkansas, to the Colorado River; the route, incidentally, that was followed by the Butterfield Overland Mail which carried mail and passengers between Tipton, Missouri and San Francisco from 1858 to 1861.

Such activity points up the interest manifested by the federal government in the improvement of the transcontinental routes to California. In May 1856, Senator John B. Weller of that state presented Congress with two leather-bound volumes containing the signatures of seventy-five thousand Californians, requesting the construction of a wagon road linking East with West. One of the results was the effort to improve the Central Overland—the Oregon-California Trail—by such means as the Lander Cutoff from South Pass to Soda Springs, completed in 1858. The work on the Central Overland was administered by the Department of the Interior, not the War Department. In four seasons of work along the central route from Fort Kearny, Nebraska, to Honey Lake, California, bridges were built, stones removed, wells and reservoirs constructed. There is no doubt that the great emigrant trail was easier to use for those pioneers who set out in the late 1850's than it had been for those who had gone before.

The thirty-fifth-parallel route across New Mexico and Arizona was also a distinct success. Completed in 1858-59, it was partly a result of the Pacific Railroad Surveys of 1853-55. The testament to the soundness of the survey of the route is that from Albuquerque to Needles it is essentially the route of the main line of the Santa Fe Railroad today. One other important army road is worth mentioning: the Mullan Road, which also grew out of the Pacific Railroad Surveys. One of the engineers working under Major Isaac I. Stephens in the Pacific Northwest was Lieutenant John Mullan, a capable young West Point graduate and engineer. He was ordered to build a wagon road from Fort Walla Walla eastward to Fort Benton on the upper Missouri River. Beginning in 1858 from the Washington end, he pushed through the bridge-making, side-hill digging, and other work that was necessary for a wagon road in those twisting ranges of mountains. By June of 1862 he had completed the road. It was never important as a military road, but its completion almost coincided with the Montana gold discoveries, so it quickly became a key emigration route. Gold seekers as well as settlers headed for the Oregon and Washington territories embarked at St. Louis; at Fort

Benton they unloaded their rolling stock or else purchased wagons and livestock there to continue the journey; some of them walked. Migration along this road, however, was never as great as along the California-Oregon trails. Again, the Northern Pacific and Great Northern (now merged as the Burlington Northern) honor the original surveyors and wagon road builders by using parts of the Mullan Road for their own rights of way.

Other roads planned and constructed, at least in part, in the 1860's, were less successful. The Interior Department had grandiose plans for roads from such upper Missouri River towns as Omaha and Sioux City, across present Wyoming and up into the Montana gold fields; but when built, these roads—Sawyer's Wagon Road and the Big Cheyenne River Road—were failures. Indian depredations, poor planning, and the coming of the Union Pacific made them untenable. The Interior Department did, however, build a successful mountain road from Lewiston, Idaho, to the gold mines at Virginia City, Montana.

It is difficult to make a proper appraisal of federal road-building activities in the trans-Mississippi West in the period after 1846. The great Central Overland Trail was already there, as was the Santa Fe Trail, and as traces so were most of the other arteries from civilized place to civilized place. The presence of federal engineers and road laborers was symbolic, however, of the rapid settlement of the new country. Side-hill excavation, the construction of bridges, the digging of wells, and the laying of plank or corduroy roads over boggy stretches certainly aided the emigrant, the freight wagon teamster, and the stagecoach driver. In the tier of states just west of the Mississippi—Minnesota, Iowa, Missouri, and Arkansas—construction definitely encouraged emigration and settlement. Perhaps the best conclusion is that the coming of the federal road builders, both military and civilian, aided an emigration that was at all events inevitable, and indicated, even in such wild parts of the West as the Powder River country of Wyoming, hotly contested between Indians and whites, that American civilization, sweeping west like a wave, could not be halted.

As long as animals were the source of power, the conveyances used along the roads remained relatively simple. Horses and mules were used for pack trains, and for many years traders and pioneers would employ these simplest of all freight carriers to transport goods into and out of the new country. Until 1800 wagons were difficult if not impossible to get through the mountains from eastern to western Pennsylvania or from Virginia or North Carolina to Kentucky or Tennessee, or up and down the Natchez Trace; so pack animals were used. As the frontier advanced, the pack trains advanced with it. Prospecting parties used this type of transportation almost exclusively, for those seeking gold and silver went where it might be found, not where the going was easiest. The army on its reconnaissances used pack animals, although supply wagons and ambulances would be drawn along also. One of the largest pack trains in the history of the American West was used when President Arthur took a vacation through the Yellowstone Park in 1883; about 180 pack animals were involved. The packer who could secure a diamond hitch in jig time, at least when he was sober, fetched good wages in the new country.

For healthy, lusty single men a pack train, plus saddle mounts, could be the quickest method of transportation. But the theory did not always jibe with the reality. If there is bound to be sickness today among a group of twenty or thirty men out facing the elements, consider the situation one to two hundred years ago. The journals, diaries, and reminiscences are full of comments about illnesses. Malaria (the ague), diarrhea, rheumatism, pleurisy, and the common cold laid men low. Add to this the probability, almost the certainty, of broken limbs, "bum legs," and gunshot wounds, and a problem arises: what does a pack train party do when a member cannot ride or walk? There is no wagon to put him in. The answer is that the party has to lay over—simply camp and await his recovery or death—or leave the poor fellow, or else make a pallet between two gentle mules or horses, one in front and one in the rear. This is not a very safe or satisfactory way to carry a sick person. Adding these considerations, the pack train loses some of its theoretical mobility, and the plodding wagon train soon catches up.

For pioneers emigrating westward the pack train was even less attractive. Theirs was a journey of three to five months, in which even the healthiest frontiersmen could take sick. Women and babies needed the comfort of a wagon. And, for such long trips as a migration of several months, something savoring of a home was needed, a place where a young wife big with child could rest, where a babe could sleep, and a sick member of the family could recuperate or be nursed back to health. A four-wheeled wagon could serve this function. A pack horse could only carry a few goods. Thus people went into the new country primarily in wagons (providing the country was accessible by wagon), rather than by pack trains. East of the Mississippi they could also go by water.

West of Philadelphia some forty-five miles is the county of Lancaster, and within it lies the fertile Conestoga Valley. By the time of the American Revolution some residents had lived there for more than two generations. The people were Germans—Pennsylvania Dutch—and English.

Their lands were productive, their homes of stone and wood built to last for generations, their livestock sleek and fat. They were artistic as well as energetic people, and from rather early times they produced a surplus. At first this included furs and perhaps some bear's oil and honey; later it included all manner of farm products. The ready market was Philadelphia, a good four days' journey away. What they needed was a wagon stout enough to stand up over bad roads, large enough to carry staples sufficient to make such a trip economically worthwhile, and light enough to be easily drawn by not more than six horses. Finally, the wagon needed some kind of cover to protect the freight from the rain. From this need arose both the wagon and the breeding of horses to pull it. The wagon was the Conestoga, and the fat, sleek, docile draft horses were likewise known as Conestogas.

The wagon was without a doubt a development from freight wagons used in Germany as well as from lighter wagons used in the English countryside. By the time of Braddock's defeat in 1755 these wagons were widely used in Pennsylvania and did faithful service for the troops. By the time the Philadelphia-Lancaster Turnpike opened, they may be said to have achieved perfection in design. By about 1820, when heavy wagons carrying three or four tons of farm produce, dry goods, iron ore, or most anything were in use, they had achieved their widest distribution. For thirty years thereafter, until railroads ended the horse-drawn long-distance freighting east of the Mississippi, these superbly designed, painstakingly constructed, tough, heavy-duty vehicles carried America's overland freight. In the process of their development and in their use, a colorful way of life evolved, but, sadly, it lacked a Mark Twain to tell us about it.

It is hardly accurate, perhaps, to call a freight wagon a thing of beauty. Yet in its flow of lines, its graceful curves, its well-proportioned white top, its wheels—the rear larger than the front—and in the bracing and the hubs and the tool box and the lazy board and the feeding trough, even in the angle at which the axe was attached to the side of the box, the Conestoga pleased the eye. Perhaps it was not beautiful, but it was a work of art. Even the hinges of the tool box were often shaped like tulips or serpents or hearts. When it was freshly painted, often with red running gear, blue box, and spotless white canvas, hemp, or Osnaburg cloth top, it was as pretty as anything that moved and was fashioned by the hands of man. Nor was this accidental. The wheelwrights, wagonmakers, and farmers of southern Pennsylvania were intensely proud of their skills.

The Conestoga was reminiscent of a boat, since its floor was curved, the deepest part rather ahead of the center. The curvature was followed in the shaping of the box, which was usually twenty-eight to forty inches deep, ten feet or more long, and forty-two inches wide. This curvature helped prevent the load from sliding out the front or back when the wagon went up and down the steep hills of the Appalachians. Each end flared outward; there was no seat at the front. The bows, anywhere from eight to sixteen of them, were flat on top—the entire canvas top of the true Conestoga was flat rather than rounded. Above the bows was the white cover, flaring out front and back at the same angle as the ends of the box. It could be puckered shut at either end with a drawstring.

The typical Conestoga had wheels sixty inches apart. The running gear was relatively complex for a horse-drawn vehicle, and was made of hardwoods, white ash being a favorite. The running gear and the box touched at only three points, and a system of suspension made it possible for the box and its contents to ride easily over bumps and ruts, up hills and down steep gorges. The wheels were beautiful examples of the wheelwright's art, and the iron tires were usually two to four inches in width (wider tires made wagons much easier to pull than narrow ones).

To pull these stately freighters or heavy-duty farm wagons the husbandmen of Maryland, Pennsylvania, and adjoining areas bred the horses possessing the traits they most wanted in a draft animal: powerful body, long sturdy legs, and a docile nature. In time, fat, sleek horses, usually bay or black but sometimes dapple, sixteen and a half or more hands high and weighing 1,650 pounds or more, became common along the eastern roads. These draft horses were called Conestogas; yet there never was a breed of them, and the horse possessing their particular attributes no longer exists. They were simply a regional product, descended from Flemish or German draft horses, very well fed—often on far more expensive grain than most farmers fed their animals; they were, in fact, given loving care by owners who appear to have possessed a genuine humanitarian interest in their welfare. Such excellent care, along with an easygoing type of selective neighborly breeding, produced these wonderful workhorses.

There were various sizes of Conestogas. Three, four, five or six horses pulled them. (With the odd number the lead horse was called a "spike.") Typically there were six horses, or three teams. Hitching up such an assemblage of horsepower required a skilled teamster, even with well-trained horses, what with chains, harness, singletrees, spreaders, collars, and so forth. The team next to the wagon was known as the wheelers, then came the middle or swing team, then the lead team. The wagoner soon had six horses, all dapple gray or bay or black, waiting patiently for his "giddap." Such a wagoner, who as a farmer might aug-

A Conestoga wagon and Pennsylvania tavern. (The Historical Society of Pennsylvania)

ment his income by doing some freighting in the slack season for farm chores, was known along the roads as a "militia man," while the full-time teamsters were known as "regulars." The latter looked with disdain upon the former.

With the horses hitched up and the wagon loaded, the teamster was ready to start. He walked on the left side, or rode in a special saddle mounted on the left wheeler, that is, the horse closest to the wagon on the left side. There was also a plank seat that could be lifted from its position flush with the box and set just ahead of the left rear wheel, jutting out from the box. This was the "lazy board." But most of the time the teamster walked alongside the left wheeler, holding loosely the "jerk line" which constituted his only actual contact with his rig. This was a long piece of leather as much as two inches wide, the other end attached to the bit in the mouth of the leader—the front horse on the left side. A good Conestoga freightman with a strong voice could so control his patient and docile draft horses that his long whip and the jerk line were mere safety devices.

Until 1850 the Conestogas were the elite of freight wagons and carried much of America's land cargo. Since the wagon might average no more than two miles an hour, it could cover only twelve to fifteen miles a day. So at these intervals taverns or inns, sometimes called "stands" or "teamster's stands," grew up along the line. While no two inns were alike, they did tend to resemble one another in design. They were often of stone, nearly square, with two stories and an attic with windows in the gable ends. Usually a porch stretched across the front, from which two doors led inside, one to the barroom and the other into a hall which in turn led to family living quarters. The barroom was often fairly small—say eighteen feet by thirty—while the dining room was larger and usually contained a huge fireplace. But more time was spent in the barroom, where whiskey was often served "on the house" and more sophisticated drinks—applejack, apple toddy, cherry bounce, peach brandy, poker'd beer, to name a few—were dispensed for the more discriminating.

Outside the inn was a watering trough and a yard large enough for many wagons. Close by was a small pasture where the horses could graze; a nearby barn furnished hay. We are speaking, incidentally, of inns catering to wagoners; for in the more settled regions there were "uppity" inns and taverns catering to the stagecoach and carriage trade. Wagoners were not welcomed at them, and genteel people might think twice before putting up at a wagoner's inn.

It was a remarkably self-contained unit—the teamster, his teams, and his wagon. The truck stops along the great highways today, catering to modern teamsters, are the continuance of a heritage.

The passing parade of land transportation in the new country down to 1850 must have offered as much variation and entertainment to those who lived by the side of the road as the combination of mass media of our time. Westward came wagons carrying iron farm implements, furniture, tools, clothing, shoes, caskets, liquors, and food—including specially built fast wagons that carried fresh oysters to inns beyond the mountains. Westward toward the new country traveled families on the move from New England and New York, from eastern Pennsylvania or Maryland or Virginia. Some traveled well; some traveled in extreme poverty, with a mangy horse and a rattletrap two-wheeled cart, and the numerous human progeny walking alongside. There were Germans, English, and Scotch-Irish, speaking thick words an American "native" could not understand and showing the timidity of peasantry out of its element—hesitant, trying to make up for misunderstanding, bewilderment, and fear by displaying a permanent smile.

Eastward came the products of the new country: whiskey, peltry, grain, timber, and herds of hundreds of hogs, cattle, sheep, horses, even turkeys and geese. These last were placed in pens at night where soft tar had been put down. The tar stuck to their feet and served as protection so the fowl could continue their walk to market next day.

Traveling now east and now west, besides the wagoners, were businessmen on good steeds, supervisors of the big freighting firms, horse traders, middlemen seeking flocks or herds to purchase, stagecoaches, occasional companies of actors, circuses with mangy wild animals. The road from Philadelphia to Pittsburgh, the Philadelphia-Lancaster Turnpike, the National Road—all were busy.

The wagons were not all Conestogas, but the Conestoga became the standard, the ideal, and variations of it appeared. By the time the westward advance had reached that area in western Missouri where the river makes a great curve to the north, many a farm and freight wagon resembled the Conestoga in many ways; yet in workmanship, symmetry, and running-gear design, it was simply not the Conestoga.

The Santa Fe trade marks the beginning of major changes from the Conestoga to the prairie schooner, or, to use a more common term, the covered wagon. Oxen were used to pull it more than horses and mules. The running gear was changed so that sharper turns could be manipulated. The fore and aft flare of the wagon was changed to a straight upright position, and a seat was added at the front. The wagon increased in size, so that the average rig owned by Russell, Majors, and Waddell (the greatest of all freighting firms) had iron tires four inches wide and held up to 7,000 pounds—three and a half tons. Plains freighters began experimenting with a second wagon, added in tandem much as trailers in tandem are allowed in many states today. Eventually a third, two-wheeled cart was sometimes added. This carried more merchandise, served as a chuck wagon or living quarters, or, in the case of the twenty-mule-team rigs (not affiliated with Russell, Majors, and Waddell) that carried borax out of Death Valley, California, it served as a water wagon.

The twenty-mule teams and the wagons they pulled were probably the ultimate in size of all animal-drawn rigs. It was 165 miles in searing heat from the mines to the railroad at Mojave in the 1890's, and there were just three springs of water on the way. A freighter could make about 18 miles a day. To make the operation profitable it was necessary to haul large amounts of borax; but in addition, hay for the stock and food for the teamster and water for both had to be carried along.

Wagons were designed weighing 7,800 pounds which were hauled in tandem, plus a water wagon at the tail end. They were huge wagons by standards of the day: beds 16 feet long, 4 feet wide, and 6 feet deep; rear wheels 7 feet in diameter with steel tires 8 inches wide and an inch thick; the front wheels were somewhat smaller. Such conveyances—

two wagons and a water trailer—carried loads including 47,000 pounds of borax, plus about 16,000 pounds worth of the wagons themselves, hay, food for the teamster, and water: about thirty-one and a half tons. It took an expert to drive such an enormous rig, which was in fact misnamed, since a typical twenty-mule team consisted of 18 mules and 2 horses.[1] (The horses, stronger and easier to control, were closest to the wagon.)

All prairie schooners used on the Great Plains demanded great skill in workmanship since the dry, rarefied air of the plains shrank the joints and loosened the box; tires came loose for the same reason. To combat this tendency the firm of Russell, Majors, and Waddell specified that the hubs should be made of Osage orange and the spokes and felloes of white oak, for these woods resisted the dryness.

A twenty-mule-team rig. The size of the borax wagons and the all-important water wagon is clear in this photo. (U.S. Borax Company)

Freight outfit at Saguache, Colorado, circa 1880. (State Historical Society of Colorado)

By the 1850's wagon manufacture had followed the normal economic tendency for concentration of production in the hands of a few companies. Three such trade names were the Pitt, which was manufactured in Pittsburgh and strongly resembled the Conestoga, the J. Murphy of St. Louis, and the Studebaker of South Bend. Most of their products were farm wagons that could carry up to two and a half tons (5,000 pounds), but occasionally they turned out freighters' wagons also, often to the buyer's specifications. Emigrants tended to use good farm wagons of the usual two- to two-and-a-half-ton capacity; these they strengthened in various ways, attached hickory hoops above the bed, canvas over the hoops, and had their emigrant's covered wagon.

The firm of Russell, Majors, and Waddell deserves at least passing mention here, for their organization demonstrates that managerial competency was approaching twentieth-century standards, although their equipment, ox-drawn for the most part, was as slow as in the days of Christ. This Missouri-based company contracted with the army for delivery of goods to the remote military forts in the new country, and in the mid-1850's its operations were phenomenal. The partners scoured the neighboring states and territories for oxen and purchased stout wagons—"Pittsburghs," made in the city of that name, J. Murphys, and others—made to their own specifications. When spring came they were ready, with a half million dollars invested in 3,500 oxen and 500 wagons. These they divided into about twenty wagon trains of twenty-five or twenty-six units each, with which they guaranteed to deliver the goods —two and a half million pounds of them. And they did.

As Majors explained in his autobiography, each wagon was carefully packed, and the load was not to be touched until the destination was reached; it was covered with three sheets of thin ducking. Twelve oxen, or six yokes, pulled each wagon, and twenty to thirty extra head always accompanied a train. Thus a complete wagon train had between 320 and 330 oxen. The personnel to supervise and guide such a caravan consisted of a wagonmaster (paid $125 a month and board), an assistant, and a teamster for each wagon (at about $1 a day plus expenses). There was also a man along to watch over the extra stock, and two or three extra men, in case of accident or illness, "the latter case being an exception for as a rule," said Majors, "there was no sickness."[2] Since the wagon beds were covered with duck and were not to be disturbed, the men placed their bedrolls and other possessions in the kitchen wagon, which also held the grub and provided a place for a sick man to ride. Once the outfit was accustomed to its routine, nearly 300 oxen, twelve per wagon or six yokes, could be hitched up and the train made ready to move in an incredibly short period of time. Once Majors timed an outfit after the cattle had been driven into the corral and allowed to calm down. It took just sixteen minutes until the wagonmaster was ready to pop the whip and start the train moving. There was, of course, a "nooning" lasting two to two and a half hours; nevertheless, in the course of a sunrise-to-sunset day, twelve to fifteen miles could be covered with loaded wagons. Night drives were also fairly common.

The firm was highly successful in its 1855 and 1856 operations, in spite of cholera that struck down a few teamsters. Then, with the coming of the Mormon war, the company fell on hard times. Troubles ranged from the burning of wagon trains by Mormons to the failure of the army to pay. The speculative schemes of one partner, William Russell, including the Pony Express experiment in 1860-61, helped into bankruptcy a company already on the ropes.

Wagon freighting continued until well after the coming of the railroads, although these did put long-distance drayage out of business. Yet large areas were not served by railroads until well into the 1880's, and the long caravans of white-topped wagons were a familiar sight on the plains and in the mountains until the railroads came. The prevalence of these wagon trains broke some of the monotony for pioneers headed west, while the ox droppings, where the train had camped for the night, provided fuel for the people of wagon trains to come. Nor did the freighters or emigrants give up quickly. Well into the twentieth century, in some remote parts of the West, families still moved short distances in wagons, and teamsters continued to haul goods from town to town.

Some people went west on business, or if they went to the new country to stay, they did it in style. For them—drummers, military men, sisters of army wives, government employees—there was transportation by stagecoach. By the nineteenth century this type of transportation was entering an era of rapid growth and development both in the United States and in Europe, including the British Isles. The "flying coachman" brought small, envious boys to the local tavern (which was also the stage station), and the reinsman was the hero of the day as he brought the stage, in a clatter of galloping hooves and squeaking wheels and a cloud of dust, to a halt in front of the inn.

The growth of stagecoaching was indicative of the settled state of the new country, for the economics of passenger transportation demand that cities with commerce, industry, and an enterprising, mobile population (as distinct from sleepy farm villages) be at both ends of the line. Philadelphia to Pittsburgh, Boston to Albany or New York, New York to Philadelphia and Washington, D.C., and Charleston to Savannah were examples of profitable stage routes in the early days of the new country. Two or three decades later Baltimore to Wheeling to Springfield to Vandalia to St. Louis, or St. Louis to Alton to Chicago were also bustling stagecoach routes.

Out West the need for stagecoaches was apparent first in the gold-mining regions of California. Here resided an unusually mobile and restless population. Moreover, the thousands of homeless miners yearned for mail and wanted transportation from one mining camp to another. As soon as a semblance of political organization existed in California, the populace began petitioning Congress for overland mail and passenger service.

Stagecoach transportation was not cheap. Horses needed changing about every twelve miles, so a route of 200 miles required sixteen or eighteen way stations. The stock had to be well trained and of top quality. In the years after 1790 the coachmen of New England developed horses just for the coach trade. Among the types most in demand were Morgans and Cleveland Bays, both of which possessed qualities of strength, endurance, and "horse sense" highly prized by coachmen. The number of such good horses was never equal to the demand, and they were costly.

Expensive too were the coaches. Whereas a good farm wagon, even a Conestoga, would rarely cost over $200, a good American coach could command $1,000 to $1,500. Here again, New Englanders developed a unit that was far more practical than the heavy, ponderous coaches used in Europe. True, springs were used in these old-world coaches, but they were not mounted scientifically; they broke easily and functioned differently with a heavy load than with a light one. They made no provision for tilting backward and forward. The harness system involved such tight control over the horses that the poor beasts suffered from the jolting as the coach wheels fell into the numerous potholes or bumped over rocks. The first long-distance stage line, from London to Edinburgh, began operations in 1785; curiously, in the same year America's first long-distance line began running between New York and Albany.

Yankee ingenuity early became apparent in the development of a greatly improved stagecoach. To make it ride easier the New England coachmakers threw out the springs and substituted leather thoroughbraces, heavy bullhide straps mounted on top of the running gear, one on each side from front to rear. The coach, which the coachmaker, who knew something of the physics of stress and strain, now made in oval shape, almost literally sat on the thoroughbraces. It rocked with the jolts, while the real bumps were absorbed by the running gear. Three seats were placed inside the enclosure; a triangular boot was placed on the outside rear for luggage; and the driver's seat was placed outside and high up in the front. A railing was added around the edges of the roof, so that luggage or six or more men could be carried up there.

The demand for these vehicles was so great that in time a master coachmaker appeared, the firm of Abbott and Downing, of Concord, New Hampshire, which was incorporated in 1826 and by 1850 was the world's leading stagecoach company. Its Concord coaches represented the ultimate in the wheelwright's and coachmaker's art. These conveyances, standing 8'6" high, with rear wheels 5'1" and front wheels of 3'10", came in a variety of sizes, though the wheel dimensions remained the same. The typical Concord held nine people inside, the driver plus two up on the driver's seat, and the men on the roof. Stories were circulated of as many as thirty passengers plus luggage on a Concord in California, and Carrie Adele Strahorn told of the Gunnison (Colorado) stage she took with her husband that carried seventeen passengers plus luggage.

When the Concords left the plant in New Hampshire, they were

A typical stage of the Concord type used by express companies on the overland trails, circa 1869. Black soldiers are on guard atop. (U.S. Signal Corps, The National Archives)

the handsomest coaches ever produced in America, and if comfort, design, practicality, and durability are virtues, then they were a far greater accomplishment than the gilt carriages in which royalty paraded in Europe. The company also produced a lesser coach called the Celerity wagon, lighter, used primarily for mail and express, as well as "mud wagons," ungainly but cheaper, without thoroughbraces or springs, yet well made and excellent on bad roads. Troy coaches, manufactured in Troy, New York, ran second in excellence to the Concords.

New England stage drivers, armed with the know-how of their trade, worked south and west, and as long as they remained sober (which often was not for long) they found steady employment. Several of them grabbed the big chance when they found themselves in such new country as California, Montana, Colorado, or Missouri. There they rousted up the best old wagon and the best four or six span of horses or mules they could find and, with nothing more, set up business as coachmen. This is specifically the story in California, where young New England-born James Birch came to dominate stagecoaching until his untimely death at sea. By the mid-1850's California had the best stagecoach service in the world. The competition was keen, and a magic ingredient—government mail contracts—brought the shrewdest kind of promoter to the fore. These lucrative agreements were let by the United States postmaster general in California even as senators, homesick miners, and businessmen anticipated a transcontinental stage service to carry mail, express, and passengers, which, of course, would have to be heavily subsidized by the government. It was in the election year of 1856 that the big petition for a good wagon road and stagecoach service was presented to Congress. Politically, something had to be done. A law was passed granting the postmaster general the power to decide upon a route from the Mississippi River to California and to pay a subsidy of up to $600,000 a year for semi-weekly coach service both ways. Since the postmaster general was Aaron Brown of Tennessee, the South won this round, for Brown would naturally favor a Southern route.

The contract was let to a New England coachman, John Butterfield, one of the founders of the American Express Company, who represented a group of seven investors, all of whom were executives of the four principal express companies in the United States at the time: Adams Express, Wells Fargo, National, and Butterfield's own American Express. But more important than this was his friendship with President James Buchanan, who was determined that Butterfield should have the contract. In spite of pressure applied on behalf of Birch, Butterfield landed it.

He accepted the terms and set out to provide service within a year of the signing. Postmaster Brown had not helped things by stipulating a preposterous trail which became known as the "oxbow route" because of its shape on a map. The eastern termini were St. Louis (actually, Tipton, Missouri, the western terminus of the railroad) and Memphis, the latter Brown's home town. Coaches from each city were to meet at Little Rock, where a single vehicle went on to Fort Smith, then via a route laid out by Captain Randolph Marcy in 1849 through the lands —now part of Oklahoma—occupied a few years previously by the Choctaw and Chickasaw Indians, forcibly moved there from their lands east of the Mississippi. The road then led to Sherman, Texas, and then to Fort Belknap on the Brazos River. The route continued through Texas; at the Horsehead Crossing of the Pecos the Overland Mail coaches advanced upstream 150 miles, then followed more or less the New Mexico–Texas border west to Franklin, on the Texas side of the Rio Grande, present El Paso. They next followed the route of the Mormon Battalion which had been led during the Mexican War by Colonel Philip St. George Cooke (and which later became known as Cooke's Road) to Tucson, advanced northwest to the Gila River, southwest by west to

Yuma, up to Los Angeles and then, via Tejon Pass and the interior valley, to San Francisco.

It was 2,795 miles in all, with the expanse from Fort Smith to Yuma a virtual wilderness. Yet the route had a few compensations. It was, as Brown had pointed out in its defense, virtually snowless; moreover, much of the terrain was easily traversed by good horses and mules and a coach in good condition, whether there was an actual road or not. Nevertheless it is a testament to Butterfield's ability that he was able to plan 200 way stations and have 139 of them operational within a year. He purchased 1,000 horses, 500 mules, 500 vehicles—Concord Celeritys and a few Troys—at a total cost of about a million dollars. He hired about 800 men; and he had men, mules, horses, hay, grain, water, and equipment stationed along the trail by September 16, 1858. The first through passenger, a newspaperman named Waterman L. Ormsby, arrived safely in San Francisco at 7:30 A.M. on October 9th, twenty-three days, twenty-three hours, and thirty minutes out of St. Louis. The Butterfield route was a success. In a short time there was a waiting list for passengers west, and initially the coaches came through with acceptable regularity.

The Pike's Peak Rush, plus the impending secession, renewed interest in a central route. The freighters Russell, Majors, and Waddell became deeply involved in stagecoaching from the Missouri to Denver, from there north to the Oregon Trail, and then to Salt Lake City and via the California Trail to San Francisco. Primarily as a publicity stunt to convince Congress of the need for daily mail service with California via the central route, Russell had launched the Pony Express on April 13, 1860. Many of the swing stations were already in existence, and only horses, a fairly simple saddle, and a light, specially designed aparejo were necessary as equipment, plus about eighty "thin, wiry young fellers." The Express, which carried the mail the 1,966 miles from St. Joseph to Sacramento, was a practical success but a financial calamity. It was a "loss leader" which, it was hoped, would aid Russell and his COC & PP (Central Overland California and Pike's Peak Express Company, humorously known as the Clean Out of Cash and Poor Pay) in landing a million-dollar-a-year subsidy. When the lush federal contract failed to materialize, and Russell was indicted for the embezzlement of bonds, the COC & PP went insolvent and pulled the firm of Russell, Majors, and Waddell down with it. After sixteen months the Pony Express also ceased to run, the telegraph having made it obsolete. It was not really such a great achievement.

The man who bought Russell, Majors, and Waddell was Ben Holladay, a hard-driving businessman who understood the value of every cent, eliminated all manner of superfluous falderal from his lines, and

This photo, believed to have been taken in the 1850's, shows the more realistic aspects of stagecoach travel: mud, dirt, unwashed humanity, and drafty hotels. (Wells Fargo Bank, San Francisco)

kept his schedules running on time. He destroyed his enemies, viciously and systematically; when he had established a monopoly, he gouged the helpless public mercilessly. But he paid his help on time and he delivered the mail, which pleased the Post Office Department; he drove his horses to death in order to boast of a faster schedule. At the height of his power, he was lord over 3,000 miles of stage line.

In combating his competitors he may have allowed robbery of their stages and even the murder of drivers and passengers. That such dark accusations were made against him implies at the least a reputation something less than honorable; but this bothered him not a whit. Like all men who deal with the federal government when the stakes are high, he had friends in the Post Office and the War departments and friends in Congress. He was never ashamed to put in preposterous claims for damages incurred by Indians, floods, or changes in route ordered by the Post Office Department. With such wheeling and dealing plus lavish entertainment, Holladay rode the crest of government subsidies of stagecoaching.

On November 1, 1866, Wells Fargo bought out Holladay, and in early 1869, with the Central Pacific and Union Pacific due to join rails, that firm sold out to a number of smaller stage companies, which for several years operated excellent stage lines: Barlow and Sanderson, in the mountains of Colorado and west to Utah, California, Washington, and Oregon; and Gilmer and Salisbury in Idaho, Montana, and Wyoming, which later managed the famous Deadwood Stage, are examples.

Gradually the locomotive and the motor car crowded out the stagecoach. With the passage of time it became a garish reminder of a departed era; and the hardships of stagecoach travel—the odor of horses; the flies, gnats, and mosquitoes; the dust (and six horses can raise a lot of it); the mud in winter; the crowding of nine people or more in a narrow box; the unpleasantness of crying children, whiskey-sodden, unshaven, unwashed men, and cranky women; the crude eating and sanitary facilities at the stops; the lurching coach that spilled people over one another—all of this was forgotten.

Water Routes
and Railroads

Many of the phases in the development of transportation in the new country went on simultaneously; thus, at the same time that more than 5,000 Conestogas were lumbering across the Appalachians from Philadelphia or Baltimore to Pittsburgh in a travel time of about three weeks, people and goods were leaving from Pittsburgh, Wheeling, or Brownsville (Redstone) on the Youghiaghany or Monongahela, from Limestone (Maysville), or from Bear Creek (Louisville) for a voyage down the western waters. Indeed, not merely river boating but water transportation in general was of tremendous importance in the settling of the new country. In some periods, in the area east of the Mississippi, its contribution to settlement certainly exceeded that of roads and trails.

This is due partly to the obvious ease of communication by water when compared with the tedious toil, the expense, the hardships, and the slow progress of travel on land. Roadmaking was in its technological infancy, and in any event it was slow and very expensive. Horses, oxen, and mules were likewise costly, and restricted in how much they could carry or pull.

The great Mississippi Valley, including the Ohio Valley as the principal eastern artery, and the Missouri Valley as its counterpart to the west, was so planned by nature as to cause some to see in it the sure hand of God, so well suited was it for the uses of man. A conservative estimate places the navigable mileage of the Mississippi and its tributaries at fifty thousand miles. What we do not realize today is that there was a time when most of those fifty thousand miles actually were used for water transportation. By the time of the American Revolution all manner of boats, or at least conveyances that floated, were being used on the western waters. Their nomenclature is hazy, and the use of various names for different types of river craft should not be considered a hard and fast or always accurate terminology.

There was first the flatboat, which in a way became a symbol of the advance into the new country. It was eminently suited for the western waters, for its displacement was considerably less than a foot; when the water was low and the sandbars appeared, the flatboatmen could still progress downstream. Although they might differ in size, all "flats" had essentially the same shape. They could be anywhere from twenty to a hundred feet long, but the average flatboat was twelve to fourteen feet wide and forty to fifty feet long. The narrowness was necessary due to the chutes at the Falls of the Ohio (Louisville, Kentucky), which were just fifteen feet wide and had stones at each side which destroyed any vessel that collided with them. A flatboat of the ordinary size could carry four to five hundred barrels of flour, apples, peaches, pork, whiskey, cider, brandy, vinegar, or even Seneca oil (a medicinal petroleum product from springs in Pennsylvania). Thousands of barrels of salt were carried down the Allegheny to Pittsburgh, where the owners, having sold their cargo, often proceeded to sell the flatboat. In crates or other containers the flats carried all manner of produce on down the river: hulled and unhulled corn, butter, tallow, pork, beef, cheese, hemp, rope, tobacco, oats, potatoes, venison, bacon, horses, cattle, slaves, shingles, glassware, iron products, and so on *ad infinitum*. Occasionally the flatboat not only contained a cabin but was protected by a broad board railing built up three or four feet from the deck.

Steering such a cumbersome craft posed problems. Basically, a pole, possibly forty or fifty feet long, with a wide flat oar fastened to it, served the purpose. The pole was slung over a forked joint on the roof of the cabin or mounted on the railing at the stern. To keep the boat in the current, similar contrivances, manipulated in the same way, extended one from each side. These "sweeps" are believed to have been the basis for one of the names given the flatboats: broadhorns. Oftentimes manipulation was improved by having a smaller oar at the bow. Well named the "gouger," it could aid considerably, in coordination with the stern oar, in guiding the boat.

The flatboat also needed a cable, forty or fifty feet of rope used to tie up on shore; a pump, to help keep dry the hold, shallow as it was; and a brick fireplace for cooking—sometimes a sandbox contrivance did the job as well. Add that proverbial American piece of furniture, the rocking chair, a jug of Monongahela rye, and a crew of at least five—two per broadhorn and a man at the helm—and the vessel was ready to float all the way down to New Orleans if that was where its captain hankered to go. They might erect a sail to help them along; in fact, all manner of variations were to be found.

However the vessel was rigged, the flatboatmen looked ahead to a

River scene showing flatboats and two keelboats. (Rare Book Department, Cincinnati Public Library)

long adventure. From Pittsburgh to New Orleans was about 1,950 miles, the mouth of the Ohio being the midpoint, a journey of five to six weeks, twenty-four hours a day; it was a month to New Orleans from Louisville. Slow as this may seem, it was the principal means of transportation downstream. In the early 1800's between four and seven hundred flatboats arrived per year at New Orleans, and the number increased until it topped 2,700 per year in the mid-1840's, after which it began to slacken off. Many never went all the way, of course; the total number of "flats" on the western waters at any given time, but especially in the spring and the autumn, was far in excess of those arriving at New Orleans.

The flatboats never went back upstream. Their crewmen, after a few dangerous, often carousing days in Natchez or New Orleans, headed home on foot or on horseback. Usually they took passage on a keelboat or a steamboat (fairly common by the mid-1820's) as far as Natchez. From there—again, if they survived a carouse at sinful Natchez-under-the-hill—they headed northeast via the "Devil's Backbone"—the Natchez Trace. They usually traveled in groups over this trail made treacherous by highwaymen, and, if all went well, arrived at Nashville after several weeks on the trail. From there they probably headed on north or northeast for the Ohio, the Monongahela, or some other tributary from whence they had set out months before.

There were professional flatboatmen who spent their lives on the western waters. They were tough, arrogant, and illiterate; they loved to exchange boasts, insults, threats, dares, and profanity with people along the shore, and in time every river town had its gambling dens, saloons, and brothels to cater to them. The boatmen often supplied free transportation, liquor, and food to one of the itinerant fiddlers who plied the river offering in exchange for the hospitality a storehouse of songs— love songs, jigs, profane ditties, but few sacred numbers—as well as river gossip. Sometimes the men all danced on the deck, or gambled, or fought.

A man could make a living on a flatboat. With his omnipresent tin or copper horn, he could notify those in other boats, or those ashore, to please take notice. There were floating dram shops in an era when hard liquor was the opiate of just about every male over the age of fourteen. There were floating medicine shows, apothecary shops, peepshows, grist mills, and general stores. There were itinerant preachers, sometimes passengers and sometimes owners of their own churchly vessels. Yankee peddlers abandoned the old nag and wagon in exchange for a "flat" loaded with tinwares, needles, thread, calico, books, shoes, and sundries. Some flatboats were devoted to transporting horses or cattle. And sometimes, for conviviality, two or three would tie up together, as they floated down the beautiful Ohio or Mississippi, and be sociable for a few hours, then drift apart.

Above the flatboat in the progression toward more complex craft were the mackinaws, barges, batteaux, and keelboats that peppered the western waters. The mackinaw was an interesting craft with a single purpose and a brief existence. It was used primarily on the Missouri by fur traders. Some of these crude boats, made of hewn planks one and a half to two inches thick, pointed at both ends, flat-bottomed, could make up to seventy-five miles a day down the Big Muddy. Four or five oarsmen manipulated the craft from the bow, while the freight, usually furs and buffalo hides and the like, was stacked in the hold amidships, covered tightly with other buffalo skins. Fifteen tons could be carried this way. St. Louis was the end of the line, however. The vessel was sold for whatever its lumber would bring.

Bateaux, sometimes called galley bateaux, were used on the Ohio, the Allegheny, and the Monongahela. They too were of plank, flat-bottomed and pointed at the ends. They could carry up to forty tons of merchandise, which was sometimes housed, along with the crew, in a cabin at the rear of the boat. Apparently a score of rowers worked the craft upstream. These awkward vessels, an improvement over the pirogue (a type of canoe), ceased to be used on the western waters after the 1790's. Native ingenuity appears to have added a keel at about this time, and thus evolved an improved vessel—the keelboat.

It is probable, then, that the most graceful and practical boats on the western waters, the light and manageable keelboats, were merely improvements of the bateaux. Keelboats were built on keels, had ribbing, and were covered with planks. Typically they were sixty or seventy feet long and had a seven-to-ten foot beam and a hold three or four feet deep. Even when loaded, they drew only a couple of feet of water. Above decks they usually had a box-like cabin that held freight and gave the crew some protection from the elements. There was a huge oar jutting out from the stern. A typical keelboat cost two to three thousand dollars.

On each side of the deck was a cleared footway twelve to eighteen inches wide, from which the crew plunged their poles into the river bottom, placed the upper end of the poles against their shoulders, and literally walked the boat upstream. Or, if the current was too great, they would be forced to cordelle. This word is both a noun, denoting a towline several hundred feet long, and a verb, denoting the pulling of the boat by men holding the line. As a towline, "one end was fastened to the top of the mast and the other passed to the crew on shore," explains Leland D. Baldwin. "The bridle, a short rope lashed at one end to the bow and at the other end to a ring through which the cordelle passed, was used to keep the boat from swinging.[1] The crew splashed along the bank, holding the rope, and pulled the vessel upstream. A typical keelboat had a crew of four, six, or even a dozen men, primarily Americans. While they worked, the captain, called the patroon, manned the tiller. On occasion a sail was used.

Between the keelers and the bargers, as flatboatmen were called, there was bad blood. The typical barger was a Creole, a French Canadian, or a halfblood with Negro strains. The fights between crews of barges (flatboats) and keelboats were legendary; if there was no opposition around, then they would fight among themselves. The semi-legendary Mike Fink epitomized the lusty life the keelers led.

These vessels lasted for years and worked upstream as often as down. They often carried passengers as well as freight; there were regular mail and passenger packets from the 1790's on. Though it was a four-month toil from New Orleans to Pittsburgh, that journey was often made. Even after the coming of the steamboat, the keelboat persisted on the upper waters of the Ohio and its tributaries because of its shallow dis-

placement. Most of the keelboats returned to their home ports upstream, loaded with European textiles and manufactured goods, which
came into the inland valley far cheaper that way than by wagon freighting over the mountains. They also carried hemp, cotton, tobacco, copper, and other raw materials from the South and West which were
processed into finished products in the Ohio River towns, and, along
with ironware and glassware, were then transported downstream again.

So vigorous was the trade and industry of the new country that
oceangoing vessels were constructed at several places along the great
rivers. Probably the first seagoing vessel was a schooner built at Elizabeth, Pennsylvania, on the Monongahela, in 1793. It is recorded that in
1800 two oceangoing vessels left the ways, one from Marietta, Ohio,
and the other from Elizabeth. The latter, christened the *Monongahela
Farmer*, was of 250 tons. Always such vessels were sent down river with
a full cargo. In the case of the *Monongahela Farmer*, it consisted of 721
barrels of flour, 500 barrels of whiskey, 4,000 deerskins, 2,000 bearskins,
plus some hemp and flax. In the years until Jefferson's hated embargo
(December 21, 1807-March 1, 1809: by its provisions no American vessels could depart for a foreign country), ships were built at Allentown,
Freeport, Wheeling, Cincinnati, Louisville, Elizabeth, and probably at
other towns on the western waters. In the 1840's there was a resurgence
of this inland shipbuilding industry, which finally petered out shortly
after the Civil War. To further expedite foreign trade, Louisville, Cincinnati, and other river cities were from time to time designated as ports
of entry.

Finally, east of the Mississippi, there was transportation on the canals.
These were never built in strictly frontier country, but they were con-
comitants of the development of the new country. They were constructed with financing and original impetus from eastern centers that
wanted to win the competition with their rival cities for the lucrative
western trade. Or, once the success of the Erie Canal was evident, they
were built because they were looked upon as the panacea that would
lower costs of transportation of produce to the eastern markets and
lower the price of finished goods in the interior—but without bankrupt-
ing the state and at the same time lowering the selling price of agricultural commodities in the East. The logic may have been distorted, but
the canal-crazy booster chose to ignore that.

But the canals did serve a need, and transportation of many kinds
has had to base its existence upon this rather than upon any claim to
great profits. Some canals—like urban transit in our own day—lost money
but nevertheless served the public. They furnished a way to convey

goods (and passengers, secondarily) cheaply and practically. In the America of the 1820's and 1830's, energetic and searching for increased mobility, canals seem to be a solution.

There was nothing new about canals; they were widespread in Europe and the British Isles. Perceptive men from Louis Joliet, who had advocated a canal connecting Lake Michigan and the Illinois River as early as 1673 (opened finally in 1836 and still in use), to Albert Gallatin, Jefferson's secretary of the treasury, had advocated them. Gallatin's "Report on Roads, Canals, Harbors and Rivers," issued in 1808, set forth an elaborate transportation system, including many canals and offering something for every section of the country. The report was forgotten in the troubles involving the rights of the nation as a neutral carrier during the Napoleonic wars. But after the Peace of Ghent, which ended the War of 1812, the needs of the new country once more became paramount. As we have seen, there was a tidal wave of migration into the West after the war. The needs Gallatin had noted in 1808 came flooding back like a recurring tide. Something had to be done.

The initial great decision was made by the forward-looking leadership of New York, headed by Governor DeWitt Clinton, which succeeded in "selling" the state's million inhabitants on a very expensive risky investment—the Erie Canal. It was to make use of a most logical route west, one that had been mentioned for fifty years and more: up the Hudson to Albany, then west via canal 364 miles all the way to Buffalo on Lake Erie, essentially along the Mohawk River Valley—the "water-level route."

Much of the risk involved in construction lay in the absence of plain know-how. The nation had no canal experts or engineers, nor did it have a labor force trained for this kind of work. But surveying was already being carried on, and on July 4, 1817, in a small clearing in a dark forest near Rome, New York, the first shovel of dirt was thrown. The speaker's platform that day was of wooden puncheons, and whale oil torches hung on nearby oaks to eliminate some of the forest gloom.

For nine years, work on the canal continued. Irish laborers filled the air with their brogues as farmers along the right-of-way contracted with laborers on the one hand, and the canal authorities on the other, to dig specified sections; the farmers usually reaped a good profit. The canal builders would attach a chain to the top of a tree and, with a windlass, pull the stubborn thing until it came crashing down. Then they mounted two drums sixteen feet high on an axle thirty feet long and twenty inches in diameter; and in the center they attached to the axle a drum fourteen feet in diameter. One end of a chain was attached to the drum

The Erie Canal. From a Bureau of Public Roads diorama. (National Youth Administration, The National Archives)

Canal locks on the Pennsylvania System. (The Historical Society of Pennsylvania)

and the other looped around a stump. Hitched to the opposite side of the drum was a team of horses; when they pulled, the drum rocked, exerting pressure on the stump, which in seconds was pulled out of the ground as neatly as a good dentist extracts a tooth. With the trees and stumps removed, the digging would begin. The ingenious Yankees used horse-drawn scrapers to remove the earth; they then attached a cutting blade to sever tree roots.

Clinton's canal-building genius was young Canvass White, whom he had sent to Europe to tour the towpaths and accumulate expertise about canals. White was responsible for the use of hydraulic cement on the canal locks, which made them so long-lasting; he also helped in the design of aqueducts which were the pride of the Erie. Forty feet wide, four feet deep, with towpaths on each side, the Erie advanced through malarial swamps and virgin forests, and was finally finished in 1825. It was an astounding success.

The most interesting reverberation of that success was the reaction in other cities along the Atlantic. Their merchants were insanely jealous of the great prosperity which the Erie was bringing to the city of New York and, conversely, apprehensive about its effect on their own economies. They all wanted the trade of the Ohio River Valley, and so set out to checkmate New York's great windfall. The Massachusetts legislature even contemplated a canal across the Berkshires to the Hudson, but better Yankee judgement fortunately prevailed.

The Pennsylvania Portage and Canal System was the most expensive and the most difficult from the engineering point of view. Its main line started at Columbia on the Susquehanna River, which it followed as far as the Juniata; it then went west along that stream until the Allegheny wall loomed ahead at Hollidaysburg. Here an ingenious but expensive system of inclined planes was constructed. The canal boat, or part of it, was put on a cable car. As the car coasted down one side, stationary engines pulled the cables that drew another car up the other. All told, there were five separate inclines up the east side and five down the west side. The rise was 1,398 feet up from Hollidaysburg and 1,171 feet up from Johnstown, the terminus on the other side. The canal also passed through a 901-foot tunnel at Conemaugh, four miles east of Johnstown.

The Allegheny Portage Railroad, as it was called, was the wonder of the age. It was also the chief bottleneck of the system, and a constant expense. Nevertheless, from March of 1834 on, Pennsylvania could boast that it was possible to ship goods from Philadelphia to Pittsburgh, or vice versa, a distance of 394.54 miles, entirely by canal boats. A lateral canal extended up to Lake Erie. For all of its canals (for in total mileage they were double the length of the Main Line) the state of Pennsylvania spent $65,800,000, much of which represented a loss, for by the 1830's the railroads were offering such stiff competition that they became the principal purchasers of towpaths for rights-of-way.

Washington, D.C., came up with the Chesapeake and Ohio Canal, and Baltimore, miffed because that canal missed that metropolis, countered with the Baltimore and Ohio Railroad. Inland, both Ohio and Indiana launched ambitious and poorly engineered systems that brought those states into serious financial straits. Altogether about 4,400 miles of canals were dug, at a cost of $188,170,000 (including repairs), down to 1860.

In design the canal boat appears to have been an offshoot of the keelboat, with substantial changes. No canal boat could have a deep rounded hull, since the water might be only four feet deep, so it was flattened. No canal boat was going to move faster than four miles an hour; the freight boats and so-called line boats (which also carried poor emigrants) made only half that time. Because speed was out of the question, the boats soon became snub-nosed at the bow and squared at the stern. Because they passed under hundreds of low bridges, their height from hull to cabin roof could not be much more than eight feet. A typical packet (the elite of the canal boats) might be seventy to seventy-five feet long, but it was rarely more than eleven feet wide.

Although there were variations, a typical Erie passenger packet began at the bow with a small crew cabin. If the captain had his family along, this constituted their apartment. Next came the ladies' cabin, which served as dressing room, dormitory, and parlor; on the best boats it was separated from the next room by a wall. More often a red curtain served the purpose. On the other side was the big main room, called the main cabin, the saloon, or the dining room—it served all these purposes and was also a dormitory for the men at night. On a typical packet containing between thirty and forty passengers, it might be anywhere from thirty-six to forty-five feet long. Further back was the bar, and behind it, at the stern, the kitchen.

To manage such a boat there were the captain and usually two steersmen, two drivers, and a Negro bartender and cook. The motive power might be horses but very often was mules. Regardless, two or three of them were used, attached to the boat by a towline seventy to ninety feet long. Every ten or twelve miles the stock was changed; occasionally spare horses were kept on the boat.

Life along the canals was quite sinful from the viewpoint of the strait-laced nineteenth century—at least if the writings of lantern-jawed divines are to be believed. Much of the work was done by boys twelve to sixteen years of age. They were illiterate and exploited; they married young and often had different wives in different canal towns. Malaria was endemic among them, along with other ailments concomitant with a mobile, unstable existence. That the boats ran on Sunday did not help the industry in the eyes of the clergy.

And yet many respectable people earned their livelihood on the canals. There were towpath walkers who checked a given expanse of the canal every day, maintenance men who kept the embankments tight, stopped the leaks, killed muskrats, and toiled long hours after storms to keep the canals open. There were captains who carried their families with them, and lock keepers who were proud of their tasks and worked sometimes eighteen hours a day. As one authority has described it, "In spite of the hard work, the long hours and the exposure, there was a fascination, a sort of freedom, a tinge of vagabondry, about the life which not only bound a man to it for all his days, but drew his sons and daughters after it as well."[2]

One common misconception is that a canal was always full of dingy, smelly, unpainted old hulks. Because photography was beginning just as the canal age was on the decline, and color photography was still just a tinkerer's dream, most photographs show old and dilapidated canal boats. In the heyday of canaling, however, those waterways were speckled with gaily decorated, fresh-painted vessels, each with a name. The horses and mules wore bangles and bells; and the passenger packets bore all the colors of the rainbow. Their captains could have them painted any color or combination of colors they desired, and it seems from descriptions by travelers that they exercised this freedom to the point of license. A black hull, red deck, white cabin, and green shutters along the narrow little windows was a fairly common combination, and blues, yellows, reds, and colors in between were not unusual.

Crowded conditions were the norm; while forty passengers constituted a good load, up to 150 men, women, and children might be crammed aboard. At night people slept in berths precariously attached to the walls, or on the floor. Ventilation was nonexistent, the mosquitoes exasperating, the bedbugs, lice, roaches, and fleas better if not thought about; the cries of children in the women's cabin and the ceaseless activity of the crew outside combined to rob all but the most exhausted of sleep. Days were spent walking along the towpaths, playing cards, lounging or conversing. It was slow but steady traveling.

In spite of all we have said about flatboats and keelboats carrying produce to New Orleans, the trans-Mississippi country was stagnating until the canals created a new market for its surplus, bringing the new country men cash and purchasing power, and as a result providing the East with a market for manufactured goods. Everyone profited.

It was the canals that widened the economic opportunities in the new country, raised land prices, and brought in a massive emigration which in turn created more wealth. The ready availability of money further stimulated the economy. Ohio, Indiana, Illinois, and Michigan grew from a combined population of 792,000 in 1820 to over 4,200,000 by 1850, concentrated in the areas that benefited most from the Erie Canal. Trade via the Great Lakes increased enormously; the Erie shipped $10 million in merchandise into the new country in 1836, $94 million in 1853. Conversely, the new method of transportation wrecked the old triangular trade pattern of moving goods down the Ohio and Mississippi, around to the eastern seaboard, and across the mountains to Ohio, for the upper half of the Old Northwest now used canals and lakes rather than the great rivers.

The wait at the docks for the coming of the canal packet, the sound of the horn, the sight of the driver trotting the horses along the towpath, and then the dexterous manipulation as the captain guided the vessel to a perfect docking, were a thrill for the midwestern boy. But for all its feverish activity the canal age was relatively short, and before it had crested the competition that would destroy all but the most successful canals had entered the fray: the steamboat and the railroad.

In spite of all the activity on the new country waterways, progress was held up by the agonizing slowness of the vessels going upstream. What was needed for river traffic was something that could go upstream fairly rapidly and under its own power, yet still be light enough to navigate the rivers when the water was low. John Fitch is said to have built a steamboat for the Ohio River at Bardstown, Kentucky, in 1798, but he died the next year. At least two other steamboats were tried on the New Orleans-Natchez run prior to 1810, but neither was a success. Meanwhile a New York firm whose officers included Robert Fulton, Robert R. Livingston, DeWitt Clinton, Daniel T. Tomkins, and an engineer named Nicholas J. Roosevelt was pushing ahead with a plan for western steamboating. They contemplated establishing a monopoly on steamboat transportation on the western waters; and though they did not succeed in this, they did get a steamboat on the Ohio and Mississippi and proved its feasibility.

Roosevelt supervised the construction of the *New Orleans* on the Allegheny side of Pittsburgh, laying the keel in the spring of 1810. Launched in March of 1811, it was 138 feet long, had a 26-foot beam, and cost about $40,000. Its capacity was 371 tons, but no one knows whether it was a side-wheeler or a stern-wheeler.

Roosevelt took it up the Monongahela to prove that it could move against the current. Low water prevented him from heading down the Ohio until October, at which time he steamed downstream from Pittsburgh. He arrived at Louisville at midnight under a huge harvest moon, blew the whistle and aroused the populace, most of whom came out to see the new water creature that could go upstream under its own power. He left his lovely wife there—she was the sister of J. H. Latrobe, of Baltimore and Ohio Railroad fame—and steamed back up to Cincinnati.

When he returned, the water had risen and he, his crew, his wife, their baby born at Louisville, and a Newfoundland dog named Tiger, all aboard the new-fangled boat, ran the chutes of the Ohio. It is said that even Tiger was frightened by the risk, and lay quietly by the feet of his mistress. They made the run safely, however, and looked forward to a relatively peaceful journey down to New Orleans. But 1811 was a portentous year in the American West. Tecumseh was beating the war drums; in that year he traveled south to enlist the aid of the southern tribes in the fight against the white man. Early in November, while he was gone, came the Battle of Tippecanoe. The night skies had been brightened by the lustrous tail of the Great Comet of 1811. People reported that gray squirrels had migrated en masse southward through the forests, and incredibly large flocks of passenger pigeons had darkened the skies. Economic conditions had been worsening since 1808. In a religious, superstitious era, people saw portents of disaster.

Suddenly the crew and passengers of the *New Orleans* witnessed terrifying, astounding things: water jumped up in waves, bluffs crumbled before their eyes, river banks fell in, the channel virtually disappeared. These were all results of the first tremors of the New Madrid earthquake, the most severe ever noted in a non-volcanic area. For two weeks the tremors continued. On the land the earth pulsated like the waves of the sea; trees whipped back and forth, snapped and fell; even the leaves on the ground swirled around. Great cracks appeared in the earth's surface from which sand, muddy water, gases, and shale spouted forth. Whole islands were swallowed by the river, and at one time the Mississippi itself backed up. Reelfoot Lake in western Tennessee remains to this day a reminder of the terrible earthquake that created it. The Roosevelts had no sensible choice but to keep going, however, and to hope that the *New Orleans* would not be the first steamboat to be a victim of an inland earthquake. Down the Mississippi they steamed, past wrecked villages and forests with fallen trees, with the river waters muddy and roily; and in mid-January they reached New Orleans safely. After that the *New Orleans* made regular runs up to Natchez until she sank after striking a stump in 1814. Yet her example was all that was needed; by 1817 fourteen and by 1819 thirty-one steamboats were said to be operating between New Orleans and Louisville.

Almost immediately changes began to be made in their construction. Nowhere in the history of the new country is there so excellent an example of the pragmatic Americans improving upon things as the story of steamboat development, unless it is that of railroading. Gradually— if a twenty-year period can be considered gradual—the river boat as we now think of it appeared. The boat got larger and the hull became nearly flat. Although the hull was made of oak and other hardwoods, the rest of the structure was usually constructed of softwoods, even of pine.

Freight, machinery, and passengers occupied, of course, the between-decks areas: lower between-decks (main deck and boiler deck) was for machinery, cargo, and deck passengers; upper between-decks (boiler deck and hurricane deck) was for cabin passengers; on the hurricane deck was the pilot house and, from the 1840's on, the texas, which was a box-like extension aft of the pilot house, serving at first as living quarters for officers; later passengers were occasionally housed there.

The cabin passengers would also have a saloon which, in some of the later boats, bordered on the magnificent, with plush Brussels carpets, expensive furniture, carved and gilt ceilings, and stained glass. Crude but affluent passengers were warned not to whittle on the wood, to please remove boots before retiring, and to use the spittoons. Even at its best, the steamboat saloon had something of the tawdry about it.

Ahead of the pilot house, rising from the deck, was the jackstaff, whose principal purpose was not as a flagstaff, but as an aid to the pilot in steering. Meanwhile the two chimneys were pushed aft and up through the superstructure rather than forward of it. Because weight was an important element in the usefulness of the boat—determining how much freight it could carry, for example—measures were taken to lighten it whenever possible. The superstructure was made of thin wooden planks, hammered together with thin nails. In the 1840's, after the essential design of a good steamboat had been perfected, gingerbread ornamentation began to appear. One writer described such a vessel as looking like "a bride of Babylon."[3] Indeed it was carnivalish and flimsy; the average life of such boats was not more than five years.

High-pressure engines were developed which generated great power relative to the size and weight of the vessels they pushed. In time the side-wheels reached forty feet in diameter and eighteen feet in width. (Side-wheelers predominated on all but the smaller boats.) The structure vibrated in even the smoothest-running vessels as the pistons turned the

The *Rosebud*, one of the last Missouri River steamboats to ply the waters above Bismarck, North Dakota. Photo taken circa 1878. (U.S. Signal Corps, The National Archives)

great paddle wheels, while the exhausts could be heard for miles down the river. A smooth-running vessel churned up a wake in the river like a shovel in soft dirt.

Many activities along the river banks were geared to serving and improving steamboating. Woodyards appeared like magic along the river banks. The wood was stacked eight feet high, four feet wide, and in long "ranks" eighty-four feet long. A rank was twenty cords; the price hovered around $2.50 a cord. The Mississippi was the great place of employment for free Negroes, as roustabouts, woodchoppers, and stevedores.

A keelboat could make no more than twenty miles a day upstream, but as early as 1825 a hundred miles a day was not considered unusual for a steamboat. By that year a journey up to Louisville took no more than ten or eleven days. A generation later (in 1853) the *A. L. Shotwell* and the *Eclipse* made the journey in four days, nine hours, and thirty minutes, an average of almost fourteen miles an hour. Freight rates fell drastically, of course—from $5 per hundred pounds, New Orleans to Louisville, to as little as 25 cents per hundred pounds.

From 1820 to 1850 the number of steamboats increased more than tenfold, in tonnage more than twelvefold. The business was immensely profitable. Possibly such stories were exaggerations, but when it was said that the *New Orleans* had cleared $20,000 in her first year over and above expenses, and that she cost but $40,000 to build, investors looked no further. For capitalists who thought in big terms financially, the move to the trans-Appalachian West had been held back until some solution was found to the transportation problem. The sight of keel-boats toiling upstream at twenty miles a day or less had discouraged eastern investors. Now that the steamboat had arrived, the problem was solved, and such people advanced with their money into the new country.

Deck passage, in which the poor had to share space with the crew, the machinery, and the freight, was taken by emigrants from abroad who swarmed into the new country with the coming of the steamboat. A Louisville editor in 1849 commented that boats had passed by with as many as 500 people packed on them. The stench was terrible, the food bad, and the people, already fatigued from the long voyage across the Atlantic, were sickly. Cholera swept some of the boats, but still the emigrants came. "It was," writes Louis C. Hunter in his monumental study of western steamboating, "as though they were given the freedom of a drafty, dirty, and more or less crowded warehouse, a hot and noisy factory, and, when livestock was part of the cargo, of an ill-smelling barnyard as well."[4]

The rapid growth of the entire Mississippi Valley is attributable in great part to the coming of the stern-wheelers and side-wheelers. The population of trans-Appalachia, just over a million in 1810, rose to more than six million in 1840 and to more than fifteen million, about half the national population, in 1860. The rise in shipping is another indication of rapid settlement. At New Orleans the receipts of western goods amounted to less than $4 million in 1801 but in 1849-50 were $97 million. As early as 1843, New Orleans had twice the tonnage of the port of New York.

As the years went by, the western steamboat made its way along almost every stream of any consequence in the vast Mississippi Valley. As early as 1831 the *Yellowstone*, owned by the American Fur Company, advanced up the Missouri above Council Bluffs, and eventually steamboats worked upstream 2,200 miles to Fort Benton. When gold was discovered in Montana and the Sioux made the overland journey hazardous, Missouri river boating experienced a brief boom. In the heaviest year, 1867, seventy-one vessels left St. Louis for the upper Missouri country. Thereafter, as the Indian danger subsided and with the coming of the Northern Pacific, the upper Missouri business fell off drastically.

The practicality of the steamboat was such that hardly had Oregon and California been opened to settlement when orders were placed for steamboats, some of which came in pieces in the holds of ships, to be reconstructed at the mouths of the western-running rivers out there. Incredible as it seems, some steamboats actually made the journey around Cape Horn on their way to being used as river boats in the West. By the end of the year 1850 there were at least sixteen steamboats active on California rivers, and at about the same time the Columbia, Willamette, and Yamhill rivers in Oregon were hosts to these practical vessels.

In many ways the river steamboat is representative of the spirit of young America—an America advancing into the new country, hastily, often thoughtlessly, establishing crude civilization where howling wilderness had existed just the day before. The American was in a hurry, and the steamboat was the fastest connection between any two points joined by a river. The vessels were risky; accidents and explosions were common. Yet few Americans were deterred. The boats were crowded, with cabin passengers often sleeping on carpets or doubling up, and the poor deck passengers suffering needless hardships. They were dirty; they had no modern refrigeration for food; they had the odors of live stock, of unwashed humanity, and of unsanitary facilities. Even the best boats did not have inside plumbing, including water closets, until the 1850's. Not only a common brush and comb for all the passengers, but even a common toothbrush, were occasionally furnished; sometimes sixty or seventy men, even though they were cabin passengers, had to use the same two wash basins and two towels. The "western itch" was not just a phrase describing a state of mind.

It was on July 4, 1828, the same day that John Quincy Adams turned the first shovel for the extended Chesapeake and Ohio Canal, that the city fathers of Baltimore launched the construction of the Baltimore and Ohio Railroad. This was not the first railroad in the United States, but it was certainly the most ambitious to date. The goal was for the B & O to surmount the Appalachians and reach the Ohio Valley. In 1830 the first few miles were opened to traffic out of Baltimore; twelve years later the line reached Cumberland, and in 1852 it reached Wheeling. Four years after that it reached St. Louis. This progress, especially in the early years, was actually very slow, but it was because of litigation with the Chesapeake and Ohio Canal Company and difficulties over financing, rather than problems of construction.

In 1831 when the York was built, steam locomotives were a novelty. Crude as it was, it won a locomotive contest. (Chessie System)

Indeed, the improvements in locomotives, cars, rails, techniques in construction of roadbeds, tunnels, and bridges, were in every way as rapid as was the concurrent development of the steamboat; probably more so. When the first stone of the Baltimore and Ohio was laid in 1828, railroading was in its infancy even in England, where it had begun. The B & O at first used horses to draw the cars, which looked like stagecoach bodies mounted on little wheels. A treadmill run by a horse and a sail using the wind were both tried for motive power, though it was the steam engine that held the great promise for the future. B & O officials sent men to England to study George Stephenson's locomotives, but their conclusion was that the English type, used on expensively laid roadbeds over flat terrain, would never function satisfactorily in the new country. The B & O must accept sharp curves and steep hills and restricted financing as facts of life.

And so the line became a virtual railroad laboratory, a growing experiment station for railroading. Since it was the leader in the field its directors allowed diagrams of equipment and road construction techniques, complete with accompanying explanations and tables, to appear in their annual reports. Progress is easily traced in them. By 1834, when the railroad was just six years into construction, its rolling stock was beginning to have a modern look. First of all, the standard gauge of 4 feet 8½ inches, used in England, was accepted. Improvements in the rolling stock were introduced by such employees as Ross Winans, who had originally come down from New Jersey to sell some horses to the company. He invented the "friction wheel" with the long flange on the inside, similar to modern railroad wheels. He balanced the weight of the locomotive so that it was equal for each wheel, developed new connecting rods, and made other innovations that improved the power and reliability of the locomotives. Even more modern looking were the passenger, freight, and new baggage cars developed by the B & O. The rolling stock was mounted on two four-wheel trucks, the same as today. Seats in the coaches were in a double row with an aisle, though the company had to overcome complaints that the aisle would become simply an elongated spittoon by providing plenty of cuspidors. And the cars were brightly painted, each with a name. Freight cars (called at first "burthen" cars) likewise had a modern look; and the baggage car was first introduced in 1834, an obvious necessity bringing on the invention.

Similarly the railroad experimented with tracks, bridges, culverts, trestles, switches, and the numerous other accouterments of railroading. The B & O was right behind the Erie Railroad in using the telegraph. In 1851 the first electric locomotive was run on the B & O tracks. At first ties were known as sleepers, and the rails were placed upon long pieces of wood called stringers; in fact so much was constructed of wood that the first workmen on the road were carpenters. One of the first, a man named Wendell Bollman, became the company's expert bridge-builder; and another employee, John Elgar, invented useful switches and turntables.

Construction of the line started and stopped as often as a slow freight, usually due to financial problems. Irish and German emigrants working for small contractors gradually acquired much construction know-how; some of them followed the railroads westward for years afterward. At one time, in 1851, the B & O had 5,000 men and 1,250 horses hacking out the main line; the payroll was $200,000 a month. When the track was finally open to Wheeling the railroad had learned how to cut tunnels, build bridges and trestles, hack roadways from hillsides, and deal with contractors and men. There had been riots, usually due to lack of pay or to hard-driving contractors, with the workmen bolstered by too much whiskey (which was available at three cents a glass).

Considering the times, the idea of railroads caught on with startling rapidity. In spite of the millions that had been borrowed for canals, the

The Kansas Pacific was proud of its freight engine number 22. Note the design between the two large wheels. (DeGolyer Library, Dallas)

public embraced the iron horse and left the canals behind. Improvements hastened public enthusiasm, which hastened construction. By 1856 the state of Ohio was interlaced by 2,593 miles of railroad completed and 2,094 miles under construction. Two years earlier, in 1854, Indiana next door had 1,278 miles operational, 1,592 under construction and 732 miles "contemplated." By 1860 Illinois had 2,867 miles of railroad, and Chicago was already the terminus for eleven lines. By 1865 there were, in round numbers, nearly 32,000 miles of railroad east of the Mississippi. Missouri, Iowa, and Texas had the lion's share of the 3,272 miles that were west of the Mississippi. The end of the Civil War opened the way for a burst of railroad construction in the trans-Mississippi West, for the problems of roadbeds and locomotives had in great measure been solved, the public had developed complete faith in the railroads, and financing was to be had both from political entities (cities, states, and the federal government) and from private sources.

In the story of this rapid expansion the Illinois Central plays a prominent role. Until its construction in the years following the granting of its charter in 1850, the fertile lands of central Illinois were sparsely set-

103

THE FINEST FARMING LANDS

CORN   COTTON   FRUITS & VEGETABLES

EQUAL TO ANY IN THE WORLD!!!

MAY BE PROCURED

AT FROM $6 TO $12 PER ACRE,

Near Markets, Schools, Railroads, Churches, and all the blessings of Civilization.

1,200,000 Acres in Farms of 40, 80, 120, 160 Acres and upwards, in ILLINOIS, the Garden State of America.

The Illinois Central Railroad Company offer, on LONG CREDIT, the beautiful and fertile PRAIRIE LANDS lying along the whole line of their Railroad, 700 MILES IN LENGTH, upon the most Favorable Terms for enabling Farmers, Manufacturers, Mechanics, and Workingmen, to make for themselves and their families a competency, and a home they can call Their Own.

ILLINOIS

Is about equal in extent to England, with a population of 1,722,666, and a soil capable of supporting 20,000,000. No State in the valley of the Mississippi offers so great an inducement to the settler as the State of Illinois. There is no part of the world where all the conditions of climate and soil so admirably combine to produce those two great staples, CORN and WHEAT.

CLIMATE.

Nowhere can the industrious farmer secure such immediate results from his labor as on these deep, rich, loamy soils, cultivated with so much ease. The climate from the extreme southern part of the State to the Terre Haute, Alton and St. Louis Railroad, a distance of nearly 200 miles, is well adapted to Winter

WHEAT. CORN, COTTON, TOBACCO,

Peaches, Pears, Tomatoes, and every variety of fruit and vegetables are grown in great abundance, from which Chicago and other Northern markets are furnished from four to six weeks earlier than their immediate vicinity.

THE ORDINARY YIELD

of Corn is from 50 to 80 bushels per acre. Cattle, Horses, Mules, Sheep and Hogs are raised here at a small cost, and yield large profits. It is believed that no section of country presents greater inducements for Dairy Farming than the Prairies of Illinois, a branch of farming to which but little attention has been paid, and which must yield sure profitable results.

AGRICULTURAL PRODUCTS.

The Agricultural products of Illinois are greater than those of any other State. The Wheat crop of 1861 was estimated at 35,000,000 bushels, while the Corn crop yields not less than 140,000,000 bushels, besides the crop of Oats, Barley, Rye, Buckwheat, Potatoes, Sweet Potatoes, Pump-

kins, Squashes, Flax, Hemp, Peas, Clover, Cabbage, Beets, Tobacco, Sorghum, Grapes, Peaches, Apples, &c., which go to swell the vast aggregate of production in this fertile region. Over Four Million tons of produce were sent out of Illinois during the past year.

CULTIVATION OF COTTON.

The experiments in Cotton culture are of very great promise. Commencing in latitude 39 deg. 30 min. (see Mattoon on the Branch, and Assumption on the Main Line), the Company owns thousands of acres well adapted to the perfection of this fibre. A settler having a family of young children can turn their youthful labor to a most profitable account in the growth and perfection of this plant.

THE ILLINOIS CENTRAL RAILROAD

Traverses the whole length of the State, from the banks of the Mississippi and Lake Michigan to the Ohio. As its name imports, the Railroad runs through the centre of the State, and on either side of the road along its whole length lie the lands offered for sale.

CITIES, TOWNS, MARKETS, DEPOTS.

There are ninety-eight Depots on the Company's Railway, giving about one every seven miles. Cities, Towns, and Villages are situated at convenient distances throughout the whole route, where every desirable commodity may be found as readily as in the oldest cities of the Union, and where buyers are to be met for all kinds of farm produce.

EDUCATION.

Mechanics and working men will find the free school system encouraged by the State, and endowed with a large revenue for the support of the schools. Children can live in sight of the school, the college, the church, and grow up with the prosperity of the leading State of the Great Western Empire.

For Prices and Terms of Payment,

ADDRESS LAND COMMISSIONER, Ill. Central R. R. Co., Chicago, Ill.

—— From the 1867 issue of the Tribune Almanac.

tled and cultivated in a most desultory manner. There was no practical way of getting the agricultural products, which were of small value in proportion to bulk, to market. A major public enterprise was therefore suggested; after years of congressional debate, and under the guiding hand of Illinois' Senator Stephen A. Douglas, the Illinois Central Bill was finally passed.

The IC was a land-grant railroad, and as such the first to attempt to stimulate emigration along its lines. Its experience with promoters in Scandinavia and England, with representatives in New York City, and among German, French Canadian, Norwegian and Swedish emigrants already settled elsewhere, and its efforts to entice and persuade using placards and illustrated informative booklets were later emulated by the great transcontinental railroads. The road also experimented with many different plans aimed at the profitable sale of lands.

Under certain circumstances it was possible for a poor farmer (from New England, for example, where soil exhaustion was widespread) to purchase his acreage—forty acres was a common amount—pay only the interest for the first two years, and make the total payment within seven years at a reasonable interest rate of 6 per cent. Moreover, the railroad would give the prospective purchaser free passage to the farm site when he chose his land, and then free transportation for his family. In addition, no state taxes had to be paid until the title was clear, that is, after full payment. For a time the IC would even accept the products of the farmer's land in payment, giving highest prices for them, and allowing him a one-third discount on freight charges.

In 1850, just prior to the coming of the Illinois Central, central, eastern and southern Illinois was new country, prairie and woodland. The railroad not only brought about settlement but also determined centers of population by its choice of station sites and its policies toward townsite speculators. Illinois more than doubled in population in the decade of the 1850's and increased by more than 600,000 people in the 1860's. And the IC increased the prosperity of Illinois as well as its population.

There was no doubt in men's minds that it was possible to construct a railroad across the continent to California or Oregon. Only politics and the war stood in the way of the "great transcontinental." Even the routes had been surveyed, in a general way, in the years 1853-55. By the war's end, the charters had been issued to the Union Pacific, the Cen-

Perhaps the most amazing fact about this Illinois Central advertisement is that it was truthful—the land was incredibly fertile, cheap, and easy to buy. (Courtesy Illinois Central Gulf Railroad)

tral Pacific, and the Northern Pacific. The UP and the CP were each
granted a four-hundred-foot right-of-way, ten alternate sections per mile
on both sides of the line, and a governmental subsidy that could be, and
often was, the established limit of $48,000 for each mile constructed in
mountainous terrain. The subsidy was at first in the form of a first mortgage loan, with payment upon completion of established sections of the
road. This was changed in 1864 to a second mortgage, in this sense: it
allowed "the railroads to sell first-mortgage bonds to private subscribers,
relegated the government to the position of the holder of a second mortgage, thereby making the rights of the private subscribers paramount in
any bankruptcy, forfeiture of contract, or other legal proceedings against
the property of the roads."[5] All told, some forty-five million acres and
sixty million dollars went to these two railroads.

Once these roads were under way, it was clear that the difference between their mode of construction and that of previously built roads east
of the hundredth meridian was minimal. Because the western builders
received government money for every mile built, they did abandon the
use of small contractors in favor of large ones employing about a thousand men and building the tracks at a rapid pace. They even created
companies, such as the Crédit Mobilier. And—again because every mile
counted—they did push construction hard when funds were available.
The principal contractors on the Union Pacific were General Jack Case-
ment and his brother Dan. It was not unusual for their crews to work
through moonlit nights and on Sundays. With 1,000 men and 500 teams
the UP proposed to build three miles a day out of Cheyenne, and eventually was laying twice that much track. Meanwhile the companies
platted towns and fixed division points; though, planned or not, a wood
pile or a water tank was fairly sure to appear every twelve or fifteen
miles along the lines. The UP tie cutters denuded the Platte Valley of
what little timber it possessed, even though the soft cottonwood rotted
away and had to be replaced in a short time.

As for the Central Pacific, it was better planned, better surveyed, and
better built than its sister road coming from the east. Leland Stanford,
Charles Crocker, Collis P. Huntington, and Mark Hopkins—the "Big
Four" (though Theodore P. Judah deserves mention also)—were men
of substantial business acumen, of which their railroad bore the marks.
They were also men of courage, for the challenge of a railroad through
the Sierras, where snowdrifts of forty feet are common, was enough to
deter lesser men.

They too hired the Irish and the Germans and anyone else who could
handle a pick or a shovel, including Celestials, whom they found to be
tractable and hard-working; 12,000 Chinese were on the CP payrolls by

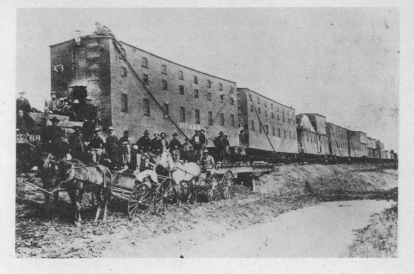

Two- and three-story bunk cars used by Great Northern Railway in late 1880's and early 1890's. These extremely high cars were provided with cables to prevent their capsizing when parked at windy locations; platforms underneath were for the more unwieldy belongings of the construction workers who lived in them. Jim Hill's line was once known as the St. Paul, Minneapolis, and Manitoba (note letters St. P. M. & M.). (DeGolyer Library/G. N. Riddy)

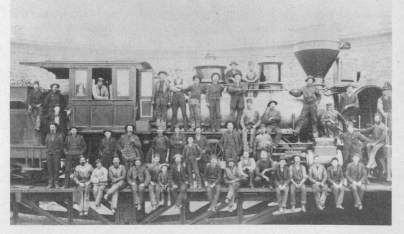

Union Pacific roundhouse employees at Green River, Wyoming, pose on a Consolidation type 221 locomotive. (DeGolyer Library, Dallas)

1869. They gathered into small groups, each with a cook, bathed in powder-keg tubs filled with near-boiling water, drank warm tea from forty-gallon barrels and drew their pay from a Caucasian whom they paid to handle their accounts.

The CP dug tunnels with nitroglycerine as well as picks and shovels; the road was cut through walls of solid rock, and it crossed chasms on trestles that at least looked precarious. The company built 37 miles of snowsheds, using 64 million feet of timber and 900 tons of bolts and spikes. On the Nevada and Utah deserts wells were dug for water which, when found, was piped to railside. When, on June 18, 1868, the gleaming engine "Antelope" pulled the first train out of Sacramento to surmount the Sierras and reach Reno, it was indeed a day of triumph. The foothills towns sped by—Newcastle, Auburn, Clipper Gap, New England Mills, Colfax, Cape Horn, Secret Town, Alta, Shady Run—until the summit tunnel was reached, 104 miles out of Sacramento. Then downward the rails led to Reno.

Ten months later the CP and the UP met at windswept Promontory Point, Utah—May 10, 1869. In getting there, partly as a stunt and partly for reasons of profit, the CP on the 28th of April, following intricate preparations, laid ten miles and fifty-six feet of rail—the most ever laid in a day. It was during these hectic days that an observer, noting the quantities of whiskey, bearing such brand names as Red Cloud, Red Jacket, and Blue Run, which was consumed, commented: "Verily, men earn their money like horses and spend it like asses."[6]

When, at eleven A.M. or a little after, the Central Pacific's No. 60 (dubbed Jupiter) and the Union Pacific's No. 119 closed the gap, and the telegraph flashed the news to the nation, a new era began in American history. The activity was feverish; so lucrative did the profits promise to be that other capitalists jumped in and launched their own plans for transcontinental railroads. Just how many little lines and hopeful promotions bore the two words ". . . and Pacific" is not known, but their number is legion compared with those that did make it to the West Coast. By 1893 there were five lines across the western mountains and deserts: the Union Pacific–Central Pacific; the Northern Pacific; the Atchison, Topeka, and Santa Fe; the Southern Pacific; and Jim Hill's Great Northern.

The optimism that brought on this proliferation of railroads had not always existed. It was at first thought that no railroad could pay its way across the plains, deserts, and mountains of the West. It was partly this belief that led the managements of both the Central Pacific and Union Pacific to create their own construction companies, which siphoned off enormous profits—the only profit, they felt, to be made out of transcontinental railroading. The best known of these corporations was the

Pennsylvania-chartered Crédit Mobilier of America, wholly controlled by Union Pacific entrepreneurs, which became the subject of a Congressional investigation.

The rapid emigration into the new country after the Civil War quickly reversed these dire predictions into equally incorrect expectations of enormous profits. The climatic cycle was passing through a wet phase at the time; farm settlement extended onto the high plains and thus provided freight and passenger revenue for the roads. Moreover, the range cattle business, hardly contemplated a decade earlier, was just emerging from trial and error into an enormous industry, covering great expanses of land where buffalo and red men had roamed at will. Even the destruction of the buffalo brought money into railroad coffers, through the hauling of hides and bones. Mining of coal and precious metals gave evidence of becoming widespread over the West, instead of being concentrated in just two or three areas as in the 1850's. Permanent towns and cities sprang into existence where Spanish bayonet and buffalo grass, horned toads, rattlesnakes, prairie dogs, and burrowing owls had existed unmolested for centuries. Tuberculosis victims began coming west to profit from the therapeutic powers of the dry air. Until the 1920's sanitariums for "lungers" dotted the West, and cured victims of the white man's plague stayed on to become productive citizens and, occasionally, leaders in the developing new country.

When it was realized that settlement could take place all over the West, the railroaders became the greatest of boosters. Farming, tourism, processing of agricultural products, and even manufacturing were encouraged. First, however, the people had to be settled; upon the success of that endeavor hinged everything else. And so the western roads undertook vigorous colonization efforts, competing with each other in attracting settlers to their shares of the western terrain. Not only did they sell their own lands; they helped to sell federal lands, state-owned school lands, and the lands owned for speculative purposes by great land companies. Emigration along a railroad's right-of-way was the key to that road's profit. Management knew this and worked to achieve it.

Each company set up its real estate business in its own way, but all of them were likely to centralize their efforts in a Land Department, a Bureau of Immigration, or, like the Northern Pacific, with both. Survey records, plats, and the legal paraphernalia for registration and issuance of abstracts of title, as well as records of payment, were handled by the Land Department. Moreover, credit—liberal credit for those times—was extended. The Union Pacific in 1870 asked 25 per cent down and the remainder in three annual payments; the Northern Pacific asked 10 per cent down, 10 per cent at the end of each of the first three years, then

15 per cent for the final four years, plus 7 per cent interest collected annually. On occasion first mortgage land grant bonds of the company were accepted, though at a premium of 5 or 10 per cent. In hard times the fortunate speculators with money could drive extremely favorable bargains. The Central Pacific followed very similar policies, but in addition often taught the emigrant how and what to farm, sank wells, and maintained several agricultural experiment farms.

Prices, no matter how low, were of little significance unless there were buyers. To entice emigrants to their lands, the railroads, some of the big land companies, and some states maintained emigration bureaus and employed hundreds of operatives to "sell" their real estate in other lands as well as to native American purchasers. European operations usually functioned out of a London office. The agents were often clergymen who had seen the new country, believed in it, and returned to their native Germany, Sweden, Denmark, Norway, Finland, Ireland, or England to advertise the company's lands. Their greatest appeal was to the peasantry and to lower-middle-class landowners.

The company representative not only met with prospects at parish meetings, country fairs, and the like but also made the frightening trip less of a horror by arranging for boat passage, assuring the emigrants that a representative would meet them at Castle Garden in New York City, and generally allaying their fears and helping them on their way. Agents of large steamboat companies were persuaded to cooperate with railroad agents. Cunard distributed thousands of pamphlets for the Northern Pacific and allowed NP agents in Europe to sell tickets via the steamship line and the railroads that led inland to where the emigrants entrained on the Northern Pacific. It is also clear that a little loose money wisely distributed to agents of the steamship lines resulted in all manner of favors being done for the railroad representative. He needed to do this, for the competition with his counterparts working for other companies was stiff. That agent was at Castle Garden not out of kindness but to prevent his prospect from meeting a persuasive agent of another line and heading for Burlington or Kansas Pacific land, for example, instead of into Northern Pacific country.

Some idea of the railroads' operations may be gleaned from Northern Pacific statistics of 1883. The company had 831 agents working in the British Isles alone. Some 632,590 copies of its publications were distributed, many of them translated into Swedish, Dutch, German, Danish, and Norwegian. In the summer of that year Rufus Hatch, a Wall Street tycoon and a heavy investor in the NP, brought more than fifty wealthy Europeans to New York and at the cost of $40,000 carried them in a special train to Yellowstone Park and back, hoping to entice them into making heavy investments in the northwest.

(Right) Title page of Northern Pacific emigration book, 1873. (Minnesota Historical Society)

(Left) Cover of a Northern Pacific recruitment booklet aimed at enticing German settlers to the new northwest. (DeGolyer Library, Dallas)

That the companies exaggerated in their flyers and broadsides is well known. They said very little about the difficulty of breaking the tough prairie sod, the absence of timber, the cold winters, or the epidemics. A critic writing in the *Chicago Tribune* described a page of an Illinois Central brochure as leading one to believe that "the real scene of Adam and Eve's interview with the apple lay . . . down about Kankakee" (a city south of Chicago).[7] A Northern Pacific advertisement said the most common ailment among Montana residents was the pangs of overeating, "resulting from the excessive indulgence of the hearty appetite attendant upon the invigorating atmosphere."[8]

Most companies also sold "exploration tickets" which carried the prospects along the railroad to search out possible farm sites. Different lines offered various deals. In general they required full fare but then deducted it from the purchase price of the land if the prospect signed on the dotted line within a given time, such as sixty days of the ticket purchase. Moreover, he could then carry his family to the nearest siding free of charge. For parties there were usually reduced rates. So extensive was the land and emigration business that a number of companies erected reception houses where the emigrants could live until their choices of land had been made.

The treatment afforded emigrants riding West differed from line to line. Most of the companies appear to have carried out their land settlement and emigration activities with at least a modicum of humanity. They felt the need for rapid settlement along their lines if they were to prosper, and because of this they really did endeavor to help the settlers decently. Yet mankind seems unable not to create class differentiations; rare was the railway conductor, ticket agent, or freight forwarder who did not offer one quality of service, courtesy, and attention to the Pullman passengers, another to coach passengers, and still a third to emigrants. The freeloading hoboes got the bum's rush, of course—if caught. The Union Pacific–Central Pacific, for example, ran emigrant cars all the way to Sacramento and, when the line reached San Francisco, to the Golden Gate. The emigrants were packed ninety to a car into the cheapest kind of conveyance, and they had to pay for it, albeit a small amount compared to the coach and Pullman passengers.

Most of these emigrants were not particularly verbal. There is a dearth of descriptive material about their experiences, though one suspects that many a bundle of old letters stashed away in a trunk somewhere narrates just such adventures. Because the Indians were no longer a menace, and because these people were absorbed in a desperate gamble, betting that they would succeed against great odds in establishing the good but simple lives of common people in the new country, historians have overlooked them.

Fortunately the Scots writer Robert Louis Stevenson has left us a poignant description of a trip across the plains and mountains and deserts to California. With a small valise, a knapsack on his back, and "the bag of a railway rug" in which he had stuffed six volumes of George Bancroft's *History of the United States*, this long-haired, stoop-shouldered, sensitive man crossed the continent in eleven days ending on the first of September, 1879. Stevenson, twenty-eight at the time, was something of a noncomformist who refused to pursue an honorable profession as befitted the only son of one of Scotland's great engineers; he was determined to succeed as a writer. He was also a traveler, a bon vivant though usually lacking necessary funds, a romantic in love with a married woman ten or fifteen years his senior. It was in reply to a cablegram indicating that his beloved "Fanny" was seriously ill in California that Stevenson determined to come to the New World. With very little money in his wallet he headed West. On ship he selected the second of three classes of accommodations. Even so he lost fourteen pounds and got the itch and chronic constipation. Since he also had incipient tuberculosis, the rigors of poor food, bad ventilation, and little rest made of him an emaciated, hollow-cheeked, feverish traveler.

Some of his narrative reflects the moroseness and dejection triggered by his physical condition. And yet Stevenson retained for the most part a remarkable balance; indeed, his sickness may have counteracted his romanticism and resulted in a more realistic appraisal of a trip across America in emigrant railroad cars.[9]

Still in his misery he saw beauty in things American. It rained so much in New York, he wrote a friend, that "one sees it is a new country, they are so free with their water." By morning, when he took some air on a station platform in Pennsylvania while the train was stopped, his spirits had risen. But he found the American sunrise different, somehow, from the European: "less fresh and inspiriting . . . it has a duskier glory," he wrote, "and more nearly resembles sunset; it seems to fit some subsequential evening epoch of the world, as though America were in fact, and not merely in fancy, farther from the orient of Aurora and the springs of day." That particular day was one of the better ones. The sky was cloudless, and in the wooded river valleys "the atmosphere preserved the sparkling freshness till later in the afternoon . . . it smelt of woods, river, and the delved earth." Stevenson listened to the sounds of place names and savored them. "There is," he wrote, "no part of the world where nomenclature is so rich, poetical, humorous, and picturesque as the United States of America. . . . [it is a] songful, tuneful land. . . ."

And a busy one. Every transfer of stations and trains was rush-rush-rush, a wearing experience. At Chicago he said he had never been as dog-tired. And at Council Bluffs he found himself being "sorted and jostled" in front of the Union Pacific Emigrant House as a busy little white-haired official read from a list and directed people to one of three emigrant cars. The hindmost one was for families, the center one for bachelors such as Stevenson, and the third for Chinese. They would rank fourth, third, and second from the end; the last car would be, of course, the caboose. Ahead of these three carloads of humanity rolled freight car after freight car—for as any railroader knows, freight is more important than passengers. The bachelors, said Stevenson, "carried the second car [the one for single men] without ceremony by simultaneous assault."

The emigrant cars of the Union Pacific were typical of the American railroad passenger car—"that long, narrow wooden box, like a flat-roofed Noah's ark, with a stove and a convenience, one at either end, a passage down the middle, and transverse benches upon either hand." If the UP car differed, it was only in the extent of its plainness. It was made entirely of wood, the dim lamps often burned out, and unupholstered, torturous benches were barely long enough for two men to sit on at the same time. Those on the UP at least had backs (some did not), and they could be arranged to face each other in pairs.

"Where there is scarce elbow-room for two to sit, there will not be space enough for one to lie," wrote Stevenson.

Hence the company . . . have conceived a plan for better accommodation of travellers. They prevail on every two to chum together. To each of the chums they sell a board and three square cushions stuffed with straw and covered with thin cotton. The benches can be made to face each other in pairs, for the backs are reversible. On the approach of night the boards are laid from bench to bench, making a couch wide enough for two, and long enough for a man of the middle height; and the chums lie side by side upon the cushions with the head to the conductor's van [the caboose] and the heels to the engine.

Once aboard, the little white-haired man therefore paired off the passengers and sold to each, if he would buy, the necessary long board and three cushions. The price at first was $2.50, which Stevenson paid; he was mortified to see it reduced to $1.50 before the cars pulled out of Council Bluffs. At North Platte, Nebraska, the same sold for 15 cents a cushion and the board gratis. Even more humiliating was his rejection as a "chum" by an American farm type. For long moments the Scotsman feared he would be rejected by the whole carload; but then a young Pennsylvania Dutchman accepted him.

Finally, towards evening of a hot summer's day, and after an intolerably long delay, the freight-and-emigrant train clickety-clacked out of the yards at Council Bluffs, rattled across the wide Missouri, through Omaha, and chugged steadily westward. "It was a troubled, uncomfortable evening in the cars," Stevenson remembered. There was the humidity and the stillness and the black outdoors of the plains, fixing for a storm. There was thunder in the air, and the men sat restless, pensive; men desperate, running westward to the new country in hopes of security, a job, and a new life. "Hunger, you would have thought, came out of the east like the sun, and the evening was made of edible gold," Stevenson commented.

Then one of the men produced a cornet and was shortly playing "Home, Sweet Home." The talk ceased, the faces lengthened, and then a goateed, hard-countenanced man turned abruptly to the player, and ordered him to stop that "damned thing. I've heard about enough of that. . . ." he growled, "give us something about the good country we're going to." The cornetist understood and played some spirited dancing tune, and the sadness faded. The lamps were dimmed.

With the morning awakening the daily routine was established. Chums made purchases from the newsboy and pooled their resources. "Shakespeare" (R. L. S.) had bought a tin washing dish, "Dubuque" (who hailed from there) a towel, and "Pennsylvania" (the Dutchman) a brick of soap. First awake and about had first usage. Here was how it was done:

> Each filled the tin dish at the water filter opposite the stove, and retired with the whole stock in trade to the platform of the car. There he knelt down, supporting himself by a shoulder against the woodwork, or one elbow crooked against the railing, and made a shift to wash his face and neck and hands—a cold, an insufficient, and, if the train is moving rapidly, a somewhat dangerous toilet.

They had also purchased coffee, sugar, and a pot, and when their turn came they prepared theirs at the stove; milk, eggs, bread, and coffeecake were sold at the stops by the natives. "Soon from end to end the car would be filled with little parties breakfasting upon the bed-boards. It was the pleasantest hour of the day." Stevenson further explained that some meals were taken at luncheon stops, and once he received the same meal as eastbound first-class passengers but paid just half as much. This was unusual, and probably a mistake. Ordinarily the emigrants were shabbily treated. "Civility is the main comfort that you miss," he recalled. "Equality, though conceived very largely in America, does not extend so low down as to an Emigrant." For example, no one ever shouted "All aboard" for the emigrants, and a man had to keep a sharp eye or he might miss the train. "The annoyance is considerable," he complained, "and the disrespect both wanton and petty."

Nebraska: "It was a world almost without a feature" to the young traveler, "an empty sky, an empty earth; front and back, the line of railway stretched from horizon to horizon, like a cue across a billiard-board; on either hand, the green plain ran till it touched the skirts of heaven." Even its incessant sounds, the chirping of grasshoppers—"a noise like the winding up of countless clocks and watches" gave no relief from the sameness. He pitied the settler in such a land. "A sky full of stars is the most varied spectacle that he can ask for. . . . His eye must embrace at every glance the whole seeming concave of the visible world." And the houses in which the people lived, in such drabness, a dozen dwellings at a time parallelling the tracks, jutted up so awkwardly in so "naked and flat a country. . . . With none of the litter and discoloration of human life; with the paths unworn, and the houses still sweating from the axe, such a settlement as this," he wrote, "seems purely scenic."

Wyoming was worse, and so was Stevenson's health. He was giddy, light-headed, feverish, nearly disoriented; the evening they left Laramie he was miserably sick. The lamps faded but did not go out, and he observed the sleepers in their "uneasy attitudes: here two chums alongside, flat upon their backs like dead folk; there a man sprawling on the floor, with his face upon his arm; there another half-seated with his head and shoulders on the bench . . . others stirred, turned, or stretched out their arms like children. . . ." Stevenson opened a window, for he needed fresh air to keep himself alive, or so it seemed. It was in Wyoming that an epileptic on the car had three fits. Some wanted to throw him off at the next station. Fortunately the conductor refused.

In the long but steady course of time the train pulled into Ogden; it was like a new life, or nearly so, to transfer to the cars of the Central Pacific, for they were somewhat better. They had been recently varnished, had boards that pulled out from the seats so that no purchases had to be made, and had an upper tier of berths. Moreover, the Union Pacific cars had "begun to stink abominably . . . [like] a whiff of pure menagerie, only a little sourer, as from men instead of monkeys."

The next few days and nights, with the train creeping along under the searing Utah and Nevada sun, with nothing but sand and sagebrush outside to gaze upon, were a nightmare and a discomfort. The car had upper and lower bunks, and Stevenson's was an upper, "immediately under the roof, and shut into a kind of Saratoga trunk with one side partly open." He could only lie awake and cough; one night he walked back and forth through the car. And then, after he had fallen into a restless sleep one night, a fellow passenger disturbed his slumber. "A fire of enthusiasm and whisky burned in his eyes; and he declared we were in a new country, and I must come forth upon the platform and see with my own eyes."

They were entering the Sierras; by morning they were moving through snowsheds, and by afternoon they were in Sacramento. "Not I only," Stevenson remembered, "but all the passengers on board, threw off their sense of dirt and heat and weariness, and bawled like schoolboys, and thronged with shining eyes upon the platform, and became new creatures within and without. . . . For this was indeed our destination; this was 'the good country' we had been going to so long."

By their own feet, by pack and saddle horses, by wagons and stagecoaches, by flatboats and keelboats and batteaux, by steamboats and canal packets, and finally by railroads did the people pour into the new country. Still not satisfied with the time it took and the bother it de-

Part of the main street of Corinne, Utah, a "gentile" town about twenty miles southeast of Promontory Point, in 1869. (U.S. Geological Survey, The National Archives)

Scene of stagecoaches meeting a train, Cisco, California, 1866. (Wells Fargo Bank,
San Francisco)

manded of its customers, the people were ready to forsake even the railroad. The frontier officially closed in 1890; within little more than a decade the internal combustion engine offered the hope of practical, individual transportation anywhere in the continental boundaries of the nation; would even offer a swift journey through the air above. But that is another story.

VI

New Country Society

Men, Women,
and Families

No one has ever questioned, let alone analyzed, the masculinity of the frontier society. Since it is as obvious as the sun in the daytime, the subject has not been discussed. And yet there were qualities of this land of mostly men which permeated all other regions of America at the time, and traces of its influence remain to this day. Therefore one of the most valid ways to build an understanding of new country society is to begin with the conscious realization of its masculinity, which was far more apparent and real than in today's society for several very obvious reasons.

In the entire history of the new country, 1776-1890, the nation as a whole had a preponderance of males, ranging from 102.2 males for each 100 females (in the census of 1870) to 105.2 males per 100 females (in 1850); in 1890 the ratio was 105 to 100. (Due to heavy emigration, 1900 to 1910, it raced up to 106 to 100.) But this is not the full story. The new country areas of the nation themselves had an overwhelming preponderance of males. In 1880, for example, Colorado had 129,131 males to 65,196 females, Oregon had 103,381 males to 71,387 females, Montana Territory had 28,177 males to 10,792 females, and Wyoming Territory had 14,152 to 6,637.

In the initial stages of the westward advance the exploration of the new country was done exclusively by men. They could move faster when they grouped for security. True explorers rarely take women along with them. It is the unusualness of Sacajawea's accompanying Lewis and Clark that contributes so much to the mystery of her personality. Further, the work involved in extracting a living from the new country was, much of it, traditionally man's work, such as hunting, for example. In the early stages of the westward movement, as in the trans-Appalachian region, hunting did not just add to the larder, it was the very basis of subsistence. It was always hoped that the corn, beans, squash and other vittles would mature out there in the clearing, but meanwhile hunting kept people alive. The domesticated animals were quite likely pigs, which rooted in the forest most of the year. After the first hard frost in October, it was time to slaughter some of them for the winter's meat supply; that, too, in its initial stages, was man's work. If there was an Indian scare, it was the man in the cabin, or the men at the stockade, who asserted leadership and did the fighting. A house raising was likewise man's work, as was rail splitting, wood chopping, road making, bridge building, sod busting, and the establishment of law and order.

True, the women were strong helpmates. But, although the pioneer woman often stepped into the breach when her man was killed, wounded, absent, or ill, the doing of the man's work was never interpreted as belonging to her by nature, nor was her doing it in any sense a part of the accepted mores of the time. Neither was she a lumberjack, a prospector, a miner, a flatboatman, an Indian trader, or a railroad builder. One or two instances of woman freight wagon drivers or stagecoach drivers such as Calamity Jane and Charlie Parkhurst are so rare as to have attracted the attention of journalists and dime novel writers. Neither were women registers or receivers of land offices, nor surveyors or assayers, nor did they ride with the cowboys.

Moreover, much of new country endeavor demanded cooperation that brought the boys together. Mining began with prospecting with a "pard," followed by several men forming a company; ranching demanded half a dozen cowboys, a horse wrangler, and a cook; lumbering involved several men working with a degree of unity and cooperation, or else someone got hurt. Much communal action, whether a roundup, the working of a sluice-box, or a hastily raised posse and a subsequent hanging, was exclusively male.

Within certain bounds, men in good health and with average personalities appear to have had, to use their own terminology, a "hell of a lot of fun" in the new country. Joseph G. Baldwin chronicled the high living of the Old Southwest in *The Flush Times of Alabama and Mississippi*, where "real estate see-sawed up as morals went down on the other end of the plank" and a typical new country village was made up of two-thirds hard-working fellows and one-third "single gentlemen who had come out on the vague errand of seeking their fortune, or the more definite one of seeking somebody else's. . . ."[1] The anecdotal *Georgia Scenes* by A. B. Longstreet likewise conveys the rowdiness and conviviality of the new country, with its drunks, horse traders, terrible fights, gander pullings, militia company musters, and shooting matches. Although Mark Twain's description in *Roughing It* of life in Virginia City bears the gloss of the master storyteller, there is no doubt of the

An 1881 class of Knights Templar in Kansas. (The Kansas State Historical Society, Topeka)

great times they had. Men drank, gambled, speculated, made deals, invested, lost, and won. Even those who were in process of becoming ten-hour-a-day industrial workers shared in the social activities of the town. There were several fire-fighting companies, and every active man of the community belonged to one of these, replete with his flamboyant uniform. Everywhere politics was a great American game, with torchlight parades, stump speakers, and plenty of whiskey. Most men participated, if only as members of the crowd; they would march with torches to the home of their candidate and cheer him, then march to the home of the opponent and utter in unison three agonizing groans.

The secret fraternal organizations, of which the Masons were the most numerous, were also part of the westward movement. Freemasonry was European in origin, but it came to the colonies at an early time; many of America's leaders were members. Although there was a serious, though short-lived, anti-Mason movement in the 1830's, by and large that organization was accepted in the new country. When strangers in a new community came to know each other, one of their happiest discoveries was being Masons in common. Instantly a mastic was present, for Masons tended to trust one another as if membership implied (as often, in fact, it did) a certain standard of conduct and ethics. Again and again in the new country the first formal social event was the establishment of a Masonic lodge. Leading citizens were members. Even later the most solid building in the town, usually constructed of native stone or expensive brick, was still the Masonic temple. Indeed, according to Muriel Sibell Wolle, who has painted the weatherbeaten structures left standing in the ghost towns of the West, the two types of building with the greatest lasting qualities were the Masonic lodges—and the cribs along Maiden Lane.

Since the Masons usually included a substantial percentage of a town's up-and-coming leaders, it follows that many policies and decisions of concern to the community emanated from the Masonic lodge. It is well known, for example, that the vigilantes of Montana Territory were initially Masons, and for good reason. Masons met in secret, they trusted one another, and the bad men were not Masons. Long after the "good" women had come to town, led campaigns for schools and churches and the closing of Maiden Lane, the Masons continued to be a powerful social force for the good in the new country, cooperating with the women and influencing the men to vote for or finance or support such improvements.

The secret fraternal order was in fact an important element of American society in the second half of the nineteenth century. More than 250 different fraternal orders existed at one time in the United States, and they were particularly strong in the new country areas. Their number crested in the 1880's and declined slowly until the 1920's, when they began rapidly dying off.

While having this "hell of a good time" some men rose to positions of wealth and prominence. In such an open period a young man who went West might be at different times a farmer, surveyor, justice of the peace (which earned him the title of "judge" for the rest of his life), railroad builder, realtor, mayor of a town, representative to the territorial legislature, member of the state's constitutional convention, builder of business blocks, deacon of a church, mining entrepreneur, and Thirty-Second Degree Mason. Montana's Nathaniel P. Langford, Cornelius Hedges, K. Ross Toole, and Sam Hauser, to name a few of them, were young and ambitious and in a new country all at once. John Evans, William Gilpin, General Larimer, and William N. Byers were similar figures in Denver and Colorado.

These vigorous fellows came closer than most to grasping the potential of the new region and making the most of it; one can pick up any of those "mug book" type state, county, or city histories for any place from Appalachia to the communities along the Pacific shores and read their eulogistic biographies. Armed with little more than the ability to read, write, and cipher, they took the measure of the new country and came to control it. Read their reminiscences; the excitement of western activity, the feverish haste to make fortunes (which also resulted in a hastily created civilization) attest to the enjoyment they found in everyday living. It was, for them, a wonderful age in which to be alive. Progress was everywhere, and success was for many easily attainable. In the balance those of the middle class seem, from this distance in time, to have been relatively satisfied with their lot.

Below them, however, was the working man, whose status has to be interpreted partly by what one reads (liberal or conservative interpretations of statistics that are often in themselves skimpy); partly by the era, for the period 1776-1890 embraced several very different eras; and partly by place, for there was a difference in pay for similar jobs in different parts of the country (southern lumberjacks earned less than northern ones, west coast textile workers more than east coast ones). Similarly, jobs in different trades paid different wages, coal miners earning less than petroleum workers in the period after the Civil War. Signs of the ending of the new country stage in the country's history were the strikes of the workers, such as the great railroad strike of 1877, and their reduction to poverty when the economic cycle was at the depression stage.

Yet there were several other elements that make the picture look somewhat more attractive. Long hours on the job did not always mean long hours of toil, and in many jobs there were enforced periods of idleness. In the areas we consider the new country, towns or relatively small cities had relatively small industrial operations. An employee whose child was sick might ask his boss for the day off, and receive it; in depression, such small companies might keep men on the payroll out of humanitarian and Christian attitudes of responsibility. Small communities lacked laws prohibiting the keeping of chickens and livestock, and many a working family had a half acre or more where they grew vegetables, raised chickens for eggs and Sunday dinners, and even kept a cow. In a day before workman's compensation and unemployment insurance, town and city families often stuck together and pooled their resources. The homes they lived in look drafty, cold, and uncomfortable to us today, but they nonetheless had room for a good-sized family, coal or wood stoves and heaters, long verandas with porch swings to sit on in the cool of summer evenings; it was tolerable. Finally, there is no longer any question that in the post–Civil War period real wages—i.e. wages equated with cost of living—rose by between 10 and 25 per cent.

But there was still a class below this one, the ranks of the unemployed. Unfortunately statistics are not accurate for the nineteenth-century years, but it is clear that during such severe depressions as 1837-41 and 1873-78, unemployment was severe. It was during these years—though not exclusively so—that there existed a mass of drifting men who suffered all the age-old hardships of the downtrodden. They were the drifters. Usually they were emigrants, their women left far across the sea. Some were native Americans, surplus from the farms. Or they were war veterans. Some of them had mucked on the Erie Canal and then followed the canal boom all over the Middle West until the bubble had burst in the Panic of 1837. Others were railroad workers; hired hands on farms, ranches, and mines; laborers everywhere. With no workman's compensation or unemployment insurance, they drifted from job to job, from place to place. They were so prevalent that they came to be recognized as a distinct type and were called tramps; an entire vocabulary, even a kind of underground culture, came into being among them.

Such a drifting life, with poor food or no food at all for long periods, drinking water of questionable purity, and lacking facilities for personal cleanliness, bred endemic sickness. If they had work and took sick—with typhoid, for example, or if incipient tuberculosis suddenly became manifest—they were laid off the job and told to leave the premises. If one of them was injured, the "boys" took up a collection. In terms of human dignity, of pride and self-respect, such men, if of average intelligence as most were, must have suffered terrible humiliation. They were also suspect whenever some "horrible crime"—rape or child molestation, for example—took place in the community near where they were encamped in a hobo jungle. Statistics are lacking, but suicides were common among these people. Anyone who has scanned the newspapers of the new country during the nineteenth century is struck by the numerous "shocking discoveries" of lone men whose emaciated corpses were found where they had hanged themselves under railway trestles, or succumbed by a railway embankment from a self-inflicted gunshot wound. Others expired from starvation or illness in a cabin or a tarpaper shack. For these masses of drifting men there was little of the pleasant, happy life that the successful men were enjoying. Most of the poor climbed out of aimlessness into lower-middle-class stability when times got good again. But many did not. For them, there was much hell but little of a good time in the new country.

A night camp of tramps near Bryan. From *Frank Leslie's Illustrated Weekly*, 1878.

That new country society was strongly masculine does not mean that women were not wanted or that women were not there. As we have noted, there were never enough women to match the men on a fifty-fifty basis, and in some parts of the new country men at times outnumbered women by two or three to one. It was their scarcity that gave women prestige. The bylaws of Yellowstone City, Montana, stated that hanging was to be the penalty "for murder, thieving, or for insulting a woman."[2] Maybe they meant it, too. There were just fifteen women in the camp that first winter of 1864-65 and three hundred men.

There exists a stock impression of the new country woman. She is pictured as tall as Kansas' Populist female orator Mary Elizabeth Lease, whom William Allen White described as "nearly six feet tall, with no figure, a thick torso, and long legs. To me," he added, "she often looked like a kangaroo pyramided up to a comparatively small head. Her skin was pasty white. . . . She had no sex appeal—none!"[3] (Of course, Mary Elizabeth had a good voice, and is remembered as the woman who told the Kansas farmers to "raise less corn and more *hell!*") Or, the new country woman is pictured as grim as Carrie Nation, destroying "dry" Kansas saloons with her hatchet (for liquor was illegal but widely sold there) and founding a home for drunkards' wives in Kansas City, Kansas.[4] To complete this rather grotesque image, the new country woman holds a babe in her arms, has numerous progeny about her, and is wearing a sunbonnet. Implied in this is woman the overburdened, over-worked, over-fecund, with a tired body, weatherworn face, and gap-toothed smile. If she had once been pretty, soft, and sexually alluring, she certainly was no longer. This stock type of frontier woman has been dubbed the "sunbonnet myth" by Dee Brown in his delightful anecdotal book *The Gentle Tamers* (New York, 1958). Brown discredits this myth, and indeed none of the women he describes fit the description.

If many women did come close to fitting the sunbonnet myth, the reason may be that the nineteenth century was a bad time for women in general, not just for the pioneer woman. In western Europe the peas-ant woman worked equally hard but with less hope. The low-class city dweller in Europe or America was subject even more to tuberculosis, skin eruptions, and social diseases and also had little hope for bettering her place in life. Only middle- and upper-class women had leisure and luxury. Yet even they were expected to live in total subservience to the male society. For many of them the search for meaning in life must have been long, frustrating, and depressing. They had no status in the law, no property, no possession of their children should the husband leave or sue for divorce.

Women's medical care was poor everywhere. The progress of medi-cine in the nineteenth century was scandalously slow, lagging far be-hind technological, social, and industrial advance. The failure to con-trol consumption, typhoid, diphtheria, smallpox, yellow fever, puerperal fever, malaria, scarlet fever, measles, chicken pox, as well as the lack of anesthesia and, when used, its crudeness by modern standards insured a degree of suffering for the eastern woman about equal to that of her sis-ter out in the new country. Not until two-thirds of the nineteenth cen-tury had passed did the medical profession understand ovulation. Child-birth was a dangerous ordeal everywhere.

The sunbonnet myth tends to inspire pity, and that it should not do. The new country woman held her head high, and her bright eyes searched the horizon for what lay ahead. She shared with her husband a faith in their future, in the "great day acomin'" which they would live to see. Beneath her linsey-woolsey or calico frock was a sturdy body. She could walk to Kentucky, or Missouri, or the Pike's Peak country, or to Zion at Salt Lake or to Oregon. She was a builder, along with her husband; she knew her value. If her life was hard, and it was, so was that of her husband. Yet both found life rewarding, and that is a most important ingredient of mental wellbeing.

There is a chronological and geographical cleavage in the story of women in new country society. Starting in the 1840's the women's rights movement began to make progress; and in that same decade settlement crossed the Missouri and jumped all the way to the Pacific coast. For the women who went west in the 1840's and thereafter, their new life must have seemed like a breath of spring. They literally put so many miles between themselves and their sisters back east that the stultifying society of the settled country never caught up with them. By the time Colorado, Montana, Oregon, California, and other western states had become settled country, the women's rights movement had already won great victories.

The sisters or mothers left back east, even if they had once been proud new country women, found that the customs of early-nineteenth-century society soon caught up with them. Men dominated everything. Segregation of races was not a bit more absolute than segregation of the sexes. River boats always had ladies' salons, and, as Mrs. Trollope discovered, the ladies were expected to stay there. Neither could women participate in political gatherings. Only in church affairs were they welcomed; there they were active participants. Without church, suggested Mrs. Trollope, the American female would be as cloistered as the women in an Arabian harem.

If the hardships of all women were substantial in the nineteenth century, it follows that for many of them the transition from life in a settled area to life in a new country was not traumatic. From the status of farmer's daughter to that of pioneer's wife was no great hurdle. The pioneer woman knew that a clearing would have to be made, a cabin built, and a community of neighbors created. But these tasks she understood; the mystery of what the new country looked like intrigued her, or attracted her positively, like a magnet. Even if she had lived all her sixteen or eighteen years without the terror of an Indian scare, she had heard stories aplenty. Yet human nature led her to believe it would never happen to her—and usually it did not. She left with her swain into the new country with no more tears than accompany the departure of a friend or relative today. She had married, which was a positive good; she had also received a dowry of excitement and hope, of freedom to be mistress of her own household. In a day of mysterious ailments and accidents somehow brought about by the sure hand of God, she also carried with her a faith that was deep and genuine, a rock of stability that would give her solace in childbirth, when babies died, husband took sick, crops failed, or she herself was ailing.

It was more than just love for a man that led Narcissa Prentiss to wed the doctor-missionary Marcus Whitman with the knowledge that they would spend their married lives amidst the heathen of eastern Washington, though as far as we know she had no premonition of their being murdered, as they were in 1847 by the Cayuse Indians. Was it a sense of adventure that led women to marry career army officers who would spend their lives being shunted from place to place on the frontier? Or was it, perhaps, a sense of destiny—of being a participant in the great migration and the building of the new country?

Or perhaps it was much simpler. Maybe it often *was* the mere attraction of a ramrod-straight, well groomed and uniformed young second lieutenant, whose desire for a warm and loving wife could not be hidden. One questions his honesty, though, as he made his pitch to the starry-eyed maiden. The diaries and letters home of military brides are filled with tearful, rude awakenings when the frontier fort was reached, and the young officer and his lady occupied their quarters. Such was the experience of Mrs. Alice Blackwell Baldwin, wed in the comfortable home of her parents in Detroit one cold December day in 1867. Her husband was a dashing young career officer whose regiment, the Thirty-Seventh Infantry, was stationed at Fort Harker, Kansas, on the Smoky Hill River, southeast of present Ellsworth.

The railroad trip from Detroit to Junction City in bitter cold weather, often in unheated cars, was bad enough, but the trip from there on, part way with a bull train (an ox-drawn freight outfit) and then in an army ambulance, was worse. Still, the assurance that soon they would arrive at their own quarters at Fort Harker bolstered her waning morale. South-central Kansas was flat, bleak, and snow-covered, and at first Mrs. Baldwin failed to see any change in the scene when her husband announced, "There, my dear, behold the site of your future home; we will soon be there." After intense scrutiny the young bride made out "the stub of a stovepipe, although no smoke issued from its top. Presently," she said, "I saw other discolorations on the landscape, which proved to be the barracks and officer's quarters. The so-called 'barracks' were mostly dug-outs, but God be praised! There floating in the storm was Old Glory."

Their "home" proved to be one of the dugouts.

I gazed with disgusted disappointment around the bare, squalid room [she wrote]. Its conveniences were limited to one camp chair, two empty candle boxes and a huge box stove, red with rust and grime, its hearth gone and the space filled with a tobacco-stained hill of ashes, the peak of which was surrounded by 'chewed-out quids' of unknown vintage. . . . The walls of the kitchen were stayed and supported by logs, while the ceiling was of the same material and covered with dirt. . . . Canvas covered the ceiling and dirt sides [of her living room]. It sagged slightly in the center and trembled under the scampering feet of pack-rats and prairie mice. The canvas cover not quite extending on one end, the pack-rats would perch on the beams, rear up on their hind legs, with their bushy tails hanging below, and survey me with their beady eyes.

It was all a bit too much, and she burst into tears at the evening meal given them at the officer's mess, "so my soldier, pitying me, and yet half-provoked at my sobs, supported me back to my dug-out."

Mrs. Baldwin may have broken down that first evening, but she had true grit. The next morning she got up and prepared her husband's breakfast. Almost nine months to the day of their wedding, she had her first child, the first white baby born in Trinidad, Colorado Territory. When her husband retired from the service many years later, he held the rank of major general.[5]

That men would bring gentle-born and town-raised young wives to such God-forsaken places speaks strongly for their love (or something akin to it but less heavenly) and harshly about their thoughtlessness. Brides from the farms of Iowa and Illinois were similarly shocked when their husbands introduced them to tarpaper-and-slab one-room dwellings, sticking up like warts on the windswept plains, or to sod houses or even dugouts with tamped dirt floors, roofs with grass and wildflowers growing on top, bedbugs and fleas and "no-see-ums" that seemed to come out of the walls. One suffragette told of her mother arriving with the children at a one-room cabin prepared by the father. She slumped to the floor in despair, hid her eyes in her hands, and stayed in that position for several hours. Then she regained her composure and set about caring for her family. The writer Hamlin Garland gave similar dismal portrayals of woman's life on the Middle Border.

A song printed in *Godey's Lady's Book* indicates that not all women were so love-struck as to marry and head for the new country with their dashing swains:

> What, fly to the prairie? I could not live there,
> With the Indian and panther, and bison, and bear;
> Then cease to torment me, I'll not give my hand,
> To one, whose abode's in so savage a land.[6]

Not all of the women who went to the new country were accompanied by husbands. The prostitutes "down on the line" or along Maiden Lane were also important in western history. No one knows the percentage that left the cribs for homesteaders' shacks, miners' cabins, and town laborers' cottages, but certainly a high number did become "honest women."

Some respectable women found the openness and breeziness of the West so invigorating and delightful that they refused to stay back East. Such a one was Carrie Adele Strahorn, whose husband was a kind of economic spotter–public relations man for the Union Pacific Railroad in the 1880's and 90's. His work took him not only along the railroad right of way but into the boondocks, hundreds of miles to either side of the rails, reached only by stagecoach, buckboard, or saddle horse. Carrie refused to marry "Pard" unless he would take her with him. His employers thought they had the solution: take her West just once, they said, and after that she will be glad to stay home. They did not figure on Carrie. She took the measure of the West, saw it at its crudest, with its unwashed and unshaven men, greasy food, smelly horses, filthy outhouses—and she enjoyed the life and met its hardships with a smile. She was perceptive, too, and wrote with a fluent pen. Her *Fifteen Thousand Miles by Stage* is a classic narration of travel—one woman's Baedeker of the far West.

For all of the painted ladies and the rather substantial number of bizarre females who moved across the new country stage, the vast majority were wives and mothers. They had in common a way of life covered in one word: toil. They cooked and baked, sewed and knitted, milked cows, tended gardens, and raised children. All of this they were expected to do. And often they were lonely, felt unappreciated, yearned for a haven of refuge where the work was all done. Some of the hymns they sang as they went about their tasks reveal their hidden loneliness, the vacuum in their hearts:

> When at last life's day is ending,
> As the ev-'ning draweth nigh,
> And the sun is slowly wending,
> Down behind the western sky.

> 'Twill be sweet to think of pleasures,
> That shall never know decay,
> In that home of joy and splendor,
> Just beyond life's twilight gray.

And the chorus:

> Rest, sweet rest, and joy and gladness,
> Comes when toil, when toil is o'er,
> Sweetest resting comes when toil is o'er,
> 'Twill be joy and rest eternal
> On the other shore.[7]

Atlantean Brown Club, Minneapolis, 1887. (The Kansas State Historical Society, Topeka)

Musical evening in a Victorian parlor in small-town Oregon. White-tie attire contrasts with animal pelt on floor. Photo by W. A. Raymond, c. 1880. (The Bettmann Archive)

A surprising number of new country women were literate, and it was they who saw to it that the children attended school and Sunday School and did their lessons; in the absence of schools, the mother served as teacher. More than that, the women were the ones who reminded the men of the world of literature and the arts. "Knowing that books were always scarce in a new country, we also took a good library of standard books," reminisced Virginia Reed Murphy, who had survived the horrors of the Donner tragedy.[8] And Jessie Benton Frémont, who said that "no man can know what a wear & tear the detail of family life in a new country is to a woman," longed for the twice-monthly mail stages that brought "brain rations" in the form of newspapers, periodicals, correspondence, and books.[9]

While the natural tendency is to mention outstanding women who made their marks, many nameless, toiling, devoted women who raised their children under primitive conditions were no less truly valiant. Many a new country man remembered his mother's sacrifices; his feeling about her even turned up in hymns, such as this one: "Can a Boy Forget His Mother?" Here is one verse:

> Can a boy forget his mother,
>   Or the parting words she said?
> As she stood with arms around him,
>   And those burning tears she shed?
> Will that scene not round him linger,
>   Tho' he far away may roam?
> Can a boy forget his mother,
>   Or his far off childhood home?

And the chorus:

> Can a boy forget his mother?
>   Can he cease her kiss to crave?
> Can a boy forget his mother,
>   Tho' the flowers bloom o'er her grave?[10]

It was the new country women who furnished the additional thought, the more carefully weighed judgments, the disciplines of household routine, that brought their husbands and children through the long journeys to new homes. Catherine Margaret Haun, whose husband later became a United States Senator from California, put the matter succinctly in her diary. "Our caravan had a good many women and children," she wrote, "and . . . they exerted a good influence, as the men did not take such risks with Indians and thereby avoided conflict, were more alert about the care of the teams and seldom had accidents; more attention was paid to cleanliness and sanitation and, lastly, but not of less importance, the meals were more regular and better cooked thus preventing much sickness and there was less waste of food."[11]

The freedom of the new country, the glaring disparity in the ratio of the sexes, and the crying need for women on an agricultural frontier did indeed lead some to demand more rights. It was a trend already under way, a result of a number of forces active in the society from the 1840's on, and so it was not initially the inspiration of the new country woman. By 1850 most states had passed some kind of legislation recognizing the right of married women to hold property; whereas in 1870 there had been 90,000 women schoolteachers in the nation, by 1890 there were 250,000. Such early women's rights advocates as Emma Willard, Frances Wright, Catherine Beecher, Mary Lyon, Sarah and Angelina Grimké, Lucy Stone, Lucretia Mott, Susan B. Anthony, and Elizabeth Cady Stanton were not women of the new as apart from the settled country.

Nevertheless it was in the new country that the early victories for woman suffrage were registered. Some of this was due to sheer serendipity, some of it was ludicrous, but nevertheless it took place. The reasons often had little relation to the pros and cons on the subject that generated so much discussion in the East. The desire to advertise the territory appears to have had as much as anything to do with the adoption of woman suffrage in Wyoming on December 10, 1869. A number of men in that vast land, where the males outnumbered the females six to one, felt that being the first territory to approve woman suffrage would be excellent public relations—would really put Wyoming on the map! Others, including a newspaper editor or two, also thought it would be a good idea in itself. Anna Dickinson and Redelia Bates, both young and attractive suffragettes, had spoken in Cheyenne shortly before the legislature convened. And finally a member of the Council of the Territorial Legislature, forty-six-year-old William H. Bright, deserves some credit. He came from lonely South Pass City, more than eighty miles from the railroad, but he apparently lived there in some bliss with his lovely twenty-six-year-old wife Julia, who was educated, intelligent, and known to favor suffrage and women's rights. Colonel Bright (as he was known) introduced the bill and politicked it shrewdly; to everyone's surprise it passed and was signed by Governor John A. Campbell, again to everyone's surprise. Men scratched their heads trying to figure out how it happened, who had got the signals mixed. But they were stuck with it: Wyoming had woman suffrage.[12] Wyoming women also obtained the right to jury duty, control over their own property, and an assurance, on paper at least, of equal pay for equal work.

While the initial suffrage victory in Wyoming was, therefore, rather a fluke, the coming of woman suffrage to Utah was, by contrast, a portent of the future pattern of suffrage victories. As Alan P. Grimes has pointed out in his study *The Puritan Ethic and Woman Suffrage*, any change in the electorate was going to affect governmental policy, local, state, and national. Some proponents saw in woman suffrage a method toward achieving their own aims, while opposition forces saw a serious threat to their position should the suffrage movement succeed.

In Utah woman suffrage was granted by the Mormon-dominated territorial legislature in 1870 with hardly any preliminary debate. The reason for its passage was quite obvious. Gentiles had formed the Liberal Party to challenge Mormon dominance. Woman suffrage in a territory where almost all the women were Mormons and most gentiles were men could secure Mormon dominance at the polls. It is a commentary on the general hostility toward the Mormons that the only Congressional act passed regarding suffrage in the nineteenth century was the so-called Edmunds-Tucker Act of 1887, which abolished woman suffrage in Utah; Wyoming was not affected.

Of further significance is the Utah constitution of 1896, which carried a provision for woman suffrage. Although the matter had received considerable discussion, the suffrage provision passed easily, by a vote of 75 to 14. Such a lopsided victory indicates acceptance of the idea as a result of the seventeen years in which woman suffrage was legal. It also tells something of the attitude of Mormons toward women and the view Mormon women held of themselves.

Although theirs was a patriarchal society that condoned polygamy (although only 2 to 3 per cent practiced it) the Mormons were extremely puritanical. The solid endeavor of that valiant people toward a successful Zion demanded that women be as productive in their way as men. Mormons taught and preached a great deal, and from as early as 1842 the women had the opportunity to converse at the church-sanctioned Relief Society meetings. While they worked no harder than other pioneer women, Mormon women gained specific recognition for their contributions and were thus made to feel valuable and respected in their calling. "Mothers in Israel," sermonized Brigham Young, "you . . . are called upon to bring up your daughters to pursue some useful avocation for a sustenance, that when they shall become the wives of the elders of Israel, who are frequently called upon missions, or who devote their time and attention to the things of the Kingdom, they may be able to sustain themselves and their offspring. . . ."[13]

Mormon women also had a social organization which was charged with constructive tasks. They were encouraged to supply midwives, and some of them apparently approached the status of general practitioners.

The Mormon frontier was certainly without many luxuries, but at least the women, unless their husbands had settled in Dixie (the region just north of the Grand Canyon) or at some lonely "stake" on the frontiers of Zion, had the luxury of female society, which was denied to many of their gentile frontier sisters.

Thus a well-organized element such as these women were, enjoying the franchise, could be a strong force for prohibition, for laws against prostitution—in short, for legislating high morals according to the Mormon code. Men who supported these ideals—and all good Mormons did —were pretty likely to favor woman suffrage also, since it was a vehicle to bolster their power at the polls in behalf of these measures.

It was in Wyoming, however, that the effect of woman suffrage as a defender of the Protestant ethic first emerged. Wyoming in the nineteenth century was a wild place. It contained nomadic Indians—Crow, Shosone, and Sioux, primarily—lonely men at military forts, more than 10,000 railroad workers, tie cutters, and the seamy characters inhabiting such hell-on-wheels towns as Cheyenne and Laramie. In the late 1860's and early 1870's there were brief gold strikes at Atlantic City, Pacific

The "hell on wheels" town of Cheyenne had assumed an appearance of stability by 1876. (U.S. Signal Corps, The National Archives)

City, and South Pass City. A few years later the territory (not until 1890 did Wyoming achieve statehood) became cattlemen's country with cowboys, most of whom were single, cattle barons, and range wars. Wyoming was a land of drifting men, few of whom planned upon permanent settlement there. There was little morality. Sunday was the best day of the week for the saloonkeeper, and the best-known, successful females were likely to be madams or sporting women. The results of woman suffrage and the accompanying women's rights legislation were soon apparent in Wyoming. A Boston clergyman wrote that he "was compelled to allow that in this new country . . . [he] had witnessed a more quiet election than . . . in the quiet towns of Vermont."[14] In March 1870, Laramie got its first women jurors. A grand jury of six women and nine men indicted every saloon for failing to close on Sunday as specified by a law passed by the territorial legislature. Pretty soon Laramie was known as the "Puritan Town" of Wyoming.

In the Utah experience woman suffrage helped maintain the Puritan ethic; in the Wyoming experience it became a force for civilizing and bringing under control the rowdy elements of new country life. The pattern was retained everywhere until well into the twentieth century. Women supported the Anti-Saloon League, they were founders of the WCTU, they fought for laws closing down gambling dens and houses of prostitution. Their movement was melded with forces favoring the initiative, referendum, and recall, and with the effort to restrict immigration—goals of the Progressive movement, and the results of changes taking place in the settled country. Still the pioneer work of these dedicated feminists also did much to soften and civilize the last of the new country—the territories and states of the Rocky Mountains and the Far West.

The new country woman's primary task, however, was to care for her family. From marriage came children, and the most elemental social unit came into being. In the new country marriage and the birth of children took place very quickly, the latter sometimes before or without the former. The people knew that America was sparsely populated, that it could provide sustenance for many millions more, that any young fellow with a rustic background could in time own a self-sustaining family farm. The posting of marriage bans, intricate family arrangements, and long engagements were all lacking from the American scene. This led some European travelers to comment, sometimes with amazement and occasionally with unusual understanding, at the flippancy with which Americans entered into marriage.

This assumption was probably not valid. Most American marriages were entered into with equal seriousness, but far more simply, than European. Since love was a prime requisite, in the absence of the social stratification and the religious formality of Europe, the marriage was usually a decision of the boy and girl involved. The Protestant ceremony was a very short one, followed by merrymaking that verged on rowdyism and rather frank emphasis on the sexual side of the union. "Health to the groom, and here's to the bride, thumping luck, and big children," ran a toast of the times, and by all appearances the bride shared in appreciating the meaning as much as the groom; she may even have shown it physically. The young couple headed for the new country with horse or horse and wagon, a few household gifts, and the best wishes of their relatives and friends.

The only tears shed when the bride and groom left home were over the parting, for everyone in the little crowd of well-wishers knew that the young couple's prospects were bright. Fine lands and a wonderful future lay ahead. With their only necessities a rifle, axe, horse or oxen, seed, a few farm implements, some cooking utensils, and bedding, the newlyweds were just about on an even par with thousands of others. If they had a little specie accumulated by the girl from sewing, or squeezed into her hand by a hard-bitten but loving father, or accumulated by the groom from the sale of peltry taken the previous winter, then they were all the better off.

So too was the coming of children anticipated with pleasure. Elsewhere in the world each child was an additional burden, another mouth to feed, another obligation that accentuated the quiet desperation of the common man's life. In the new country children were welcome. "Here, 'more the merrier,'" wrote a correspondent for the *Democratic Review* in 1844. "For six months of the year hats and shoes are out of fashion, and drapery of almost classical simplicity is quite sufficient for the younger children. . . . Our poor man counts each one of his half dozen or half score a blessing . . . stout hands and active heads are the very thing we need."[15]

Many of the families were large. "Brides who were as Rachels in the Atlantic states, having migrated to the west, became as Leahs; and . . . they esteem it no unusual compliment to receive even the double blessing of Rebeccas," a traveler wrote in 1824.[16] It has been estimated that the state of Kentucky, where families of twelve or sixteen were not unusual, had furnished a million human beings to other states by 1860. So favorably did Tennessee look upon new families that in 1829 it passed a law granting a father of three or more children at one birth the privilege of 200 acres of state lands for each child. Infant mortality was high; many a frontier woman suffered from the unclean hands of clumsy midwives or physicians; and epidemics of typhoid, diphtheria, smallpox and scarlet fever sometimes left a hiatus of three to five years in a community in which the malady had killed off every child between two and five, but still most of the progeny lived, matured, and entered the mainstream of American life. The boys very soon shared in the chores of the head of the household, while the girls helped the mother with household tasks.

Generalizations are very questionable in such cases as this, but the best description of the new country family is that it was an easygoing, pleasant unit, a haven of love and companionship in which the bond of common blood was so deeply understood that the insipid manifestations of affection were seldom seen. This led some observers to describe the American family as cold and unresponsive, a strange social unit in which members would leave for distant places with no more than a shake of the hand, where "the father of the frontier bride gave her a bed, a lean horse, and some good advice; and having discharged his duty . . . returned to work." But in fact, wrote Arthur Calhoun, this apparently frigid attitude was "evidently due . . . to the economic largeness of the new world which made family wealth and backing less significant. . . . The abundant opportunities of the new country, the relative ease of getting along, the certainty that the children would be able to find good openings, tended to loosen family attachments. . . . The family ceased to be an economic unit: each member could follow a calling to taste."[17]

In such a family children grew up very quickly. By age four they could carry a bucket and collect the eggs from the nests of the hens in the barn; a little later the boys could harness a horse, yoke up a team of oxen; they learned to plant and weed and harvest, to milk cows and slaughter a few pigs after the first frost, to butcher them, salt them down, and preserve the meat. The handling of gun and axe came with growing up.

Sometimes the father was a sadistic tyrant, and some fiction has rather emphasized him as such. Such men did exist then, as they do today. But he was more likely to be, at the worst, a benevolent despot in an admittedly patriarchal society; and much more often than supposed he was permissive—though by nineteenth-century rather than mid-twentieth-century standards. This is apparent because of what we know of the new country child. At age 4-7 he was looked upon as a little rascal rather than as an angel or cherub. A few years later, in his early teens, possibly because he had chores to do and actually knew the basics of farming by the time he reached puberty, he struck Europeans as being remarkably self-confident, independent, and fearless. There was no time in the new country for the prolonged infancy that existed in European society. Most parents raised their children with the implicit understanding that they were expected to sprout their wings early and leave the home roost to establish themselves, with their own family units, elsewhere.

And the parents wished them all the best. Their generation had slaved to create a society out of the wilderness; "for the children" was a common phrase they used in justifying their toil. It was concern over the threat posed by the "slavocracy" to their continued right to free lands in the West that crystallized the opposition of the rural people of the Old Northwest to the South and thus hastened the coming of the Civil War.

The family was of especial importance in the new country, for it was the one social structure that provided stability. It antedated the coming of government, law and order, schools and churches. When children were orphaned due to disease, accident, or Indian depredations, or left destitute by desertion, it was not at all unusual for a neighboring family to take them in and raise them with their own. The land was bountiful, and another mouth or even several more to feed constituted no great problem; while extra hands at the harvest and more helpmates in the kitchen just about compensated for the expense.

For all of this importance of the family, the social wrenching of divorce was more common than is usually supposed. Indiana, which had lenient laws, was the divorce center of the pre-Civil War era, but divorce was possible in all of the states. Usually it was by way of private statute —that is, a divorce was provided for in a statute passed by the state legislature for that specific case. All manner of politicking and underhanded tactics accompanied this process. The clergy took umbrage to the system, so that a trend set in to place jurisdiction in the hands of the courts, where it remains today. There was, of course, a double standard, and more wives were the unhappy victims of philandering husbands than the other way around, though it was not uncommon for husbands to return home to find their wives had left with another man. If the stories from frontier Texas are the norm, one did not ask too many questions in that frontier state about a neighbor's background. Interspersed in local papers "back east" among notices of strayed heifers and horses, and occasionally runaway slaves, are statements like this: "The subscriber announces that he is no longer responsible for debts incurred by his wife Matilda who has left his bed and board. . . ." In spite of a few divorces, a good many desertions, and a substantial number of brutal, drunken husbands, there is general agreement that marriage and family was a happy and honorable institution in the new country, and morality within that realm was high.

Society Beyond the
Family

While the family was in sound condition as an institution in the new country, the physical condition of its members may be described as precarious. Initially the inhabitants were young, for the most part, and so possessed the resiliency of those still fresh in years. Men and women both worked hard, which gave them a muscle tone that would be the envy of any jogging man or health-spa-frequenting woman of today. The health and strength resulting from an outdoor existence with its hard physical labor pulled through many a frontiersman, Kentucky farmer or Colorado cowboy, suffering from accident or disease. Gruesome shotgun and rifle wounds, premature blasts in a mine, cuts from an axe that had glanced off an unnoticed knot in the wood, broken bones from a mule's kick, all mended quickly, if not always correctly. Teeth did acquire cavities, and many a medical doctor acted as dentist until he was almost as adept as men trained in the profession. In some parts and at certain periods in the history of the new country, a doctor spent most of his time patching up wounds and mending broken bones, because the residents were mostly young and free of the diseases of old age.

Yet the years took their toll, and by the time the young had become thirtyish fathers and mothers with progeny playing about the dooryard, even the best physiques would likely have suffered a bout of fever, fallen victim to some contagious disease, or begun to show the debilitating effects of too much raw whiskey, too much fried and greasy food, or too much anxiety, worry and childbearing. Moreover contagious and deficiency diseases came into the new country along with the people. Scurvy, with its swollen gums, fever, anemia, and weakness, was common enough to be readily identifiable on the Oregon and California trails. Hookworm was endemic in the South. Malaria was common and extended well up the Mississippi and Ohio river valleys. What the settlers called the "ague" and "the shakes" were usually this disease, and so common were they that travelers commented on the sallow and jaundiced complexions, the lackadaisical attitudes toward life, of their victims. A disease especially prevalent in the Ohio Valley was "milk sickness" or "cow sickness," which gave a person chills, a fever of 103.5 degrees or more, vomiting, a swollen abdomen, and delirium. Not until the 1920's was its source discovered: cows that eat rayless goldenrod and snakeroot have in their milk the poison tremetol which afflicts humans. Probably Lincoln's mother, Nancy Hanks Lincoln, suffered from this sickness. Tetanus, better known as lockjaw, blood poisoning, the lingering typhoid fever, erysipelas, yellow fever, Asiatic cholera, and the usual run of childhood diseases all added to the precariousness of family health.

Probably in no aspect of western civilization did knowledge so lag in the nineteenth century as in the realm of medicine. Thus the ignorance and suffering in the new country was very little different from that in the centers of population in the East and in Europe. However, due simply to the shortage of physicians in the West, the prevalence of Indian remedies and the practice of folk medicine were probably greater. Whether the net result of the administration of these local nostrums was any worse than the overuse of the lance for bleeding and calomel for purging—the established practices of the Eastern physician—is conjectural. From ailments that went under such names as bilious fever, stagnant-water effluvia, malignant and putrid diseases, the westerners suffered much. Those who survived had nothing to thank but their own strong constitutions, though some gruesome concoction which they had downed probably received the credit, along with the doctor who made them swallow it.

What seemed to be lacking was plain common sense. The treatment of illnesses was a case of the blind leading the blind, and a resort to something akin to if not actually plain superstition was the result. Peter Smith's *The Indian Doctor's Dispensary*, Dr. Richard Carter's *Valuable Vegetable Prescriptions for the Cure of All Nervous and Putrid Disorders*, Robert L. Foster's *The North American Indian Doctor*, or Peter C. Gunn's *Domestic Medicine or Poor Man's Friend, in the House of Affliction, Pain, and Sickness* were all published west of the Appalachians between 1813 and 1830; the last volume had sold over a hundred thousand copies by 1839. Some of their prescriptions were sensible—over sixty of the drugs used by the American Indian are to be found in the modern materia medica and among the products of present-day pharmaceutical companies—but others, which constitute the overwhelming majority, are simply horrendous.

Besides these there were the folk nostrums handed down from generation to generation in families. For baldness, rub fresh peach leaves on the head; for bed-wetting, eat a handful of sumac berries twice a week; for fever, gather a bunch of "dollar leaves"—dollar-sized leaves of a southern plant that grows very close to the ground— steep them in water, strain, and drink.

In the new country family it was usually the mother who dispensed these nostrums. In a village or among a range of villages in a valley, one woman would very likely become known as a midwife; she often served as a practical nurse as well. One of the widows of John D. Lee, a notorious Mormon, was such a person down in "Dixie." Puerperal fever was common, for basic sanitation was not practiced. If a woman in labor faced a breech birth or the foetus was slow in coming, there was little help for the hours of agony that awaited her. Sometimes a quill of snuff was held to the mother's nostrils, the resulting paroxysm of sneezing bringing forth the child.

Not until an illness defied all the nostrums known to the mother or the local quack was a doctor called. If the sick in the community were lucky, he was a man of high intelligence, great compassion, and had acquired most of the limited knowledge that a year or so in a medical college could offer. This meant that he had some understanding of anatomy and could set bones and clean a wound. A doctor could inspire confidence and give hope to the sick, even if the illness puzzled him and his pills were nothing but sugar-coated opiates. If he possessed in addition some common sense, then the sufferer was indeed fortunate. Oftentimes such a new country doctor rode a circuit much as Methodist preachers did. People looked forward to his coming and awaited his diagnosis and prognosis. When epidemics of diphtheria, typhoid, smallpox, or children's diseases were not rampant, then broken bones, axe cuts, and the lingering terminal illnesses commanded his skills.

Some of the doctors were indeed men of intelligence and common sense, and some of their contributions have been recorded. Dr. Ephraim McDowell successfully removed an ovarian tumor in 1809. The operation was performed at his log cabin office in Danville, Kentucky. Dr. John Sappington's pills contained quinine, which helped contain malaria in the Mississippi and Ohio valleys. Dr. William Beaumont studied the functions of the stomach, his specimen being a patient whose wound refused to heal. Chloroform and ether, the stethoscope, and smallpox vaccinations were early used by doctors practicing in the interior of the continent.

It is clear, however, that nineteenth-century medicine was of unforgivably low standards everywhere, and the horrid nostrums, purging, and bleeding could not save many. Those who recovered had been strong

A nineteenth-century doctor's saddle bag and bottles. They belonged to James E. Talbot, a pioneer physician of Green County, Indiana, who began practice in the 1870's. (Courtesy Lilly Research Laboratories)

enough to overcome both the illness *and* the prescription. Among the tragedies recorded in graveyards is one told by this epitaph for an infant:

Vera Grace
Born June 24, 1881
Died August 30, 1881
Weep not papa and mama for me
For I am waiting in heaven for thee

Or:

GONE BEFORE US
OH OUR CHILDREN
TO THE BETTER LAND
VAINLY WAIT WE
FOR OTHERS IN YOUR PLACE TO STAND

And all across the new country this one appeared:

> REMEMBER FRIENDS AS YOU PASS BY
> AS YOU ARE NOW SO ONCE WAS I
> AS I AM NOW SO YOU MUST BE
> PREPARE FOR DEATH AND FOLLOW ME[1]

To bear up under these tragedies, in this life full of mystery, the women turned to faith, to religion, to the compassionate Jesus. To a lesser degree so did the men; and from the ranks of the new country males came the preachers of a new religion.

Some formal establishment of religion, whatever the sect, was the next step in social organization above the family. Local lay readers or licensed preachers held services in their cabins before even a semblance of a village had appeared in the area. Itinerant Baptists or circuit-riding Methodists might at almost any season of the year appear out of the forest, down at the ranch house in the swale, in the upper part of a valley, or at a remote mining camp in the Rockies. Indeed, the Christian faith was strong, a potent social force in the new country. This was true equally in 1776 and in 1890, with only the geography changing.

The basic concepts of Christianity were especially applicable to a new, sparsely settled country, a wilderness, an essentially agricultural society. It was easy for people in such a situation to identify with the participants in the great Biblical dramas, for the multitudes of old were no larger than such a gathering as assembled at Cane Ridge, Kentucky, August 6-11, 1801. This Great Revival, as it has been called, took place about seven miles from the town of Paris in Bourbon County, and is often considered (though it was actually not) the first of that frontier phenomenon, the camp meeting. It was certainly the largest, estimates of attendance varying from ten to twenty-five thousand; it "was, in all probability, the most disorderly, the most hysterical, and the largest revival ever held in early-day America."[2] And the ancient herds of livestock were not unlike the pioneers' herds, and the ancient ethics—the Ten Commandments—the same. This identification was greatest among the Mormons migrating to the Great Basin.

But while Christianity of a certain kind was applicable in the new country, formalized, stereotyped organizations of the established churches were not—at least not in the trans-Appalachian country where the pioneers advanced too rapidly for Catholicism and the Episcopal Church to keep pace; when it was settled country both of these faiths caught up, and rapidly, but their parishioners were no longer pioneers. The type of Christianity that was so successful in the new country, at least east of the Mississippi, was pietistic and highly individualistic. A man or woman could make peace with God without a mediator. This has been called the Universal Priesthood of All Believers, and although it had been practiced by certain persecuted peoples in Europe—the dissenters of the Rhine Valley in particular—it achieved its greatest acceptance in America, where the formal priesthood of established churches was missing. Moreover it was a faith of the heart, of the emotions, rather than of reason and intellect. It was an optimistic faith in spite of the numberless sermons that stressed hellfire and brimstone, for its theme was redemption. The individual had the power within him to suffer personal repentance for his sins, and thus to gain redemption.

Pietism was not restricted to a few minor sects in Europe, however. It was intrinsic in the faith of the Quakers. Later many aspects of pietism appeared as ingredients of the Methodist persuasion; to some extent this was a result of John Wesley's experience on a voyage to America. Some Moravian emigrants had been aboard, and while the ship floundered about in an Atlantic gale he had noted their peace of mind; they quietly prayed and were clearly unafraid to die. Wesley was impressed; he searched for their secret and incorporated it into his own faith and that of his followers. It was just one condition, which was, he said, "a real desire to save the soul."[3] This idea gave great impetus to the movement in England and was of prime significance when Methodism came to America. It should also be noted that in saving the soul a person experienced deep emotion which often included erotic or at least strange and, to the outsider, ludicrous manifestations.

Methodism was not originally a church per se; it was a movement in England among Anglican churchgoers, stressing morality and soul-saving, and designed, besides that, to send people back to the established Anglican church. There was much lay preaching, often in fields because no hall was available, and there were "class meetings" where the preachers or exhorters pleaded with people to save their souls. Eventually, of course, the movement got out of hand and Methodism became an independent Protestant sect.

Although John Wesley had been in America from 1735 until 1738, and Methodism in England is usually dated from 1739, nearly a generation elapsed before it was planted in the American colonies, primarily because from about 1732 until the 1780's there was a lull in British emigration to America. Controversy surrounds the claimants to the honor of being first Methodist exhorter or preacher in America, but whoever deserves the credit, he arrived in the 1760's. Again, the Methodists came as helpers rather than as competitors, and they got along very well, initially, with established sects. They were most successful in the southern colonies, working as adjuncts of the Episcopal Church; they were not so successful in the Piedmont, where Presbyterians and Baptists were already entrenched.

Almost by accident a system began to appear. The Methodist preachers, of whom there were few, became itinerants. They whipped up religious enthusiasm in the populace, left lay preachers to conduct classes, and then moved on. In Virginia in 1774-75 they brought about a real revival, complete with the "falling exercises" in which the participants fell to the ground, often writhing, sometimes as if dead. In 1771, meanwhile, Francis Asbury had arrived in America. This incredible man of the cloth set an example for all Methodist preachers to emulate. He was a tireless itinerant, traveling 270,000 miles in his lifetime, preaching in village squares, at executions, wherever he could muster an audience.

In 1784-85 the Methodist Episcopal Church was founded, and the activities of the preachers were controlled by establishing geographical circuits that they could cover in one to six weeks. "The itinerant system was admirably suited to the spreading of the gospel in a new country," wrote the historian of religion on the American frontier, William Warren Sweet.[4]

In Edward Eggleston's novel *The Circuit Rider* (1874), that personage is described as he approached a residence near the pioneer settlement and shouted the usual new country greeting, "Hello! Hello the house!" The owner came out to meet the stranger. "He was a broad-shouldered, stalwart, swarthy man, of thirty-five, with a serious but aggressive countenance, a broad-brim white hat, a coat made of country jeans, cut straight-breasted and buttoned to the chin, rawhide boots, and 'linsey' leggings tied about his legs below the knees. He rode a stout horse, and carried an ample pair of saddlebags."[5]

Such a preacher brought not only the Gospel but news of the neighboring settlements and the outside world. He carried some books in his saddlebags for sale to the few individuals who thirsted for knowledge, for the Methodists were energetic in publishing and selling books with a pro-Methodist slant. Since he preached every day but one (which was often Monday, when he washed his clothes and took care of his own affairs) in a different place the preacher could deliver the same sermon over and over again. "This made for the development of effective oratorical preaching," writes Sweet, "the type particularly well adapted to the frontier."[6]

For indeed the Methodist preacher did exhort. He could paint livid pictures of the torments of the sinners writhing in agony in a fiery hell. Salvation was up to the individual, and in this salvation business there was complete equality before God. Rich man, poor man, sick man, ro-

A Methodist circuit rider. (From *The Methodist Publishing House: A History*, Volume 1, by James P. Pilkington. Used by permission of Abingdon Press)

bust man, it made no difference; Methodism subscribed to a most democratic gospel, one peculiarly attractive to the equalitarian new country
man. And—as might be expected considering the origins of Methodism—
when camp meetings were called, even if initiated by the Presbyterians,
the Methodists were there. Their hymns—John Wesley's brother wrote
more than 6,000—were constantly heard in the wilderness.

Such high-voltage proselytizing had great effect upon the new country
people, especially those of trans-Appalachia in the period before the
Civil War, who faced loneliness, illness, death, and the mystery of it all.
People were superstitious, and their highly emotional faith reflected this.
Eggleston mentions two events which, he suggests, are both based upon
actual events that were said to have occurred in "a valley in Ohio." In
one, the heroine, in a ride through several miles of dreadful dark woods,
is accompanied and protected by two beautiful dogs which appear from
nowhere and disappear after the woods are traversed, the assumption
being that the Lord has sent them; in the other a white pigeon flies in
an open window "and light[s] upon the bed of the dying man," then
flies out again and disappears into the sun, apparently taking his soul
with it. Eggleston footnoted this passage: "I have followed strictly the
statement of eyewitnesses. E.E."[7]

Probably too much attention has been given to the Methodist circuit
riders, for just as the enlisted men do the actual fighting in wars and the
generals win, so are the local preachers and exhorters who carried on after
the itinerant had left the forgotten "enlisted men" of Protestantism in
the new country. But as the generals are remembered, so have the great
Methodist circuit riders such as Francis Asbury and Peter Cartwright
been recorded in the annals of history. Most leaders have their share of
egotism; Asbury had himself designated a bishop in the Methodist
Church, and Cartwright wrote a most immodest autobiography, which,
however, includes some splendid descriptions of camp meeting excesses.

It is worth noting also that circuit riders and itinerants of other faiths
were likewise busy later, on the other side of the Mississippi River. In
the mining country of the Rockies, for example, the appearance of an
itinerant preacher was often followed—with surprising rapidity—by the
formal organization of a church and subsequent construction of a
church building. In fact, the more formal sects such as the Catholics
and Episcopalians, who had temporarily lost out in the trans-Appalachian new country, were quite capable of holding their own in the post–
Civil War trans-Mississippi and Far West.

Not always were the visits of "Sam Singers" (psalm singers) anticipated with relish. The fictional Reverend McBride, who preached for an
hour to the cowboys at Sunk Creek Ranch on the text from Psalms,

"They are altogether become filthy; there is none of them that doeth good, no, not one," was one of the stolid, hellfire-and-brimstone types who always somehow found everything and everybody about them subject to criticism. As Owen Wister said of him in his classic novel *The Virginian*, "Stone upon stone he built the black cellar of his theology, leaving out its beautiful park and the sunshine of its garden." How the Virginian dispensed with the "Sam Singer's" services after one night and one sermon is left for the reader to discover by reading the novel.[8]

But others were notably successful. One beloved Methodist circuit rider was the Reverend Wesley Van Orsdel, who arrived at the Blackfoot reservation in northern Montana in June 1872, a fledgling parson from Pennsylvania. He had a good voice and had earned his passage on a Missouri River steamboat by singing hymns. The Blackfeet dubbed him "Great Heart" because he was so warm, sympathetic, and understanding to them; white settlers, who took to him with equal affection, called him "Brother Van." After a year the young Methodist concluded that the whites needed religion more than the Indians. Thus was launched the most beloved circuit rider in Montana history; before he crossed the great divide (Brother Van would have appreciated the phrase), he had established more than a hundred Methodist churches in Montana. In 1918, when he was nearing the end of his ministry, some of his followers arranged a birthday party for him. One of the invited who could not attend, because, he said, he was "on the jury"—and in truth he was, at Great Falls, Montana—was the great cowboy artist Charles Russell. Here is part of his letter saying he could not attend, bad spelling and all:

The evening you came [to Babcock's ranch in Pigeye Basin] there was a mixture of bull whackers and prospectors who welcomed you with hand shakes and rough but friendly greetings

I was the only stranger to you so after Bab interduced Kid Russell he took me to one side and whispered

Boy, says he, I dont savy many samsingers but Bro. Van deals square and when we all sat down to our elk mcct, beens, coffee and dryed apples under the rays of a bacon grease light, these men who knew little of law and one among them wore notches on his gun, men who had not prayed since they nelt at their Mothers Knee bowed there heads while you Bro Van gave thanks and when you finished someone said Amen. I am not sure but I think it was a man who I heard later was ore had been a rode agent

I was 16 years old then Brother Van but have never forgotten your stay at old Bab's, with men whose talk was generly emphasised with fancy profanity but while you were with us altho they had to talk slow and careful there was never a slip. the outlaw at Bab's was a sinner and none of us there was saints but our hearts were clean at least while you gave thanks when the Hold-up said, Amen.

You brought to the minds of these hardened homeless men the faces of their Mothers and few can be bad while she is near.

I have met you many times since that Bro. Van, sometimes in lonely places but you were never lonesome or alone for a man with scarred hands and feet stood beside you and near him there is no hate so all you meet loved you.

Be good and you'l be happy is an old saying which many contradict and say that goodness is a rough trail, over dangerous passes with windfalls and swift deep rivers to cross.

I have never ridden it very far myself but judging from the looks of you its a cinch bet that with a horse called faith under you its a smooth flower growen trail, with easy fords where birds sing and cold clear streams dance in the sunlight all the way to the pass that crosses the great divide.

Bro. Van you have ridden that trail a long time and I hope you will still ride to many birthdays on this side of the big range.

With best wishes from my best half and me.
C. M. Russell[9]

Out to the Colorado mining town of Irwin in the early 1880's came Bishop Spaulding of the Episcopal Church. The faithful erected a tent for him, spread sawdust over the bare earth, placed candles around an improvised altar, converted a packing box into a pulpit, and borrowed someone's prayer book. Trouble was, next door was a gambling hall. "You could hear the clink of the chips and the shouts of the dancehall caller as he sang out 'Honors to your partners, allemande left, ladies and gents waltz up to the bar,'" an oldtimer reminisced. Of course it frustrated the bishop's sermonizing, and he asked the manager of the hall if business could be suspended for an hour. "No!" shouted the clientele. But the manager yelled out, "You fellows, plug up the kitty and give the Bishop the benefit of the next play." This was done, and the sermon was delivered.[10]

The itinerants, whether circuit-riding Methodists, drifting Baptists, highly educated Roman Catholics, or cultured Episcopalians, played a critical role in bringing religion to new country society. Yet one suspects that their notoriety has caused the role of the sedentary preacher to be neglected. Crossroads communities grew up quickly in the new country; or, if communities in the sense of towns were missing, then there were glens or vales in which a church might be situated for a farm area of twenty square miles or so. The itinerants established churches at such communities, made them part of the larger church organization, and

Episcopal church, Wichita, 1869. (The Kansas State Historical Society, Topeka)

provided superior sermons as well as a sort of inspection service for the larger organization. Yet the lowly community church, Methodist, Baptist, Presbyterian, or some other sect (such as Lutheran in a German settlement, Swedenborgian in a Swedish settlement, etc.), with its local parson, has been overlooked in most literature on the movement west.

Such churches sprouted all over the new country. Methodist settlers who had been exhorters or had done some preaching "back East" noticed the vacuum and announced that they would hold classes in their crude cabin homes. Often the Methodist circuit rider found a flourishing class already in existence, led by a local preacher or class leader. Thus Sunday services were held on a regular basis, even though the circuit rider might appear no more than half a dozen times a year. In time the country was so settled that a circuit rider was no longer necessary.

Other prolific church founders were, of course, the Baptists. American Baptists rightly date their church from the one founded by Roger Williams at Providence Plantation in 1639. Their growth was slow during the next century, for they were considered radical and were persecuted. A split in the most established churches, especially the Presbyterian and Congregational, following the Great Awakening of the 1730's, gave the Baptists an opening.* Groups that stressed emotionalism in personal

* The Great Awakening was an evangelical wave of religious fervor that affected the Atlantic seaboard and frontier settlements equally. Its emotionalism included repentance, prayer meetings, and hysterical manifestations. The Second Great Awakening is a term often applied to a similar wave that began in the 1790's, of which the Great Revival at Cane Ridge in 1801 represents a peak. The first awakening burned out with the coming of the French and Indian War; the second died down in the 1820's.

salvation separated from the main bodies of their churches and became independent, and many began to consider themselves Baptists.

These Separate Baptists began to increase with feverish rapidity in Virginia and North Carolina, where in 1760 they formed a loose organization, the Sandy Creek Association. They appealed to the poor settlers of the Piedmont, the preachers exhorting them in a cultivated "holy whine," a singsong mode of preaching which can still be heard on the radio of a Sunday morning in the Southern Bible Belt. The communicants indulged in all the excesses of the shakes, barks, falling exercises, rolling exercises, and speaking in tongues. Their great meetings antedated Cane Ridge by many years, but the very same religious excesses occurred at them. By the end of the American Revolution they were a well-established sect, very pro-patriot, becoming politically involved and pushing for religious liberty. By 1781 they had crossed the mountains; by 1785 there were eighteen Baptist churches in Kentucky and five or six in eastern Tennessee. And they multiplied mightily.

In fact, the Baptists, rather than the Methodists, were the most American church. Their government was an example of pure democracy, each congregation choosing its preacher and rewarding him for his efforts and sacrifices as it saw fit. It chose its elders; it passed moral judgment on its members; it accepted into membership those it wanted and rejected those it did not want; it decided when, how, and where to build its church edifice or whether to abandon it, pack up, and trek elsewhere like the Jews of old, headed for greener pastures. If a member desired to enter the ministry he "exercised his gifts" and preached. If the congregation judged him competent, he was "raised up" and given by the church a license to preach, which might embrace his own church or extend to the boundaries of the church association. Later, if successful, he could go through a more formal ceremony making him an "ordained" preacher and granting him the privilege of administering the sacraments.

Membership in loose organizations such as the Sandy Creek, Elkhorn, or South Kentucky associations represented very little loss of total freedom, and in fact the association existed more to strengthen the sect than to control the membership. Association membership implied agreement upon certain doctrinal concepts—"1st. That the Scriptures of the Old and New Testaments are the infallible word of God, and the only rule of faith and practice"—and included in the terms of membership that "each [church] may keep up their associational and church government as to them may seem best."[11]

The preachers were invariably farmers like their neighbors, men who may well have been illiterate, but who had had a religious experience and desired to carry the Good Word to mankind. Since their belief was strong that "one does not get to Heaven with a wet finger"—meaning a finger wetted to turn the pages of a book—there was actually a prejudice against educated preachers. Neither were they salaried, though a good preacher received aid in building his house or barn, planting or harvesting his crops, and occasionally—on his leaving or in the event of some family crisis—his communicants might take up a collection of thirty or forty dollars for him.

Often there were several licensed preachers in a given church. When these men of the cloth moved elsewhere they established new congregations, or, if they remained in a growing community, they would leave their home church and be instrumental in the founding of a new one. The itinerant preacher, whose character has suffered a good deal in fiction writing, was often a Baptist. His particular brand of Baptism might be Regular, Separate, United, General Particular, Primitive, or Free Will, but all were still Baptists. He was not like a Methodist circuit rider, who did possess some education and was somewhat held in tow by his church organization.

There can be no question that the churches of all denominations were a civilizing influence in the new country. If people were ardent believers, fearful for the destiny of their eternal souls, then to be expelled—"churched"—was a terrible thing, the Protestant equivalent of Catholic excommunication. It also carried with it a social stigma. Thus when a man or woman was charged with excessive drinking, adultery, quarreling, blasphemy, or shabby treatment of a brother member in a horse trade, and was ordered to appear and explain, many sobbed and repented. Charges were often ironed out in appearances before the deacons. Falsehood, bearing false witness, heresy, shrewishness, the disobedience of children to their elders, child neglect—these and other wanderings from the path of morality were examined and decisions and reprimands often made.

If a generalization can be made, most of the Protestant churches practiced a mild Calvinism, as demonstrated by their moral code and some emphasis on hard work, temperance, faith leading to success on earth combined with some Arminianism, which, of course, rejected predestination. Methodists took pride in being anti-predestinationists. The Presbyterians were a bit too stringent for the new country, save for one branch, the Cumberland Presbyterians, which broke away and practiced a faith that accepted emotionalism and enlarged the scope of human frailty and activity beyond the limitations of the Westminster Confession. Congregationalists tended to be too coldly intellectual for the rampaging West and did not fare so well.

What is disconcerting about the new country religion is the way it seemed to freeze as an effective social force, ceased offering a challenge, and hardened at so low an intellectual level. To quarrel over doctrine and split over money was common. To accept social responsibility in the realms of race, business, education, health, or community needs was the exception rather than the rule, and when such commitment was made, it was too often on the side of bigotry and prejudice. Many church organizations represented the limits to which the members were willing to go in any kind of unified endeavor. Any manifestation of government larger than the membership of a neighborhood church was anathema to them—an expression of the traditional American hatred of government in all its forms.

A good example of this is the case of the Anti-Mission Baptists. When some Baptist preachers began drives to raise money for missionary purposes, strong dissent arose among some of the Baptist churches in the new country, especially those congregations in which the people were poorly educated and out of touch with the usual cultural influences. This movement, they said, was un-Baptist; it was, they felt, the first move toward centralized control of their fiercely independent churches. Praiseworthy as it might be, they would have none of it.

Whatever their professed faith, the people of the new country took their beliefs seriously. The occasion of a camp meeting or the more sophisticated revival, which met in a formal church building but retained the nightly evangelical services, was reason for excitement. If nothing else, it represented a change in the humdrum of life. Sunday meetings with "dinner on the ground"; lusty singing with the leader "lining the hymn" (singing a line or two and the congregation repeating it until it was learned); the presence of a visiting divine such as the great Charles Grandison Finney or Alexander Campbell; a wedding; a funeral; a christening—all of these religious events were also social events for the congregations.

But in the vigorous three or four decades prior to the Civil War even the activities of the Baptists, Methodists, Campbellites, Presbyterians, Congregationalists, and other Sunday-go-to-meeting sects left reservoirs of unexpended energy. And it was, after all, a free country. The boundaries of acceptable religious behavior had never been fixed; on the contrary, the First Amendment to the Constitution implied that there were no limits. With no deterrent, therefore, save the disapproval of a society that was fluid, expanding, and new in a new country, the ground lay fertile for innovative, radically different religious movements. Shakers and Perfectionists, Rappites and Millerites who thought they knew the date of the Second Coming, all had their day. Established sects allowed

A camp meeting. (The Methodist Publishing House)

splinter groups and heresies to occupy many an hour of hot debate at ministerial conferences. Alexander Campbell persuaded ten thousand of Kentucky's Baptists to join the Disciples of Christ.

The most energetic and unstable religious activity centered in western New York. This was a "New England extended" area, rapidly changing but prosperous with the increased activity engendered by the construction of the Erie Canal. It had achieved settled country status by the 1820's, but it was still predominantly rural and agricultural. For the times it had a good educational system, and literacy among both men and women was high.

By and large the inhabitants there did not succumb to the extreme physical manifestations that characterized religious activities farther to the south. But in the way of the Yankee intellect they were nevertheless obsessed with religion; their enthusiasm would rise to a high pitch, then decline, but, upon the advent of some new preacher, rise once more. So often had their religious excitement burst into flame that people came to call the area the Burned-over District.

In their background was nearly two hundred years of Yankee religious development. From the rigorous faith of John Winthrop, who spoke of the Puritans as "a city upon a hill, the eyes of all people upon us," through the decades of harsh Calvinist theology, the period of decline, then the Great Awakening of the 1730's, and the continuing emphasis upon Puritan ideals of hard work, sobriety, and morality down into the nineteenth century, these Yankee people had preserved a strong interest in the Christian faith. Concepts of a new Zion, of a Second Coming, of the achievement of God's country on earth, had always been latent in the Puritan mind.

Changes in time and place resulted in new ideas, but they tended to grow out of these primary concepts. By the 1820's, as sociologist Thomas O'Dea has pointed out, there were four identifiable tendencies to be found in the fluid religious ideas rampant in the Burned-over District: sectarianism, ecumenism, communitarianism, and the recognition of human freedom and striving.[12] Present in addition to this was the frenzied, uncontrollable energy of a free people. Should they—or a segment of them—direct this uncontrolled enthusiasm in the support of a new sect, it could become a religion of great force, yet be substantially different from any other on earth. So strong was the Christian faith that any such group would, however, probably build upon the Judeo-Christian tradition. But whatever it added would be distinctly American and, granted the freedom of spirit in the new country, startlingly different.

When the new sect arose, it was founded and first led by a most American type, Joseph Smith, Jr. He was born to a New England couple whose farming-class antecedents went back to the 1630's and 1660's in Massachusetts. Grandfather Smith had moved to frontier Vermont, and it was there, in a crude but still Yankee society, that his son, Joseph Smith, Sr., grew up. He married a young woman née Lucy Mack, and the fourth of their children was a boy christened Joseph, Jr., born at the village of Sharon in 1805. In 1815 the family moved to the vicinity of Palmyra, New York, in the heart of the Burned-over District.

To earn money both Joseph and his father hired out as treasure-seekers, for Indian mounds abounded thereabouts and people were convinced that there was buried treasure in the region. In time Joseph became quite a necromancer, and thus further developed his already unusual imaginative powers. This work brought him to the farm of Isaac Hale, whose daughter Emma the future prophet married; with Emma soon pregnant, Joseph was confronted with a real need for income.

His solution was the publication of a religious book. This was an unusual recourse for a young husband of twenty-five, though not so much then as it would be now. He lived in a day when religion was for most people not only a testament of faith but entertainment, recreation, social intercourse, emotional outlet, and the limit of intellectual or philosophical activity. Many a youth in Joseph's day concentrated upon religion alone.

The young man had quite a story to tell, involving the appearance of angels, the uncovering of golden plates, and their translation with some "seeing stones." He came up with a narrative, the Book of Mormon, which purported to be the history of the family of Lehi, covering American history from 600 B.C. to 421 A.D. Whether the book—275,000 words, 522 pages in the most recent edition—was a manifestation of true faith and revelation or merely the product of a fertile and imaginative mind applying its capacities to Christianity, Indian mounds, and the Lost Tribes of Israel, it was quite an achievement for so young and poorly educated a man.

Mark Twain read a few pages of the Book of Mormon and pronounced it "an insipid mess of inspiration," and for nearly 150 years critics have made similar derisive statements. Such ridicule does not, however, answer the question of why three million Mormons believe in it, why it has been translated into dozens of languages, and why it has been such a force in the lives of men. The fact is that Mormonism succeeded when other sects failed partly because it possessed something the others did not have—a written narration, a canonical book.

In its fourteen books and an editorial note, the Book of Mormon relates the journey of Lehi, his wife Sariah, and their four sons from Jerusalem to the New World. Two of the sons, Laman and Lemuel, rebelled, and in time their descendants, called Lamanites, developed darker skins; their present descendants are the American Indians. These Lamanites caused a lot of trouble for the white descendants of the good son, Nephi. After many bloody battles the Angel Moroni, son of Mormon, the compiler of the plates, sealed them on the hill Cumorrah, convenient to Joseph Smith's home. There Joseph found them. The plates told the story of what happened to the good Nephites. The Book of Mormon also contains books relating the history of a land called Zarahemla, an editorial note entitled "The Words of Mormon," another book narrating the history of people called Jaredites, and finally the Book of Moroni in which some of Mormon's teachings and rituals are elaborated upon. The times were far too Christian for any faith to abandon Christianity, and the Mormon sect was no exception. It embraced a good deal of the Old Testament, some of the New, and had Lehi and his progeny, both good and bad, as descendants of the Hebrews. (Mormon success with the Indians was due in large part to their belief in a Hebraic Indian origin and the consequential desire to convert them.)

Within the framework of these strange tales of ancient and exotic peoples, presented in an awkward King James style, are the ideas, statements, concepts, and answers to contemporary questions which explain much of the book's attraction; they also place a "made in America" stamp on the work. And they point up, as Thomas F. O'Dea has said, the intellectuality of the book: "There is nothing obscure or unclear in its doctrine. . . . The revelation of The Book of Mormon is not a glimpse of higher and incomprehensible truths but reveals God's words to men with democratic comprehensibility."[13]

Moreover, as Alexander Campbell, who knew something about religion and had led his own flock into a new church, The Disciples of Christ, pointed out, the Book of Mormon committed itself ex cathedra on almost every religious controversy of the times: infant baptism, ordination, the trinity, regeneration, repentence, justification, the fall of man, the atonement, transubstantiation, fasting, penance, church government, religious experience, the call of the ministry, the general resurrection, eternal punishment, who may baptise, free masonry, republican government, and the rights of man. Many people feel insecure in the face of controversy; conversely they feel secure in the presence of positive stands. Surely this is especially true in the realm of faith. Mormonism provided such absolutes at a time of intense religious controversy, and this was one source of its strength.

The careful reader will also find in the Book of Mormon a strong link with the camp-meeting type evangelism of the new country. Repentance and redemption were the very hallmarks of frontier religion, and the problems of good and evil, the continuing circle of success and virtue, pride, fall, repentance, and righteousness restored, are clearly portrayed again and again. In the fourteen books are a number of sermons which have all the thumping impact of New England's brand of evangelism. There is a general sense of optimism, of a great future, of thanks to the Lord for the wonderful new country, and an assumption that the new land will be occupied—a Mormon equivalent to the concept of manifest destiny. The Puritan work ethic is likewise stressed; all Mormons work and there is no professional clergy. Eventually the Puritan element was extended, to the extent that a good Mormon does not touch alcoholic liquors, tea, or coffee; there is emphasis on family and on Puritan concepts of morality. What is lacking—and this too is a most American defect—is heady philosophy. The theological intricacies of the faith can be analyzed by scholars if they wish, but Mormonism was an earthy story, easily understood, for a simple and agrarian people.

Since the narration of the Book of Mormon stops in 421 A.D., it skips about fourteen hundred years of European history and then, with Smith's discovery of the golden plates, renews the story in America; this ignoring of Europe places an American stamp on the faith. Further, statements of democratic belief are sprinkled throughout the fourteen books. In 2 Nephi 10:11 we read: "And this land shall be a land of liberty unto the Gentiles, and there shall be no kings upon the land, who shall raise up unto the Gentiles." Further on in the same book we read: "For none of these iniquities come of the Lord; . . . and he denieth none that come unto him, black and white, bond and free, male and female; and he remembereth the heathen; and all are alike unto God, both Jew and Gentile" (2 Nephi 26:33). And in the Book of Mosiah (29:25-26): "Therefore, choose you by the voice of this people, judges, that ye may be judged according to the laws which have been given you by our fathers, which are correct, and which were given them by the hand of the Lord"; and "therefore this shall ye observe and make it your law—to do your business by the voice of the people." There are also references to such historic events as the coming of the Pilgrims and the American Revolution.

The Book of Mormon was published early in 1830 and on Tuesday, April 6th, the Church of Christ—the name was later changed to the Church of Jesus Christ of Latter-day Saints—was formally established. Joseph Smith was its absolute head. From the very beginning the church grew rapidly, although as a result of its insistence upon the sacredness of the Book of Mormon, its acceptance of Joseph Smith as the Prophet and, in turn, Smith's acceptance of this epithet, and its marked clannishness, the church also suffered persecution from the start. Here was a final test of the limits of religious freedom in America; for, aside from its peculiarities, the Mormon church was the ultimate institution for the religiously directed American, who, in the new country, was a wellspring of energy. If thousands joined this sect and expended their energies to its greater glory, what would prevent Mormonism from ultimately dominating America? And, with all that power, what could prevent the church from adopting unusual practices?

Smith exerted a pragmatic leadership which enabled his church to grow for the next fifteen years in spite of continual persecution, or possibly partly because of it. Persecution led the Mormons to gather unto themselves, to abandon secular society, thus setting up a progressive movement, for the more they kept together the more they changed and the more complex became the institution of Mormonism, its governance, its economic and social base. First to chilly Kirtland, Ohio, close to Lake Erie, then to Independence, Missouri, then to a community at Far West north-northeast of Independence, and finally to a segment of land jutting into the Mississippi on the Illinois side, the Mormons moved. At this last place they established the city of Nauvoo. Armed with a charter from the state that gave him great authority,

Joseph Smith reached the height of his power. By 1842 Nauvoo and its environs had a population of about 15,000 Saints.

This was just twelve years after the founding of the church, but in that period the sect had grown, been persecuted, suffered about forty casualties and lost hundreds of thousands of dollars in farmland, crops, livestock, and buildings. But the Saints persevered. Nor were they meek about it: they founded the Danites, a group of fighting men sometimes known as the Avenging Angels, and gave at times as much violence as they received.

For two more years, until his execution at the hands of a mob at the jail at Carthage, Illinois, on June 27, 1844, Joseph Smith continued to elaborate Mormon theology. By this time, besides The Book of Mormon, there was a growing source of Mormon practice embodied in the *Doctrine and Covenants* and *The Pearl of Great Price*, the latter including purported books of Abraham and Moses. Mormon ritual was made more sophisticated, with some portions kept secret save to Mormons in

Mormon version of persecution by gentiles. (Historical Department of the Church of Jesus Christ of Latter Day Saints)

Mormon emigrants circa 1879, exact location unknown; note the telegraph poles. (U.S. War Department General Staff, The National Archives)

Main Street, looking south, in Salt Lake City in the 1860's. The Mormons laid out their towns with wide streets. (Historical Department of the Church of Jesus Christ of Latter Day Saints)

good standing. And finally polygamy, rumored as a practice of the church almost from the beginning, was officially sanctioned: it came out in the open at Nauvoo. Once more the extent of religious freedom allowed by American society was tested; Joseph Smith was martyred, and the Saints, now led by Brigham Young, had to leave again.

Young was a natural leader of men, organizer, and administrator. Under his masterful guidance the Mormons advanced westward and settled on the western side of the Wasatch Mountains, close to the barren Great Salt Lake. The Quorum of Twelve, of which Young was president, continued to rule. The obvious danger of death by starvation or thirst in the parched Great Basin was now what kept the Mormon people working together; the previous reason, persecution, was temporarily lacking, since they had marched westward beyond their persecutors. Salt Lake City was laid out according to Joseph Smith's plans (which had been followed at Kirtland, Far West, and Nauvoo, though with some changes), and a temple was begun. New arrivals continued to appear, many from England and the Scandinavian countries. Some came in the 1850's pushing handcarts.

Meanwhile Mormon farmers mastered the ancient art of irrigation. Some Saints were sent along the migration trails to establish ferries at river crossings and charge what the market would bear, while others staked out ranches where springs issued forth and created lush meadows where grass could be harvested or livestock grazed. The hay could be sold to emigrants and a charge for grazing rights levied. Iron was smelted and even sericulture attempted. So independent, different, and self-supporting did they desire to be that a Mormon alphabet was created, though it was not successful.

Zion was, almost from the first, much more than just Salt Lake City. It is clear that the Saints envisioned a realm extending from Idaho and western Wyoming southwest all the way to southern California, a long line of settlement at least two hundred miles wide. Brigham Young had visions of an outlet to the sea in southern California, and later by way of the Colorado River and the Gulf of California. By now long forgotten, and fortunately so, are statements by Mormon leaders implying ambitions which embraced an early return to the site of the original Zion at Independence, Missouri, and hinted at even greater triumphs.* Such was the result of a free people expending their energies in a new country, concentrating upon the greater glory of a religious sect which itself was a product of the land of freedom. Their faith had gone beyond the lim-

* Independence is today the headquarters of the smaller Reorganized Church, which splintered off from the main body after Smith's death.

its of religious freedom in America, they had suffered and been forced to flee into the wilderness, and there had taken hold and flourished.

With what must have been to the Saints a shocking rapidity, the Mexican War and the California gold rush swept Zion right back into the mainstream of American life. Some gentiles settled in the Great Basin, even in Salt Lake City; the Territory of Utah was created. For a time affairs went smoothly, but in 1855 three bitterly anti-Mormon federal judges arrived, and troubles began anew. Charges and counter-charges fired emotionalism on both sides. Finally in 1857 an American army was sent to Utah to enforce federal authority there; serious bloodshed was narrowly averted. Mormon reaction was militaristic and violent. The whole situation was highly volatile, and one horrendous incident occurred. A California-bound wagon train, loosely known as the Fancher train but actually consisting of two parties, was betrayed and disarmed, then destroyed by Mormons and Indian allies at Mountain Meadows in southern Utah. Between 120 and 150 men, women, and older children were massacred in cold blood, while 18 smaller children or infants were spared.

This incident, which occurred on or about September 11, 1857, has been called the blackest day in Mormon history. Yet it also may mark a critical turning point for a movement which until then had thrived on persecution. Mormon hands were no longer clean; both sides had drawn blood—the gentiles at Haun's Mill in Missouri where, on October 29, 1838, seventeen Mormons were killed by a mob, and at the Carthage jail, and the Mormons now at Mountain Meadows. To wage warfare against the gentiles, who were backed by the federal government, was futile. Would not cooperation, some *modus vivendi*, work better? The Mormons tried it, and it did work; a hostile situation that could have resulted in a western civil war gradually faded away. For another generation, until 1890, the Mormons defended polygamy, but then, in the face of a Supreme Court ruling, they gave way. Thus did a religion, a society, a state, and *almost* a nation—a product of new country energy and freedom—accept life within the federal system.

While all of this was happening, the great majority of the Mormon people went about their tasks in peace. Toiling and sharing, they built clean villages that put the gentile's grubby frontier communities to shame. They dug thousands of miles of irrigation ditches and built reservoirs and dams. They trudged out into their sagebrush acres at dawn and pulled up the tenacious shrubs with the unpleasant odor and the spines that worked deep into the hands, until finally a few acres were cleared. They plowed and seeded and ran water in from the irrigation ditch, and the desert began to blossom. The Saints, working together, built Zion from sagebrush and sand. Historian Bernard De Voto's grandfather, Jonathon Dyer, was such a Mormon pioneer. What can be said about him? asked De Voto.

He was a first-class private in the march of America—a unit in the process that made and remade the nation. . . . he had raised seven children who, with their children, had merged with the frontier into the republic. . . . The earth was poisoned, and Jonathon made it sweet. It was a dead land, and he gave it life. Forever. Following the God of the Mormons, he came from Hertford [in England] to the Great American Desert and made it fertile. That is achievement.[14]

Joseph Smith had transformed the idea of manifest destiny into an image of the Kingdom of God, and Brigham Young saw to it that it embraced a massive area of land. There was a great deal of worldliness in Mormonism, which had direct relation to the pragmatism of American life. While they believed in the Second Coming of the Lord, and in heaven and hell, much of their attraction for potential converts, and their general success, lay in their ability to master the new country. The Mormons knew what to do with a fallow field, a forest, a lake or free-running Wasatch Mountain creek; with a stud horse, a prize bull, or a blooded lamb. They accepted authority because it produced satisfactory results. While heaven awaited the coming of the Elect, an irrigated field and a full granary supported the Saints on earth—and very well.

Thus one could argue that Mormonism succeeded because it was the most American of faiths, emphasizing equality, manifest destiny and a sense of mission (of which adventism was a part), worldliness, and a belief in hard work. Its group emphasis appealed to the lonely and alienated souls who comprised a noticeable percentage of Americans. Persecution, the result of their own cliquishness, the exotic beliefs which made the outward forms of their faith so different from all others, and finally, the practice of polygamy, brought them strength. Mormonism was also a most American faith in the mediocrity of its sermons and music. Mormons sang a lot, but most of their songs were old tunes with new words. They danced a lot and enjoyed sports, reflecting the growing American emphasis on the enjoyment of life. Their faith was, in truth, a product of unwashed, unrefined, rural America; it was a product of the new country.

Today a legend exists about schooling in the first fifty or sixty years of the nineteenth century: that school was held in a crude, one-room schoolhouse dominated by a schoolmaster who punished the rowdies and the slackers with a birch rod that raised red welts and disciplined the

Informally posed teacher and pupils grouped outside schoolhouse. Darkroom wagon of C. R. Monroe, traveling photographer, in background. Photo by Charles Van Schaick. (State Historical Society of Wisconsin)

lesser miscreant by propping him on a stool wearing a dunce cap. There is some accuracy in this. Sometimes the schools were abandoned cabins or even brush arbors, since the eight or ten weeks of schooling was often in the summer. The itinerant Irish, Scot, or English schoolmaster was likely to be an eccentric personage. Yet "spare the rod and spoil the child" was a widely accepted nineteenth-century aphorism, and an occasional birching was part of growing up. Probably the sadistic school-master was the exception to the rule. In any event, whether kind and capable or cruel and incompetent, he was boarded at the homes of the children and paid a pittance by their parents' contributions. This arrangement usually antedated the formal school district.

The fault in the one-room-schoolhouse-disciplinarian-schoolmaster legend lies in its aura of permanence; it was actually a rather short-term arrangement. Much of the new country filled up with startling rapidity, and as soon as it became settled country, the citizenry took steps toward improved educational facilities and better teachers. And well they might: when the Morrill Act land-grant colleges were established in the

1860's, one of their problems was finding adequately prepared students. Approximately one-fourth of the applicants, most of them from farm areas where they had been taught in one-room schoolhouses, were found to be unqualified for college work. Many were just barely literate. A further reason for the inaccuracy of the legend is that after the Civil War the schoolmaster gave way to the schoolmarm.

When a substantial county or village population existed, more sophisticated forms of local government and taxation arose to support the schools. However, the school tax was something new, and new taxes are always the ones most bitterly assailed. People wondered why they should be taxed to educate their neighbors' children. Others felt that private schools were best; for them, the common school (as the public schools were first known) had about it the aura of a pauper's school. Yet the common school rapidly made headway, especially during the equalitarian 1830's during which the West so prevailed upon national policies. By 1850 every state had a permanent school fund, the interest of which was used for school support, and a system of taxation for school maintenance. Such complete support had come about because of a general belief that "a school common to all, teaching a body of materials considered necessary to all, was vital to the maintenance of a healthy republic."[15]

With this public acceptance of the citizen's obligation to support the common schools (and by 1850 over 90 per cent of all schoolchildren were attending such schools) came a demand for better teachers and better texts. The teachers were usually hired by a community after being "examined" by a principal, a superintendent, or a school board; sometimes some kind of statement of good moral behavior was also required. Gradually statewide certification gained ground, and with it came higher requirements. As for textbooks, the total number available for reading, grammar, geography, arithmetic, bookkeeping, composition, surveying, history, logic and metaphysics, and moral philosophy jumped from 93 in 1804 to 407 in 1832, and the proliferation continued.

Yet of all those sources of knowledge, the *Readers* composed by William Holmes McGuffey are best remembered. Indeed, they were so successful—an estimated 122 *million* were sold between 1837 and 1920—that to them can be attributed a substantial share of the molding of nearly three generations of the American people in a common educational experience. What this means in terms of the homogeneity of a people brought together from different places and of many races is of extreme importance; it helped unify the new country.

The *Readers* are of particular interest here because McGuffey, a professor of ancient languages at Miami University in Ohio, compiled his texts for the students of the West and South—the new country. His *Readers* set out to teach spelling, enunciation, and grammar while at the same time providing enjoyable reading. They first appeared in 1837 and were an immediate success.

Altogether there were six *McGuffey Readers*. Their first contribution consisted of the simple but, at the time, unusual fact that they were graded. McGuffey accomplished this by reading to a group of children of different ages and noting what appealed to each age. Thus sorted, each set of texts was the basis for a graded *Reader*. In the *First* as well as the *Sixth Eclectic Reader* (as his texts were called), McGuffey challenged his students; he rarely "talked down" to them. When a selection contained unusual words the student would find at the end of the selection their pronunciation and meaning: "1. Em′ i-grāte, to *remove from one country or state to another for the purpose of residence, to migrate*," and so on.[16]

Finally, what of the content? The selections were products of the Victorian age, moralistic, sentimental, materialistic, worldly, and some of them morbid about death. Virtue was rewarded and sin punished. The Puritan work ethic appeared again and again:

> Work, work, my boy, be not afraid;
>   Look labor boldly in the face;
> Take up the hammer or the spade,
>   And blush not for your humble place.
>
> There's glory in the shuttle's song;
>   There's triumph in the anvil's stroke;
> There's merit in the brave and strong,
>   Who dig the mine or fell the oak.[17]

McGuffey's prose selections were arranged in sequences of paragraphs illustrating a theme. Selection XLIX of the *Fifth Eclectic Reader* was entitled "Behind Time"; it contained the story of a train wreck caused by the engineer being late, of the Battle of Waterloo lost because Marshal Grouchy failed to appear on time, a commercial house bankrupt because the money from California arrived too late, and a prisoner hanged because the messenger with the governor's pardon arrived—too late.[18]

There was religion in the *Readers*, but McGuffey avoided dogma and dry sermons; there was patriotism—Bancroft's description of the Boston Massacre, for example—but considerably fewer patriotic selections than our generation believes. Finally there was good prose and poetry that took the student out of backwoods Indiana or Iowa or the plains of

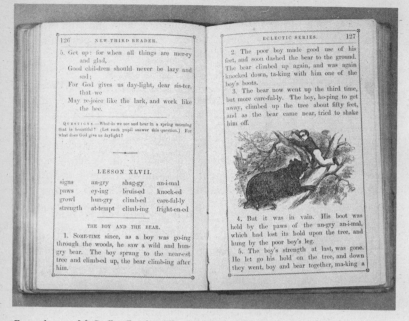

Pages from a McGuffey Reader. The Protestant ethic is apparent in the lines at the top of page 126. (Miami Collection, Miami University)

Texas and carried him all over the world and into all periods of history. There was Southey's "The Battle of Blenheim," Bryant's "The Death of the Flowers," Washington Irving's description of a thunderstorm, a description of "The Relief of Lucknow" from the London *Times*, the play *William Tell*, and even the old rhymes about "The Blind Men and the Elephant."

One hundred and twenty-two million copies, 1837-1920: the *Readers* made their mark. They were, Hamlin Garland reminisced, "almost the only counterchecks to the current of vulgarity and baseness which ran through the talk of the older boys, and I wish to acknowledge my deep obligation to Professor McGuffey, whoever he may have been, for the dignity and literary grace of his selections. . . ."[19]

Between the common schools, which were essentially grade schools, and the colleges, there were Latin schools in the East in the colonial period, but at first little or nothing west of the Appalachians. In the early 1800's the academy came into vogue and remained until the public high school replaced it, for the most part after the Civil War. There were many academies in the new country; they were usually private, being either sectarian or simply owned by an ambitious pedagogue; usually they were chartered by states, charged tuition, and ranged in scholastic standards from a few good ones to the majority of poor ones. There were female academies (as they were called) and military academies, academies teaching all grades through the second year of college. Some states granted them the right to stage lotteries to raise money— and more than a few times pedagogue and lottery money vanished with no academy in sight. If men with rudimentary educations had nothing else to do, they formed academies. Many a successful minister felt that an academy bearing such a name as Wesleyan, Asbury, Cokesbury, Ebenezer, or Bethel should be an adjunct to his church building. In 1840 North Carolina had 140 academies with 4,400 students and Alabama had 114 with 5,018 students; in 1860 Alabama had 206 with 10,778 pupils. The Tennessee legislature chartered twenty-seven county academies in the year 1806 alone.

The demise of the academies was slow, but as the public gradually accepted the concept of tax-supported education the high schools made increasingly rapid headway; by 1880 there were 800 public high schools and by 1900 there were 6,000. Yet in spite of all the weaknesses of the academies, they represented some sense of obligation to the young for education beyond the three R's on the part of the new country people (though high schools were prolific in the East also), and they did assure the ambitious student an education beyond the common school, should he really desire it.

Neither the common school nor the academy was a product of the new country, although both took hold and thrived there. The American four-year-college, on the other hand, developed primarily in the West. It was usually sectarian and may be described as a concomitant of denominational competition. So many were started—one authority places the number at 516 prior to the Civil War—that the term "neighborhood colleges" is almost acceptable for them. Of that number just 104, or about 19 per cent, became permanent institutions. Why so many begun, and why so heavy a mortality?

Part of the reason was the impact of the western movement upon the more staid society of the East. Such intellectuals as Timothy Dwight and Edward Everett deplored the population drain of their New England. Dwight predicted dire consequences when the political power of those "restless inhabitants . . . whose vanity persuades them that they are wise and prevents them from knowing they are fools"[20] was felt in

Washington. The solution, in the minds of many Easterners, was active
financial and missionary aid to these western people. "It is plain," said
Everett, "that this extraordinary rapidity of increase requires extraordinary means, to keep the moral and intellectual growth of the people
on an equality with their advancement in numbers and prosperity."[21]

The aid was forthcoming, and there was a proliferation of western
colleges. Yale and its graduates are said to have had a guiding hand in
establishing sixteen of them in the name of orthodox Congregationalism,
and Princeton, in the name of Presbyterianism, twenty-five. The new
country people, usually led by local divines but strongly backed by town
speculators who saw prosperity and growth in the existence of a college
nearby, led the campaigns. The most common contribution of the local
gentry was that which was most plentiful: land. If the land included the
highest hilltop around, so much the better.

With the land donated, the next task, and the harder one, was raising
money for the construction of a single building, finding a faculty that
would teach for a pittance (and often preach on Sundays), and corral-
ling a student body. It was in raising money that the Westerners especially looked to the East. The more successful college presidents or
boards of trustees preyed upon the fears of their eastern brethren, with
a "save yourself by saving us" attitude. In the years just prior to the
Panic of 1837 this argument was very successful. With the Panic, and
the consequential drying up of funds, a number of colleges closed their
doors. The peak of college founding was in the 1850's, but again the depression of 1857 put a number of them out of business.

After the Panic of 1837 some eastern elements made an appraisal of
their western colleges and discovered that there had been much duplica-
tion and waste. To prevent it—and to a degree, they did succeed—they
organized the Society for the Promotion of Collegiate and Theological
Education in the West, which attempted to restrain new country enthusiasm and channel eastern funds more wisely. Simultaneously various Home Mission Societies sent into the West educated preachers who
rounded out their meager salaries by teaching Greek and Latin, ethics,
and political economy at local denominational colleges; many of them
were well educated and thus raised standards.

There were factors other than economic jeopardizing the lives of new
country colleges. Competition, poor location (for reasons of health as
well as population), catastrophes such as fires (which were very common), and dissension in matters of faith and teaching were all common
sources of weakness. Transylvania College, by far the most successful
early institution of higher learning west of the mountains, lost its pres-

University of Minnesota, 1889. (Minnesota Historical Society)

tige through religious controversy. A fire which destroyed a college's one and only building often destroyed the institution also, for no incentive arose to replace it. Nor was it always easy to assemble a tuition-paying student body, and rowdyism—such as removing all the doorknobs—was common. Yet for all this the colleges made a distinct contribution to the intellectual life of the new country, demonstrated by the substantial percentage which kept their doors open and became permanent institutions.

State universities originated in the South; Georgia was the first to enact a charter, its legislature passing the act on January 27, 1785. It justified its course on the grounds of support of the principles of religion and morality. The first state university to be operational was the University of North Carolina, which opened in 1795; the University of Tennessee likewise claims an early beginning. The University of Michi-

Hunting party, Jewell County, Kansas, 1888. (The Kansas State Historical Society, Topeka)

Fun in the new country: a horse race down the main street of Gunnison, Colorado in the 1880's. (Duane Vandenbusche Collection)

gan, a temporary victim of the classical revival, was established in 1817; the chartering act called it a *catholepistemiad* with thirteen *didaxiim*— or professorships.

In the 1840's a movement got under way for the establishment of colleges devoted to the agricultural and mechanical arts, to be supported by federal land grants. Today the two areas of learning do not seem affiliated, but a century and more ago the farmer was a jack-of-all-trades and the term "mechanical arts" covered many of his tasks. This movement culminated in the passage of the Morrill Act of 1862, by which a total of 16,000 square miles of the public domain was granted to the states on the basis of 30,000 acres to each state for each representative and senator it sent to Congress, the proceeds from the sale of the land to be used for establishing agricultural and mechanical (A & M) colleges. Twenty-eight states established such colleges under the act, many of them in new country areas where such federal aid was greatly appreciated.

The sum total of new country education—common schools, academies, colleges and universities plus a few manual labor schools and the numerous Sunday schools in which Scripture was learned by rote—adds up to a massive, though unstructured, drive toward producing a literate citizenry. By our standards today the education it provided may appear wooden and uninspired. But its accomplishment, which was nothing less than an instant, viable educational system in a new country where everything needed to be done at once, was tremendous.

The Puritan work ethic plus the great tasks to be accomplished left, it would seem, little time for recreation in the new country. True, the people did work hard, but they played hard too. The men and boys looked forward to hunting excursions after the harvest was in. So, too, was fishing a principal sport of the new country. Horse racing, shooting matches, and card playing were common forms of gambling.

All sections had annual celebrations, most of them on the Fourth of July. Local talent competed in local tournaments or contests: hard-rock mining in the Rocky Mountains, for example, or birling and other specialties of lumberjacks in timbered areas. At other times there were corn-shucking contests, watermelon-eating tournaments, and the like. Women had their sewing bees, church dinners, and choir practices. Marriage, with the accompanying shivaree, could be a raucous occasion. Even funerals ended in big family dinners or, in cowboy country, in a horse race from the graveyard to the nearest saloon. Halloween from earliest times included such high jinks as the buggy in the hayloft and the privy on the schoolteachers' front yard. An occasional circus, the county fair, and, in later years, a traveling Tom show could add to the interest of life.

It was, after all, the Victorian era in the new country as elsewhere; yet the exuberance of an optimistic and energetic people barely restrained itself within the tight bonds of correct society. In the balance, the new country people had a good society, and good times, too.

VII
The Urban Frontier

In terms of the span of recorded history the conquest of the American wilderness from 1776 to 1890 is an incredibly short period of frenzied activity. Its aim was nothing less than building a wilderness into a civilization equal to the civilization of western Europe or its counterpart, the states of the settled country on the eastern seaboard. This activity was as multifaceted as the human condition of the times was complex, and its goal was an instant civilization. What is perhaps more significant is the existence in the new country of men who could earn their livelihood at all of the tasks necessary to bring that civilization about; many never planned to be involved in agricultural pursuits, and when they advanced into the wilderness they were bound for communities, settlements, urban places, no matter how crude. Their destinations could have been as rustic as Boonesboro, as old as Vincennes or Kaskaskia, St. Augustine or Santa Fe, or as metropolitan as New Orleans, St. Louis, Denver, or San Francisco.

Regardless of size, the little stations, small towns, and cities grew with —as a part of—the settling process. There is really no mystery about this. It would be reason for discussion if urban centers had not arisen. Yet the historians of the American frontier have consistently ignored these urban places in their narrations of the developing new country; and this failure to take the cities into account has contributed to a distorted view of the American move West.

This omission demands some explanation. Why is it that Frederick Jackson Turner failed to mention cities until late in his career, when he is quoted as suggesting a need for urban history? Why is it that not one of the half dozen or so college texts in the history of the American frontier makes an issue of the urban centers? Only one such book, in a recent edition, devotes as much as a single chapter to the urban frontier.[1] This is commendable, even though the chapter consists of a mere chron-

icling of the early history of a few great cities of the trans-Mississippi
West, and there is no attempt made to explain the role of the city in
the growth of the new country. It would appear that the principal reason for the failure to discuss cities is a certain romanticism, a love of the
unusual and exotic. The majority of the population, which resides in
towns and cities, finds them dull. Problems of water supply, sewage,
streets, lighting, fire prevention, and law enforcement are details of administration, none of which fire the imagination. But the wide open
spaces do.

Still another explanation has to do with the fact that the nineteenth
century was a period of explosive population increase all over the world,
a concomitant of which was the phenomenal growth of cities. The phenomenon did not, therefore, represent a peculiarity of the new country—
save for the fact that many of its cities started from scratch. But the
conquering of a last vast temperate-zone country uninhabited and unoccupied by western man—that *was* a matter of interest.

In 1776 the wilderness west to the Pacific was already spotted with the
first signs of the disease that would destroy it: urbanization. St. Louis
had been established for more than a decade, the Sieur de Bienville had
founded New Orleans in 1718, and the Spanish had located at San Antonio in the same year. Santa Fe dated back to 1609, Vincennes to 1702.
Cadillac, a French administrator, founded Detroit in 1701, and in 1703
the Jesuits established Kaskaskia and started a college there. Cahokia
began in 1699 as a small French Catholic mission founded by priests
from the Seminary of Foreign Missions at Quebec. Fort Pitt, which had
started out as Fort Duquesne in 1753, had by 1776 residences outside
its walls, portents of the city that would grow at the forks of the Ohio.
Fort Fincastle, later Fort Henry, was chartered as the town of Wheeling
in 1806. In 1775 Daniel Boone forgot about surveying and hunting long
enough to establish Boonesborough, which was but one of several Kentucky stations in existence in 1776. Add the towns of the more sedentary Indians such as the Five Civilized Tribes of the Southeast, the missions of the Spanish in the extreme Southwest including San Francisco,
Monterey, San Diego, and San Francis Xavier at present Tucson, plus
the previously Spanish communities at Pensacola and St. Augustine in
Florida; add the fur-trading posts, first of the French and then of the
British in the Great Lakes country, such as Niagara and St. Joseph, and
it becomes clear that a sprinkling of population centers already existed
across the length and breadth of the United States-to-be, even in 1776.

One hundred and fourteen years later—that is, in 1890, when the
census considered the frontier at an end—the new nation was peppered

with urban centers, villages, towns, and cities small and large. In 1790 the first decennial census gave the new nation nineteen towns with a population in the 2,500-10,000 range; the eleventh census in 1890 listed 994 such towns. The 1790 census listed five cities with a population of 10,000 to 50,000; a hundred years later there were 296 such cities. By then there were also forty-seven medium-sized cities with a population of 50,000 to 250,000, eight "large" cities with 250,000 to 1,000,000 inhabitants, and three "great" cities with over a million. Needless to say, there were none in the last three categories in 1790, and just one in the smallest of the three in 1800. Not until 1840 was there a single "large" city; not until 1880 a "great" city, although ten years later there were three of them. It is interesting to note that the decade of greatest increase was 1840-50, during which the number of towns nearly doubled (from 94 to 174), and the number of medium-sized cities more than doubled, from four to nine.

There are few surprises in the origins of these cities. Speculators and their grandiose plans lay behind most of America's urban centers. These moneyed men, controlling massive areas of land, studied their plats and retained certain sites for themselves, sites which, due to naturally favorable locations, held great promise for the growth of successful communities. Thus in 1787 did the Reverend Manassah Cutler, representing the Ohio Company of Associates, peruse an early map of Ohio and observe an inset of a city to be built at the mouth of the Muskingum River where the company had set aside 6,000 acres for "a city and commons." In the spring of 1788 a party of New Englanders under the leadership of Rufus Putnam, who was superintendent of the group under the auspices of the Ohio Company, arrived there. They found that the long-gone Mound Builders had preceded them in using the site for a town. Putnam took advantage of the earthen changes that had been made by the earlier inhabitants by using their processional way as a wide street; he preserved for the public lands on the river and laid out blocks of land for settlers. Today Marietta, Ohio, reflects its New England ancestry as well as the wise town planning of Rufus Putnam.

In 1773 Captain Thomas Bullitt of Fauquier County, Virginia, laid out a town near the present Municipal Bridge in Louisville, Kentucky. Subsequent Indian troubles prevented his plan from materializing, but Bullitt's choice was a good one, for it lay on the Kentucky side of the Falls of the Ohio where boatmen would be landing. Then in 1778 George Rogers Clark came down the Ohio with about 160 soldiers, headed for the British outposts in the Ohio country; Clark was accompanied by about twenty families of emigrants. He landed the whole entourage on an island in the Ohio, constructed cabins and blockhouses,

By 1846 Louisville was a settled, prosperous city. (U.S. Bureau of Public Roads, The National Archives)

and planted corn—which gave the place its name: Corn Island. (It has long since been swept away by Ohio flood waters.)

In June Clark and his men shoved off, leaving the settlers behind on the island. He and his men subsequently captured Kaskaskia, Cahokia, and Vincennes. In the fall of 1778, with the Indians cowed temporarily, he sent word to the families on Corn Island to go ashore on the Kentucky side; there they constructed a blockhouse dubbed "Fort-on-Shore." By April of 1779 the little community agreed upon a simple town plan which included streets and about 116 half-acre lots, which were distributed by chance on April 24. When Clark returned shortly thereafter he laid out a much more sophisticated plat for a town. By 1780 it had perhaps 100 settlers. In that year the Virginia assembly passed an "Act for Establishing the Town of Louisville at the Falls of the Ohio"; the name honored King Louis XVI of France, for that nation had given aid to the Americans.

Cincinnati was the winner among three embryo communities all situated at or near the confluence of the Big or Little Miami rivers and the Ohio. Columbia was founded by a speculator named Benjamin Stites and others at the confluence of the Little Miami and Ohio rivers; Losantiville—the name is described as "a curious mixture of Greek, Latin, and French supposed to represent *the city opposite the mouth of the*

Licking,"[2] which flowed in on the Kentucky side—was founded by a speculator named Mathias Denman, close to Columbia; and finally, on the Big Miami, the land promoter John Cleves Symmes founded North Bend. Cincinnati grew out of Losantiville and absorbed Columbia; in 1790 the absurd name was changed to Cincinnati in honor of the politically prestigious Revolutionary War veterans organization, the Society of the Cincinnati. The city was a purely speculative enterprise, laid out unimaginatively in a grid pattern that ignored more practical plans suggested by the terrain. When the Queen City of the West (as it was later known) became the seat of Hamilton County and had the economic, if not the social, good fortune of having Fort Washington erected nearby, its success was assured.

Up on the Tennessee River a frontiersman-speculator named James White constructed a log house in 1786, added three guest houses, and connected them with a stockade, so that by 1788 his residence and adjoining cabins were known as White's Fort. Three years later, in cooperation with William Blount, a town with sixteen blocks and sixty-four lots was surveyed and christened Knoxville in deference to the political sagacity that understands the massive egos of public men. In this case the honored one was Major General Henry Knox, Washington's secretary of war, who sanctioned the establishment there in 1793 of a blockhouse and small garrison. A painting made more than a century later (in 1901) by an artist named Lloyd Branson depicts not only White's Fort but also two signs tacked onto the stockade: Gay Street and Main Street. It is unlikely that such signs existed, but in placing them there on a corner of the stockade the artist certainly depicted James White's aspirations. The streets became thoroughfares in the proposed town and remain today the principal arteries in Knoxville.

Marietta, Louisville, Cincinnati, Knoxville, and hundreds of other aspiring communities on the frontier possessed many similarities. Contrary to what is perhaps common belief, they did not "just grow"—they were planned, surveyed, and then platted in an unimaginative grid of streets laid down north and south, east and west, at right angles. The towns were invariably speculative enterprises. The plats usually anticipated a common, or square, sometimes a public promenade along a river or lakefront, and depicted highways entering and leaving. Unfortunately, speculative mania usually gobbled up the promenades, and often the squares were victims of the same disease. In only a few instances were there remaining signs of aesthetic considerations, or an attempt to blend streets with the terrain. That sameness that irritated Toqueville so much about America was ever-present in the common grid-type layout of so many towns and cities. It is still so.

Map of Westervelt, Goodhue County, Minnesota, 1857. (Minnesota Historical Society)

Some towns did provide for a progressive increase in the size of lots as one worked out from the center, a kind of early-nineteenth-century ancestor of modern suburbia, with individual house lots gradually blending into farmland. This was done in Joseph Ellicott's plans for Buffalo and in Brigham Young's Salt Lake City, to mention just two examples. Speculators often held onto strategic lots which, with success, would yield enormous unearned increment, while they made business lots so attractive, even giving them away upon the promise of construction and opening of a business, that prospective bankers, printers, blacksmiths, and general storekeepers submitted to such enticements and came to settle.

Once in a while speculators do appear to have possessed some sense of the aesthetic. John Overton and General James Winchester laid out Memphis with an initial 362 lots, with wide north-south and east-west streets and four squares: Auction, Court, Exchange, and Market. They even provided initially for a promenade along the summit of the bluff overlooking the Mississippi; for Memphis, after all, was at the site of one of the famous Chickasaw Bluffs. Thomas Jefferson's plan for Jeffersonville, across the Ohio from Louisville, provided that each alternating square should be perpetually devoid of man-made construction, and every house would face outward upon such a square. He felt that such a town would be free of the miasmas that brought so much disease and death to most crowded communities. Alexander Ralston, who had worked for Pierre L'Enfant in designing Washington, D.C., laid out Indianapolis according to a design that shows the influence of his mentor. Circleville, Ohio, was ambitiously planned as a circle tangent to a square. Detroit began with a plat calling for many triangles. And finally, there was a charm to the New England villages that proliferated across the northern counties of Ohio, Indiana, Illinois, and Iowa and southern Michigan. They were geometrically simple, always with a common, but their elm-shaded streets, white churches with steeples rising simply toward the blue sky, and general neatness and calmness, created a pleasing impression.

Some communities did, however, grow spontaneously. The site of Chicago, on Lake Michigan at the head of a portage to interior Illinois and the Mississippi Valley, was a meeting-place of Indian trails long before the white man arrived. In the winter of 1682-83 La Salle built a stockade there; a century later a Frenchman named Jean-Baptiste Point Sable had a fur-trading establishment there. In 1795, in the Treaty of Greenville, General Anthony Wayne exacted from the Indians "one piece of land six miles square at the mouth of the Chikago river, emptying into the south-west end of Lake Michigan. . . ."[3] By 1804 Fort Dearborn was constructed and occupied, with an Indian agency and a factory (trading post) attached; by 1805 Ebenezer Belknap, a Connecticut Yankee, was managing the factory there. Soon other traders, notably one John Kenzie, arrived and set up their cabins and stores outside the stockade. Before long several farmers had established themselves nearby, so that by the outbreak of war in 1812 there must have been a dozen cabins and forty or fifty people, not including Indians, in the settlement. In 1812 the fort was abandoned, and a massacre of the departing inhabitants ensued a mile and a half away—soldiers, civilian

This was Chicago in 1831. (U.S. Bureau of Public Roads, The National Archives)

men who had formed a militia, women, and children, about a hundred
in all, though a few survived—while all but the magazine of the fort was
destroyed. It was rebuilt in 1816. A vigorous Indian trade arose again,
which was soon dominated by John Jacob Astor's American Fur Company. Although the trade declined in the 1820's and the garrison was
withdrawn between 1823 and 1828, a tiny community continued to
exist. In 1831 Cook County was created by the state legislature (Illinois
had achieved statehood in 1818) and Chicago was named a county seat.
The year before, the town had been platted by a civil engineer, James
Thompson, in anticipation of growth that would result from the digging of the Illinois and Michigan Canal. In the autumn of 1833 a jail
was built. Black Hawk's War in 1832, a tragic incident involving the
Sauk and Fox Indians in northwest Illinois, turned national attention
to the Old Northwest; Chicago profited by the publicity as well as by

Currier & Ives lithograph of Chicago in 1892. (Courtesy Chicago Historical Society)

the influx of soldiers and refugees. The population of 40 to 50 in 1830 rose to 4,470 in 1840, 29,963 in 1860, nearly 300,000 by 1870, and by 1890, 1,100,000. In a century of phenomenal urban growth, even in the world's fastest-growing nation, Chicago's rise was simply incredible. To paraphrase an old saying, you can't keep a good location down. A good location? The site was swampy and wet, cold in winter and full of insects in summer. But it was strategic, and that made most of the difference. Such boosters as William B. Ogden, Philip Armour, and Cyrus McCormick aided Chicago's growth in many ways. Most especially was Ogden's contribution important in making the city a transportation center.

Ogden was a New Yorker who was already a successful businessman when he went to Chicago in June 1835. He was its first mayor, and from the beginning was a heavy investor in Chicago real estate. Realizing that the key to the city's future lay in transportation, he led the way in promoting railroads that would aid Chicago. He was president of a Pacific

Railway Convention that met at Philadelphia in 1850, organizer of the
Chicago and Northwestern, and first president of the Union Pacific. He
was also active in promoting canal and waterway development. He profited immensely, of course, from the policies he shaped and promoted.

San Francisco is also a city which grew naturally from the shores of
the magnificent bay and the Golden Gate. Writing in 1776, Fray Pedro
Font, Juan Bautista de Anza's diarist, described the harbor as "a prod-
igy of nature." From the cliff at Fort Point (as it is known today; it is
the northernmost point of the San Francisco Peninsula, and is within
the Presidio) the men gazed down upon the sea and observed spouting
whales, schools of dolphins or tuna, sea lions, and sea otters. Near their
camp deer grazed. Healthful herbs were discovered amidst the dense
shrubbery. Indeed, wrote the Father, "the port of San Francisco is a
marvel of nature, and might well be called the harbor of harbors."[4]

Yet its potential was not to be realized until the Americans half a
century later swept into what for them was new country. Neither the
presidio nor the mission founded by the Spanish flourished, the former
because it was on the fringe of a declining empire, and the latter because of poor soil and lackadaisical Indian wards. When ships did pay
a visit, they usually dropped anchor in a protected place the Spanish
had named Yerba Buena Cove, which is where the city of San Francisco, as apart from the military and religious installations, got its start.
In 1836 the hide-and-tallow ship carrying Richard Henry Dana as one
of its crew put in there; he described the town of Yerba Buena as "a
newly begun settlement, mostly of Yankee Californians . . . which
promises well."[5] Five years later it was visited by detachments of Lieutenant Charles Wilkes' U.S. naval exploring expedition. Although
whalers and hide-and-tallow ships were frequenting the bay more often,
they found Yerba Buena still a settlement hardly deserving the designation of town. There was the Hudson's Bay Company building; a
store run by Nathan Spear; a grog shop sporting a billiard table; William
Hinckley's hotel, made of the poop cabin of a ship; a blacksmith shop;
and assorted outbuildings—perhaps twenty buildings in all. Yerba Buena
—"good herbs"—had a long way to go.

Yet even then the town was obviously growing. The *alcalde* (a mayor,
justice of the peace, and sheriff all in one) was prompted in 1839 to
commission a local Frenchman, Jean Jacques Vioget, to survey the area
and lay out streets, designating such property as was already owned.
Thus was fixed the pattern of San Francisco, and the streets later named
Montgomery, Grant, and Sacramento became identifiable. A few years
later, in 1845, the town plat was doubled by extending the length of the

streets. In the previous year had come the first government building, the custom house. Yerba Buena was on its way.

On July 9, 1846, Captain John B Montgomery of the U.S.S. *Portsmouth* landed and took possession for the United States. He named one of his officers, Lieutenant Washington A. Bartlett, as the new American *alcalde*. Bartlett ordered the survey of the town extended once more. In most instances the streets were once again lengthened, though a notable departure from Vioget's plan was the creation of Market Street. Many of the streets received names which have been retained to the present. In the January 30, 1847, issue of the *California Star*, the town's first newspaper (founded by Sam Brannan, a Mormon who had led 238 Mormons to California by sea in 1846) was the announcement that henceforth the settlement would be known as San Francisco.

The town was growing on the strength of whalers, hide-and-tallow boats, and trade with the ranches of the back country. Settlers and American officials sensed its future greatness, but no one could have envisioned the changes wrought by the gold discovery at John Sutter's sawmill. With the deluge of Forty-niners the town became the liveliest settlement on the eastern side of the Pacific. There was one period in which for several months the population doubled every ten days. The newcomers bustled from tented saloon to false-fronted hotel to one-story offices of lawyers, assayers, quacks, and small merchants. There was dust or mud and continual discomfort, which seemed to be forgotten in the feverish excitement of the populace.

By 1850 San Francisco had 35,000 inhabitants; by 1860 about 57,000; in 1870 nearly 150,000; in 1880 235,000; and 300,000 by 1890. Its mixed population included Chinese, Malays, Mexicans, Peruvians, Hawaiians, Indians (from India), Russians, French, Germans, English, and the predominant Americans. Not only did it make fantastic gains in population, it suffered all the ills of cities, but crowded into a concentrated period of time. San Francisco's first depression came in 1853-54 when the placers in the mining areas gave out. Business declined, and unemployed miners flocked to the city. Then prosperity returned with the discoveries of the Comstock Lode in Nevada, from which more than $300 million worth of precious metals was extracted in a twenty-year period. The city was the great entrepot for those fabulous mining centers of the Washoe: not only was finance capital furnished by the city's businessmen, but everything needed for mining and smelting, and supplies for the population working in the Nevada towns was shipped over the Sierras from San Francisco.

Mining is a highly speculative industry, and the city by the Golden Gate, as the center of mining investments, suffered from gambling and

By 1851 San Franciscans were boasting of their new and impressive streets and buildings. From *Gleason's Pictorial*. (Well Fargo Bank, San Francisco)

San Francisco in the 1850's. (Wells Fargo Bank, San Francisco)

speculation, from booms and busts, wild rumors, runs on banks, and bank failures. San Francisco contained probably the most gullible populace in the world in those early decades. It was there that two con men, Philip Arnold and John Slack, persuaded the city's best financiers of the validity of a diamond mine in a secret spot in the western mountains or deserts, sold their own "interests" for $600,000, and then left town. In late 1872 the hoax was exposed. "Philip Arnold had found investors willing to believe absolutely anything," wrote A. J. Liebling. "He left them willing to believe not quite everything. . . . The Age of Innocence was over."[6] Well, almost over. The San Francisco financier William C. Ralston also invested in such harebrained schemes as sericulture and tobacco growing before his own Bank of California failed in 1875.

The 1870's were bad times for California as well as for the rest of the country, and the experience of several years of depression probably did act as a kind of catharsis, purging many a fool from the ranks of the heavy investors. There was as well frustration in San Francisco because the completion of the transcontinental railroad failed to bring to California the anticipated immigration. Speculators inland went bankrupt. And there was irritation at the failure of the Central Pacific to come to the bay area: it stopped at Sacramento. Even worse, goods for the interior now came in increasing quantities west via the railroad rather than east from San Francisco. With the eighties came more stability, for the boosters of the city had been correct: it did become the great port city of the eastern Pacific.

Besides its boom-and-bust existence, San Francisco suffered from racial violence, crime, and fires during these early years. The Chinese had evoked some hostility from the very first years of the gold rush, but when depression struck and the city filled with unemployed laborers, the smoldering antagonism burst into flames. From the 1850's into the 1880's there were sporadic eruptions of anti-Chinese feeling. First a rabble-rouser named James d'Arcy, then an Irishman named Dennis Kearney, led the mobs. They wrecked Chinese laundries and other property, physically abused the Celestials, and cut off their queues. A city that was half wooden buildings and half tents was sure to suffer conflagrations, especially when open cooking fires and whale oil lamps were the rule; there were six major fires between 1848 and 1851. Soon efficient volunteer fire companies were formed, the water supply was improved, and solid brick and stone structures began to replace the inflammable wooden ones.

Some of the fires were started by the criminal elements of the city. San Francisco's underworld was as polyglot as its respectable population, but escaped criminals from the penal colonies of Australia constituted one of the more common types. The thugs congregated in a section known as the Barbary Coast, but their activities threatened the entire city. One group, the Hounds, was organized in semi-military fashion, and made nocturnal raids on the city's poorer foreign colonies. Corrupt city government seemed incapable of handling the situation. It is in considering this problem and how it was handled that we become aware of the difference between San Francisco and other new country cities. Twice in the 1850's the better elements—what we would today call the Establishment—formed vigilance committees and in a most business-like manner reestablished law and order, then disbanded. Such actions were unusual and the efficiency, group solidarity, and integrity of the participants indicates a quality of citizenry far above that of most new country cities. There were other indications of unusual leadership among the city's better elements. The volunteer fire departments, for example, competed with respect to who had the finest equipment and constructed brick and stone firehouses with living quarters as posh as a gentlemen's club.

Literacy must have been high. By the mid-1850's there were a dozen daily newspapers, plus weeklies; there were already French- and German-language newspapers. San Francisco was known as a good theater town as early as the mid-fifties. By 1854 there were two libraries in the city, two historical societies, and the California Academy of Sciences. These are signs of an active civic pride, of organizational ability surmounting personal interests, and of a cultural atmosphere—all of which was substantially above the level of the typical new country city. Some of it may be attributed to the enormous wealth that was concentrated in San Francisco, but this does not quite answer the question, why this good leadership? It would seem that the populace was in some way different from that of the rest of the new country. The difference was one of degree, but it was sufficient to give San Francisco a distinction, a character all of its own.

One explanation has to do with distance. By comparison with new country cities of the South or the Middle West, San Francisco was a long way from the settled country. Between the lower Missouri River towns and the Golden Gate lay eighteen hundred or more miles of high plains, mountains, and deserts. Until 1869 the only way to traverse this expanse was in ox-, mule-, or horse-drawn conveyance, or on muleback or horseback. The announced duration of the Butterfield stage run from Tipton, Missouri, to San Francisco was twenty-six days. The distance was 2,700 miles, and the cost ranged from $150 to $200.

To go the 15,000 miles by way of Cape Horn cost, for passage alone, $250 to $600 and required, even aboard the beautiful clipper ships, 90 to 120 days at sea. After completion of the Panama Railroad in 1855 the hardships and the time of a sea voyage were both reduced, but it still took two to two and a half months and involved passage on two ships and a train trip. Probably $750 constituted a minimum sensible sum for a single man to take for the whole passage, via either Panama or Cape Horn, and a thousand dollars was widely held to be a safer amount. Thus going to California was a different proposition from the emigration of the pioneer husbandman from, say, Ohio to Wisconsin, or that of a drifter riding the rails toward Chicago. It involved a substantial cash outlay, a great distance, and a long time en route.

Moreover, this was a migration which was at first predominantly male, which again differentiated it from the traditional movement of American agricultural pioneers. Finally, the lure was different. It is safe to assume that men investing seven hundred or a thousand dollars at mid-nineteenth-century value were shrewd, ambitious fellows headed for a new country to seek a fortune; and from the prosperity many of them achieved in San Francisco, it is clear that they abandoned mining for more lucrative, if less romantic, ventures. They came to realize the potential of business in the city with the wonderful harbor. World trade, marketing agricultural products, servicing the mines, and profiting from the local population all offered these entrepreneurs the opportunity of great wealth, or at least a better and more prosperous life than they had known before. The nabobs were relatively few—Flood, Fair, Mackay, Huntington, Crocker, Hopkins, Stanford, Ralston, Colton, Sutro—but for each of them were dozens of others who earned lesser but still substantial fortunes.

Such intelligent, educated, and enterprising men in the prime of life gave to San Francisco the elixir that made it great. Being separated from the East by long distances, the high expense of travel, and slow transportation, the San Franciscans possessed a civic pride that reflected a fierce love of what they considered their new, permanent home. This explains the existence of vigilantes to clean out the thugs and coerce the mobs, the volunteer fire companies to protect the city from fiery holocausts, the construction of stone mansions and business blocks and, for lesser residents, attractive wooden homes with big bay windows. It explains the pursuit of culture manifested by an active theater, a dozen newspapers, libraries, and even historical associations. The men of San Francisco were determined that it would be a better town than the ones they had left.

Finally, because of the great wealth concentrated there, the boosterism, though extravagant, was rooted in a concept of permanence. Yerba Buena Cove soon disappeared, the victim of businessmen cre-

ating more space for wharves, warehouses, and business blocks. Then
there was William C. Ralston's Palace Hotel, opened in 1875. It cost
$6-7 million, and its vital statistics are staggering even today. It boasted
850 rooms and had walls of white marble from Vermont and black
marble from Tennessee and an interior court measuring 144 by 84 feet
into which coaches could drive, and which was covered over, above the
seven stories, with glass. The hotel's water supply came from an artifi-
cial underground lake fed by four artesian wells; it was said that the
reservoir was big enough to launch a boat on. Unfortunately, Ralston
did not witness the grand opening. A few months before, his bank closed
and his fortune wiped out, he had gone for a swim at North Beach. He
was brought to shore unconscious, and died. Whether it was his form of
suicide or a result of natural causes no one will ever know.

The cattle town of Dodge City seemed to sprout right out of the buffalo grass. In June of 1872 two liquor dealers found out where the Santa
Fe Railroad would shortly be building west of Fort Dodge, chose a site
beside the right of way, on a gentle rise above the Arkansas River, and
that very day pitched a tent and were in business. Before the day was
out a couple of other men established a general store there. In July,
1872, a corporation was formed to develop the site. By then there were
already a couple of hundred occupants, and Dodge City was flourishing. Although it is usually considered a cattle town, its first bonanza was
as a shipping center for buffalo hides, more than 200,000 being sent out
in the winter of 1872-73 alone. When that business declined, Dodge,
like such other cattle towns as Wichita, Abilene, Ellsworth, and Ogallala, took up the slack by becoming a farming community. Incidentally,
as Robert Dykstra has pointed out in his study *The Cattle Towns*, most
of them were platted by speculators, men such as Joseph P. McCoy,
who plunged heavily and were both rich and poor several times in their
lives.
    All the cattle towns developed reputations for violence, and in the
popular mind Dodge City, "The Wickedest Little City in America,"
comes to mind first. But under the analysis of no-nonsense historians,
much of the aura of wickedness has been dissipated—in fact, they may
have overdone it. Dykstra produces statistics which pretty well destroy
the tradition of a violent death a day, of a Boothill Cemetery running
out of room. He finds that in the years 1870 through 1885 the cattle
towns of Abilene, Ellsworth, Wichita, Dodge City, and Caldwell had
a total of just forty-five homicides, and Dodge City, while leading the
others had just fifteen. Considering that Dodge during most of those
years was the whoop-up place for soldiers and buffalo hunters, and the

end of the trail as well for the Texas cattlemen, the homicide rate was surprisingly low. Moreover, in-depth studies of such towns reveal the sobering, dull facts about conflicting pressure groups (farmers versus cattlemen, businessmen versus the farmers) and opposing forces within the towns. The presence of churches and schools, problems of taxation and law enforcement, and such mundane nuisances as stray dogs and unemptied privy vaults were all part of the history of these towns as well as of many others, but the chronicling of these matters robs the cattle towns of much of their flamboyant romance.

For the sake of accuracy this is good, if it does not result in an overreaction. There must have been a reason why railroad passengers were warned not to leave the station platform and many wisely remained in their cars while their train was stopped. There *was* a substantial transient population, it *was* predominantly male, and it was bubbling over with energy. There *were* plenty of saloons and gamblers, and if there were fewer prostitutes than are usually portrayed, then those who were present were kept very busy. It was new country, and everyone was on the make. The faro tables and saloons stayed wide open far into the night, every night, and there were places where a law-abiding man with common sense did not go. "Experience soon indicated that whoring, gambling, and overindulgence in liquor were the three main causes of cattle town violence," writes Dykstra,[7] and shows how the town fathers channelled and controlled the whoring, gambling, and alcoholism. They learned how to make money out of it while at the same time preventing its excesses, such as shoot-outs and murders. Such sobering analyses of these towns still do not make of them sleepy little religious communities. When the herds arrived, there was plenty of noise, fights, gambling, whoring, and general carousing—but it was under control.

Some towns prospered, with little justification of place to aid them. Perhaps the best case is Los Angeles, today a massive, sprawling, smog-ridden, overgrown small town. It is true that, in the days before anyone had ever heard of temperature inversion, the city of the Angels could boast of a most salubrious climate. But many another settlement in southern California could boast of that. What made Los Angeles the biggest was the activity and dedication of a small group of local boosters whose single-minded pursuit was to raise their city to high status.

Indeed, every successful urban center could point with pride to city fathers. Dr. Daniel Drake in Cincinnati comes to mind, William Clark and the Francis Preston Blair family in St. Louis, William Byers, William Gilpin, General Larimer, and John Evans in Denver, Brigham Young in Salt Lake City. Often ten or a dozen men were involved, sometimes actually connected by a common investment in a joint-stock

By the 1850's Salt Lake City was a thriving metropolis. The Wasatch Mountains are in the background. (Historical Department of the Church of Jesus Christ of Latter Day Saints)

Salt Lake City in the 1890's; view from South Temple and Main. (Historical Department, Church of Jesus Christ of Latter Day Saints)

company which had purchased the land, platted the town, and used its funds to advertise and promote the sale of the real estate. Such an arrangement was as common in small towns as in the big cities. Take Martin, Tennessee; in many ways its founding was typical of thousands. The Martin family owned several hundred acres thereabouts. When they heard that a railroad would shortly be coming through the area, one of the family headed for the main offices of the railroad in Chicago and made such an attractive offer, including land for depot, yards, and so forth, that the right of way was surveyed through Martin land. The town was laid out, the railroad came, and a village appeared. When a college was established there, Martin's future was assured. It never grew into a great city, but it is small-city America at its best, and was once called by *Look* magazine "the happiest town in America."

The man important in the development of Memphis was one of its original founders, Judge John Overton. He lobbied vigorously with the Tennessee legislature, fostered improvement, criticized the local newspaper editors for their lack of boosterism, and chided other citizens for not providing sufficient wood for steamboats. The judge was also typical of many nineteenth-century town builders in his narrow-minded, mercenary views. "It must be said," writes an historian of early Memphis, "that Overton's motives do not seem to have included any concern for the welfare of the people or the future of the country, but to have been the mere desire for the accumulation of wealth. . . . Working for Memphis, he was working for himself, and that was the limit of his horizon."[8] Memphis suffered from terrible yellow fever epidemics in 1873 and 1878; one foreign visitor said the city smelled worse than Cairo, Egypt.

It is a fact that nearly every town and city had its champions. It is also true that many of them were a predatory breed. They were happy in their wheeling and dealing, but also, like Judge Overton, far too busy to pay attention to the needs of a growing metropolis. About the best that can be said for such individuals was that their best interests and the best interests of their community often coincided. Thus a town booster who for his own reasons promoted a plank road, a canal, harbor improvements, dredging of a river, or a railroad was also aiding the growth of the town. A reputation for sickness and disease was harmful to business, so a booster might get behind a bond issue for a sewer or waterworks. But if he could not see a direct connection between the improvement and his own welfare, then he was likely to be lackadaisical in his support, or even an opponent. After all, everyone hated taxation.

Even so, many a town or city can point with pride to a founder who at least occasionally transcended his mercenary pursuits and worked actively for such things as parks, schools, colleges, churches, and hospitals. Such a man was John Evans, for whom Evanston, Illinois, is named, as well as the hamlet of Evans, Colorado, and 14,260-foot Mount Evans west of Denver. Evans, a physician, came from Pennsylvania Quaker stock, though he changed to the Methodist persuasion while he was still a young man. His search for a lucrative practice took him to Indiana, where he led the movement for a state hospital for the insane. In the struggle he was introduced to the varieties of politics—Methodists versus Presbyterians, mercenary motives versus idealistic aims, corruptionists versus men of integrity—and discovered that he enjoyed the turmoil of public life. He not only witnessed the construction and operation of the Indiana Home for the Insane as a result of his successful campaigning, but became increasingly involved in both politics and business affairs because he enjoyed them.

In 1845 Evans accepted a chair at the Rush Medical College in Chicago. The city in that year had a population of 12,000, which was 50 per cent more than it had numbered a year before. Evans either led or was a vigorous supporter of the efforts to establish hospitals, pass quarantine laws, regulate the medical profession, and form the Chicago Medical Society. He invented an obstetrical extractor that was considered an improvement over the forceps then in use. By 1848, when he made Chicago his home (he had previously commuted from Attica, Indiana), he was already established as a leading physician and a prominent citizen. Within less than a decade his real estate holdings and other activities led him to abandon medicine. Even as he was accumulating a fortune from his investments, he was busy helping Chicago grow, and grow better.

Evans was elected a member of the Chicago City Council in 1852. He used his position to gain permission for the Ft. Wayne and Chicago Railroad, in which he was a heavy investor, to enter the city. He led the campaign to upgrade Chicago's educational system and the forces advocating a Board of Sewerage Commissioners. He also spearheaded a campaign for a Methodist college, the ultimate result of which was Northwestern University, near which he built his home. The community, just north of Chicago, took the name Evanston. In all, Evans bequeathed over $106,000 in cash and property to the new institution.

Even Chicago and adjacent Evanston did not satisfy his ambitions, however, and in 1857 he became involved in a town platted on the south bank of the Platte near where it flows into the Missouri. Oreapolis, as the embryonic city was named, was helped on its way by Evans through plans for a Methodist university to be situated there; if the transcontinental railroad passed through the town, Oreapolis stood to grow and be great. But the great transcontinental bypassed it, and it suffered the fate of most of the hundreds of paper towns of Nebraska's early years; in this project even Evans lost out.

When he settled in 1862 in Denver, a lusty frontier community of about 5,000, 600 miles of Indian-infested plains from the nearest towns along the lower Missouri, Evans was already a man of wealth and broad business and political experience. His tour as territorial governor of Colorado (April 1862–August 1865), was a mixture of success and failure, but his grasp of Denver's potential was sure. He purchased real estate and plunged into railroad affairs, determined to bring the steel rails to the new city. He profited immensely, and so did Denver. A feeder line, the Denver Pacific, from the Queen City of the Plains to Cheyenne was the result of his efforts, as was a link southward to Fort Worth, called the Denver, Texas, and Fort Worth; all of this is today known as the Colorado and Southern Railroad. He also built into the Rockies southwest of Denver, and in one transaction apparently realized a profit of $800,000, which figured at 2,500 per cent of his initial investment. Evans had a fixed policy of helping churches of all denominations in their construction costs. He was the prime mover for the establishment of the University of Denver; advocated more parks for the city; and was, as his biographer Harry Kelsey points out, one of the incorporators of the State Historical Society, the Denver Chamber of Commerce, and the city's United Charities.

Most of the men who figured in the rise of the new country cities belong somewhere between Judge Overton of Memphis and John Evans of Chicago, Evanston, and Denver. They were men of reasonable honesty, some imagination, considerable courage—meaning a willingness to risk their fortunes in daring endeavors—a considerable amount of ego, as may be ascertained by the large numbers of them who paid to have their adulatory biographies included in expensive town or county histories, and some civic pride. Too often, however, their civic interest faded when it interfered with their personal interests. So the booster platted the city, built the hotel, ran a general store and a livery, invested in real estate, and dipped into railroad bonds. But at the same time he fought taxes, school bond issues, waterworks, and sewage plans; if he were in mining, he hacked off the forest cover, polluted the streams, and filled the air with noxious fumes from his smelter; and yet he convinced himself that he was an Upright Town Leader, a Good Citizen. Frederick Jackson Turner's oft-quoted description of the American frontiersmen fits the new country urbanite best of all: "That coarseness and strength combined with acuteness and inquisitiveness; that practical, inventive turn of mind, quick to find expedients; that masterful grasp of material things, lacking in the artistic but powerful to effect great ends; that reckless, nervous energy; that dominant individualism, working for good and evil, and withal that buoyancy and exuberance which comes with freedom . . ."[9]—such a man was rarely the hard-working farmer or the lone pioneer out in the wilderness. Turner's man was the urbanite: the doer, the booster, the ambitious man with a multitude of plans. He was Mark Twain's Colonel Sellers, the best-known character from Twain's and Charles Dudley Warner's *The Gilded Age*.

Urbanization in the new country did not always mean teeming cities or even fast-growing ones. It also meant small towns with a population of 2,500 or more—the criterion the census considered acceptable for denoting a town. Many villages never grew fast or very much; some remained nearly stationary in population; and more than a few withered and died. Many are still languishing in the terminal state.

Since agriculture was the basic endeavor in the new country, the town of the agricultural frontier should draw our attention first. Depending on the era, its location was very likely to be on the banks of a river, at a strategic point on a canal, at a crossroads, or along a railroad. In large sections of the Middle West and along the Middle Border (western Minnesota, Dakota, Nebraska, and Kansas), a prime consideration was distance, for no farmer wanted to be more than a half day's wagon ride from a settlement. Generally this meant that a town must exist not more than twenty miles from the farm. The beauty of the system of land survey was the crossing of survey lines every six miles. Often those crossroads became two streets of a town, as Main and First Streets, and made possible with the utmost simplicity the grid-type patterning of the city blocks. If, however, the center arose due to a railroad station or a canal or river landing, there would be instead a Front Street, a Canal Street, a Railroad Avenue, or a River Street. Then there might be streets parallel to it, bisected by cross streets more or less at right angles, in a semblance of city blocks. The street along the railroad served as the crossing of a T, with the long stem extending as Main Street at right angles to the railroad and, perhaps, turning into a straight-as-an-arrow road leading out from the shaded paths of Great Plains Small Town and extending north or south for fifty or a hundred miles or more. Add the grain elevators in the 1880's, cattle chutes and yards, a water tank in the "tank town," and the little burgs were as they still are out on the plains today, shimmering in the heat from the summer sun and shivering in the winter blizzards.

Although such towns occasionally sprang up out of need, with no preliminary surveying or systematic platting of lots, most new country agricultural communities were, like other urban centers, planned and platted by men of vision who hitched their futures to the sale of lots and the growth of their speculative acreage. Town planning and selling was as much a part of the nineteenth-century scene as the flamboyant high-pressure sales of retirement communities are of the twentieth. Colorful lithographs depicted hundreds of such places: there was always the steepled church, the academy, the fine business blocks, the neat, geometrically laid out residential areas, the clean, neat streets replete with full-grown trees, fine carriages, and prancing horses; and, if the intercity transportation was the railroad, then a fine station and sophisticated railroad yards were in view. If the transportation was by river, then the bird's-eye view included half a dozen fine, glistening white steamboats busily entering, leaving, or being serviced at the wharves.

Most such paper cities never made the grade. The streets were never more than furrows drawn by a plow along the survey lines, the little wooden "lot" signs weathered, rotted, and fell to the ground, and the potential city became farmland just like the acres adjoining it. Many of those that did make it did so out of the luck of location. Sometimes a railroad determined townsites along its line and surveyed and platted its own town lots, although even this did not always assure success. Often a struggling town's populace raised funds and purchased railroad bonds as well as granting the company lands for right-of-way, depot, and yards, the town fathers realizing full well that without the railroad the embryonic city would die, and with it their investments and hopes. The competition for county seats, for colleges, even in a few cases for state capitals, became so intense that bribes and even murders accompanied it.

Most new country towns possessed a drab sameness that passed through two stages. The first was the early period of town growth, in which wooden buildings predominated, including those on Main Street. They were board-and-batten structures with wooden signs; little one-story real estate offices, law offices, barber shops and the like were squeezed in between such two- or three-story wooden structures as, for example, a business block (really a single large building) holding a general store on the first floor and law offices and physician's and dentist's offices on the second and subsequent stories. Such larger buildings might also include the community hotel, often the largest structure in town, or the Masonic temple. A furniture store featuring stoves and caskets would not be out of the realm of possibility; nor must we forget the feed stores, one or two saloons, a restaurant or two, a couple of livery stables, a watchmaker, and a harness shop. To make them more imposing, some of the one-story business blocks had false fronts giving the

Iola, Kansas, 1871. (The Kansas State Historical Society, Topeka)

A typical high country town: Gunnison, Colorado, 1882. The community served
agricultural, grazing, and mining interests. (State Historical Society of Colorado)

impression of a two- or three-story structure. Add Baptist, Methodist, Presbyterian, in some areas Roman Catholic, and, if the town was substantial, Episcopal churches. Add a school. Prior to the 1860's the upper grades were probably housed in an academy, a privately supported institution which was attended by the youth of the town's elite. Such institutions usually perched on top of the highest hill around; they so proliferated in the 1830's and 40's that they were known as hilltop academies. After the 1860's, when the growth of the public high school was phenomenal, this institution became the pride of the town.

Such a town might have cobblestone streets, but the probability was that dust was the norm in summer, mud in the other seasons. People walked more than they rode in those days, and the ten-to-thirty-minute jaunt to and from the office offered fine mental and physical therapy that is sadly missed today. The homes were of wood, had front porches and lawns and back yards which contained, possibly, a stable for the horse that pulled the buggy in which the family rode to church, a chicken coop and small chicken yard, and, until the 1870's at least, a common privy.

Such was the first phase of the new country town. Its second phase was marked by signs of permanence, especially by the replacement of wooden business structures with brick or stone ones. Anyone who has traveled through America has seen hundreds—thousands—of such buildings, along Main Street, which have outlasted their usefulness; today many are being wrecked for their brick, which is prime building material for new homes. The streets were paved; Main Street now appeared as it

In most new country towns the hotel was the largest building. Southwestern stage at Humboldt, Kansas, in the 1870's. (The Kansas State Historical Society, Topeka)

Long Branch Saloon, Dodge City, 1880's. (The Kansas State Historical Society, Topeka)

Men in front of saloon mimicking drinking. Photo by Charles Van Schaick. (State Historical Society of Wisconsin)

would last into the 1940's or even later. Wooden churches gave way to those deep-red brick edifices located on the fringes of the business districts, those gloomy buildings that seemed to announce, "Funerals, come to me!" Class lines hardened; there was a dividing line between the "right" people and the others, who lived on "the other side of the tracks," "over by the stock yards," or in "niggertown" or "the east end" (whatever designation the area was known by); and there was a mansion or two or three belonging to the really rich.

There could be a park with a grandstand, or a courthouse square, if the town was a county seat, with long park benches along the sidewalk where men could sit and talk of a spring afternoon, or, on a Saturday, hear about politics and the price of grain or discuss the latest horrendous crime and the trial that was pending. Still another place of concentration was the railroad station, to which men repaired to see who got on and who got off, and to receive one of the first copies of the big-city newspaper—the Chicago *Tribune*, Boston *Globe*, Atlanta *Constitution*, New York *Tribune*, San Francisco *Chronicle*, Rocky Mountain *News*. Still another gathering place was the barber shop. Mounted trophies from the hunt, lithographs of pugilists and race horses, copies of the *Police Gazette*, some firearms mounted on the wall behind the oak chairs for those waiting their turn, brass spittoons, one for each waiting chair and one for each barber chair, and mirrors, of course, fairly well furnished the shop. A back room may have offered baths for farmers, miners, or cowboys who were in for the day and smelled rankly of active unwashed manhood.

The saloon is well known as a place of conviviality, although some authorities suggest that their number has been grossly exaggerated. But Livingston, Montana, in 1883 boasted thirty-three saloons for a population of about 3,000, while Gardiner, next to Yellowstone Park, at the same time had six or seven; Leadville, Colorado, in 1879 had 120 saloons and nineteen beer halls. Drinking appears to have been heavy throughout the new country; where men predominated the saloon was a place of importance.

Perhaps fiction has overdone the frontier *maison de joie*; still there is no question of the prostitute's presence in the new country. The town of the Middle West or Middle Border always had a painted lady or two who was a source of much gossip—and apparently an available source of sex for men who dared risk being seen entering or leaving her premises. For cattle towns, mining towns, and towns near military installations there was a sufficient number of girls to warrant a "line," a "maiden lane," a "boarding house" or two, or a hotel in a declining section of the business district which was known all around as the local whorehouse.

Moro, Oregon, in the northwestern wheat country. Photo by W. A. Raymond, circa
1890. (The Bettmann Archive)

Census statistics and police blotters do not indicate any great preponderance of these ladies of the night, and this has prompted some authorities to play down the number of prostitutes around, as they have
questioned the number of saloons. But such women rarely advertised
themselves as such. Moreover, their prevalence at a given place was
often periodic or seasonal. Dodge City or Abilene may have had barely
a dozen during much of the year, but during those weeks when the cattlemen arrived up the trail from Texas, their numbers were certainly
greatly increased by reinforcements out of Kansas City, St. Louis, or
even New Orleans. Up in Montana the girls traveled a circuit, hitting

Gardiner when the soldiers at Fort Yellowstone got paid, moving to Helena when the miners were paid, then perhaps to Butte where the copper mines and smelters employed hundreds of lonesome men, and then back to Gardiner again.

Other places of importance in the new country towns were the general store; the livery stable, a hangout for the town's gay blades (and where, according to Lewis Atherton in his delightful *Main Street on the Middle Border,* nice little boys were forbidden to go because of the talk of mares, stallions at stud, and other earthy items); and the feed store, where sodbusting farmers talked of crops and prices. In the South there was still another gathering place, the local cotton gin. There, after the cotton was in, the men could lounge under a nearby magnolia, live oak or longleaf pine and enjoy a ripe watermelon and a noonday snooze. In the mining communities the assay office was often a source of news, as were the newspaper office and the post office.

Such was the town as it appeared to the residents of a twenty-mile radius who used it as a trading center. It was to the town also that there came what little culture there was in those days. At its highest level, from the 1830's through the 1860's, this was the lyceum, a sort of nineteenth-century version of the modern Artist's Series that come to colleges and towns of America today. Farm and townspeople alike attended. Emerson was a highly successful lyceum lecturer, as was Hall J. Kelley, who spoke long and convincingly in the 1830's and 1840's on why the country must have Oregon. Others spoke of phrenology and women's rights and temperance. Visiting evangelists livened up the Lenten season for many a Baptist or Methodist family. Traveling medicine shows supplied crude entertainment and nostrums containing a high percentage of alcohol. Occasionally a theatrical troupe, complete with tent and props, came through: *Ten Nights in a Bar Room* and *East Lynn* were perennials from the 1840's on. Finally there was the circus, which offered dazzling sights to the country and town folk.

In the 1870's a new form of enlightened instruction and entertainment, the Chautauqua, added much to the cultural life, such as it was, of the new country towns. Beginning as a summer school for Methodist Sunday School teachers amidst the sylvan beauties of Chautauqua Lake, New York, it was soon transformed and expanded. Soon every up-and-coming midwestern town, and a few southern, Rocky Mountain, and far western towns as well, boasted a local Chautauqua. Some kind of a rustic setting was basic. There, for a period of one to six weeks in the summertime, people camped and listened to lecturers, singers, musicians, and entertainers of various respectable talents, while attending courses in literature, religions of the world, political theory, ethics, and other popular subjects of the day. A big tent served as the auditorium, though later some permanent buildings were added at places where the idea took hold. Such was Chautauqua's first phase; a second one, much more commercialized, flourished into the 1920's.

The picture we have so far of the new country town is hardly one of hustle and bustle. By the farmer's standards it was a busy place, but that could have been because he headed for town on the same day, Saturday, as all his fellow farmers did. The general store and feed store, the restaurants and saloons, the waiting rooms of physicians and dentists, and the chairs at the barber shops were full. Yet, even on a busy Saturday, there was a great deal of time left over for talk. There was time to enjoy nature, the first robin of spring, a new colt down at the livery, the dry leaves of autumn. Men died at an earlier age in those days, but not so much from heart attacks.

Not everyone moved so slowly, however. There were the hustlers, the drummers, the wheeler-dealers even then, whose names filled the hotel registers. At the hotel or its adjuncts—coffee shops, bars, exhibition rooms—deals were made, as well as sins committed. Drummers representing far-off firms contacted local merchants; politicians conversed with the local Republicans or Democrats. They packed their gladstones hastily to make the 5:40 train—or whatever time the train left town. James Bryce, a discerning British traveler who wrote about America, noted, after visiting the American West in the late 1870's, that "men usually drop off the cars before they have stopped, and do not enter them again till they are already in motion, hanging on like bees to the end of the tail car as it quits the depot."[10]

The populace struck Europeans as living on the verge of frenzy. James Bryce, visiting the Pacific Northwest in the early 1880's, found the inhabitants of Seattle and Tacoma feverish in their efforts to create an instant civilization. He found Seattle's business in full swing at seven A.M., "the shops open, the streets full of people."[11] Real estate was on the lips of everyone, and everyone seemed to be an investor. There were instances in which the premium for subscription to the local newspaper was clear title to a lot in one of the developing subdivisions. Such land madness had always been characteristic of new country cities; in 1871 a Chicago newspaper estimated that every other male and one in four females owned real estate in that booming metropolis.

About the only thing anyone feared was the growth of a rival town. Thus Seattle and Tacoma, Minneapolis and St. Paul, and, later, Dallas and Fort Worth vied for power. The optimism of the boosters was inamazing. The capitol building at Bismarck was to be built on a hilltop a mile from the town. But it was assumed that since, as one of the speakers at the cornerstone-laying ceremonies said, "Bismarck was the centre of Dakota, Dakota the centre of the United States, and the United States the centre of the world," then surely Bismarck would become "the metropolitan hearth of the world's civilization.' "[12] James Bryce was skeptical, and Bismarck today is hardly the hearth of the world, but as for growth, the speaker was right; the capitol is today surrounded by the city.

The populace of the new country urban centers was irritatingly transient, and every man with a stake in the town's success worked with his fellow investors to insure permanence and prosperity. The biggest edifice, as Daniel Boorstin has pointed out, was the hotel; this alone suggests the ephemeral air of many a town. But unlike the European inn, the American hotel was the center of activity, which sometimes enabled it to carry the surrounding community into permanence. Newspapers were encouraged; they publicized boosterism, for if the town failed they failed; it was not unusual for a small community to have several. If a railroad came through, a college or some state facility such as an insane asylum (as such institutions were called in the nineteenth century) was located there; if a military post existed nearby, if an industry located there, then the town had a chance of becoming permanent. Thus the significance of an ugly red brick or granite business block or two instead of false-front business buildings, the rooting out of stumps in the main street and its being paved with cobblestones, the construction of a water supply and sewers, the building of a court house, or the aid of a good representative in the state legislature was that they helped achieve permanence or were evidence of the permanence of a new country community.

It was from observing the town builders and real estate promoters, believers in the great day coming, that Bryce sensed the coming greatness of America. "It is the same everywhere from the Mississippi to the Pacific," he wrote. "Men seem to live in the future rather than in the present; not that they fail to work while it is called today, but that they see the country not merely as it is, but as it will be, twenty, fifty, a hundred years hence, when the seedlings shall have grown to forest trees." It was, he said, a "constant reaching forward to and grasping at the future."[13] Such men could be found at the hotel and railroad station; they rented horse and buggy from the livery, did business at the bank, laid plans, then departed for another town in the new country, quite similar to the one they had just left.

The small towns of the South were different from their northern and western counterparts, yet they were still clearly American. The southern town was very often located on a navigable river. When the railroads came, new towns arose at junction points; but there were not many railroads in the new country of the South. Atlanta was the principal recipient of benefits from the railroads. Originally there had been a post office called White Hall where the Georgia Railroad and the Central of Georgia met and formed the Western and Atlantic. The name was changed to Terminus, then Marthasville, and finally Atlanta.

But most southern towns existed because of rivers, and their activities were dictated in large part by the waterways. In the fall when the crops were in there was a flurry of activity, with yeomen farmers and planters coming to town to have the cotton ginned or to confer with lawyers, realtors, and merchants. When the produce had been sent downstream, when deliveries had been made to the small town merchants and planters of goods which had been ordered from Memphis, New Orleans, Pittsburgh, or Cincinnati and been carried up the smaller rivers by steamboat to the town, then lethargy took over. Southern towns seemed to hang in the hot, humid air, thick with the fragrance of camellia, jasmine, magnolia, and honeysuckle, in suspended animation. Still their lethargy was hardly greater than that of an Iowa agricultural community at midweek between seasons.

What was different about the southern town was its probable lack of planning, so that the geometric grill of streets and blocks was missing. Another characteristic was the area of shacks and poverty where domestics and a few free blacks lived; they were all "free," of course, after the Civil War. Sometimes it was not a separate area, but a kind of residential alley behind the white people's residences. The whites lived in wooden houses, often unpainted or needing paint, with spacious porches and plenty of shade trees and shrubs giving the house some protection from the fierce sun.

Such a new country town was Columbus, Mississippi, in the northeastern part of the state. Settled in 1817 and incorporated four years later, in its prime it vied in activity and population with Vicksburg. Columbus served a flourishing, developing, cotton-growing region, with timber industries adding to its prosperity. Located at the head of navigation of the Tombigbee River, which was also the site of the crossing of the Nashville-Natchez road, it had as well the advantage of being the seat of Loundes County. Even though the Tombigbee was open at Columbus just three months of the year, that was sufficient. Saturdays and the autumn weeks when the crops were in witnessed a flurry of activity. Litigation, court days, and other governmental activities provided business throughout the year. Physicians, lawyers, merchants, and retired

Vicksburg, 1876: mud and stagnant water when it rained, dust when the weather was clear—these conditions added to Vicksburg's location on the Mississippi to ensure illness and such plagues as yellow fever. (Mississippi Department of Archives)

Business was vigorous on the Mississippi waterfront at Vicksburg in 1890. (Mississippi Department of Archives)

planters provided the town with solid business blocks and spacious residences; it also had the Franklin Academy, the first free school in the state. With its churches, its quiet streets, its beautiful trees and, by nineteenth-century standards, acceptable sanitation facilities, Columbus was a pleasant southern new country town, a good place to live.

But most southern towns were not as prosperous as Columbus, Vicksburg, Natchez, Atlanta, or Shreveport. They lacked proper lighting, water, and sewage; located in a warm climate and on trade arteries, they suffered from plagues of cholera and yellow fever which swept the South again and again in the nineteenth century. Malaria was practically endemic in the population, and typhoid was common. Religion of a particularly volatile kind seemed to be the principal diversion, along with politics. Still, the town in the South was not as influential politically as it was in the North; it was secondary in this respect to the surrounding agricultural countryside.

There was one type of new country community that was so different as to warrant special notice. This was the mining town of the Far West, which sprouted wherever "color" was found, or very close by. Virginia City, Nevada, on the slope of Mount Davidson, is a well-known example, but such places as Helena and Virginia City, Montana; Lead and Deadwood, South Dakota; and Leadville, Central City, Black Hawk, and Cripple Creek, Colorado, were typical of hundreds of such camps (as they were often called). Often they were established along the gulches and ravines where waters tumbled down from the high mountains. Some towns perched precariously on bleak mountaintops or windblown plateaus; the towns around the White Pine Mining District in Nevada received every breath of cold air without any barrier or buffer. Caribou, Colorado, was at just about the same altitude as the timberline.

In these very unlikely places a form of instant civilization sprang up. Miners came from all points of the compass and hastily staked out their claims. Tents, tarpaulins, wagon beds, wickiups, and crude log cabins appeared. Sometimes a town speculator staked out a settlement in a gridiron pattern, but rarely was his claim to ownership honored. More likely the town presented a haphazard collection of dry goods, grocery, assay, barber, saloon, hardware, powder and mining supply, blacksmith, feed, and hotel establishments, all situated along both sides of a vacant strip of mud or dust that was more or less accepted as the main street. In the midst of the boom this thoroughfare would be filled with oxen, mules, and horses drawing white-topped freight wagons, buggies or stages carrying people. Plank walks appeared fairly soon along the sides of the street, out of necessity.

Into this new community came also the drifting men of the age, many with their worldly belongings on their backs. Referred to by the more permanent residents as "idlers and roaring reprobates," they slept on the plank sidewalks, in empty barrels, on lumber piles, on saloon floors. Gamblers arrived, and possibly a stage came in one day carrying a madam and three or four prostitutes. At least a couple of fortunetellers or mediums would set up shop to offer advice about claims and investments, for a price. A phase of intense speculation, when properties changed hands hourly and values soared, was always a feature of the boom. Then, in a few days or weeks, the community's first crisis arrived. Was the strike valid? Was there *really* gold and/or silver? How rich were the deposits? What did the professional geologist who had been sent in by outside capital have to say about it? Was someone getting under way with a mill or a smelter? Did the ore react favorably to processing?

If the strike appeared valid, if there apparently really was an abundance of precious metal, then the tent and wagon town changed with almost miraculous rapidity into a clapboard and false-front one, many of whose buildings had from the very first a weather-beaten, windblown look. Businessmen secured valid titles to their properties, and soon even a brick or stone business block began to appear here and there.

As consolidations took place and the drifters accepted employment with the few big mines and mills or else left for other climes, the bustle of new wealth continued. Streets and saloons were full, stores did a thriving business, and violence occasionally flared. There actually were occasions when a saloon was shot up, or drunks galloped on their mounts through the streets firing their pistols. Men were killed or maimed by faulty blasting operations, and fires were great and fairly common spectacles. Observing them was doubly dangerous because several stores selling miner's supplies kept their stocks of powder right in town. When the heat set off the powder, not much was left. The masses of men present provided plenty of spectators for street fights; at Treasure Hill, Nevada, one of them attracted an estimated 2,000 men. Prostitutes were often the cause of the disputes.

The extensive energy and activity in these remote communities are difficult to imagine. More than 13,000 claims were estimated to have been filed in the White Pine Mining District of east central Nevada in 1865-67, the years of the initial discoveries. Lawyers soon appeared, for litigation over disputed claims was certain to arise. In 1869 the Land Office required some twelve documents for the certification of a single title; such red tape was grist for the barrister's mill. Firewood, sold by the jackass load, was three to five dollars in the district, while flour was sixteen or seventeen dollars a hundred-pound barrel, and potatoes twelve and a half cents apiece.

As the town showed signs of becoming permanent, those who stayed sorted out into two classes, wageearners and owners or managers. The town boosters now came to the fore. They could usually be identified by occupation. The general storekeeper, who probably had a larger cash investment in the community than anyone else, was likely to be a town leader. The saloonkeeper or liquor dealer was also frequently a booster, as was the newspaper editor. For these people brick or stone edifices for the bank, the Masonic lodge, or even stores and saloons were symbols of permanence and portents of future population stability.

With stability all the problems confronted by all new towns swooped down upon the mining community. Streets required grading or cobblestoning. Sanitation, involving both water supply and sewage, became a crying need, especially as spring breezes marked the end of ice and snow, and the filth from privy vaults, the droppings from horses, mules, and oxen in the streets, and the garbage dumped behind the homes and hostelries began to thaw and smell and attract myriads of flies. Smallpox, pneumonia, and typhoid were common in the camps, while intestinal disorders and deficiency diseases such as scurvy were not unknown. Sensitive to the sure loss of their investment if the town got a bad name, a few men with vested interests arose to lead the way towards municipal improvement. A calamity helped: a bad fire created civic interest in a water system and a good firehouse; an epidemic made it easier to float a bond issue for a city sewer, or raise tax money to maintain a city scavenger. Competition from a rival community—and often goldfields had two or three towns vying for business—motivated civic activity for better streets, or even for toll roads or narrow-gauge railroads connecting the camp with the outside world. In these communities, above all else, suitable transportation was a must; it was necessary to convey ore to the smelters and also to bring human needs in from the rest of the world. Therefore bonds were floated for roads or railroads.

These requirements plus a bit of leadership led to municipal government, usually consisting of a council and a mayor. Day-by-day government was handled by a town treasurer, a clerk, a marshall, an attorney; sometimes there would be a street commissioner, an engineer, a physician, and, as noted above, a town scavenger. All of the problems of administering the community were augmented by the usual one of money. Where, for taxing, would the squawk be least? Usually there was a tax on all businesses; and usually the highest tax was on saloons, dance halls, gambling joints, breweries, and theaters. There was often a general property tax also; poll taxes were fairly common, and fines added somewhat

Gold Hill, Nevada, 1868. Photo by O'Sullivan. Notice his "dark room" at lower left.
(Office of the Chief of Engineers, The National Archives)

to the treasury. All of this, however, was rarely sufficient. Delinquencies running as high as 30 per cent of the potential were not unknown. The fact that extensive improvements were inaugurated while the community was on the upgrade, and had to be paid for while the mines were in decline and population was drifting elsewhere, forced the remaining citizens to shoulder an enormous tax burden.

Politics in the mining towns was initially a form of entertainment. Men listened to orators and drank free beer or harder persuaders, and staged torchlight parades as local bands beat the drums and blew their trumpets. Later local elections tended to fall into the hands of a few, and, as with most local elections today, it was almost impossible to get out the vote. As W. Turrentine Jackson says of the camps, "all things considered, the democracy of the mining camps appears self-interested, politically passive except where property and patronage are concerned, dedicated to materialism, careless of democratic theory, ideals, and institutions, and insensitive to minority interests, like those of foreign citizens."[14]

With stability (which in this case is relative, for a mining community is by its very nature ephemeral) other changes took place. The old glad-handed camaraderie gave way to a class society. Lines of demarcation were fuzzy, but pretty soon there were "one-bit" and "two-bit" saloons, and "two-bit" and "four-bit" barber shops, and the Very Important Men were not seen in the cheaper places. There were workers versus idlers, laborers versus capitalists, whores versus "dramatic artists." The successful man frequented a bawdy house with a ridiculous air of refinement about it; the other class paid calls on the girls down on the line. Respectable women, wives of mine foremen and metallurgists and businessmen, began to reduce the sin of the town—or at least make it less noticeable. A school system was formed. The original activity on Sunday, which had been the great gathering day when the miners converged from the nearby diggings to get their mail, do their laundry, purchase supplies, chat, and watch grudge fights, began to give way to church, until one day Sunday was, as elsewhere in nineteenth-century America, a day of rest.

On the lighter side the mining frontier included a potpourri of entertainment. There were footraces and horse races, boxing, cockfights; in winter there was sledding and ice-skating. Roller-skating was popular from the 1870's on; there was croquet (Presbyterian billiards), pool, hard-rock-drilling contests. There were lyceums and lectures and debates, glee clubs, minstrels, and plays, by both local and traveling companies. Tent shows appeared in Idaho and Montana as early as 1865. There was money in the camps, and an audience of lusty and lonely men; entertainers gravitated to such places. They were of varying quality, of course; one busty performer held an anvil to her breast while her partner hammered out a horseshoe on it. And there were holidays, the Fourth of July and Christmas being the two most important ones.

There were in addition the fraternal organizations. Many joined them for the sake of security, since most offered members cheap life insurance —$2,000 of straight life, plus membership, for around $16 a year. The Masons, Odd Fellows, Ancient Order of United Workmen, Woodmen of the World, Order of the Red Man, Knights of Pythias, and other such groups flourished in the camps, as did German Turnverein societies, Irish Fenians, and the Ancient Order of Hibernians; smaller racial groups had their own organizations where their numbers warranted.

Finally, the mining town was a school in Americanization for its large concentration of foreign-born. In many camps well over 50 per cent of the inhabitants were emigrants. Cornish ("Cousin Jacks" and "Cousin Jennies"), Irish, and Germans predominated, but men of all races were to be found in these isolated new country Babylons. Moreover, they were young; and the newer the camp, the younger was the population. A median age of twenty-eight was not unusual, and in such a place a man of forty was considered old.

In their democratic poverty the citizenry got along remarkably well. Only the Chinese suffered severely, although there was discrimination against Mexicans and Indians too. The arrival of Chinese in town was considered a sign of decline; many Celestials left these towns much more rapidly than they entered, for violence against them was common and cruel; lynching was not unknown. Those who stayed lived in an area soon designated "Chinatown" and took to washing clothes or cooking. They mastered enough English to be understood.

Most mining towns went into extremely rapid decline. Often within two or three years from the initial strike the town was deserted, the entire district a dismal scene of abandoned mining claims, vacated tunnels into the mountains, and empty, drab, unpainted false-front stores leaning as the wind blew. The heavy mining and milling machinery stood still, rusting in the wintry blasts. What had been accomplished? Much more than a few holes dug in the ground and some precious metals extracted. "The camp," writes Duane Smith, "was a nucleus that attracted, encouraged, and transmitted intellectual, social, economic, and political foundations from which a rich harvest has been reaped."[15]

Indeed, the urban mining frontier accomplished this and more. The towns were dependent from the very first upon the products of other places. They raised no fruits or vegetables or livestock for meat. Therefore they provided a nearby market for ranchers and farmers who saw farms in the mountain valleys rather than mines in the hills as a way of making a living. Thus the remote farm and ranch lands of the new country were developed decades earlier than they would otherwise have been. Because the mining towns needed transportation, the railroad and wagon roads were constructed deep into the Rockies and Sierras years before such conquest of the mountains would otherwise have taken place. And finally, the little towns which served the mines depended upon larger towns which became distributing centers for the mining country, towns which grew into cities such as Sacramento, Stockton, Salt Lake City, and Denver.

Whether they were mining towns, cattle towns, agricultural hamlets, or growing cities with commerce and industry flourishing, the new country urban centers had much in common. All of them were (to borrow a mod-

ern phrase) where the action is. Progress was Boone building Boonesborough, Ogden building Chicago, Evans boosting Denver, Brigham
Young laying out Salt Lake City, civic organizations advertising Los Angeles. The existence of towns and cities gave incentive to transportation
plans, and the long distances between them spurred steamboat, canal,
stagecoach, and railroad development. More even than the farm, ranch,
mine, or lumber camp, the towns and cities were the symbols of civilization's advance into the new country.

ᎤVIIIᎤ
From New Country
to Settled Country

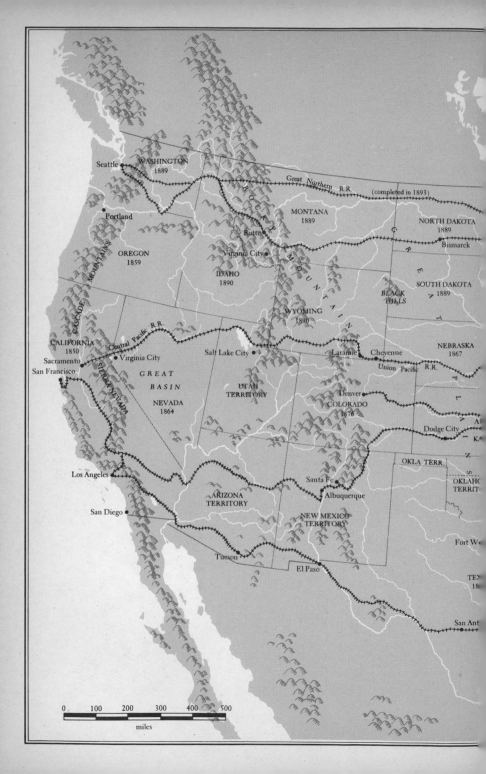

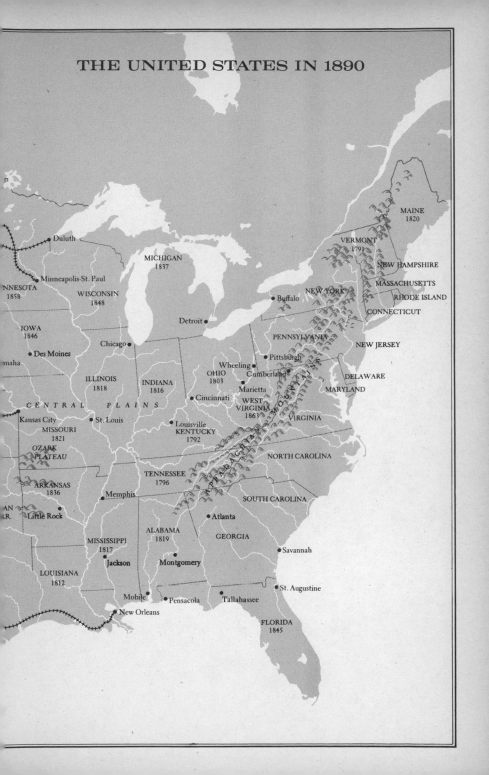

THE UNITED STATES IN 1890

MAINE
1820

VERMONT
1791

NEW HAMPSHIRE

MASSACHUSETTS

RHODE ISLAND

CONNECTICUT

• Duluth

MICHIGAN
1837

NEW YORK

• Buffalo

• Minneapolis-St. Paul

MINNESOTA
1858

WISCONSIN
1848

Detroit •

PENNSYLVANIA

NEW JERSEY

IOWA
1846

• Chicago

Wheeling •   • Pittsburgh

DELAWARE

• Des Moines

OHIO
1803

Cumberland •

MARYLAND

maha

ILLINOIS
1818

INDIANA
1816

Marietta •

WEST
VIRGINIA
1863

• Cincinnati

C E N T R A L   P L A I N S

VIRGINIA

Kansas City •   • St. Louis

• Louisville
KENTUCKY
1792

MISSOURI
1821

OZARK
PLATEAU

NORTH CAROLINA

ARKANSAS
1836

TENNESSEE
1796

• Memphis

SOUTH CAROLINA

AN
R.   • Little Rock

• Atlanta

ALABAMA
1819

GEORGIA

MISSISSIPPI
1817

• Savannah

Jackson

Montgomery

LOUISIANA
1812

St. Augustine •

Mobile •   • Pensacola   • Tallahassee

• New Orleans

FLORIDA
1845

Chicago: May 1, 1893. In blustery, wet weather, "the city of great superlatives" opened the gates to its proudest display, the World's Columbian Exposition, a world's fair in celebration of the four hundredth anniversary of Columbus' great voyage. From the muck of Jackson Park had risen a $30-million white city displaying everything the world had to offer, at its very best, right up to the time of the fair, from May 1 to October 31. "Rolling chairs" pushed by students from more than a hundred colleges carried the more affluent from the Agricultural, Transportation, or Fine Arts Buildings to Machinery Hall, the Manufacturers and Liberal Arts Building, various structures of the states, a Mining Building, an Electrical Building, or to the gaudy Midway Plaisance.

Of course there were frustrations and criticisms. The fair was not all ready by opening day. And Chicagoans, it was noted, were out to "cash in." They were, to quote *Frank Leslie's Weekly*, "on the make." They had surrounded the grounds with "ramshackle temporary structures," mostly hotels (some of which by mid-May had already blown down), and were charging outrageous prices. As for the city of Chicago, its streets were terrible, its water supply abominable ("a dirty, milk-like color, not transparent"), its atmosphere smoke-befouled.[1] But it was a *hustling* city. Seventeen years before, Philadelphia had presented a great Centennial Exhibition which had cost about $8 million. Chicagoans had raised four times that much for their show, and even this they considered no great achievement.

There was also at the fair that long summer a series of exhibitions of "things unseen" in the "annex of pure intellectuals," as the writer for *Frank Leslie's Weekly* referred to the various congresses which were held in Chicago in connection with the fair and attended by intellectuals; they were exhibits, he wrote, which extended "into the region of ideas not susceptible of ocular demonstration."[2] In a single week, there were meetings of instructors of the deaf, of the blind, of stenographers, of higher education, of university extension courses, of manual and art education, of kindergarten educators, of social settlements, of college fraternities, of business college teachers. Among the "things unseen," hardly given a line of publicity in the local press, was a "World's Congress of Historians and Historical Students," which would include a special meeting of the American Historical Association. This organization was not very old, having been organized in 1884, and it was pretty staid and Waspish (as it remained until relatively recently); it was also dominated by the Ivy League colleges. However (and with some reluctance, one suspects), its leadership had decided to accept the invitation to meet out West in Chicago, beginning July 10.

It was natural that an occasional Westerner should be on the program, and one of them was a young professor from the University of Wisconsin, Frederick Jackson Turner. We do not know for sure if he had occasion to browse through the fair exhibits—his biographer says that he remained in his room putting the final touches on his paper, which was presented, the fifth in a row, on Wednesday evening, July 12.[3]

Possibly on the following day, however, relieved of his obligation, he found time to stroll through the fair grounds. If he did, then his spirits must have been bolstered by the accomplishments he saw, for it was indeed a massive, though garish, display of human progress. Possibly he paused at the exhibit of the Boone and Crockett Club, a sportsman's association founded a few years before by Theodore Roosevelt; its membership was a roster of outdoorsmen from the nation's financial, political, and scientific élite. The club had already become a lobbying force preaching conservation. Someone had felt that so prestigious an organization should be represented. And it was: amidst all the massive buildings and the glitter of the super-carnival the club erected a crude log cabin, in front of which stood an old Conestoga. We do not know if many of the twenty-one million visitors took much notice of it. A good guess would be that they did not, because such a dwelling with such a conveyance in front was a commonplace of the remembered past. But the contrast between it and, say, the white palace that housed the mining display led at least one journalist to take up his pen and philosophize.

> The log cabin [editorialized *Harper's Weekly*] represents an actuality in this country even today, but so does the colossal and beautiful triumph of skill in architecture which forms one of the groups of palaces of the World's Fair. The modest hut of logs represents that humble beginning which in this country may easily lead to the fruition that the other stands for, and if we look no farther away than Chicago itself we will find palatial buildings in plenty on ground that supported log cabins only a little more than forty years ago.[4]

Boone and Crockett Club exhibit at World's Columbian Exposition, Chicago, 1893.
(Courtesy Chicago Historical Society)

Of course, there were some Indians to remind the visitors of the wild frontier; and a group of cowboys set out from Chadron, Nebraska, on a 900-mile horse race to the fair. But the fair, with its electric lights, electrically propelled boats on the lagoon, great Ferris Wheel, and displays of machinery and merchandise, made few people think of the age just past. Instead they marveled at the wonders which just a few years, such a very few years, had wrought on the American land. If Turner did pause at the Boone and Crockett Club exhibit, he may well have gained confidence in the validity of the thesis he had set forth in his paper delivered the night before.

He had titled his paper "The Significance of the Frontier in American History." In it Turner, proud of the American accomplishment, seemed to sense the pulse of the people, and used history to offer them an explanation of why as Americans they felt superior to the peoples of the Old World. He said that the key to American development was the existence of an area of free land and its continual recession westward; the real America was to be found in the great Mississippi Valley, not along the Atlantic seaboard. He elaborated on this theme in great detail, ending his paper with the following statement: "And now, four centuries from the discovery of America, at the end of a hundred years of life under the Constitution, the frontier has gone, and with its going has closed the first period of American history."[5] This was confirmed by the remarks appearing in the Introduction to the Census Report for 1890:

> Up to and including 1880 the country had a frontier of settlement, but at present the unsettled area has been so broken into by isolated bodies of settlement that there can hardly be said to be a frontier line. In the discussion of its extent, its westward movement, etc., it cannot, therefore, any longer have a place in the census reports.[6]

Thus 1893 was indeed a fitting time for an historian to present such a thesis; and for nearly forty years, until the depression of the 1930's, Turner's thesis had few critics and many defenders. Turner was a master teacher: first at the University of Wisconsin and later at Harvard, graduate students flocked to his seminars; more than a score of his protégés became leading American historians, their monographs and textbooks so permeated with the Turner thesis that at least two generations of Americans came to believe that America was different, and better, than the rest of the world because its people had passed through the frontier experience. Although the thesis today has many critics, it is probably accurate to say that most American historians still subscribe to it, at least in part.

I too accept the Turner thesis, but in nearly a quarter century of teaching the frontier, or, as it is also known, the westward movement in American history, I grew to believe that the thesis also functioned as a kind of container into which all studies of the frontier first had to fit. Once boxed in, the course of the westward movement was presented in frontier history texts, in the frontier chapters in U.S. history texts, and even in ordinary writing, both fiction and non-fiction, in almost identical format. Indian troubles loomed large; so did the diplomacy that rounded out the geographical limits of the original forty-eight states. Transportation included mention here and there of turnpikes, canals, boating on the rivers, stagecoaches and freight haulers, and finally the railroads. The narration devoted time here on the emigration to Kentucky and Tennessee, there to the Old Southwest or the Old Northwest, Florida, Texas, Oregon, and California. Farming, ranching, and mining bore mention, as did social life in a chapter or two. Somehow this format, essentially unchanging through the years, was distorting the meaning of the great westward movement, hardening some myths and legends, and ignoring the wider view that was opening before us through the distance of time. As I write this (1974) it is eighty-four years since the end of the frontier. The view is broader, and there is also greater depth of perception. Different aspects need to be stressed, some old illusions destroyed, and attention called to some new ones. Events that loomed large to historians in 1893 today no longer dominate the historical landscape. It is time for someone to present the story of the explosive filling in of this great temperate zone area in new and different ways: that has been the object of this book.

First, we have viewed the vast country from the Appalachians to the Pacific as a single entity. This seems justified by the rapidity of its occupation, for from 1776 to 1890 is just 114 years—a ridiculously short period in terms of the three to five thousand years of recorded history. At the time of the signing of the Declaration of Independence the Spanish were in what became San Francisco; before Ohio achieved statehood in 1803 an American named Philip Nolan had already lost his life fighting Spaniards along the Brazos River in Texas; while Wilson Price Hunt was leading the Astorians overland to man a proposed fur-trading post at the mouth of the Columbia, William Henry Harrison was destroying Prophet's Town on Tippecanoe Creek. While the National Road was extending westward in the 1820's, American hide and tallow ships were cruising off California, trading with the Spaniards; in the same year the Alamo fell (1836), Dr. Marcus Whitman and Henry Spalding led a party including their wives, the first white women ever, across South Pass and on to Oregon. While some farmers hesitated over settling on the Great Plains, others emigrated to Oregon and Texas; while the Civil War raged in 1862, the Sioux went on the warpath in Minnesota; two years later Denver was virtually under siege by the Indians. The year Wisconsin achieved statehood (1848), James Marshall found gold in a mill race in northern California; in the year of the Custer fight on the Little Big Horn (1876), Colorado achieved statehood and the first transcontinental railroad had been in operation for seven years. The view of the westward movement, from our position at eighty-plus years since frontier's end, is, then, of a rapid sweep across a continent already salt-and-peppered with white men here and there all over the vast new country.

And it is clear that, even as of 1776, English, French, Spanish and Russians, as well as such Americans as Thomas Jefferson (as a scholar) and George Rogers Clark (as a doer) possessed in the aggregate (had it been assembled) a pretty good idea of the geographical outlines of the country, of its Great Lakes, the Mississippi-Ohio-Missouri river system, the Great Plains, Rocky Mountains, Great Basin, the Sierras and Cascades, and the Pacific slope. The aborigines had so many paths that it would have been possible (though no one, so far as we know, ever did it) to follow their paths from coast to coast, or almost so. And the Indian? He was considered but a nuisance, swept aside in the oncoming rush of the whites; so too were the French in the Mississippi Valley and the Spaniards and Mexicans in Texas and California. What chance had the fur-trading elements of the Hudson's Bay Company to hold off the Americans who came to cut the forest, build farms, construct villages, and create an American civilization in Oregon? The sweep across the continent was inevitable. The complexities of the Louisiana Purchase, the Florida Treaty of 1819-21, the Mexican War, the Oregon question; the numerous "inviolable" treaties with the Indians guaranteeing them new lands to the west "in perpetuity" were likewise mere incidents washed away by the flood tide of the white man's advance.

And what of the people? The emigration was by a polyglot population, most from European peasant stock, but in which the English-speaking percentage carried the day in language, law, and government. The different nationalities that came are not so important individually as the story of their acculturation and adjustment to the new country, of their joyful hard work in a land where there were few taxes, priests, soldiers, or other European signs of restrictive authority. Here was a new country with incredible opportunity for the reasonably healthy, stable, and hard-working person. Millions of such individuals made the most of the opportunity.

In retrospect it was an exciting 114 years. It was, by today's standards, a simpler time, a more challenging time in the sense that the individual saw so much of the challenge within his reach. Maybe—without getting lost in the semantics involved—it was the happiest time for a whole people in all history.

And now we are back again to that Boone and Crockett Club cabin and Conestoga, so incongruous amidst the white palaces and pavilions, the Midway Plaisance where Little Egypt shocked the country with her oriental dancing, the fabulous Ferris Wheel, the dazzlingly bright electric lights. How many times, that summer, did men and women of forty, fifty, sixty or more years linger there, and recall days of yore, of their own childhood or young adulthood, of moving from one homestead to a land of greater promise farther west in the new country, in such a Conestoga wagon, living as a family unit in just such a crude cabin? I like to think that many paused there, showing it to their children who were impatient to see something else, but insisting that the young ones take a good look, hear the tale of their parents' beginnings. And how many of the women stood there with thoughts that were a combination of the bitter and the sweet; and how many men said vocally, "Those were great days!" and then under their breaths added, "Didn't we have a helluva good time?"

Notes

This Land Is Ours: The Sweep Across the Continent

1. Herbert Bolton and Thomas Maitland Marshall, *The Colonization of North America, 1492-1783* (New York, 1922), p. 288.
2. Theodore Roosevelt, *The Winning of the West*, 4 vols. (New York, 1900), Vol. I, pp. 107-8.

The Problem of the Native American

1. No. 857, Vol. XXXIII (New York: March 2, 1872), pp. 385, 391.
2. James D. Richardson, *A Compilation of the Messages and Papers of the Presidents, 1787-1897* (Washington, 1900), Vol. I, pp. 104-8.
3. I U.S. *Statutes at Large*, 329-31.
4. *Ibid.*, p. 470.
5. Richardson, *A Compilation* . . . , pp. 184-85.
6. *Annals of Congress*, Second Congress (1791-93), House of Representatives, January 26, 1792, pp. 338 ff.
7. Alexis de Toqueville, *Democracy in America*, ed. J. P. Mayer and Max Lerner (New York, 1966), p. 312.

The Sweep Across the Continent: First Phase

1. Glen Tucker, *Tecumseh: Vision of Glory* (New York, 1956), p. 211. This is but one of several versions of Tecumseh's statement.
2. Quoted in Samuel Flagg Bemis, *John Quincy Adams and the Foundations of American Foreign Policy* (New York, 1949), p. 327.

Ownership and Order: Land Legislation and Provision for Government

1. Malcolm Rohrbaugh, *The Land Office Business* (New York, 1968), pp. 298-99.
2. Quoted in Payson Jackson Treat, *The National Land System, 1785-1820* (New York, 1910), p. 345.
3. Quoted in William D. Pattison, *Beginnings of the American Rectangular Land Survey System, 1784-1800*, published dissertation, University of Chicago, Department of Geography, Research Paper No. 50 (Chicago, 1957), note 2, p. 50; p. 51.
4. Lowell O. Stewart, *Public Land Surveys: History, Instructions, Methods* (Ames, Iowa, 1935), p. 94.

5. Theodore C. Pease, "The Ordinance of 1787," *The Mississippi Valley Historical Review*, Vol. XXV, No. 2 (September 1938), pp. 170-71.

The Sweep Across the Continent: Final Phase

1. Thomas Jefferson Farnham, *Travels in the Great Western Prairies, the Anahuac and Rocky Mountains, and in the Oregon Territory*, in *Early Western Travels: 1748-1846*, ed. Reuben Gold Thwaites, 32 vols. (New York, 1904-7), Vol. 28, Editor's Preface, pp. 12-13, and pp. 309, 333; Vol. 29, pp. 23, 27. The petition may be found in 26 Cong., 1st Sess., Senate Doc. 514 (Serial set no. 360).
2. Allan Nevins, *Frémont: The West's Greatest Adventurer* (New York, 1928), I, p. 273.

The Basic Mix

1. Stewart H. Holbrook, *The Yankee Exodus* (New York, 1950), p. 3.
2. John Francis Hamtramck Claiborne, *Mississippi as a Province, Territory, and State* (Jackson, Mississippi, 1880; reprinted Baton Rouge, Louisiana, 1964), Vol. I, pp. 107-9.
3. Frances Trollope, *Domestic Manners of the Americans*, ed. Donald Smalley (New York, 1960), p. 370.
4. Charles Woodmason, *The Carolina Back Country on the Eve of the Revolution*, ed. Richard J. Hooker (Chapel Hill, 1953), p. 39.
5. *The Carolina Back Country . . .* , pp. xxvi, 15, 30, 52, 61.
6. Henry Marie Brackenridge, *History of the Western Insurrection in Western Pennsylvania, Commonly Called the Whiskey Rebellion, 1794* (Pittsburgh, 1859), pp. 16, 47.
7. James Hall, *Letters from the West* (Gainesville, Fla., 1967), p. 5.

Basic Traits and New Ingredients

1. John Bradbury, *Travels in the Interior of America*, March of America Facsimile Series, No. 51 (Ann Arbor, 1966). p. 310.
2. Morris Birkbeck, *Notes on a Journey in America*, March of America Facsimile Series, No. 62 (Ann Arbor, 1966), pp. 30-31.
3. Zadoc Cramer, *The Navigator . . .* , 8th ed., March of America Facsimile Series, No. 61 (Ann Arbor, 1966), pp. 33 ff.
4. James Hall, *Letters from the West* (Gainesville, Fla., 1967), p. 31.
5. *Ibid.*, pp. 139-40.
6. Birkbeck, *Notes on a Journey in America*, pp. 36-37.
7. *Letters from the West*, p. 118.
8. *Ibid.*, p. 124.
9. Timothy Flint, *The History and Geography of the Mississippi Valley* (Boston, 1833), Vol. I, p. 142.
10. Frederick Marryat, *A Diary in America, with Remarks on Its Institutions* (New York, 1839). Quoted in George E. Probst, *The Happy Republic* (New York, 1962), p. 165.
11. Theodore C. Blegen, ed., *Land of Their Choice: The Immigrants Write Home* (Minneapolis–St. Paul, 1955), p. 312.
12. Stephen Byrne, *Irish Immigration to the United States* (New York, 1873), pp. 3-4.

13. William H. Goetzmann, ed., *The American Hegelians* (New York, 1972), p. 3.
14. Carl Wittke, *Refugees of Revolution: the German Forty-Eighters in America* (Philadelphia, 1952), p. 120.
15. Andrew F. Rolle, "The Italian Moves Westward," *Montana: The Magazine of Western History*, Vol. XVI, No. 1 (Winter, 1966), pp. 13-24; quote from p. 19.
16. This phrase was used in Europe during the nineteenth century. A collection of such letters is the substance of Theodore C. Blegen, ed., *Land of Their Choice: The Immigrants Write Home* (Minneapolis–St. Paul, 1955).
17. Rufus Learsi, *The Jews in America: A History* (New York, 1954), p. 65.
18. Andrew Rolle, *The Immigrant Upraised* (Norman, Okla., 1969), pp. 256 ff.
19. A. L. Rowse, *The Cousin Jacks* (New York, 1969), p. 9.
20. Lynn Perrigo, "The Cornish Miners of Early Gilpin County," *Colorado Magazine*, Vol. XIV, No. 3 (May, 1937), pp. 91-101; Cornishman quotation on p. 95.
21. Gunther Barth, *Bitter Strength: A History of the Chinese in the United States, 1850-1870* (Cambridge, Mass., 1964), p. 56.
22. Patricia K. Ourada, "The Chinese in Colorado," *Colorado Magazine*, Vol. 29, No. 4 (October 1952), p. 281.
23. Clarence King, *Mountaineering in the Sierra Nevada* (Boston, 1872), p. 110.

Farming the Appalachian Plateau

1. Lyman Draper (1815-91) collected Revolutionary War and pioneer Appalachia manuscripts until they comprised 478 volumes of material on the frontier from 1765 to 1815. He was also head of the Wisconsin State Historical Society. See William B. Hesseltine, *Pioneer's Mission: The Story of Lyman Copeland Draper* (Madison, Wis., 1954).

Farming the Middle West and the South

1. Weymouth T. Jordan, *Rebels in the Making: Planters Conventions and Southern Propaganda* (Tuscaloosa, 1958), p. 19.
2. Quoted in Clifford C. Norse, "The *Southern Cultivator*, 1843-1861," unpublished doctoral dissertation, Florida State University (Tallahassee, 1969), p. 352.
3. Lewis C. Gray, *History of Agriculture in the Southern United States to 1850* (Washington, 1933), Vol. II, p. 831.

Far Western Farmers and Cattlemen

1. Kathryne L. Lichty, "A History of the Settlement of the Nebraska Sand Hills," M.A. thesis, University of Wyoming (Laramie, Wyo., 1960), pp. 79-80.
2. Frank L. Owsley, "The Pattern of Migration and Settlement on the Southern Frontier," *Journal of Southern History*, Vol. XI, No. 2 (May 1945), pp. 160-62.
3. Wilson M. Rockwell, "Cow-Land Aristocrats of the North Fork," *The Colorado Magazine*, Vol. XIV, No. 5 (September 1937), pp. 163-64.

Far Western Spoliation

1. Tom McHugh, *The Time of the Buffalo* (New York, 1972), pp. 16-17. Dr. McHugh, a zoologist, has a convincing rationale for arriving at this estimate.
2. Sir William Drummond Stewart, *Edward Warren* (London, 1854), pp. 3-6.
3. I acknowledge my indebtedness to Robert L. Kelley, whose *Gold vs. Grain: the Hydraulic Mining Controversy in California's Sacramento Valley* (Glendale, 1959), is the definitive work on the subject. Mention should also be made of Rodman W. Paul, *California Gold* (Cambridge, Mass., 1947), Chapter X; the entire book, however, is an excellent study.

Travel by Road

1. W. A. Chalfant, *Death Valley: The Facts* (Stanford, Cal., 1933), pp. 120-23.
2. Alexander Majors, *Seventy Years on the Frontier*, ed. Prentiss Ingraham (Columbus, Ohio, 1950), p. 103. Raymond W. and Mary Lund Settle, *War Drums and Wagon Wheels* (Lincoln, Neb., 1966), p. 44.

Water Routes and Railroads

1. Leland D. Baldwin, *The Keelboat Age on Western Waters* (Pittsburgh, 1941), p. 64. Archibald Hulbert, *The Ohio River: A Course of Empire* (New York, 1906), p. 226, says that it is impossible to describe adequately the "canoes, pirogues, skiffs, dugouts, galleys, arks, keelboats, flatboats, 'broadhorns,' 'sneak boxes,' and rafts" that were used on the western waters. So individualistic was construction that authorities differ on specifications and terminology. The best that can be attained might be termed "accurate generalities."
2. Alvin W. Harlow, *Old Towpaths: The Story of the American Canal Era* (New York, 1926), p. 341.
3. Quoted in Herbert Quick, *Mississippi Steamboatin': A History of Steamboating on the Mississippi and Its Tributaries* (New York, 1926), p. 326.
4. *Steamboats on the Western Rivers* (Cambridge, Mass., 1949), p. 426.
5. Leslie E. Decker, *Railroads, Lands, and Politics: The Taxation of the Railroad Land Grants, 1864-1897* (Providence, R.I., 1964), p. 15.
6. Quoted in George Kraus, *High Road to Promontory* (Palo Alto, 1969), p. 258.
7. Quoted in Paul W. Gates, *The Illinois Central Railroad and Its Colonization Work* (Cambridge, Mass., 1934), p. 177.
8. James B. Hedges, "The Colonization Work of the Northern Pacific Railroad," *Mississippi Valley Historical Review*, Vol. XIII, No. 3 (December 1926), p. 315.
9. This section is based upon Robert Louis Stevenson, *From Scotland to Silverado*, comprising "The Amateur Emigrant" and "Across the Plains," ed. James D. Hart (Cambridge, 1966), pp. 100-47.

Men, Women, and Families

1. Joseph G. Baldwin, *The Flush Times of Alabama and Mississippi* (New York, 1957), p. 36.
2. E. S. Topping, *The Chronicles of the Yellowstone* (St. Paul, 1888), p. 28.
3. *The Autobiography of William Allen White* (New York, 1946), pp. 218-19. Others disagree: historian John D. Hicks described her as a "tall, slender, good-looking woman" as of 1890. *The Populist Revolt* (Minneapolis, 1931), p. 159.
4. It is interesting to note that the definitive *Dictionary of American Biography* contains about 115,000 entries, but has biographies of fewer than 700 women. See Elizabeth Cochran, "Hatchets and Hoopskirts: Women in Kansas History," *The Midwest Quarterly*, Vol. 2, No. 3 (April 1961), pp. 229-49.
5. Alice Blackwood Baldwin (Mrs. Frank D. Baldwin), *Memoirs of the Late Frank D. Baldwin, Major General, U.S.A.* (Los Angeles, 1929), pp. 123 ff.
6. *Godey's Lady's Book*, Vol. XXI (September 1840), pp. 141-42. The song, by a W. D. Brincklé, M.D., bears the title "To the Prairie I'll Fly Not."
7. Charles K. Langley and R. H. Randall, *Bethel Chimes: A Collection of New Songs* (Marion, Iowa, 1891), p. 114.
8. Virginia Reed Murphy, "Across the Plains with the Donner Party (1846): A Personal Narrative of the Overland Trip to California," *Century Magazine*, Vol. XLII, No. 3 (July 1891), p. 410.
9. Jessie Benton Frémont, *Mother Lode Narratives*, ed. with Foreword by Shirley Sargent (Ashland, Cal., 1970), pp. 13, 19.
10. D. C. John, D.D., *The Corona* (Milwaukee, 1893), p. 124. This and the previous hymn are from hymnals in the John Shaw Collection of Childhood in Poetry, Robert Manning Strozier Library, Florida State University, Tallahassee.
11. Quoted in Georgia Willis Read, "Women and Children on the Oregon-California Trail in the Gold Rush Years," *Missouri Historical Review*, Vol. XXXIX, No. 1 (October 1944), p. 9.
12. For the strange way in which a Mrs. Esther Morris gained the credit, see T. A. Larson, *History of Wyoming* (Lincoln, 1965), pp. 89-94.
13. Quoted in Leonard J. Arrington, "The Economic Role of Pioneer Mormon Women," *Western Humanities Review*, Vol. IX, No. 2 (Spring 1955), fn. p. 145.
14. Quoted in Alan Grimes, *The Puritan Ethic and Woman Suffrage* (New York, 1967), p. 66.
15. Quoted in Arthur W. Calhoun, *A Social History of the American Family* (Cleveland, 1918), Vol. II, *From Independence Through Civil War*, p. 22.
16. *Ibid.*, p. 20.
17. *Ibid.*, p. 132.

Society Beyond the Family

1. Muriel Sibelle Wolle, *Stampede to Timberline* (Boulder, Colo., 1949), pp. 281, 505.

2. Charles A. Johnson, *The Frontier Camp Meeting* (Dallas, 1955), pp. 62-63.
3. William Warren Sweet, *Methodism in American History* (New York, 1933), p. 41.
4. *Ibid.*, p. 144.
5. Edward Eggleston, *The Circuit Rider: A Tale of the Heroic Age* (Lexington, Kentucky, 1970), p. 88.
6. Sweet, *Methodism in American History*, p. 146.
7. Eggleston, *The Circuit Rider*, fn. p. 312.
8. There are so many editions of Owen Wister's *The Virginian* that the reader is referred simply to Chapter XXI, "In a State of Sin."
9. Original letter in custody of the Russell Museum, Great Falls, Montana; reprinted by permission.
10. Wolle, *Stampede to Timberline*, p. 211.
11. Quoted in William Warren Sweet, *Religion on the American Frontier* (New York, 1931), Vol. I, *The Baptists*, p. 23.
12. Thomas F. O'Dea, *The Mormons* (Chicago, 1957), p. 18.
13. O'Dea, *The Mormons*, p. 30.
14. Bernard De Voto, "Jonathon Dyer, Frontiersman," in Ray B. West, Jr., ed., *Rocky Mountain Reader* (New York, 1946), pp. 69, 76.
15. Lawrence A. Cremin, *The American Common School: An Historic Conception* (New York, 1951), p. 220.
16. For my examples I have used the Signet edition (New York, 1962) of *McGuffey's Fifth Eclectic Reader*. The definition used is on p. 98.
17. *Ibid.*, p. 71.
18. *Ibid.*, p. 173.
19. Hamlin Garland, *A Son of the Middle Border* (New York, 1923), p. 112.
20. Timothy Dwight, *Travels in New England and New York*, 4 vols. (1832; reprinted Cambridge, Mass., 1969), Vol. II, p. 323.
21. From "Education in the West," speech given at a public meeting in Boston, May 1833, on behalf of Kenyon College, Ohio. In Edward Everett, *Importance of Practical Education and Useful Knowledge* (Boston, 1840), p. 164; available on microfilm in American Culture Series, Film 79, Reel 235, no. 10.

The Urban Frontier

1. LeRoy Hafen, W. Eugene Hollon, and Carl Coke Rister, *Western America*, 3rd ed. (Englewood Cliffs, N.J., 1970), pp. 517-56.
2. Clara Longworth de Chambrun, *Cincinnati: The Story of the Queen City* (New York, 1939), p. 52.
3. Charles J. Kappler, *Indian Affairs, Laws and Treaties* (Washington, D.C., 1904), Vol. II (*Treaties*), p. 40.
4. Quoted in Herbert Eugene Bolton, *Outposts of Empire* (New York, 1931), pp. 257-58.
5. Richard Henry Dana, *Two Years Before the Mast* (numerous editions). The quotation is from the first paragraph of chapter 26.
6. A. J. Liebling, "The American Golconda," *The New Yorker*, Vol. XVI, (November 16, 1940), p. 48.
7. Robert R. Dykstra, *The Cattle Towns* (New York, 1970), p. 125.

8. Gerald M. Capers, Jr., *The Biography of a River Town* (Chapel Hill, N.C., 1939), pp. 42-43.
9. Frederick Jackson Turner, "The Significance of the Frontier in American History," Ray Allen Billington, ed., *Frontier and Section: Selected Essays of Frederick Jackson Turner* (Englewood Cliffs, N.J., 1961), p. 61.
10. James Bryce, *The American Commonwealth* (New York, 1897), Vol. II, fn. p. 837.
11. *Ibid.*, pp. 830-31.
12. *Ibid.*, pp. 836-37.
13. *Ibid.*, p. 837.
14. W. Turrentine Jackson, *Treasure Hill: Portrait of a Sliver Mining Camp* (Tucson, 1963), p. 94.
15. Duane Smith, *Rocky Mountain Mining Camps: The Urban Frontier* (Bloomington, Ind., 1967), p. 245.

From New Country to Settled Country

1. *Frank Leslie's Illustrated Weekly*, Vol. LXXVII, No. 1966 (May 18, 1893), p. 321.
2. *Ibid.*, August 10, 1893, p. 84.
3. Ray Allen Billington, *Frederick Jackson Turner: Historian, Scholar, Teacher* (New York, 1973), pp. 124-31.
4. *Harper's Weekly*, Vol. XXVII, No. 1902 (June 3, 1893), p. 531 (photograph on p. 532).
5. Turner's paper has frequently been reprinted, especially in books of readings for college students. Any good library should have it, quite possibly in Frederick Jackson Turner, *The Frontier in American History* (New York, 1920), pp. 1-38.
6. *Eleventh Decennial Census* (Washington, 1893), p. xxxvi.

Bibliographical Essay

When a man writes on a subject he has been teaching for a quarter of a century, it is clearly impossible for him to list all the sources he has consulted for his many statements of fact and interpretation. He does not know or recall all of them. Often his ideas are a result of his own analysis, and he can only guess at which readings influenced him. Moreover, the historiography of the new country is simply too massive for anyone to list completely. Ray Allen Billington's great frontier text, *Westward Expansion* (4th ed., New York, 1974), contains 142 pages, double-columned and in fine print, of bibliographical notes. What I am presenting here, then, are sources that have made an impression upon my thoughts and have sometimes directly influenced my interpretations.

Let me first note a few general sources which will be found in any reputable public library of a city with over a quarter million population and in any good college or university library. Two bibliographies are of great help: Thomas D. Clark, *Travels in the Old South* (3 vols., Norman, Okla., 1956-1959), and Henry W. Wagner and Charles L. Camp, *The Plains and the Rockies* (San Francisco, 1937). The books noted in these bibliographies have been printed in full on microcards by the Lost Cause Press and are thus available to many libraries whose financial condition would preclude their having the actual books in their custody. Another excellent bibliographical guide is Oscar O. Winther, *The Trans-Mississippi West: A Guide to its Periodical Literature* (Bloomington, Ind., 1942), and Winther and Richard A. Van Orman, *A Classified Bibliography of the Periodical Literature of the Trans-Mississippi West: A Supplement* (1957-1967) (Bloomington, Ind., 1970).

One of the best sources of description and travel is Reuben Golde Thwaites, ed., Early Western Travels, 1748-1846 (34 vols., Cleveland, 1904-7). A delightful collection of 100 important works on the westward movement is the March of America Facsimile Series (Ann Arbor, Mich., 1966). Ray Allen Billington is editor-in-chief of a new series of monographs by various specialists under the general heading of Histories of the American Frontier (New York, 1966-72; Albuquerque, N.M., 1973–). The following volumes pertinent to the period 1776-1890 have been published at this writing: Ray Allen Billington, *America's Frontier Heritage* (1966); John Francis Bannon, *The Spanish Borderlands Frontier, 1534-1821* (1970); Jack M. Sosin, *The Revolutionary Frontier, 1763-1783* (1967); Reginald Horsman, *The Frontier in the Formative Years, 1783-1815* (1969); Oscar O. Winther, *The Trans-*

portation Frontier, Trans-Mississippi West, 1865-1890 (1964); Gilbert C. Fite, *The Farmer's Frontier, 1865-1900* (1966); and Rodman W. Paul, *Mining Frontiers of the Far West, 1848-1880* (1963). Dale Van Every's four volumes tracing the frontier from 1754 to 1848: *Forth to the Wilderness, A Company of Heroes, Ark of Empire,* and *The Final Challenge* (New York, 1961-64) have also appeared in paperback and are informational. So too are John A. Caruso's *The Appalachian Frontier, The Mississippi Valley Frontier, The Southern Frontier,* and *The Great Lakes Frontier* (Indianapolis, 1959-66). In the New American Nation Series, ed. Henry Steele Commager and Richard B. Morris, the following volumes are pertinent: John R. Alden, *The American Revolution: 1775-1783* (New York, 1954); Clement Eaton, *The Growth of Southern Civilization: 1790-1860* (New York, 1961); Louis B. Wright, *Culture on the Moving Frontier* (New York, 1961); Francis S. Philbrick, *The Rise of the West: 1754-1830* (New York, 1965); and Ray Allen Billington, *The Far Western Frontier: 1830-1860* (New York, 1956). Besides the historical journals that exist for the various states, and the well-known national ones, special mention should be made of *Agricultural History,* a quarterly which has been in publication since 1917 and constitutes the best single source for many types of information on the developing new country.

I
This Land is Ours:
The Sweep Across the Continent

For the Spanish in North America the best general sources are the works of Herbert E. Bolton, whose bibliography is extensive but, disappointingly, does not include a good one-volume detailed history. His *The Spanish Borderlands* in the Chronicles of America Series (New Haven, 1921) gives a simplified overview; John Francis Bannon, ed., *Bolton and the Spanish Borderlands* (Norman, Okla., 1964), gives a better impression of Bolton's mastery of the subject. A recent, beautifully illustrated book tracing Anza's journey is Richard A. Pourade, *Anza Conquers the Desert: The Anza Expeditions from Mexico to California and the Founding of San Francisco* (San Diego, 1971), though Theodore E. Treutlein, *San Francisco Bay: Discovery and Colonization, 1769-1776* (San Francisco, 1968), is far more scholarly. Warren L. Cook, *Flood Tide of Empire: Spain and the Pacific Northwest, 1543-1819* (New Haven, 1973) incorporates the most recent research on the subject. Spanish knowledge of the Great Basin is discussed in Gloria G. Cline, *Exploring the Great Basin* (Norman, Okla., 1962). The Russians and their push down the Pacific coast can be traced in Hector Chevigny, *Russian America: The Great Alaskan Venture, 1741-1867* (New York, 1965). The French, like the Spanish, have many chroniclers. John Bartlet Brebner, *Explorers of North America, 1492-1806* (New York, 1933), covers both the Spanish and the French phases. Francis Parkman, *LaSalle and the Discovery of the Great West* (Boston, 1898), and Hodding Carter, *Doomed Road of Destiny* (New York, 1963) in the American Trails Series, cover Spanish-French rivalry in the Southwest very well. See also Noel M. Loomis and Abraham P. Nasatir, *Pedro Vial and the Roads to Santa Fe* (Norman, 1967). For the upper Missouri country, see Abraham P. Nasatir, ed., *Before Lewis and Clark* (St. Louis, 1952).

British and colonial (or American) knowledge of the trans-Appalachian country is considered in Jack M. Sosin, *The Revolutionary Frontier, 1763-1783* (New York, 1967); Dale Van Every, *A Company of Heroes: The American Frontier, 1775-1783* (New York, 1962); Clarence W. Alvord, *The Mississippi Valley in British Politics* (2 vols., Cleveland, 1917); James Leitch Wright, *Anglo-Spanish Rivalry in North America* (Athens, Ga., 1971); Beverley W. Bond, Jr., *The Civilization of the Old Northwest* (New York, 1934); and Thomas P. Abernethy, *Western Lands and the American Revolution* (New York, 1937).

The Floridas under British rule are ably presented in Cecil Johnson, *British West Florida* (New Haven, 1943). A good description of the American colonies on the eve of the Revolution is Herbert L. Osgood, *American Colonies in the Eighteenth Century* (4 vols., New York, 1924-25). The flora and fauna of the new country are admirably described in Richard Lillard, *The Great Forest* (New York, 1947); Theodore Roosevelt, *The Winning of the West* (6 vols., New York, 1889-96 and subsequent editions and abridgements); and John Bakeless, *The Eyes of Discovery* (Philadelphia, 1950). Robert L. Kincaid, *The Wilderness Road* (Indianapolis, 1947), is excellent on that early trail. See also Archer Butler Hulbert, *Historic Highways of America* (16 vols., Cleveland, 1902, especially Vol. 2, *Indian Thorofares*).

Although there are many works on the American Indian in general, none are entirely satisfactory. Ruth M. Underhill, *Red Man's America* (Chicago, 1953), is well organized and well balanced in its attitude, geographical coverage, and subject matter. Nearly every major tribe from coast to coast has been the subject of more or less scholarly monographs. The University of Oklahoma Press lists some 111 entries in its Civilization of the American Indians series. As for Indian policy, Francis P. Prucha, *American Indian Policy in the Formative Years: The Indian Trade and Intercourse Acts, 1780-1834* (Cambridge, Mass., 1962), and Reginald Horsman, *Expansion and American Indian Policy, 1783-1812* (East Lansing, Mich., 1967), are both excellent. Robert S. Cotterill, *The Southern Indians* (Norman, Okla., 1954), and Grant Foreman, *Indian Removals: The Emigration of the Five Civilized Tribes of Indians* (Norman, Okla., 1932) and *The Last Trek of the Indians* (Chicago, 1946), are all good on the removals of the 1830's and 40's. Henry E. Fritz, *The Movement for Indian Assimilation, 1860-1890* (Philadelphia, 1963) deals with post–Civil War Indian policy. Indian treaties are to be found in Charles J. Kappler, *Indian Affairs, Laws, and Treaties* (5 vols., Washington, D.C., 1904-41). The lobbying activities of the fur traders are well presented in Kenneth W. Porter, *John Jacob Astor, Business Man* (2 vols., Cambridge, Mass., 1931).

The best overall study of land policy is Roy M. Robbins, *Our Landed Heritage* (Princeton, 1942; reprinted Lincoln, Nebr., 1962). Other general studies are Benjamin Horace Hibbard, *A History of the Public Land Policies* (New York, 1924, 1939, reprinted Madison, Wis., 1965); Payson Jackson Treat, *The National Land System, 1785-1820* (New York, 1910); Vernon Carstensen, ed., *The Public Lands: Studies in the History of the Public Domain* (Madison, Wis., 1963); and Everett Dick, *The Lure of the Land: A Social History of the Public Lands from the Articles of Confederation to the New Deal* (Lincoln, Nebr., 1970). The manipulations of the early land speculators are well presented in Thomas P. Abernethy, *From Frontier to Planta-*

tion in Tennessee (Chapel Hill, N.C., 1932); *The Formative Period in Alabama, 1815-1828* (University, Ala., 1965); and *The South in the New Nation: 1789-1819* (Baton Rouge, 1961). Land speculation in Tennessee is ably discussed in Stanley J. Folmsbee, *Tennessee: A Short History* (Knoxville, 1969). An excellent study of the Yazoo land frauds in Georgia is C. Peter McGrath, *Yazoo: Law and Politics in the New Republic: The Case of Fletcher vs. Peck* (Providence, 1966). Two books by Beverly W. Bond, Jr., give information on land schemes in the Old Northwest: *The Civilization of the Old Northwest: A Study of Political, Social, and Economic Development, 1788-1812* (New York, 1934), and his edition of *The Correspondence of John Cleves Symmes* (New York, 1926). Two excellent articles on land issues are Jack Sosin, "The Yorke-Camden Opinion and American Land Speculators," *Pennsylvania Magazine of History and Biography*, Vol. 85 (1961), pp. 38-49; and Paul W. Gates, "The Role of the Speculators in Western Development," *Ibid.*, Vol. 66 (1942), pp. 314-33. Superficial but readable is Aaron M. Sakolski, *The Great American Land Bubble* (New York, 1932). The role of the General Land Office is ably presented in Malcolm Rohrbaugh, *The Land Office Business* (New York, 1968). A brief, earlier study is Milton Conover, *The General Land Office: Its History, Activities, and Organization* (Baltimore, 1923). For the post–Civil War period, Paul W. Gates, *Fifty Million Acres* (New York, 1966), and Edgar I. Stewart, ed., *Penny-an-Acre Empire in the West* (Norman, Okla., 1968), are worth reading.

Western intrigue is described in Samuel C. Williams, *History of the Lost State of Franklin* (rev. ed., New York, 1933). The Ordinance of 1785 is discussed in William D. Pattison, *The Beginnings of the American Rectangular Land Survey System, 1784-1800* (Chicago, 1957). The intricacies of the public land survey are described in David Greenhood, *Down to Earth: Mapping for Everybody* (New York, 1944) and Lowell O. Stewart, *Public Land Surveys: History, Instructions, Methods* (Ames, Iowa, 1935). For the Ordinance of 1787, see Theodore C. Pease, "The Ordinance of 1787," in *The Mississippi Valley Historical Review*, Vol. XXV, No. 2 (September 1938), pp. 167-80; there is an excellent survey of the history of the application of the ordinance through the years in Howard R. Lamar, *The Far Southwest, 1846-1912* (New Haven, 1966). An overview is John Porter Bloom, ed., *The American Territorial System* (Athens, Ohio, 1973).

The history of the West in the general period 1776-1860 is told in great detail in Francis S. Philbrick, *The Rise of the West, 1754-1830* (New York, 1965); Thomas P. Abernethy, *The South in the New Nation, 1789-1819* (Baton Rouge, La., 1961); Frederick Jackson Turner, *The Rise of the New West, 1819-1829* (New York, 1906); and Ray Allen Billington, *The Far Western Frontier, 1830-1860* (New York, 1956). Samuel Flagg Bemis is the authority on *Jay's Treaty* (New York, 1923) and *Pinckney's Treaty* (Baltimore, 1926). Philip C. Brooks, *Diplomacy and the Borderlands* (Berkeley, 1939) gives an excellent overview of the Adams-Onís Treaty of 1819. On the Louisiana Purchase both Arthur P. Whitaker, *The Mississippi Question, 1795-1803* (New York, 1934) and Elijah W. Lyon, *Louisiana in French Diplomacy, 1759-1804* (Norman, Okla., 1934), are good.

Of the many books on Lewis and Clark, John Bakeless, *Lewis and Clark: Partners in Discovery* (New York, 1947) and Paul Russell Cutright, *Lewis and Clark: Pioneering Naturalists* (Champaign-Urbana, Ill., 1970) are very well done; Charles G. Clarke, *The Men of the Lewis and Clark Expedition* (Glendale, Cal., 1970) takes an enlightening approach.

The Fort Mims massacre (August 30, 1813), and the defeat of the Creeks are presented in Angie Debo, *The Road to Disappearance* (Norman, Okla., 1941). Florida difficulties are covered in Rembert W. Patrick, *Florida Fiasco* (Athens, Ga., 1954); Julius W. Pratt, *The Expansionists of 1812* (New York, 1925); and Isaac Cox, *The West Florida Controversy, 1798-1813* (Baltimore, 1918). See also Samuel Flagg Bemis, *John Quincy Adams and the Foundations of American Foreign Policy* (New York, 1949).

There is a whole library of material on the fur trade. Hiram Martin Chittenden, *The American Fur Trade of the Far West* (3 vols., New York, 1935), and Paul Russell Phillips, *The Fur Trade* (2 vols., Norman, Okla., 1961) are basic. Everett Dick, *Vanguards of the Frontier* (New York, 1937), is good on the subject. LeRoy Hafen, ed., *The Mountain Men and the Fur Trade of the Far West* (10 vols., Glendale, Cal., 1965-72); Robert Glass Cleland, *This Reckless Breed of Men: The Trappers and Fur Traders of the Southwest* (New York, 1950); Harvey L. Carter, *"Dear Old Kit"* (Norman, Okla. 1961); M. Morgan Estergreen, *Kit Carson: A Portrait in Courage* (Norman, Okla., 1962); Dale Morgan, *Jedediah Smith and the Opening of the West* (Indianapolis, Ind., 1953); James C. Alter, *James Bridger* (Salt Lake City, 1926); W. A. Ferris, *Life in the Rocky Mountains*, ed. by Paul R. Phillips (Denver, 1940) and Osborn, Russell, *Journal of a Trapper*, ed. Aubrey L. Haines (Lincoln, Neb., 1955), are but a few of a large number of excellent studies. John E. Sunder, *The Fur Trade of the Upper Missouri, 1840-1965* (Norman, Okla., 1965), describes that phase of American expansion.

For Texas, Rupert Richardson, *Texas: The Lone Star State* (New York, 1943, 1955), is good. W. Eugene Hollon, *The Southwest Old and New* (New York, 1961), Odie B. Faulk, *Land of Many Frontiers* (New York, 1968), and Lynn Perrigo, *The American Southwest* (New York, 1971), are good surveys. The Texas revolution is adequately covered in William C. Binkley, *The Texas Revolution* (Baton Rouge, 1952); two other books on Texas history are T. R. Fehrenbach, *Lone Star: A History of Texas and the Texans* (New York, 1968), and Eugene C. Barker, *Readings in Texas History* (Dallas, 1919). Josiah Gregg, *Commerce of the Prairies*, ed. by Max Moorhead (Norman, 1954), and Robert L. Duffus, *The Santa Fe Trail* (New York, 1930), are good on the subject. For activities of the army, William H. Goetzmann, *Army Surveys of the American West* (New Haven, 1966), is definitive.

Oregon is discussed in Oscar O. Winther, *The Great Northwest* (New York, 1950) and Dorothy O. Johansen, *Empire of the Columbia: A History of the Pacific Northwest* (New York, 1957). Expansion to the Pacific is the subject of Norman Graebner, *Empire on the Pacific* (New York, 1955), Frederick Merk, *Manifest Destiny and Mission in American History* (New York, 1963), and Albert K. Weinberg, *Manifest Destiny* (Baltimore, 1955). A good general history of the Pacific West is Earl Pomeroy, *The Pacific Slope* (New York, 1965). Frémont's part in the taking of California is well described in Allen Nevins, *Frémont: The West's Greatest Adventurer* (2 vols.: New York, 1928). The Mexican War is treated in Alfred Hoyt Bill, *Rehearsal for Conflict* (New York, 1947), Otis Singletary, *The Mexican War* (Chicago, 1960), and Seymour V. Connor and Odie B. Faulk, *North America Divided: The Mexican War, 1846-1848* (New York, 1971), the lat-

ter having an admirable bibliography of Mexican War literature. Bernard
DeVoto, *The Year of Decision: 1846* (Boston, 1946), is an intriguing his-
toriographical exercise in which a single but very important year is scru-
tinized.

The story of the final settlement is adequately told in Gilbert Fite, *The
Farmer's Frontier: 1865-1900* (New York, 1966), Robert G. Athearn, *High
Country Empire* (New York, 1969), and W. Eugene Hollon, *The Great
American Desert* (New York, 1966). Hollon's book updates Walter Prescott
Webb's *The Great Plains* (New York, 1931).

II
The People

A good source of statistics on the population in colonial times is Everts B.
Greene and Virginia D. Harrington, *American Population Before the Fed-
eral Census of 1790* (New York, 1932). So is United States Department of
Commerce, *Historical Statistics of the United States, Colonial Times to 1957*
(Washington, D.C., 1961). See also Stella H. Sutherland, *Population Dis-
tribution in Colonial America* (New York, 1936). Some idea of colonial life
and thought on the eve of the trans-Appalachian thrust can be found in
Louis B. Wright, *The Atlantic Frontier* (New York, 1947) and Herbert L.
Osgood, *The American Colonies in the Seventeenth Century* (3 vols., New
York, 1904-7). A number of new viewpoints are suggested in Daniel Boorstin,
The Americans: The Colonial Experience (New York, 1958). Since an understanding of Americans must begin with their European backgrounds, Edward P. Cheney, *European Background of American History* (New York,
1904), is useful. The expansion of New England is ably presented in Lois
Kimball Mathews (Rosenberry), *The Expansion of New England* (Boston,
1909), while Stewart Holbrook, *Yankee Exodus* (New York, 1950), presents
a delightful story of Yankee influence. Donald Smalley's annotation of Mrs.
Frances Trollope, *Domestic Manners of the Americans* (New York, 1949),
does justice to this classic. Redemptioners are treated in Abbott Emerson
Smith, *Colonists in Bondage, White Servitude and Convict Labor in America, 1607-1776* (Chapel Hill, N.C., 1941). Southern colonials are ably described in Thomas P. Abernethy, *The South in the New Nation, 1789-1819*
(Baton Rouge, 1961).

The troubled early history of the black man in the new country is related
in Kenneth G. Goode and Winthrop D. Jordan, *From Africa to the United
States and Then . . . : A Concise Afro-American History* (Glenview, Ill.,
1969), and Winthrop D. Jordan, *White Over Black: American Attitudes
Toward the Negro, 1550-1812* (Chapel Hill, N.C., 1968). See also John
Hope Franklin, *From Slavery to Freedom* (New York, 1948), and Clement
Eaton, *The Growth of Southern Civilization, 1790-1860* (New York, 1961).
An early study is W. Sherman Savage, "The Negro in the Westward Movement," *Journal of Negro History*, Vol. XXV, No. 4 (October 1940), pp.
531-39. William H. Leckie, *The Buffalo Soldiers* (Norman, Okla., 1967)
and Philip Durham and Everett L. Jones, *The Negro Cowboys* (New York,
1965), are good beginnings at the story of the black man in the trans-
Mississippi country.

The best study of the early emigration to the new country is Marcus Lee

Hansen, *The Atlantic Migration, 1607-1860* (New York, 1940). The Scotch-Irish have had many chroniclers. Charles Woodmason, *The Carolina Back Country on the Eve of the Revolution* (Chapel Hill, N.C., 1953), gives an Anglican priest's views of the back-country people as he observed them in the early 1770's. James G. Leyburn, *The Scotch-Irish: A Social History* (Chapel Hill, N.C., 1962) is excellent. See also Ian Charles Cargill Graham, *Colonists from Scotland: Emigration to North America, 1717-1783* (Ithaca, N.Y., 1956); Duane Gilbert Meyer, *The Highland Scots of North Carolina, 1732-1776* (Chapel Hill, N.C., 1961); Henry Jones Ford, *The Scotch-Irish in America* (Princeton, N.J., 1915); and, for the Scotch background, William Edward Hartpole Lecky, *A History of England in the Eighteenth Century* (8 vols., London, 1920), Vol. 2. The Paxton Riots are discussed in Wilbur R. Jacobs, *The Paxton Riots and the Frontier Theory* (Chicago, 1967). John S. Bassett, "The Regulators of North Carolina," American Historical Association, *Annual Report for 1894*, pp. 141-212, is satisfactory on that subject, and Richard Maxwell Brown, *The South Carolina Regulators* (Cambridge, Mass., 1963) is definitive on that group. Consult Leland D. Baldwin, *Whiskey Rebels* (Pittsburgh, 1939), for that frontier incident.

Much has been written about the Germans, or the "Pennsylvania Dutch." Two good studies are by Carl Wittke, *We Who Built America* (Cleveland, 1964) and *Refugees of Revolution: The German Forty-Eighters in America* (Philadelphia, 1952). See also Adolph E. Zucker, *The Forty-Eighters* (New York, 1950). For the intellectual contribution of the Germans, see William H. Goetzmann, ed., *The American Hegelians: An Intellectual Episode in the History of Western America* (New York, 1973). The Irish are treated in Stephen Byrne, *Irish Emigration to the United States* (New York, 1873). For the Swiss, see Albert B. Faust, "Swiss Emigration to the American Colonies in the Eighteenth Century," *American Historical Review*, Vol. XXII, No. 1 (October 1916), pp. 11-44. The Huguenot emigration is treated in Charles W. Baird, *History of the Huguenot Migration to America* (2 vols., New York, 1885). For Scandinavians, see Theodore C. Blegen, *Land of Their Choice: The Immigrants Write Home* (St. Paul, 1955) and Carlton C. Qualey, *Norwegian Settlement in the United States* (Northfield, Minn., 1938). The Jews are treated in Rufus Learsi, *The Jews in America: A History* (New York, 1954), and the Italians in Andrew F. Rolle, *The Immigrant Upraised* (Norman, Okla., 1969). The Cornish are discussed in A. L. Rowse, *The Cousin Jacks: The Cornish in America* (New York, 1969) and in Lynn I. Perrigo, "The Cornish Miners of Early Gilpin County," *Colorado Magazine*, Vol. 24, no. 3 (May 1937), pp. 92-101.

George Sagic-Fisher is discussed in Nikola R. Privic, "George Sagic-Fisher: Patriot of Two Worlds," *The Florida State University Slavic Papers*, Vol. 1 (Tallahassee, 1967), pp. 35-47. For the Chinese, see Andrew F. Rolle, *California: A History* (2d ed., New York, 1969); Rodman W. Paul, "The Origin of the Chinese Issue in California," *Mississippi Valley Historical Review*, Vol. XXV (September 1939), pp. 181-93; Hubert Howe Bancroft, *Works*, Vol. XXV, *History of Nevada, Colorado, and Wyoming, 1540-1888* (San Francisco, 1890), p. 292; Gunther Barth, *Bitter Strength: A History of the Chinese in the United States, 1850-1870* (Cambridge, Mass., 1964); Stuart Creighton Miller, *The Unwelcome Immigrant: The American Image of the Chinese, 1785-1882* (Berkeley, 1969); Robert F. Heizer and Alan F. Almquist, *The Other Californians: Prejudice and Discrimination Under Spain, Mexico, and the United States* (Berkeley, 1971); Shien Woo Kung, *Chinese in American Life: Some Aspects of Their History, Status, Problems, and Contributions* (Seattle, Wash., 1962); and Patricia K. Ourada, "The Chinese in Colorado," *Colorado Magazine*, Vol. 29, no. 4 (October 1952), pp. 273-84. Clarence King's "The Newtys of Pike" is in his *Mountaineering in the Sierra Nevada* (Boston, 1872).

Travelers' accounts in which emigrants are mentioned include Timothy Flint, *The History and Geography of the Mississippi Valley* (Boston, 1833); John Bradbury, *Travels in the Interior of America* (London, 1817; reprinted Ann Arbor, Mich., 1966); Charles Dickens, *American Notes* (London, 1846; numerous editions); Morris Birkbeck, *Notes on a Journey in America* (London, 1818, reprinted Ann Arbor, Mich., 1966); James Hall, *Letters from the West* (London, 1828, reprinted Gainesville, Fla., 1967); and Frederick Marryat, *A Diary in America, With Remarks on Its Institutions* (New York, 1839, reprinted Bloomington, Ind., 1960), as quoted in George E. Probst, *The Happy Republic* (New York, 1962). There were many editions of Zadoc Cramer's *The Navigator* (Pittsburgh, 1801); an easily obtainable one is the reproduction of the eighth edition (Ann Arbor, Mich., 1967). A final reference is Harriet Martineau, *Society in America* (London, 1837; reprinted, ed. by Seymour Lipset, New York, 1962). See also her *Retrospect of Western Travel* (2 vols., London, 1838; reprinted New York, 1942).

III
Agriculture: The Basic Endeavor

As is true in general, references given for other topics may be valuable here. In addition, the following sources round out the sources of information on agriculture.

Richard G. Lillard, *The Great Forest* (New York, 1948), is excellent on the "backwoods system," Lillard's phrase for the way of life of the trans-Appalachian pioneer agriculturalist. He also describes the evolution of the American axe. Franklin's timing of a tree cutting is in *The Autobiography*, American Heritage Series (Indianapolis, 1952), p. 146. A good description of the agricultural frontier in western New York is Jared Van Wagenen, Jr., *Golden Age of Homespun* (Ithaca, N.Y., 1953). The literature on new country firearms is extensive though often faulty because it is written by hobbyists who know much about guns but little about writing history. Joseph W. Shields, *From Flintlock to M-1* (New York, 1954), is adequate. Though he exaggerates the blood and gore of the frontier, Theodore Roosevelt's *The Winning of the West* (New York, 1889-96) is still enjoyable reading and within (though just barely) the limits of accuracy necessary to justify its inclusion here. My source for the average size of a city block is correspondence dated December 4, 1972, from Mr. Robert L. Funk, Assistant Director of Information, Municipal Finance Officers Association, Chicago. On the log cabin, see C. A. Weslager, *The Log Cabin in America* (New Brunswick, N.J., 1969).

There are a number of excellent studies of nineteenth-century farming, especially in the Middle West. Particularly good is Allen G. Bogue, *From Prairie to Corn Belt* (Chicago, 1963, 1968); Paul W. Gates, *The Farmer's*

Age: 1815-1860 (New York, 1960); Fred Albert Shannon, *The Farmer's Last Frontier: Agriculture, 1860-1897* (New York, 1945); Gilbert Fite, *The Farmer's Frontier: 1865-1900* (New York, 1966); and Joseph Shafer, *The Social History of American Agriculture* (New York, 1936). The quarterly journal *Agricultural History* is crammed with information. Percy Wells Widwell and John I. Falconer, *History of Agriculture in the Northern United States, 1620-1860* (Washington, D.C., 1925), is encyclopedic. There are excellent essays in Wayne D. Rasmussen, *Readings in the History of American Agriculture* (Urbana, Ill., 1960). The U.S. Department of Agriculture *Yearbook, Farmers in a Changing World* (Washington, D.C., 1940), contains useful information. Nor should one miss the work of James C. Malin, *The Grasslands of North America: Prologomena to Its History, with Addenda* (Lawrence, Kans., 1961). Most of my material on farm animals came from the works above, but see also Harry J. Carman, ed., *American Husbandry* (New York, 1939).

Technological improvements are discussed in Roger Burlingame, *March of the Iron Men* (New York, 1938) and *Machines That Made America* (New York, 1953). A provocative essay is Harold U. Faulkner, "Farm Machinery and the Industrial Revolution," *Current History*, Vol. XXXIII (1931), pp. 872-76. An old general account is Robert L. Ardrey, *American Agricultural Implements* (Chicago, 1894; reprinted New York, 1972). The definitive biography of the reaper king is W. T. Hutchinson, *Cyrus Hall McCormick* (2 vols., New York, 1939), but Herbert N. Casson, *Cyrus Hall McCormick: His Life and Work* (Chicago, 1909), is also of interest. See the *Dictionary of American Biography*, "John Deere," Vol. V, pp. 193-94, for a good biography of that personage.

Nearly every historical study of the South devotes considerable space to southern agriculture. Of special importance is Lewis C. Gray, *History of Agriculture in the Southern United States to 1850* (2 vols., Washington, D.C., 1933). Excellent specialized studies are Weymouth T. Jordan, *Rebels in the Making: Planter's Conventions and Southern Propaganda* (Tuscaloosa, Ala., 1958); Frank L. Owsley, "The Pattern of Migration and Settlement on the Southern Frontier," *Journal of Southern History*, Vol. XI, No. 2 (May 1945), pp. 147-76; E. Merton Coulter, "A Century of a Georgia Plantation," *Agricultural History*, Vol. III, No. 4 (October 1929), pp. 147-59; and Clifford Norse, "The Southern Cultivator, 1843-1861," unpublished doctoral dissertation, Florida State University (Tallahassee, 1969). A superb study is John Hebron Moore, *Agriculture in Ante-Bellum Mississippi* (New York, 1958).

For the Middle Border and the Great Plains, two books give excellent information, Walter Prescott Webb's *The Great Plains* (New York, 1931) and W. Eugene Hollon's *The Great American Desert* (New York, 1966). Slightly more restricted in geographical area described is Robert Athearn, *High Country Empire: The High Plains and the Rockies* (New York, 1960; Lincoln, Nebr., 1965). Everett Dick, *The Sod-House Frontier, 1854-1900* (New York, 1937), is especially good on the social life of that area. An interpretive sociological study is Carl Frederick Kraenzel, *The Great Plains in Transition* (Norman, Okla., 1955). Joseph Kinsey Howard, *Montana: High, Wide, and Handsome* (New Haven, 1943), is good on the settlement there. The Southwest is adequately treated in W. Eugene Hollon, *The Southwest,*

466   Bibliographical Essay

Old and New (New York, 1961), and Odie B. Faulk, *Land of Many Frontiers: A History of the American Southwest* (New York, 1968). The Far West is well handled in Earl Pomeroy, *The Pacific Slope* (New York, 1965). Two books touching on land acquisition are Paul Wallace Gates, *Fifty Million Acres: Conflicts Over Kansas Land Policy, 1854-1890* (New York, 1966), and Edgar I. Stewart, *Penny-an-Acre Empire in the West* (Norman, Okla., 1968). A good history of the sod-house frontier is Kathryn L. Lichty, "A History of the Settlement of the Nebraska Sandhills," unpublished M.A. thesis, University of Wyoming (Laramie, 1960).

The cattleman's frontier has many historians. Ernest Staples Osgood, *The Day of the Cattleman* (Minneapolis, 1929), Louis Pelzer, *The Cattlemen's Frontier* (Glendale, Calif., 1936), and Edward Everett Dale, *The Range Cattle Industry* (Norman, Okla., 1929) are basic. Philip Ashton Rollins, *The Cowboy: An Unconventional History of Civilization on the Old-Time Cattle Range* (New York, 1922, 1926) and Joe B. Frantz and Julian E. Choate, Jr., *The American Cowboy: The Myth and the Reality* (Norman, Okla., 1955) are both good; the bosses are discussed in Lewis Atherton, *The Cattle Kings* (Bloomington, Ind., 1961; reprinted Lincoln, Nebr., 1972) and Gene M. Gressley, *Bankers and Cattlemen* (New York, 1966). Some specialized sources include Andy Adams, "The Cattle on a Thousand Hills," *The Colorado Magazine*, Vol. XV, No. 5 (September 1938), pp. 168-79; John M. Kuykendall, "The First Cattle North of the Union Pacific Railroad," *The Colorado Magazine*, Vol. VII, No. 2 (March 1930), pp. 69-74. The cattle frontier in western Colorado is described in Wilson M. Rockwell, "Cow-Land Aristocrats of the North Fork," *The Colorado Magazine*, Vol. XIV, No. 5 (September 1937), pp. 161-70.

IV
Despoilment:
The Rape of the New Country

A good beginning for an understanding of the conservation movement are Roderick W. Nash, *Wilderness and the American Mind* (New Haven, 1967) and Hans Huth, *Nature and the American* (Berkeley, Cal., 1957; reprinted Lincoln, Nebr., 1972). A good overview is Stewart L. Udall, *The Quiet Crisis* (New York, 1963). Basic to forest history is John Ise, *The United States Forest Policy* (New Haven, 1920). John Quincy Adams as conservationist is discussed in William R. Adams, "Florida Live Oak Farm of John Quincy Adams," *Florida Historical Quarterly*, Vol. LI, No. 2 (October 1972), pp. 129-42. Excellent descriptions of the land in its natural state are found in John Bakeless, *The Eyes of Discovery* (New York, 1961). Two superior books of readings are Robert McHenry with Charles Van Doren, *A Documentary History of Conservation in America* (New York, 1972), and Roderick Nash, *The American Environment: Readings in the History of Conservation* (Reading, Mass., 1968). A good unpublished doctoral dissertation in Herbert D. Kirkland, "The American Forests 1864-1898: A Trend Toward Conservation," Florida State University (Tallahassee, 1961).

There is information on grasses and their use in the United States in U.S. Department of Agriculture *Yearbook, Grass* (Washington, D.C., 1948). For bees see Colin G. Butler, *The World of the Honeybee* (London, 1954), and for the horse, Robert Moorman Denhart, *The Horse of the Americas* (Norman, Okla., 1948), and Walker D. Wyman, *The Wild Horse of the West* (Lincoln, Neb., 1945). There is a comprehensive essay on the chestnut fungus in National Audubon Society, *The Audubon Nature Encyclopedia* (Philadelphia, 1944), Vol. II, pp. 408-15. For bird life see George J. Wallace, *An Introduction to Ornithology* (New York, 1955), and Arlie W. Shonger, *The Passenger Pigeon: Its Natural History and Extinction* (Madison, Wis., 1955).

The Carolina deerskin trade is described in Vernon W. Crane, *The Southern Frontier, 1670-1732* (Ann Arbor, Mich., 1956). The American bison are discussed in Martin S. Garretson, *The American Bison* (New York, 1938); E. Douglas Branch, *The Hunting of the Buffalo* (Lincoln, Neb., 1963); and Tom McHugh, *The Time of the Buffalo* (New York, 1972). Paul Russell Cutright, *Lewis and Clark: Pioneering Naturalists* (Urbana, Ill., 1969), is excellent for its descriptions of the flora and fauna observed by the two explorers. Mari Sandoz, *The Beaver Men: Spearheads of Empire* (New York, 1964), is exceptionally evocative. For the fur trade Hiram Martin Chittenden, *The American Fur Trade of the Far West* (2 vols., New York, 1902, 1935, 1954), and Paul C. Phillips, *The Fur Trade* (2 vols., Norman, Okla., 1961) are basic. LeRoy Hafen, *The Mountain Men and the Fur Trade of the Far West* (10 vols., Glendale, Calif., 1965-72), is biographical; the "Brief History" in Vol. 1 is superb. Other good works on the fur trade are John Sunder, *The Fur Trade of the Upper Missouri, 1840-1860* (Norman, Okla., 1965), and Kenneth Wiggins Porter, *John Jacob Astor: Business Man* (2 vols., Cambridge, Mass., 1931). Very descriptive of the Far West in the 1840's is a novel by Sir William Drummond Stewart, *Edward Warren* (London, 1854).

The Federal Writers Project, *Montana* (New York, 1939), contains good descriptions of Butte, but Butte has its own publication by the Federal Writer's Project, *Copper Camp* (New York, 1943). Hydraulicking is dealt with admirably in Robert L. Kelley, *Gold vs. Grain: The Hydraulic Mining Controversy in California's Sacramento Valley* (Glendale, Calif., 1959), but there is additional information in Rodman W. Paul, *California Gold: The Beginnings of Mining in the Far West* (Cambridge, Mass., 1947).

V

Transportation

Although there are many monographs on special aspects of transportation, no scholarly, well-written survey of the subject, in terms of modern standards of historiography, has yet appeared. An old source is Archer B. Hulbert, *Historic Highways of America* (16 vols., Cleveland, 1902-5). Hulbert also has a brief survey, *The Paths of Inland Commerce*, Vol. 21 in The Chronicles of America series (New Haven, 1921). Another survey is Seymour Dunbar, *A History of Travel in America* (New York, 1915, reprinted 1937). Two surveys of the pre–Civil War period are Balthasar Henry Meyer, ed., *History of Transportation in the United States Before 1860* (Washington, D.C., 1917), and George Rogers Taylor, *The Transportation Revolution, 1815-1860* (New York, 1951), but the latter is unduly heavy on economics. One good study for the post–Civil War era is Oscar O. Winther, *The Transportation Frontier. Trans-Mississippi West, 1865-1890* (New York, 1964). A regional survey is Charles Henry Ambler, *A History of Transportation in the Ohio Valley* (Glendale, Calif., 1932).

Robert L. Kincaid, *The Wilderness Road* (Indianapolis, 1947), is satisfactory for that artery, while Philip D. Jordan, *The National Road* (New York, 1948), is well done and readable. Other studies of roads or trails are Jonathan Daniels, *The Devil's Backbone: The Story of the Natchez Trace* (New York, 1962); Hodding Carter, *Doomed Road of Empire: The Spanish Trail of Conquest* (New York, 1963); George R. Stewart, *The California Trail: An Epic with Many Heroes* (New York, 1962); and David Lavender, *Westward Vision: The Story of the Oregon Trail* (New York, 1963). Irene D. Paden, *The Wake of the Prairie Schooner* (New York, 1943), gives much information on day-to-day life on the trail. See also, in the American Guide Series, *The Oregon Trail: The Missouri River to the Pacific Ocean* (New York, 1939). An artistic pictorial presentation is Ingvard Henry Eide, *Oregon Trail* (Chicago, 1972). Definitive on the Platte River section is Merrill J. Mattes, *The Great Platte River Road* (Lincoln, Neb., 1969). The discovery of South Pass is dealt with in Robert Stuart, *On the Oregon Trail: Robert Stuart's Journey of Discovery*, ed. Kenneth A. Spaulding (Norman, Okla., 1953) and Marshall Sprague, *The Great Gates: The Story of the Rocky Mountain Passes* (Boston, 1964). Works on the Santa Fe Trail are Josiah Gregg, *Commerce of the Prairies*, ed. by Max Moorhead (Norman, Okla., 1954), Robert L. Duffus, *The Santa Fe Trail* (New York, 1930), and Noel M. Loomis and Abraham Nasatir, *Pedro Vial and the Roads to Santa Fe* (Norman, Okla., 1967). The definitive work on wagon roads is W. Turrentine Jackson, *Wagon Roads West* (Berkeley, 1962).

George Shumway, Edward Durell, and Howard C. Frey, *Conestoga Wagon 1750-1850* (York, Pa., 1964) is satisfactory. Early inns and taverns are described in Elise Lathrop, *Early American Inns and Taverns* (New York, 1926), and Alice Morse Earle, *Stage-Coach and Tavern Days* (New York, 1902). There are some excellent descriptions of travel and social life in Solon J. Buck, *The Planting of Civilization in Western Pennsylvania* (Pittsburgh, 1939). Travelers had much to say about conditions along the roads. Harriet Martineau, *Retrospect and Western Travel* (2 vols., New York, 1838), and the peripatetic Mrs. Frances Trollope, *The Domestic Manners of Americans* (New York, 1949) both have amusing experiences to tell. Nick Eggenhofer, *Wagons, Mules and Men* (New York, 1961), answers many questions about the methodology of handling and the hardware of nineteenth-century vehicles. Raymond W. and Mary Lund Settle, *War Drums and Battle Wheels: The Story of Russell, Majors, and Waddell* (Lincoln, Nebr., 1966), is adequate. So also is Alexander Majors, *Seventy Years on the Frontier: Alexander Majors' Memoirs of a Lifetime on the Border*, ed. by Prentiss Ingraham (Chicago, 1893, reprinted Columbus, 1950).

For stagecoaching see James V. Frederick, *Ben Holladay, The Stagecoach King* (Glendale, Calif., 1940), Captain William Banning and George Hugh Banning, *Six Horses* (New York, 1930), and especially Ralph Moody, *Stagecoach West* (New York, 1967). Amusing travel experiences are found in Carrie Adele Strahorn, *Fifteen Thousand Miles By Stage* (New York, 1911). Some information is also available in John L. Ringwalt, *Development of*

Transportation Systems in the United States (Philadelphia, 1888, reprinted New York, 1966). For the overland stage see Roscoe P. Conkling and Margaret B. Conkling, *The Butterfield Overland Mail* (3 vols., Glendale, Calif., 1947), and Le Roy Hafen, *The Overland Mail, 1849-1869* (Cleveland, 1926). Waterman L. Ormsby, *The Butterfield Overland Mail*, ed. by Lyle H. Wright and Josephine M. Bynum (San Marino, 1962), narrates the experiences of that line's first through passenger. Raymond W. and Mary Lund Settle, *Saddles and Spurs: The Pony Express Saga* (Harrisburg, Pa., 1955), and Robert West Howard, *Hoofbeats of Destiny* (New York, 1960), are acceptable works on the Pony Express.

Two or three works stand out among the histories of water transportation. Definitive and scholarly is Louis C. Hunter, *Steamboats on the Western Rivers: An Economic and Technological History* (Cambridge, 1949), and Leland D. Baldwin, *The Keelboat Age on Western Waters* (Pittsburgh, 1941), while Zadoc Cramer, *The Navigator* (first published in 1801, most recently at Ann Arbor, 1966) provides a fascinating journey into a past era. An early work of interest is Archer Butler Hulbert, *The Ohio River: A Course of Empire* (New York, 1906), as is his article, "Western Shipbuilding," *American Historical Review*, Vol. XXI, No. 4 (July 1916), pp. 720-33. Steamboating on the Missouri is chronicled in William E. Lass, *A History of Steamboating on the Upper Missouri River* (Lincoln, Nebr., 1962), and in Hiram Martin Chittenden, *A History of Early Steamboat Navigation on the Missouri River* (2 vols., New York, 1903). Three good books on canals are Madeline Sadler Waggoner, *The Long Haul West: The Great Canal Era, 1817-1850* (New York, 1958), Alvin F. Harlow, *Old Towpaths: The Story of the American Canal Era* (New York, 1926), and Carter Goodrich, ed., *Canals and American Development* (New York, 1961).

For railroads, see Edward Hungerford, *The Story of the Baltimore and Ohio Railroad, 1827-1927* (2 vols., New York, 1928); Stewart Holbrook, *The Story of American Railroads* (New York, 1947); John F. Stover, *American Railroads* (Chicago, 1961); Leslie E. Decker, *Railroads, Lands, and Politics: The Taxation of the Railroad Land Grants, 1864-1897* (Providence, 1964); James Marshall, *Santa Fe: The Railroad that Built an Empire* (New York, 1945); and Fred Erving Dayton, *The Age of Steam* (New York, 1925). Histories have been written of most major railroads. Because of the centennial of the first transcontinental in 1969, there are several studies of the Union Pacific–Central Pacific: see Gerald M. West, *Iron Horses to Promontory* (San Marino, 1969); George Kraus, *High Road to Promontory* (Palto Alto, 1969); Robert Athearn, *Union Pacific Country* (Chicago, 1971); and David E. Miller, ed., *The Golden Spike* (Salt Lake City, 1973). On the entrepreneurs of the Central Pacific, see Oscar Lewis, *The Big Four* (New York, 1938). Colonization is discussed in Paul Wallace Gates, *The Illinois Central Railroad and Its Colonization Work* (Cambridge, Mass., 1934). There are two good articles on the subject by James B. Hedges: "The Colonization Work of the Northern Pacific Railroad," *Mississippi Valley Historical Review*, Vol. XIII, No. 3 (December 1926), pp. 311-42, and "Promotion of Immigration to the Pacific Northwest by the Railroads," *Ibid.*, Vol. XV, No. 2 (September 1928), pp. 183-203. A description of travel on an emigrant car is in Robert Louis Stevenson, *From Scotland to Silverado*, ed. by James D. Hart (Cambridge, Mass., 1966).

VI
New Country Society

The boisterousness and masculinity of the new country is ably presented in
Everett Dick, *The Dixie Frontier* (New York, 1948), and *The Sod House
Frontier: 1854-1890* (New York, 1937). See also Hariette L. S. Arnow,
Seedtime on the Cumberland, 1763-1803 (New York, 1960); Thomas D.
Clark, *The Rampaging Frontier* (Indianapolis, 1939); William S. Greever,
The Bonanza West (Norman, Okla., 1963); and even Mark Twain, *Rough-
ing It* (various editions). Both Joseph G. Baldwin, *The Flush Times in
Alabama* (New York, 1957), and A. B. Longstreet, *Georgia Scenes* (New
York, 1957), are excellent for their descriptions of boom times in the South.
Arthur M. Schlesinger, *Paths to the Present* (New York, 1949), has an in-
teresting chapter on masonic-type associations. The first six volumes of
Montana Historical Society, *Contributions* (Helena, 1876-1940, reprinted
New York, 1966), contain biographies of a number of Montana's early
leaders. For Colorado, Harry Kelsey, *Frontier Capitalist: The Life of John
Evans* (Boulder, 1969), and Thomas L. Karnes, *William Gilpin: Western
Nationalist* (Austin, Texas 1970), are good. E. S. Topping, *The Chronicles
of the Yellowstone* (St. Paul, 1888), tells much about frontier mining life.
Dee Brown, *The Gentle Tamers: Women of the Old West* (New York,
1958), is amusing, but his choices are not average new country women. Alice
Blackwood Baldwin (Mrs. Frank J. Baldwin), *Memoirs of the Late Frank D.
Baldwin, Major General, U.S.A.* (Los Angeles, 1929), is excellent; Fairfax
Downey, *Indian Fighting Army* (New York, 1941), contains a delightful
chapter on the army women, "They Also Served."
    Home and family life on the Middle Border was the subject of most of
Hamlin Garland's writings. A *Son of the Middle Border* (New York, 1917)
and A *Daughter of the Middle Border* (New York, 1921) are especially good.
Anyone interested in the world of women in the nineteenth century should
study *Godey's Lady's Book*, a fascinating periodical of the mid-century
period. The women of the Donner party command attention in Virginia
Reed Murphy, "Across the Plains with the Donner Party (1846): A Personal Narrative of the Overland Trip to California," *Century Magazine*, Vol.
XLII, No. 3 (July 1891), pp. 409-26. Jesse Benton Frémont, *Mother Lode
Narratives* ed. by Shirley Sargent (Ashland, Cal., 1970), gives a good picture of an aristocratic young woman in the new country. I consulted the
collection of hymnals in the John Shaw Collection of Childhood in Poetry
at Florida State University for the hymns from which I quoted. Women on
the trails are treated in Georgia Willis Read, "Women and Children on the
Oregon-California Trail in the Gold Rush Years," *Missouri Historical Review*, Vol. XXXIX, No. 1 (October 1944), pp. 1-23. Two sources are good
on the frontier woman and the suffrage movement: Alan P. Grimes, *The
Puritan Ethic and Woman Suffrage* (New York, 1967), is a gem; T. A.
Larson, *History of Wyoming* (Lincoln, Nebr., 1965), is good on the Wyoming phase. A delightful essay on the Kansas new country women is Elizabeth Cochran, "Hatchets and Hoopskirts: Women in Kansas History," *The
Midwest Quarterly*, Vol. 2, no. 3 (Spring, 1961), pp. 221-49. Mormon
women are discussed in Leonard J. Arrington, "The Economic Role of Pioneer
Mormon Women," *Western Humanities Review*, Vol. IX, No. 2 (Spring

1955), pp. 145-64. Two general treatises on the woman's rights movement are Eleanor Flexner, *Century of Struggle: the Woman's Rights Movement in the United States* (Cambridge, Mass., 1959) and Andrew Sinclair, *The Better Half: The Emancipation of the American Woman* (New York, 1965).

For the family the study by Arthur W. Calhoun, *A Social History of the American Family*, Vol. II, *From Independence Through Civil War* (3 vols., Cleveland, 1918), proved indispensable.

There are a number of good studies of frontier medicine: Urling C. Coe, *Frontier Doctor* (New York, 1939); Morris Fishbein, *Fads and Quackery in Healing* (New York, 1932); James Thomas Flexner, *Doctors on Horseback: Pioneers of American Medicine* (New York, 1937); Robert F. Karolevitz, *Doctors of the Old West: A Pictorial History of Medicine on the Frontier* (Seattle, 1967); Madge E. Pickard and R. Carlyle Buley, *The Midwest Pioneer; His Ills, Cures, and Doctors;* and Charles Fox Gardiner, M.D., *Doctor at Timberline* (Caldwell, Idaho, 1940). All kinds of information about mining camp society from births to tombstone epitaphs is in Muriel Sibelle Wolle, *Stampede to Timberline* (Boulder, 1949).

The leader in historical writing on religion in frontier America is William Warren Sweet, whose principal contribution is embodied in a four-volume series, *Religion on the American Frontier: A Collection of Source Materials;* Vol. I, *The Baptists* (New York, 1931); Vol. II, *The Presbyterians* (Chicago, 1936); Vol. III, *The Congregationalists* (Chicago, 1939); and Vol. IV, *The Methodists* (Chicago, 1946). See also his *Methodism in American History* (New York, 1933). Edward Eggleston, *The Circuit Rider: A Tale of the Heroic Age* (New York, 1873, reprinted Lexington, Ky., 1970), gives an excellent though fictional portrayal of these men. Peter Cartwright, *Autobiography*, Introduction by Charles L. Wallis (Nashville, 1956), is amusing. Owen Wister, *The Virginian* (various editions) gives still another picture of the circuit rider. Of the tremendous bibliography of books on religion in America, the following are particularly useful for their emphasis on the nineteenth century: Gilbert Seldes, *The Stammering Century* (New York, 1928, reprinted 1965); Bernard Weisberger, *They Gathered at the River: The Story of the Great Revivalists and Their Impact on Religion in America* (Boston, 1958); Walter Brownlow Posey, *Frontier Mission: A History of Religion West of the Southern Appalachians to 1861* (Lexington, Ky., 1966); O. K. Armstrong and Marjorie M. Armstrong, *The Indomitable Baptists: A Narrative of Their Role in Shaping American History* (New York, 1967); and Charles Albert Johnson, *The Frontier Camp Meeting: Religion's Harvest Time* (Dallas, 1955).

There is an abundance of material on the Mormons, much of it biased, and surprisingly little written by professional historians. This fact is discussed in Rodman W. Paul, "The Mormons as a Theme in Western Historical Writing," *The Journal of American History*, Vol. LIV, No. 3 (December 1967), pp. 511-23. The best studies include Thomas F. O'Dea, *The Mormons* (Chicago, 1957); Nels Anderson, *Desert Saints: The Mormon Frontier in Utah* (Chicago, 1942, 1966); Leonard J. Arrington, *Great Basin Kingdom, An Economic History of the Latter-Day Saints, 1830-1900* (Cambridge, Mass., 1958); Ray B. West, Jr., *Kingdom of the Saints: The Story of Brigham Young and the Mormons* (New York, 1957); Kimball

Young, *Isn't One Wife Enough?* (New York, 1954); and Fawn Brodie, *No
Man Knows My History: The Life of Joseph Smith, the Mormon Prophet*
(2d ed. New York, 1971); an excellent book of readings is William Mulder
and A. Russell Mortensen, *Among the Mormons: Historic Accounts by
Contemporary Observers* (New York, 1958). Juanita Brooks, *The Mountain
Meadows Massacre* (Norman, Okla., 1961), and a novel by Amelia Bean,
The Fancher Train (Garden City, 1958), do justice to that tragic incident.
And then there is Joseph Smith, Jr., *The Book of Mormon* (Salt Lake City,
many editions).

Studies of education in the new country include Lawrence A. Cremin, *The
American Common School: An Historic Conception* (New York, 1951);
Donald G. Tewkesbury, *The Founding of American Colleges and Uni-
versities Before the Civil War* (New York, 1932); H. G. Good, *A History of
American Education* (New York, 1956); Edgar W. Knight and Clifton L.
Hall, *Readings in American Educational History* (New York, 1951); and
Louis B. Wright, *Culture on the Moving Frontier* (New York, 1961). Wil-
liam Holmes McGuffey, *McGuffey's Fifth Eclectic Reader*, Introduction by
Henry Steele Commager (New York, 1962), is good both for the Intro-
duction and for the amusing contents of the book. Foster Rhea Dulles, *A
History of Recreation* (New York, 1940, 1965) is good on that subject.

VII
The Urban Frontier

Although the situation is rapidly improving, there is a dearth of good scholarly studies on American cities. Part of this shortage may be because urban
history is unromantic; it does not fire the imagination of the historian, nor of
readers of history. A good beginning for an understanding of the specialty is
a book of readings edited by Alexander B. Callow, Jr., *American Urban History: An Interpretive Reader with Commentaries* (New York, 1969). Very
interesting are John W. Reps, *Town Planning in Frontier America* (Princeton, 1969); Richard C. Wade, *The Urban Frontier: The Rise of Western
Cities, 1790-1830* (Cambridge, Mass., 1959); Charles A. Glaab and A.
Theodore Brown, *A History of Urban America* (New York, 1957); Con-
stance McLaughlin Green, *American Cities in the Growth of the Nation*
(New York, 1957); Stefan Lorant, *Pittsburgh: The Story of an American
City* (Garden City, N.Y., 1949); and Bessie Louise Pierce, *History of Chi-
cago* (3 vols., New York, 1937-57). Gerald H. Capers, Jr., *The Biography of
a River Town; Memphis: Its Heroic Age* (Chapel Hill, N.C., 1939) is excel-
lent. Some other studies of cities are Betsey Beeler Creekmore, *Knoxville*
(Knoxville, Tenn., 1967); Clara Longworth de Chambrun, *Cincinnati: The
Story of the Queen City* (New York, 1939); and American Guide Series,
Louisville: A Guide to the Falls City (New York, 1940). John Francis Mc-
Dermott, *Old Cahokia: A Narrative and Documents Illustrating the First
Century of Its History* (St. Louis, 1949) and *The Early Histories of St. Louis*
(St. Louis, 1952), are excellent on the French and Spanish in the Mississippi
Valley. Arthur L. Schlesinger, *The Rise of the City, 1878-1898* in the
History of American Life series (New York, 1933), is a trailblazer in the
history of American urban history.

Towns of the Middle West and Middle Border area discussed in Lewis

Atherton, *Main Street on the Middle Border* (Bloomington, Ind., 1954), Robert R. Dykstra, *The Cattle Towns* (New York, 1970), and Richard Van Orman, "The First Ten Years: Successes and Failures of Kansas City, Omaha, and Denver," a paper delivered at the 1970 meeting of the Western History Association in Reno, and which he has kindly allowed me to read. Some good descriptions of far western cities are in James Bryce, *The American Commonwealth* (2 vols., New York, 1901).

A number of books have been written on mining communities, but two stand out: Duane Smith, *Rocky Mountain Mining Camps: The Urban Frontier* (Bloomington, Ind., 1967), and a brilliant monograph by W. Turrentine Jackson, *Treasure Hill: Portrait of a Silver Mining Camp* (Tucson, 1963). See also James B. Allen, *The Company Town in the American West* (Norman, Okla., 1966).

VIII
From New Country to Settled Country

Both *Frank Leslie's Illustrated Weekly* and *Harper's Weekly Magazine* are rich sources of material on the last thirty-five years of the nineteenth century. Two books by Wilbur Jacobs, *Frederick Jackson Turner's Legacy* (San Marino, 1965), and *The Historical World of Frederick Jackson Turner* (New Haven, 1968), give insight into the life of that brilliant historian. The definitive biography is, however, Ray Allen Billington, *Frederick Jackson Turner: Historian, Scholar, Teacher* (New York, 1973). Two of the easily available volumes of Turner's most significant writings are edited by Ray Allen Billington: *The Frontier Thesis: Valid Interpretation of American History?* (New York, 1966), which includes critical essays of the thesis, and *Frontier and Section: Selected Essays of Frederick Jackson Turner* (Englewood Cliffs, N.J., 1961). Two other studies by Billington are important: *America's Frontier Heritage* (New York, 1966), and *The Genesis of the Frontier Thesis: A Study of Historical Creativity* (San Marino, 1971). Some idea of the immensity of the material on Turner is found in Gene M. Gressley, "The Turner Thesis— A Problem in Historiography," *Agricultural History*, Vol. XXXII, No. 3 (October 1958). Two interpretive studies are Henry Nash Smith, *Virgin Land: The American West as Symbol and Myth* (Cambridge, Mass., 1950), and Leo Marx, *The Machine in the Garden* (New York, 1967).

Index

Fort Mims massacre, 52
Forts: Benton, 288, 321; Bridger, 107,
  286; Cahokia, 6; Caroline (Fla.),
  6; Clatsop, 49; Confederation, 44;
  D. A. Russell, 151; Dearborn, 407-
  8; Dodge, 416; Duquesne, 402; Fet-
  terman, 151; Fincastle, 402; "Fort-
  on-Shire" (early Louisville), 404;
  Hall, 108, 286; Harker, 352; Henry,
  402; La Jonquière, 6; Kaskaskia, 6;
  Leavenworth, 31, 287; Massac, 6;
  Pitt, 402; Miami, 6; Morgan, 227;
  Nashborough, 39; Ouiatanon, 6;
  Pierre, 87; Point, 410; Rosalie, 6;
  St. Stephens, 44; St. Louis, founded
  by La Salle, 6; Scott, 31; Smith, 31,
  287; Snelling, 31, 287; Toulouse, 6;
  Towson, 31; Union, 86; Vancouver,
  32, 89, 101; Walla Walla, 101, 288;
  Washington, 405; Worth, Texas,
  85
"Forty-niners," 108, 411
Fraeb, Henry, 88
Franklin, Benjamin, 62, 136, 177
Franklin, ship, 89
Franklin, state of, 65
Fraternal organizations, 345, 438
Fredonia, 98
Freemasonry, 345
Free Timber Act, 241
Frémont, Jessie Benton, 356
Frémont, John C., 91, 101, 105
French and Indian War, 136
French Canadians, 123, 257
Frontier, 126, 131, 135, 175, 188;
  "permanent" Indian, 31, 58
Fulton, Robert, 317
Funk, Isaac, 193
Funk Island, 250
Fur trade, 85-91; in Old Southwest, 42;
  personnel of, 257; posts, 257; risks
  of, 256

Gadsden Purchase, 107
Gaines' Trace, 284
Gallatin, Albert, 74, 312
Gallatin Valley of Montana, 112, 222,
  227
"Gandy dancers," 167-68
Gannett, Henry, 114
General Land Office, 73-77
Georgia, 43, 63, 124; establishes univer-
  sity, 395
Germans, 118, 124, 126, 140, 214; and
  cultural heritage, 154; character-
  istics, 142, 149; develop prairies,

123; settle in cities, 153; immigra-
  tion after 1848, 152; in western
  states, 151; as laborers, 324
Gerry, Elbridge, 67
Gervais, Jean, 88
Ghiradelli, Domenico, Italian candy
  maker, 163
Giannine, A. P., Italian banker, 163
Gila River Valley, 107
Gila Trail, 287
Gilmer and Salisbury, stage lines of, 305
Gilpin, William, 346, 417
Giorda, Italian Jesuit Father, 157
Glass, Hugh, 91
Glidden, Joseph, 220
Godoy, Manuel de, 45-46
Gold, 266, 321. See also Hydraulicking
Gold Hill, Nevada, 110
Goliad, 100
Goodnight-Loving Trail, 228
Grand Tetons, 86
Grangers, 233
Grass Valley, California, 152
Gray, Captain Robert, 55, 83
Grayson, William, 69
Great American Desert, 83, 112, 388;
  for Indians, 31
Great auk, 250
Great Awakening, 380
Great Basin, 5, 386
Great Comet of 1811, 318
Great Medicine Road (Platte River
  Trail), 110. See also Oregon Trail,
  Platte River Trail
Great North Trail, 15
Great Northern Railroad, 214, 284,
  330
Great Philadelphia Wagon Road, 126,
  134
Great Plains, 110, 112, 130, 213, 262-
  63
Great Revival, 43-44, 368
Great Salt Lake, 89, 120, 386
Great Valley, 126, 134, 141
Great Western Trail, 228
Greeks, 143
Greeley, Colorado, 212
Greene, General Nathaniel, 64, 68
Gregg, Josiah, 91
"Ground sluicing," 268
Grover's Island, 239
Gulla tongue, 128
Gutierrez-Magee expedition, 96
Gwin, Samuel, 76

Hague, Arnold, 245

Hall, James, 140, 146-47
Hamilton, Alexander, 47, 73, 139
Handcock, Forrest, 85
Hare, Joseph Thompson, 281
Harmer, General Josiah, 42
Harpe, Big and Little, 281
Harrison, Benjamin, 245
Harrison, William Henry, 30, 50
Harrison Land Act of 1800, 74
Harrowing, 199
Hauser, Sam, 346
Hayden Survey, 114
Hay mower, 206
Hays, John, 161
Health in new country, 159, 364-66
Heath hen, 250
Hedges, Cornelius, 346
Heinze, F. Augustus, 263
Helena, Montana, 152, 429
Henderson, Judge Richard, 9, 64, 176
Henry, Andrew, 86, 257-58
Henry's Fork, 88, 258
Herders, 224
Hessian mercenaries, 143
Hide and tallow trade, 84
Hide and tongue trade, 260, 262
High schools, 393
Hilgard, E. W., 213
Hinckley, William, 410
Hoboes, 170. See also Tramps
Holladay, Ben, stagecoach tycoon, 303-4
Home Mission Societies, 394
Homestead Act of 1862, 78, 113, 214, 241
Hopkins, Mark, 328
Horn, Tom, 232
Hornaday, William T., 262
Horses, 194, 247-48
Horseshoe Bend, Battle of, 18, 43, 53
Hotels, 431
Houston, Sam, 53, 99
Howell, David, 67
Hudson's Bay Company, 88, 410
Huguenots, 6, 117, 124, 133, 142
Humboldt River, 108
Hunter, George, 48
Hunting, 148, 344
Huntington, Collis P., 328
Huntsville, Alabama, 76
Hutchins, Thomas, first government surveyor, 72
Hutton, N. Henry, and military road, 288
Hydraulicking, 268-72

Iliff, George, 112, 227
Illinois, 6, 190

Illinois and Michigan Canal, 408
Illinois Central Railroad, 240; and settlement, 325-27
Indiana, 190, 363
Indianapolis, 407
Indian Chutes (Falls of the Ohio), 144
Indians, 13, 19-37, 101, 121, 175, 260. See also individual tribes
Infant mortality, 361
Interior Department: and G.L.O., 74; and wagon roads, 289
Iowa, 113, 287
Iowa Indians, 6
Irish, 143, 150; population of in West, 151; laborers on B & O, 324
Irrigation, 212, 222, 386
Iroquois Indians, 25, 42, 121
Iroquois Trail, 13-14
Irving, Washington, 91, 101
Italians, 143, 162, 163

Jackrabbits (hares), 254
Jackson, Andrew, 99, 149; and California, 105; defeats Creeks, 43, 53; and G.L.O., 76; and Indian removals, 30; and Specie Circular, 58; and timber policy, 239; recognizes Texas, 100; speculates in lands, 61
Jackson, David E., 88
Jackson, Helen Hunt, 37
Jackson's military road, 54, 127, 284
James, Dr. Edwin, 91
Jay, John, 43, 45, 142
Jay Cooke's Banana Belt, 214
Jay's Treaty, 43, 45, 50
Jefferson, Thomas, 9, 47; and exploration of Louisiana, 49; and Northwest Ordinance, 80; and plows, 199; and Texas, 85; Indian policy of, 29, 30; plans for Jeffersonville, 407
Jesuits, 6, 402
Jews, 143, 160-62
Johnson, Willard D., 213
Johnson, Sir William, 25
Johnson County Range War, 232
Judah, Theodore P., 328

Kansas, 113, 352
Kansas Pacific Railroad, 34, 113, 332
Kaskaskia, 402
Kearney, Dennis, 169, 413
Kearny, Stephen W., 105
Keelboats, 309-10, 320
Kelley, Hall J., 91, 102, 429
Kelsey, Harry, 421
Kenton, Simon, 9